Africa
Overland
4x4 • Motorbike • Bicycle • Truck

the Bradt Travel Guide

**Siân Pritchard-Jones
and Bob Gibbons**

edition
5

www.bradtguides.com

Bradt Travel Guides Ltd, UK
The Globe Pequot Press Inc, USA

Morocco: Atlas Mountains & Sahara fringes

Egypt/Sudan: River Nile culture & pyramids

Ethiopia: mountain highlands & rock churches

The Sahara: Algeria, Libya, Niger & Chad

Mali: mud cities of Timbuktu & Djenne, Dogon people & Bandiagara escarpment

West Africa: a melting pot of tribal people & lively music

ATLANTIC OCEAN

Caspian Sea

Black Sea

Persian Gulf

Gulf of Aden

Gulf of Guinea

Mediterranean Sea

LISBON
MADRID
RABAT
CASABLANCA
MARRAKECH
ALGIERS
ORAN
TUNIS
TRIPOLI
ROME
NAPLES
PALERMO
ANKARA
ISTANBUL
ATHENS
DAMASCUS
AMMAN
RIYADH
CAIRO
ALEXANDRIA
SUEZ
PORT SAID
JEDDAH
SANAA
ADEN
DJIBOUTI
BERBERA
MOGADISHU
ASMARA
ADDIS ABABA
KHARTOUM
PT SUDAN
KAMPALA
BANGUI
YAOUNDE
LIBREVILLE
MALABO
BATA
LAGOS
PORTO NOVO
ACCRA
LOME
ABIDJAN
MONROVIA
FREETOWN
CONAKRY
BISSAU
BANJUL
DAKAR
NOUAKCHOTT
BAMAKO
OUAGADOUGOU
NIAMEY
N'DJAMENA
ABUJA
YAMOUSSOUKRO
KANO
TANGIER
FES
RABAT

Africa
Overland

Don't
miss...

A melting pot of people and culture, west Africa
Bride wearing a traditional outfit, Soma, the Gambia
(AZ)

The fabulous desert vistas of the Sahara
Crabe d'Arakao, Niger
(SPJ & BG)

Tropical rainforests and exciting driving, central Africa
Overlanding near Mamfé, Cameroon
(SPJ & BG)

Game viewing, east Africa
Lion in Queen Elizabeth National Park, Uganda (AZ)

Southern Africa – a variety of adventures in more comfort
Camping at Kalambo Falls, Zambia (BH)

above	Benin bronze sculpture, Nigeria (DH)
above right	West African mask, Senegal (AZ)
right	Kente weaving in Ho, Volta region, Ghana (AZ)
below right	_Kikoi_ for sale in the market, Blantyre, Malawi (AZ)
below	Man carving wooden sculptures, Mozambique (DE)

AUTHORS

Both born in Britain, Siân and Bob met in Kashmir in 1983. Bob's overland adventures began in an ancient (1949) Land Rover, which he drove from England to Kathmandu way back in 1974, before he even thought about settling down into a 'proper job' like writing guidebooks for Bradt! He subsequently worked as an overland driver, travelling extensively all over Asia, Africa and South America, driving trucks as well as decrepit old buses in India and Nepal. Siân worked in computer programming and systems analysis for far too long, until overland travel and particularly the Himalayas captivated her on a trip to Nepal in 1982.

Since they met, they have been leading and organising treks in the Alps, Nepal, Algeria and Niger. They have hitched across Tibet, driven their overland bus with ageing clients to Nepal, explored the Sahara and driven through Africa six times in their own 1983-vintage Land Rover. Every autumn they work for Pilgrims Book House in Kathmandu, editing and writing. They have produced a cultural and trekking guide to the Kathmandu Valley, as well as guides to Ladakh in India and Mount Kailash in Tibet. Mount Kailash was also the subject of their first Cicerone trekking guide, and for something completely different, they updated the Cicerone guide to the Grand Canyon. Other Bradt projects have included updating the Maldives and Cape Verde guides. Some of this was real work, but luckily that 'proper job' has not yet materialised!

AUTHORS' STORY

The story of African overland travel since the first intrepid explorers of the 18th and 19th centuries has always been one of risk, adventure, challenge and intrigue. Africa, more than any other continent, still presents hard choices and rugged travel. In publishing this guide, Bradt, with the help of the authors, other experts and input from current travellers, is at the cutting edge of adventure travel in the 21st century.

As a client on a bright pink truck in 1975, Bob was stuck in central Africa for weeks after the drivers and half of the other passengers caught hepatitis and left. There were preposterous visa delays, border closures and civil wars. The truck also became very sick. Bob instigated some drastic, if optimistic, repairs and somehow drove it on to Nairobi. The same could still happen to anyone crossing Africa today, over 30 years later, but with the combined experience and knowledge found within this Bradt guide, such debilitating and drastic dramas can be more easily avoided.

We have explored much of the Sahara together, and our most recent longer journeys in Africa have been in our now 25-year-old Land Rover. In 2003 we drove from England to Gabon, a trip that took us to the mysterious central African rainforests. In 2004 our route went across north Africa to Cairo then south to Cape Town, a trip that was the basis of the fourth edition of the Bradt *Africa Overland* guide. In 2008 our plan was to drive down the entire west coast through Congo and Angola, but in the event visa problems restricted the trip to previously unexplored corners of west Africa, such as Sierra Leone, Guinea and Liberia. This journey, despite its problems, became the basis of this new, even more comprehensive, edition.

And of course it leaves much more for us to discover and share with our readers in the sixth edition!

PUBLISHER'S FOREWORD *Hilary Bradt*

When I was a child a colleague of my father visited us once a year, having driven his Land Rover from Ghana across the Sahara. I was amazed that it was possible to drive from Africa to England, and enthralled by his stories. This remains the ultimate adventure, yet Bob Gibbons and Siân Pritchard-Jones have done it more than once and have used their experiences to update *Africa by Road* by Charlie Shackell and Illya Bracht. The combined expertise of these four Africa travellers, along with contributions from cyclists and bikers, has produced the book that may literally save the life of a trans-Africa traveller and will certainly enhance the enjoyment of this once-in-a-lifetime trip.

When George and I travelled from Cape Town to Cairo in 1976 there were no guidebooks, so each border was approached with trepidation. We had no idea what to expect, nor even what there was to see in each country. We were using public transport, but occasionally hitched a lift with adventurous souls driving their own vehicles, and envied their freedom to go where they chose and stop when they wanted. But freedom is wasted without knowledge. And knowledge is what this book is about.

Fifth edition April 2009 First published 1991
Bradt Travel Guides Ltd, 23 High Street, Chalfont St Peter, Bucks SL9 9QE, England
www.bradtguides.com
Published in the USA by The Globe Pequot Press Inc, 246 Goose Lane,
PO Box 480, Guilford, Connecticut 06475-0480

Text copyright © 2009 Bradt Travel Guides Ltd
Maps copyright © 2009 Bradt Travel Guides Ltd
Illustrations copyright © 2009 Individual photographers and artists

ISBN-13: 978 1 84162 283 5
British Library Cataloguing in Publication Data
A catalogue record for this book is available from the British Library

Photographs Stuart Butler (SB), Danny Edmunds (DE), Bob Hayne (BH), Darren Humphrys (DH), Siân Pritchard-Jones & Bob Gibbons (SPJ & BG), Ariadne Van Zandbergen (AZ), World Pictures/Photoshot (WP/P)
Front cover Namib-Naukluft National Park, Namibia (WP/P)
Title page Lion (AZ), Karamojong girl, Uganda (AZ), Sand dunes, Libya (SPJ & BG)
Back cover Zambezi River, Zambia (AZ); Hombori, Mali (SPJ & BG)
In-text photos All SPJ & BG

Illustrations Illya Bracht & Bob Gibbons
Maps Alan Whitaker and Dave Priestley

Typeset from the authors' disk by Wakewing, High Wycombe
Printed and bound in India by Nutech Photolithographers

Acknowledgements

Thanks to all at Bradt Travel Guides for giving us this opportunity to share some of our experiences with other would-be travellers across the great Dark Continent. Special thanks to David Mozer, Ariadne Van Zandbergen, David Lambeth and Alex Marr.

To the previous authors of *Africa by Road*, first and second editions, Bob Swain and Paula Snyder, and third edition, Charlie Shackell and Illya Bracht, thank you for allowing us to use your existing material. For our own fourth edition we were very grateful to Arnout and Saskia, for their time and valuable contributions to this book, with information about buying and preparing a vehicle in South Africa. Special thanks to Martha, Charles, Angella and Titus in Nairobi, for rescuing us from the roadside! To Dr Liz Molyneux in Blantyre, Malawi, for tea and reminiscences in Doogles. To professors Kathryn and Larry, and Annette in Durban, for their exceptional hospitality at the end of a long journey.

En route in 2008, thanks to the Dar Daif Hotel, Ouarzazate and Fort Bou Jerif, Guelmime in Morocco; Zebra Bar in St Louis, Senegal; L'Auberge in Segou and Hotel Via Via in Sevare, Mali; Pastor Joseph T Kolleyan in Oasis Lodge, Salala, Liberia; Madame Raby in Hotel Tata, Labé, Guinea; Fiekpani Akim in Kande, Togo; Patrice Pasquier at Mistral Voyages in Libreville and Paul Telfer of WCS Gabon; Peggy at SRP Shipping in Durban. In the UK, thanks to Paul Gowen at the RAC, Michelle at P&O Ferries, Sue at Shewee, Valerie and Sam at Haynes Manuals, Phil Haines of Chichester 4x4 and Dr Martin Ridley in Chichester. Thanks also to Amanda of Travcour, for her help with ever-changing visa prices.

Particular thanks for added route information to Debs and Thiemo of Africa Expedition Support in Nairobi, Kenya, as well as Andi, Grant and Jeff at Oasis Overland. Thanks also to Mike Stead in Luanda for information about Angola. (Look out for his new Bradt guide to Angola.)

To any others whose stories are in here without their knowing it, thanks; and if you are in here, let us know if you'd like a copy.

A special thanks to our parents, Beryl and Tony, Marianne and John, who have, with a knowing resignation, mostly encouraged and supported us to seek out new horizons. We could not have written this book without the help of Rama and Pushpa Tiwari, of Pilgrims Book House in Kathmandu, Nepal, where much of the latest writing work was done.

And, lastly, thanks to the land and peoples of Africa for making our trips memorable, fascinating and so addictive that we can't wait to go back there again.

Contents

LIST OF MAPS

KEY TO SYMBOLS

■	Capital city
□	Capital (non-autonomous area)
●	Important town
○	Other town
	Described main route – sealed
	Other main road – sealed
	Described route – unsealed
	Other road – unsealed
	Described piste route (4x4 track)
	Other piste (4x4 track)
S3	Trans-Sahara routes (pages 23–30)
W1	West African routes (pages 31–6)
C2	Central African routes (pages 37–41)
WE1	Central African west–east routes (pages 41–4)
E1	East African routes (pages 44–5)
ES1	East–southern African routes (pages 46–8)
	International boundary

	Ferry route
	Ferry (vehicular)
	Dry or salt lake/pan
Mt Kenya 5199m	Mountain (height in metres)
	National park or reserve
	Beaches
	Camping
	Fishing area
	Historic/archaeological site
	Mosque/s
	Mountain pass
	Roman site
	Snorkel/scuba diving
	Viewpoint
	Walking/hiking/trekking area
	Waterfall
●	Other places of interest

Introduction

To contemplate an overland expedition across any continent in this modern era is one of travel's greatest challenges, and if that continent is Africa, it is doubly so. Africa is vibrant, exciting, fascinating, beautiful and inspiring, yet it can also seem at times depressing, arduous, hot and gruelling. Some days you will be floating with joy at those little things that make it such a worthwhile venture – the children's welcoming smiles, the happy villagers, the tall, incredibly shaped trees, the fabulous desert landscapes, the shady beaches, driving on a fun dirt road, that cold bucket 'shower'. The next day – struggling with the heat, the dust, the flies, the corrupt border officials, the endless bush with nowhere to camp, the mayhem of a capital city with no signposts and, of course, the absurd visa problems – you might want to be somewhere else.

If you are reading this book, you are either planning an exciting but perhaps slightly crazy journey across a vast continent, or at the very least would like to read about it. For those who at this stage may still be armchair travellers, we have included some anecdotes taken from our various trips. These may or may not encourage you to get out of that armchair and do it for yourself!

Why do it? Is there any rational answer to this question? There are so many features of the trip to inspire, so many to add a tinge of sadness. Perhaps if more people had a true spirit of adventure and tolerance for other ways of life, the world might be a safer, better place. As it is, you must be aware that you are taking different sorts of risks from those encountered every day in the Western world, but then nothing worthwhile in life is completely risk-free. There is so much to be gained by off-the-beaten-track travel. Whatever you have read about other early or more recent explorers will only awaken your imagination to the endless possibilities. You will never have enough time to do everything, so decide your main objectives and be prepared to change your plans as you go along.

Don't necessarily think it will be a once-in-a-lifetime trip; when you return life will never ever be quite the same again. We apologise for any 'incurable infections' of a life-changing nature that this book may impart. Africa may grab you wholeheartedly; you may find it hard not to return time after time. It is likely that few back home will understand or be interested in your travels beyond a quick 'Where did you go? What did you see? What was the weather like?' But your memories will live on forever and you will find inspiration and understanding that no book alone can ever hope to provide.

This book – the first three editions were entitled *Africa by Road* – describes the various ways to travel overland through Africa. The overall cost will vary widely according to your abilities and facilities, your luck in finding the right type of vehicle, as well as the length of time you have available. Different routes are described in some detail; though the possibilities are endless, some routes may be impossible for a time due to political considerations. Planning and preparation, both before and during your trip, are important; you don't want to miss some vital

At dawn a grey fog envelops the town, a place of verdant forest in a sea of desert. The heavy dew cloaks everything with a damp veneer. A monkey scurries away, disturbed outside the lodge by the guests' early morning preparations for the day's journey. Breakfast is a tasty affair; greasy fried eggs cooked in days-old ghee, dubious butter with blackened sweet bread toast and Lipton's tea. It could have been any railway station breakfast in India, but this was northern Kenya, a land of wild-eyed colourfully clad tribesmen, spectacular but harsh desert scrub and stunning isolated boulders the size of mountains.

As the first cracks appeared in the heavy fog clouds, we began the long descent from the island of hills that make Marsabit such a rich oasis. We had 'our man' Mohammed from the Kenya security forces, a gregarious family man, our armed guard, with us. We had been advised to travel with an armed guard in view of the fact that bandits frequent the route between Moyale on the Ethiopian border and Isiolo just north of Mount Kenya. Whether Mohammed would deter any determined rogues or make an armed robbery more dangerous was not something on which we cared to ponder. At the very least we were providing Mohammed with a comfortable trip to his family home near Isiolo, and ourselves with a chance to gain an insight into life in these torrid zones of northern Kenya.

Once we were down out of the cool hills, the sun broke through and a crystal-clear sky accompanied us across the dry plains. Dramatic rocks reared skyward; acacia scrub and low bushes provided suitable cover for wild animals and bandits. Just beyond a small village we passed groups of Rendille heading to the market. These amazingly dressed semi-nomadic tribal clansmen and women carried long spears; all of them wore brilliant red sashes decorated with silvery-coloured braids, ornaments and bangles. Tall and slender, they presented a picture-perfect image of a proud, self-assured independent people. Our guard suggested we should not stop here to say hello, which seemed a great pity.

The road deteriorated from a sandy strip into an unbelievably dreadful rough and rocky gash through the boulder-strewn countryside. Even at 15mph the Land Rover lurched in disgust; the suspension was banging and wearing itself away, the doors rattling constantly. Slowly we progressed into the low hills that marked the approach to the northern slopes of Mount Kenya. Its jagged peak, with icy snowfields, peered out above a wispy band of clouds in the hazy distance.

From Isiolo, where we parted company with Mohammed, the desert gave way to the rolling farmlands of the white highlands, where quaint colonial farmhouses illustrated the remarkable change in atmosphere. Gone were the tense testing hours in hostile country, replaced with scenes almost reminiscent of the rolling farmlands of Wiltshire. We passed

spare part, or forget that favourite bar of chocolate for emergencies! For example, we almost forgot our mashed potato and had to dash to Sainsbury's on the way to the ferry. Although there are more vital things, instant mash is just that, and doesn't use much fuel for cooking, so don't mock it!

Because of politics and other world issues, your route may have to change once you're on the road, so you should always build as much flexibility into your planning as possible. You'll meet other travellers, who may tell you of something they have just discovered and which you really shouldn't miss. But you should certainly have a good outline plan before you start out. Don't rush off without thinking it all over carefully. Try to avoid disasters before they happen.

If you don't think driving your own vehicle is for you, then you may want to join an organised trip. The tour companies will do most of the planning for you, leaving you just to find the money and set off to enjoy yourself – although you should still be prepared to do your share of hard work while on the road.

a smoke-belching old Bedford truck, not a local model but a British army training vehicle; it was none too healthy.

We sailed on by, all the cares of the world blown away by the cool air, the homely farms and a super tarmac highway with fuel stations, shops and animated markets. We galloped along the miles; the Kenyan capital with all its modern towers, coffee houses and vivid happy memories beckoned. We would make it before sunset at this rate. Nairobi at last!

But perhaps one should never be quite so confident of anything happening to plan in Africa. Just 12 miles from the city, in the bright lights of the northern suburbs, a cruel twist to the day unfolded. At the crest of a rise, just before some obviously poor shanty areas, the clutch gave out with a shocking suddenness. With little prior warning, we were engulfed with impatient traffic, horns blasting, drivers fuming. Desperately we pushed the stricken vehicle to the side of the road. What a crowning frustration to a day of incredibly mixed emotions!

'Nairobi is a city with substantial areas best avoided at night, with rampant crime,' quotes a line in a guidebook. Our thoughts were racing, with a sudden sense of dread. What if this had happened earlier in the day? Then a nanosecond of comic concern followed, a barely controlled fit of humour and, as ever, that thought – why are we doing this? And then, in a few short minutes, a reality check, a detached sense of resignation, of being in the hands of a higher force and then the need for practical solutions, a wiping of the slate of fear.

Within five minutes we were approached by Charles and Martha, a local couple on their way home from work. They provided an amazing breath of humanity within the sea of hurried, detached masses of evening commuters. Within an hour the Land Rover had been pushed and cajoled into the armed-guard security of the local supermarket, and the night staff had been happily rewarded for their kindness and help. Charles and Martha had invited us to stay with them, their enquiring young son Titus and Martha's younger sister Angella. The flat was in a secure compound on a third floor. They offered us a sumptuous dinner, a comfortable bed and a hot shower, heated by a giant electric ring set in a bucket. The unbelievable kindness we were shown was embarrassing. Could we ever imagine such unashamed humanity in our own country?

On this one day we had enjoyed a homely breakfast, endured a harsh, hot and dusty desert crossing, passed sombre nomadic tribal clans, avoided bandits, experienced stress-relieving exhilaration in the highlands, broken down 12 miles from Nairobi and been welcomed as honoured guests into a private house of strangers.

Although written some time ago, this introductory story still encapsulates the essence of Africa Overland. We remain close friends with Martha, Charles and their family.

This book is tailored towards planning, preparation and other details specific to travel in Africa, rather than towards information about particular countries. It does not aim to replace country guides and we strongly recommend that you take along other relevant books.

FEEDBACK REQUEST

With ever-changing variables like road conditions, border closures and costs throughout Africa, we at Bradt always welcome any updates and suggestions from travellers. Please send your feedback by email to e info@bradtguides.com, or write to us at 23 High Street, Chalfont St Peter, Bucks SL9 9QE.

Bradt Travel Guides

www.bradtguides.com

Africa

Access Africa: Safaris for People with Limited Mobility	£16.99
Africa Overland	£16.99
Algeria	£15.99
Benin	£14.99
Botswana: Okavango, Chobe, Northern Kalahari	£15.99
Burkina Faso	£14.99
Cameroon	£15.99
Cape Verde Islands	£14.99
Congo	£15.99
Eritrea	£15.99
Ethiopia	£16.99
Gambia, The	£13.99
Ghana	£15.99
Johannesburg	£6.99
Madagascar	£15.99
Malawi	£13.99
Mali	£13.95
Mauritius, Rodrigues & Réunion	£13.99
Mozambique	£13.99
Namibia	£15.99
Niger	£14.99
Nigeria	£17.99
North Africa: The Roman Coast	£15.99
Rwanda	£14.99
São Tomé & Príncipe	£14.99
Seychelles	£14.99
Sierra Leone	£14.99
Sudan	£13.95
Tanzania, Northern	£14.99
Tanzania	£16.99
Uganda	£15.99
Zambia	£17.99
Zanzibar	£14.99

Britain and Europe

Albania	£15.99
Armenia, Nagorno Karabagh	£14.99
Azores	£13.99
Baltic Cities	£14.99
Belarus	£14.99
Belgrade	£6.99
Bosnia & Herzegovina	£13.99
Bratislava	£9.99
Britain from the Rails	£16.99
Budapest	£9.99
Bulgaria	£13.99
Cork	£6.99
Croatia	£13.99
Cyprus see North Cyprus	

Czech Republic	£13.99
Dresden	£7.99
Dubrovnik	£6.99
Estonia	£13.99
Faroe Islands	£15.99
Georgia	£14.99
Helsinki	£7.99
Hungary	£14.99
Iceland	£14.99
Kosovo	£14.99
Lapland	£13.99
Latvia	£13.99
Lille	£6.99
Lithuania	£14.99
Ljubljana	£7.99
Luxembourg	£13.99
Macedonia	£14.99
Montenegro	£14.99
North Cyprus	£12.99
Riga	£6.99
River Thames, In the Footsteps of the Famous	£10.95
Serbia	£14.99
Slovakia	£14.99
Slovenia	£13.99
Spitsbergen	£15.99
Switzerland without a Car	£14.99
Tallinn	£6.99
Transylvania	£14.99
Ukraine	£14.99
Vilnius	£6.99
Zagreb	£6.99

Middle East, Asia and Australasia

Borneo	£17.99
China: Yunnan Province	£13.99
Great Wall of China	£13.99
Iran	£14.99
Iraq: Then & Now	£15.99
Israel	£15.99
Kazakhstan	£15.99
Kyrgyzstan	£15.99
Maldives	£15.99
Mongolia	£16.99
North Korea	£14.99
Oman	£13.99
Shangri-La: A Travel Guide to the Himalayan Dream	£14.99
Sri Lanka	£15.99
Syria	£14.99
Tibet	£13.99
Turkmenistan	£14.99
Yemen	£14.99

The Americas and the Caribbean

Amazon, The	£14.99
Argentina	£15.99
Bolivia	£14.99
Cayman Islands	£14.99
Chile	£16.95
Colombia	£16.99
Costa Rica	£13.99
Dominica	£14.99
Grenada, Carriacou & Petite Martinique	£14.99
Guyana	£14.99
Panama	£13.95
St Helena	£14.99
Turks & Caicos Islands	£14.99
USA by Rail	£14.99

Wildlife

100 Animals to See Before They Die	£16.99
Antarctica: Guide to the Wildlife	£15.99
Arctic: Guide to the Wildlife	£15.99
Central & Eastern European Wildlife	£15.99
Chinese Wildlife	£16.99
East African Wildlife	£19.99
Galápagos Wildlife	£15.99
Madagascar Wildlife	£16.99
New Zealand Wildlife	£14.99
North Atlantic Wildlife	£16.99
Peruvian Wildlife	£15.99
Southern African Wildlife	£18.95
Sri Lankan Wildlife	£15.99
Wildlife and Conservation Volunteering: The Complete Guide	£13.99

Eccentric Guides

Eccentric Australia	£12.99
Eccentric Britain	£13.99
Eccentric California	£13.99
Eccentric Cambridge	£6.99
Eccentric Edinburgh	£5.95
Eccentric France	£12.95
Eccentric London	£13.99

Others

Your Child Abroad: A Travel Health Guide	£10.95
Something Different for the Weekend	£9.99

Part One

BEFORE YOU LEAVE

The Basics

You're dreaming of starry desert nights, of wild animals on the plains, of tropical beaches and of camping in the bush hearing the distant beat of drums, but where do you begin? If you have opened this book, the chances are that Africa will lure you on. Will it be worth every moment and every pound, euro or dollar? Very probably. Planning a big trip to Africa begins with dreams, but eventually the practical necessities, the basics, have to be considered.

Time and money, those salient facts of modern life, are the criteria that will influence the type of trip you plan across Africa. Your budget will determine where you plan to go, for how long and in how much comfort you wish to travel. Once these factors have been thought through, you can begin to look at the other issues. Top of these will be which countries are currently accessible; which routes avoid troublesome hotspots? How will local weather patterns influence the timing of your trip? You will need to take a long look at some maps in order to work out an outline itinerary. Calculating the time to get from place to place will depend on the state of the roads, the nature of the terrain, how many mountainous sections there are and the type of transport you have, as well as the inevitable bureaucratic delays *en route*. Some countries are expensive, imposing high visa fees or border charges; others are much less costly. Already you can see the difficulties in estimating a budget. You really do need to keep in mind any number of unexpected costs that will inevitably arise on the way. Of course sometimes it works in your favour, but don't plan on it.

Taking your own vehicle affords you unrivalled freedom, but you will undoubtedly find that the cost is surprisingly high. Most of it will probably be before you even set off. All the peripheral things add up; spare parts, visa fees, insurance, the *carnet*, etc (see *Chapter 5*). Basic day-to-day expenses can be very low; fuel is often dirt cheap and food, where available, is also often very cheap. But if you decide to visit a game park, or the vehicle breaks down, the costs can go sky high.

Taking a motorcycle or bicycle is much cheaper, but you will need to sacrifice comfort, choice of some destinations and some personal space to do it. It is of course possible to cross most of Africa on very public local transport. It will not always be easy and is often extremely uncomfortable. The other option is to join an overland truck group. This is a good option for a first-time trip if you are happy to mix in with other like-minded travellers and can forgo the independence you have when travelling on your own.

What you can't budget for are changes according to 'African factors'. These might be border closures and the necessity of some unexpected shipping, which could add considerably to the cost. There might be other delays, whether due to bureaucracy, road damage, breakdowns, border closures or just bad luck. Try to make a realistic assessment of all known costs and then add a couple of thousand dollars or more in case. Then make sure you can get extra funds on a debit or credit card if necessary.

EXPENDITURE Trying to predict expenses and work out a budget is very difficult for an overland expedition. Each person has different needs and expectations. Some can survive on only US$15 per day excluding fuel, while others cannot survive on less than US$80 or more per day. You probably need to find a balance between the two. It's possible to find out many fixed costs in advance, such as visas, border entry fees, ferries, an estimate of fuel costs and planned shipping expenses. You can estimate the cost of spare parts, equipment and tools. You can decide which vehicle to take, but remember that the cost of the vehicle *carnet* bond will relate to the value of the vehicle chosen. This can be one of the most significant considerations when choosing which vehicle to buy. The level of comfort you plan can affect costs – camping or hotels or a mix of both. You can map out a route and check costs for each country from relevant guidebooks (Bradt of course!)

We have indicated below some of the costs involved before you go. Some are more or less fixed; others are very variable, such as the vehicle chosen. We have also estimated the *en route* costs, but these too are highly variable according to personal needs.

We spent an average of US$70 per day, of which US$40 was fuel and other costs for the 4x4 vehicle, and the remaining US$30 was for expenses such as accommodation and living expenses for two people. This was for a three-month trip from London to Lomé and sadly back again during early 2008, driving over 24,000km with a total on-road expenditure of US$6,000. The previous trip – a three-and-a-half-month trip from London to South Africa, worked out cheaper because the Nile route down through east Africa is less expensive for both fuel and accommodation. If you camp in the bush where possible, avoiding air-conditioned rooms, the costs can be reduced. But it would be better to assume a daily expenditure of nearer US$80 for two people, with fuel prices likely to rise continually in future. Make sure you always have a way of getting more money if you need it. If you have a major breakdown you may need more than you could possibly foresee or carry; be prepared just in case.

As you travel, you will find that in some countries, like Sudan, your expenses will be minimal, as fuel is almost free and there isn't much else to spend money on. But countries like Kenya, Tanzania and Botswana can be much more expensive because of the activities on offer, like climbing Mount Kenya or visiting the various national parks. We found that at times we would spend as much as US$100 one day, and the next only US$12 (sometimes nothing at all in the desert), while famous game parks will be over US$100 per person. It will usually balance itself out. West Africa is expensive, with fuel prices almost as high as in Europe. Food costs virtually nothing if bought in local markets, but buy imported food in a French supermarket, add an air-conditioned room and the cost becomes considerable.

Realistically, if you are buying a vehicle specifically for this trip, you will need to budget for around US$15,000–25,000 in total before you leave, plus US$300–400+ per person per week in your own 4x4 vehicle. Even with a bicycle, the total initial investment will be over US$2,000. Planning a trip by motorbike will fall somewhere between the two.

Your preparation costs will quickly add up, with the purchase of a vehicle, equipping it appropriately, getting a *carnet*, full medical insurance cover and a medical kit, and many other hidden costs that you might not have considered. It is possible to do it more cheaply, but the less you invest, the harder your trip is likely to be. At the other extreme you could buy a fully converted six-wheel drive and spend something like US$100,000 before you even start. We would

The costs listed below are based on taking your own vehicle. Information on taking your own motorbike or bicycle is discussed further in this chapter and *Chapter 3*, pages 79 and 87. The figures below will vary enormously according to the amount of work you can do yourself, and where you get the vehicle, parts and tools. A toolbox bought in a car boot sale will cost much less than one from a good stockist, but be careful. You don't want your cheap spanner to crack up in a dodgy place.

BEFORE YOU LEAVE
Vehicle
Based on a secondhand Toyota Land Cruiser or Land Rover 110/Defender

Fully equipped, ie: overland ready	US$8,000–16,000
Vehicle only	US$6,000–12,000

Vehicle preparation
If you were lucky enough to find a fully equipped vehicle, you may only need to check everything works and fine-tune the vehicle for your trip. If you are starting from scratch you may be up for this full amount.   US$4,000–7,000

Equipment   US$2,000–3,000

Spares and tools   US$2,000–5,000

Medical insurance
Based on each person for one year full cover   US$500–1,000

Medical kit
The lower amount if buying in Africa   US$200–600

ON THE ROAD
Per person, per day, based on two people in one vehicle   US$50–80

not recommend this, as the more complicated the vehicle, the harder it will be to fix if it does go wrong and even an expensive vehicle is not immune to breakdowns. Also remember the cost of the *carnet* is directly related to the cost of the vehicle.

But don't be put off! If you have the abilities and facilities to do most of the preparation yourself, you can reduce your expenses considerably. The following are some of the major costs you will have to meet, but the figures quoted are only a rough guide. Ideally, you should look at your own requirements under each of the headings listed in *Chapter 3* and check out what these are likely to cost.

SPONSORSHIP You might think that sponsorship will fall into your lap as soon as you announce to the world that you are off to explore Africa. Be under no illusions; obtaining sponsorship is a tough nut to crack. Most obvious companies have been approached in the past. They will want you to demonstrate exactly how they are going to get a return on their investment. Local firms are more likely to be sympathetic than nationally known names, but they are also unlikely to have as much to offer. You must ask yourself whether the massive investment of time you will need to find any sort of sponsorship is worth it.

The Basics **THE BUDGET**

IN AID OF CHARITY With a great deal of forward planning, some travellers have managed to raise cash for charities by approaching sponsors and private donors. Some benefits can be derived from this approach, but a lot of effort will be required. Some of the larger charities such as CARE have given help to overland travellers who have raised money for them. This could be one way of raising awareness and giving something back to Africa. (See *Giving Something Back to Africa*, page 195.)

ROUTE PLANNING

It has been lamented by some famous travellers that the planning and the expectations of the journey are sometimes greater fun than the execution of the subsequent travel itself. Maybe – planning the trip is certainly a lot of fun. Hasty preparation should be avoided; the more information you have, the greater the chances of avoiding problems later. This applies to all aspects of the trip. The website www.africa-overland.net hosts links to independent travel websites, which may give you some ideas.

MAPS Africa is big and distances are massive. Make a mental note that travel times in Africa can be several times longer for a given distance than they are in areas with more developed transport infrastructures. Michelin probably make the best, most easily obtainable maps of Africa. Most travel bookstores stock them. Try to get all the maps you need before you set off, as they are difficult and often impossible to obtain in Africa (except perhaps in places in southern Africa).

Although the Michelin maps we highly recommend are excellent for planning, they have been found to have a few surprisingly significant errors. We mention some of these later in the route sections. You will need at the very least the following map numbers: 741 (Africa North and West), 745 (Africa North East and Arabia) and 746 (Africa Central and South). These maps have a wealth of mostly accurate information on them, showing all the salient points, distance, type of road surface, wells and quality of water, dunes, possible fuel and rest stops, altitudes, scenic routes, etc. Other Michelin maps that may be of some use are 742 (Morocco), 743 (Algeria and Tunisia) and 747 (Ivory Coast).

Be aware that, although some roads shown as a tarmac highway may be exactly that, quite often they will be appallingly pot-holed, with broken sections and rough uneven surfaces. At worst they may be just plain diabolical with little tarmac left. Other roads shown as gravel might be new super-highways. Some gravel roads are excellent, such as those in Namibia; others, like those in Ethiopia, are exceedingly rough, stony, rocky and tyre-eating.

In the central African rainforest zone, roads can be extremely muddy, with large puddles often the size of ponds. Bridges here may be broken, have planks missing or be constructed of logs. During the wet seasons, some roads are impassable and others might be closed off to vehicles by 'rain barriers' (*barrières de pluie*) across the road until the muddy surfaces have dried sufficiently.

CLIMATE On the Michelin maps you will see charts indicating the approximate average temperatures, high and low, as well as the rainfall for various cities and towns in Africa. When you are planning the best time of year for your trip, these give a very good basic insight into the climatic conditions of each area.

Attempting to cross the Sahara in summer between late April and early October is pretty crazy. If you plan to invest a lot of money in driving across the Sahara, why go when the dangers are high and the journey exceedingly uncomfortable? The Sahara has a wonderful winter climate, but be aware that in the midwinter months

Where was the road to Khartoum? Maps are a wonderful thing until you realise that a road on a map in northern Sudan is in reality the sand beside the railway, and on which side of the line does it go? This road is a complete figment of Michelin's imagination. We followed the railway line but, even before leaving Wadi Halfa, we were in quite deep sand. More by luck and guesswork than map-reading, we found the way by following the line of telegraph poles alongside the railway tracks. For 200 miles we followed the tracks; occasionally the sand was very deep. We met just one vehicle all day and that was only ten miles out of town. Despite the fact that there is a railway here, which offered some comfort, this route is surprisingly remote and devoid of life.

At Station Four we encountered some workmen preparing the line for the expected train. They were sweeping sand off the tracks, and were not pleased with us as we pulled into the station astride the lines, carefully avoiding the points and steel cables. 'Which way to Khartoum?' They were not amused and directed us out into the deepest sand 100m from the station. Horribly bogged now, we discovered that the low-ratio gears on the Land Rover would not engage. Fortunately some digging and then diff lock got us out. Away from the station, we again headed as close to the railway tracks as possible, sneaking on to the embankment at the next deep sand. The track was surprisingly smooth as the rails were buried by hard sand and the only problem was avoiding touching the lines themselves. It was lucky for us that the train comes only once a week in each direction, as we were stuck on this embankment for many miles with no way off. And today there were no trains, because of a mass wedding party in Wadi Halfa, to which all were invited and no-one could leave.

It was great to camp wild in the desert at last, below some low rocky hills with a tremendous view. Having just parked and made a cup of tea, Bob said to me, 'Look, what's that over there? It looks almost like a train!'

'It is a train,' I replied.

Thank goodness we were no longer on the lines. It was a large freight train, which was obviously too late for the wedding party!

it gets very close to freezing overnight, so good bedding is essential. Remember too that altitude can play a significant part in the effects of temperature and climate. In Ethiopia or on the slopes of Mount Kenya, for example, the highlands bring a welcome relief from the sometimes oppressive heat of the plains.

Further south, planning a trip through any areas subject to seasonal rains really can wreak havoc on daily schedules, particularly where roads are not paved. It is surprising what a short sharp rainstorm can do to some roads. In the Sahel, on the southern fringes of the Sahara, this can mean seriously sticky conditions, where sand and soil are mixed. In the humid rainforests it can manifest in hours of digging away thick heavy mud while up to your waist in brown water. There is a certain amount of masochistic fun to be had in these predicaments, but not for three weeks continuously.

No departure date is likely to suit all the optimum weather patterns fully. If you plan to be on a long journey across Africa, it becomes more difficult. Somewhere *en route* is going to be awkward; you will just have to work around these things at the time. But time is what you might have most of.

OTHER FACTORS AND LIMITATIONS Below are some of the parameters that you need to determine: total number of days available, daily travel distance, acceptable range of climate, geography, road conditions, level of accommodation, flexibility with food, availability of fuel and water, delays obtaining visas *en route*, unexpected festivals and even what wildlife you want to see.

Timing is important. Because of the large number of fascinating destinations in Africa, your inclination might be to try to fit too much into too little time. Seven game parks in seven days in a 4x4 can be as gruelling as a European bus tour of seven countries in seven days. Some travellers suggest that quality is better than quantity, but if you don't want to miss anything, it's amazing how much you can pack in with some determination.

Don't be surprised if your planning chart begins to look a complete mess with rows of 'if, then, maybe' conditions for each separate possible itinerary. It's a good idea to use an Excel spreadsheet if you have it, then you can shift the options and dates around easily and view them side-by-side.

ROUTE OUTLINES With regard to actual routes, things change constantly. In the heyday of African overlanding in the late 1970s and the 1980s, almost all the continent's big routes were open, except for those via Angola, Mozambique and, at various times, southern Sudan. In the early '90s the superb trans-Saharan routes across Algeria closed, due to Islamic insurgents in the north and the Tuareg rebellion in the south. The route into Mauritania opened via Western Sahara, so trans-Africa remained possible. When the turmoil of Zaire erupted, combined with instability in the Central African Republic, the routes across the great rainforests of the Congo basin became history.

Yet routes did remain tenuously possible, as is often the way of African travel. Chad and Sudan allowed a trickle of adventurous travellers to cross from Cameroon to Ethiopia a few years ago, but hostilities in Darfur closed that route in 2004. The Nile route through Egypt to Khartoum, so long a big no-go area, opened. More recently, some have tried to drive south from Cameroon into

Gabon, across the two Congos and into Angola, a route that was expected to be a good option until Angola stopped giving out visas to overland travellers in 2008.

With the kidnappings in Algeria in 2003, vast tracks of the **Sahara** became effectively off-limits to independent overlanders. During 2007–08, and still continuing, Niger and Chad had their own problems, so most of the Sahara remains a distant dream for the time being. Nevertheless, the potential for great overlanding in those countries remains, and we have been privileged to go there during safer times, so we include some details later.

Across **west Africa** some great routes are now safe, exciting and practical. Relatively good routes from Mauritania lead to Mali and Burkina Faso, fascinating Sahel countries with spectacular mud-walled towns, picturesque mosques and varied scenery. Along the coast, only Ivory Coast remains very unsafe. Liberia is at last creeping out from the disasters of the war years. Senegal, Gambia, Guinea Bissau, Guinea and Sierra Leone are currently as safe as Africa gets. Ghana, Nigeria, Cameroon and Gabon complete the coastal route and are also to be contemplated when planning your route. The chance of encountering crime in all the big coastal cities (Lomé, Cotonou, Lago, Douala and around Port Harcourt) should be borne in mind, though.

East Africa has become a delight for overlanders, safari enthusiasts and just about anyone looking to experience Africa at its secure best. Now that the lingering conflict between opposing groups in Burundi is said to have been resolved, most of east Africa – Kenya, Tanzania, Uganda, Burundi and Rwanda – can be visited with keen anticipation. Heading south, the routes to the Cape in South Africa and Namibia are all politically stable, with only Zimbabwe presenting dilemmas about any serious security issues. All this is not to say that muggings in big cities and opportunistic crime cannot be ruled out, but that happens in cities all across the globe now.

For **access to Africa**, don't dismiss the route across Europe to Istanbul and then south to Egypt via Syria and Jordan, both exceedingly hospitable countries despite the bad images portrayed in the media. Don't go through Israel, though; you will not be able to get into Sudan later. On the downside, the Egyptian authorities have increased the *carnet* duties percentage from 500% to 900%, making it very expensive to obtain the paperwork necessary for travelling there.

By linking up the different options, almost any type of trip can be contemplated. Over the past 30 years, one route at least has always seemed to be possible, enough to keep the flickering candle of African travel passion alive. Check out various websites for travellers' stories as well – many people now carry computers with them and update their blogs as they go. In the end, though, the latest security circumstances will usually dictate your final choice.

In **planning your route** you need to be fully informed about the latest political situations in the countries on the way. You need to find out whether visas for the countries you want to visit are required and being issued – and where. You should definitely consult the various government foreign travel advice websites, such as the British one at **www.fco.gov.uk**. Of course, if you took complete notice of the information given out in these websites, you might never go anywhere at all. They are by their very nature somewhat cautious, over-protective and sometimes out-of-date. The nanny state is all around – one is not supposed to be this adventurous.

A good example of the difficulties in assessing the risk was illustrated by previous warnings about Chad north of the capital N'djamena. These warnings suggested that travel anywhere in the whole area was unsafe. While the Tibesti region certainly was dangerous, the Ennedi area was not, except for the existence of mines in known places. If we had heeded the FCO warnings when we planned to visit the Ennedi in 2002, we might have missed an incredible experience. Maybe we were lucky that time! This is not to say we recommend that everyone should go to Chad at the moment, as the situation has once again deteriorated.

Things need to be put into context and, above all, good and reliable local advice must be sought for such areas. Some places in Africa are frankly best avoided by people like us in our own cars, and are better visited with experienced local operators, as we did in both Chad and parts of Niger.

New for this fifth edition, we have set out in *Chapter 2* more detail on the routes that exist across Africa. We include some details covering the Middle East – a varied and pleasant introduction to the ways of Third World motor travel. A number of options cover the Sahara and west Africa; others concentrate on the west-to-east routes. Outline details are also given about possibilities within the Congo basin, and of course the routes south of Kenya to South Africa, on which political instability is fortunately not an issue. Whether you are planning a short foray into north Africa, a longer trip through west Africa and back via the Sahara or the complete trans-Africa, the planning will re-ignite the dreams that you had when you first decided that this journey was for you.

Of course, no trip will ever go exactly to plan. Well, it might, but anyway the travellers and local people you meet along the way are sure to provide you with invaluable up-to-date information about roads, routes, new ideas and safety concerns.

Note on place names Confusion inevitably arises between the Democratic Republic of the Congo (DRC) – formerly Zaire – and the People's Republic of the Congo. For the purposes of this book we have used Democratic Republic of the Congo or DRC for the former and Congo or Congo Brazzaville for the latter.

GETTING TO AFRICA

Ferry routes At the beginning or end of your trip, you will probably need to consider the ferry routes from Europe into Africa or vice versa; most people will be looking for the cheapest and most convenient routes.

One popular route is **Spain to Morocco** from Algeciras, Malaga or Gibraltar to Ceuta or Tangiers. Those with a vehicle or motorbike will probably opt to go via

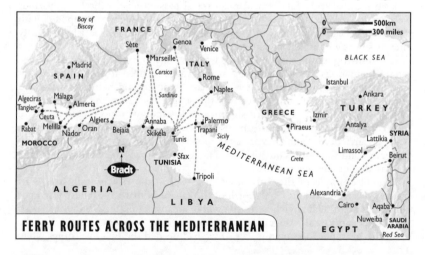

FERRY ROUTES ACROSS THE MEDITERRANEAN

Ceuta, because the fare to Ceuta is cheaper than to Tangiers and the journey time shorter. The city forms part of Spanish Morocco; its tax-free status means that fuel is cheap, but costs more than in Morocco. It's always a good idea to fill up those jerrycans if you're going north.

Other popular routes are from **France** (Marseille) **to Morocco or Tunisia.** Ferries to Algeria are currently not advised. From **Italy** good ferries run to **Tunisia.** These go primarily from Genoa, Naples and Trapani (in Sicily) to Tunis. Ferries also connect the Italian ports of Genoa, Livorno and Naples with Palermo, meaning you can visit Sicily on the way without driving all the way down through Italy.

Ferries were operating from **Greece and Turkey to Egypt.** But recent reports suggest that these, if they still exist, are best avoided. In 2004 some people shipping vehicles into Egypt were kept waiting at the dockside by the authorities for more than a few days; one party was held up for two weeks. This may not be a wise option. It might be possible to ship a vehicle from **Malta to Libya,** but this is unlikely to be of any benefit unless you are going to Malta anyway. It's better to ship your vehicle into Tunis, a very well-organised port, and take the excellent road from Tunis to Libya.

It is quite easy to ship a vehicle from Aqaba in **Jordan to Nuweiba in the Egyptian Sinai**, making a route possible across Europe through Turkey and Syria to link in with the Nile route to Khartoum.

One final ferry route that might be of some use to those travelling north from **Sudan** to the Middle East is the one from Port Sudan to Jeddah in **Saudi Arabia**. It's shown as route ME2 on the map of trans-Sahara routes on page 24. This cannot be done southbound because of difficulties in obtaining the Saudi transit visa, which is only valid for three days and is not given to unmarried couples. This visa was issued in Khartoum for direct travel from Jeddah to Jordan only – again for three days. Security issues may affect this option. Do not attempt it during Hajj, the annual Muslim pilgrimage to Mecca.

Ferries run daily from Brindisi and Bari in southern **Italy** to Igoumenitsa near Corfu in **Greece**, for those heading to Africa via the Middle East who want to avoid the cold in eastern Europe.

For more information on these routes, see *Chapter 2*, page 21.

Ferry prices For the Algeciras–Ceuta ferry it is not necessary to book in advance in winter, the off-season. Getting a place is not likely to be a problem at this time of year. Shop around when you arrive, though. At most ports, there are salespeople representing the major ferry companies who can sell you a ticket there and then. In fact, even many miles away on the main road leading to Algeciras, you will pass numerous travel agencies offering tickets at unbelievably low prices. We heard that at least one of these was genuine. Most ferries running the Spain–Morocco routes run regular services every 30 minutes both ways. A standard ferry crossing from Algeciras to Ceuta usually takes up to 45 minutes; a fast ferry to Tangiers takes just over one hour. The standard price for the short ferry crossings, for example Spain to Morocco/Ceuta for two people in a car, is around US$200 at the time of writing in 2008. However, it could be as low as US$50 or as much as US$300. For the Algeciras–Tangiers fast ferry, we were quoted US$240 in advance, but on the spot paid US$150. You take your chances.

Ferries to Tunisia are cheaper from Italy than France, and the drive to Genoa is almost as quick (allow three days from London). For the best prices these routes should be booked well in advance if possible. They are very heavily booked in summer, but most overlanders will not be going then anyway, unless they are masochists or want a totally mad experience. Return fares are particularly good value, although none are that cheap. The ferries take about 24 hours. Approximate prices are US$1,000–1,400 return (within four months).

From Trapani (Sicily) to Tunis the ferry takes about nine hours. This ferry is best booked in advance, but beware! It can be delayed by rough weather at times. It is much cheaper as a cabin is not required.

Some of the ferry companies offer concessions, depending on the season.

Ferry companies Below is a list of ferry companies with international representation.

France to Morocco or Algeria

🚢 **SNCM Ferryterranee**; BP 90, 13472 Marseille cedex 2, France; 📞 0891 701 801, +33 4 91 56 32 00; f +33 4 91 56 35 86; www.sncm.fr

Greece, Turkey, Middle East to Egypt

For Greek ferries, look at the website www.greekislands.gr and further links. At the time of writing, most ferry services to north Africa were suspended.

Italy to Tunisia

We have personally used both of these agencies successfully. Viamare act as agents for Grandi Navi Veloci and Grimaldi, while Southern Ferries deal with SNCM (French), CTN (Tunisian) and Trasmediterránea (Spanish). Check with them for any changes or updates to ferry schedules and routes.

🚢 **Southern Ferries** 1st Floor, 179 Piccadilly, London W1V 9DB; 📞 020 7491 4968; f 0870 499 1304; e info@southernferries.co.uk; www.southernferries.co.uk

🚢 **Viamare UK Ltd** Graphic Hse, 2 Sumatra Rd, London NW6 1PU; 📞 020 7431 4560, 0870 410 6040; f 020 7431 5456; e ferries@viamare.com; www.viamare.com

Spain to Morocco

🚢 **Compañia Trasmediterránea** Head office: Av de Europa 10, Parque Empresarial La Moraleja CP 28108 Alcobendas; 📞 +34 91 423 8500; f +34 91 423 8555, information & booking: +34 90 245 4645; e correom@trasmediterranea.es; www.trasmediterranea.es.

Other offices & agents: *Algeciras* (Cádiz) Recinto del Puerto, s/n, CP 11201; 📞 +34 95 658 7517; *Ceuta* Muelle Canonero Dato 6, CP 51001; 📞 +34 95 652 2239; *Málaga* Estación Maritima, Recinto del Puerto, Local E1, CP 29016; f +34 95 206 1218; *Morocco* Limadet; 13 Av Prince Moulay Abdellah, Tangiers;

📞 39 931142; *UK* Southern Ferries; 1st Floor, 179 Piccadilly, London W1V 9DB; 📞 020 7491 4960; f 0870 499 1304; e info@southernferries.co.uk; www.southernferries.co.uk

🚢 **Ferrimaroc SA** www.ferrimaroc.com; *UK* e helpdesk@ferrimaroc.com; *Morocco* Voyage Wasteels SA, Port of Beni Enzar, 62050 Post du Beni Enzar, Nador; 📞 56 348786; f 56 348781; & Ferrimaroc Nador SA, BP 96 Beni Enzar, Nador; 📞 56 348100; f 56 349520; *Spain* Ferrimaroc Agencias SL, Muelle Ribera s/n, 04002 Almeria; 📞 +34 95 027 4800; f +34 95 027 6366, e info@ferrimaroc.com

Other international companies

🚢 **MBendi Information Services** PO Box 23498, Claremont 7735, South Africa; 📞 021 671 9889; f 021 671 6316; www.mbendi.co.za

🚢 **Grimaldi** www.grimaldi-freightercruises.com & www.grimaldi.co.uk. Services to west Africa into Accra,

Abidjan, Lomé, Douala & Luanda have been recommended.

🚢 **P&O** www.poferrymasters.com & www.routesinternational.com

Finally, at the end of the trip, what happens to the vehicle to which you could well have become sentimentally attached?

4X4 VEHICLES If you are planning to ship your vehicle back at the end of the trip (or indeed to start your journey by shipping one out), this can be a major expense. The lowest prices from Mombasa, Dar es Salaam, Accra, Durban or Cape Town to Europe are around US$4,000 for a container (there are a lot of other African countries that also offer freight service, but the above are the largest and most popular). Also beware of all the hidden extras; these can add as much as another 50%.

Shipping a vehicle from Europe to South Africa is reasonably easy, if a little more expensive. We found the shipping companies and agencies fair, even with all the extra costs, which were quoted in advance. For shipping a vehicle to either east or west Africa, hidden costs may be an issue, as problems can occur later at the African ports where red tape is complex and almost certainly some large bribes may be necessary.

Whether in east, west, central or southern Africa, you will probably need to use a shipping agent. Although this may add to the cost, it should give you peace of mind and save a lot of time.

It would be advisable to try to find other travellers who want to ship their vehicle, as a container can be shared, depending on the size of the vehicle.

For shipping from Mombasa we have been told that dealing with the bureaucracy and corruption needs a lot of patience and the costs are extortionate. In west Africa, Accra seems to be the least difficult place to sort out shipping. Other ports are Lomé and Douala, with both Libreville and Pointe Noire also offering irregular services. Coming back from or going out to South Africa, there are roll-on roll-off ferries between Durban and Rotterdam/Southampton in the UK.

We shipped our vehicle back from Durban in 2004 through P&O and a local agent. This service is offered approximately once a month. The vehicle was put onto a ship bringing hundreds of new cars into Europe, to Southampton, Zeebrugge or Hamburg. Vehicles are driven on and off and are not in containers. It took three weeks. At the time, the cost was US$1,250, plus various port charges at each end adding around US$400. It does, of course, cost more now, but is certainly less than the cost of a container.

This can be arranged through P&O Ferrymasters in the UK (as above, page 12, and below), or SRP Shipping in Durban, South Africa (see below).

MOTORBIKES Of course, shipping a bike can be much cheaper, particularly if you share a container. It is even possible to hitch a lift by putting a bike inside a vehicle already being shipped. Airfreight for motorbikes is also pretty reasonable.

BICYCLES It is generally possible to take a bicycle as luggage on most airlines.

WEBSITES/CONTACTS The following are good website addresses for shipping lines, agents and costs.

An Mbendi Profile – African Shipping Industry
www.mbendi.co.za
Complete online freight services (international)
www.freightquote.com
P&O Ferrymasters www.poferrymasters.com

Grimaldi www.grimaldi.co.uk; www.grimaldi-freightercruises.com
SRP shipping ✆+27 (011) 304 5791/6; f +27 (011) 304 5840/5114; e srpship@mweb.co.za

STARTING A TRIP FROM SOUTH AFRICA *Arnout Hemel and Saskia de Jongh*

YOUR VEHICLE Whether you buy your vehicle at home or in South Africa, each option has its benefits and disadvantages. Assuming home is Europe or any Western country, it's worth considering the following factors.

Availability In South Africa you'll mainly find petrol cars; diesel cars are less common and more expensive. Toyota Hilux and Land Cruisers, and Land Rover Defenders are common. South Africans like the outdoors and 4x4s, so there is plenty of outdoor equipment.

Cost Cars cost about the same in South Africa as in Europe. Equipment is much cheaper (rooftop tents, fridges, etc). Labour costs are lower in South Africa, so it's cheaper to add an extra fuel tank, get things fixed or get your rooftop tent installed.

Time The time you need to prepare your vehicle depends on the state of the car and the level of perfection you want to achieve. It can be done in two to three weeks, while some people spend over a year. If you belong to the second category, prepare your car at home! Preparations are easier to plan and you can spend any free hour you have available.

In South Africa you need a safe place to prepare your vehicle to avoid theft. The best option is to find a guesthouse with a parking lot, a spacious campsite or friends with a big home. You may feel that your preparations in South Africa take time from your actual trip. Try to see them as part of your holiday; enjoy the good weather and finish your day with a sundowner and *braai* (barbecue).

Shipping/selling Unless you make a round trip, there will always be a time when you have to ship your vehicle or sell it at the end of your trip. Selling a South African car is easy in South Africa, but more difficult elsewhere. Shipping in either direction between Europe and South Africa seems relatively straightforward (see *Shipping your vehicle*, page 13).

BUYING AND PREPARING A CAR IN SOUTH AFRICA If you have decided to arrange everything in South Africa, then bear the following things in mind.

Before you leave home Check whether your local automobile association issues a *carnet de passage* for a foreign vehicle (normally they do not, but for example the Dutch ANWB does). If they do, it gives you the flexibility to sell the car in your home country as well as in South Africa. Also the process for depositing the money is easier and more reliable.

Check out the web to get an impression of the cars on sale. Two good websites are www.autotrader.co.za and www.ananzi.co.za.

Buy guidebooks and maps. The Michelin series (746, 741 and 745) are very good, or check out MapStudio's *Southern & East Africa Atlas*. Maps are not easy to find in South Africa. However, detailed 4x4 maps with GPS co-ordinates for southern Africa are available in Johannesburg and Cape Town. Here you can also find a very interesting book from Getaway Magazine: *Getaway Guide Cape to Cairo*, with a description of the whole trip including GPS co-ordinates.

Check at your local bank to see if it is possible to transfer money to South Africa. The easiest way is by internet banking, otherwise you can order an international payment. If you want to be on the safe side, arrange a credit or debit card with which you can withdraw money from a local bank in South Africa (not the cheapest option, but it will work).

Finding the right car The best markets to buy a car in South Africa are either Cape Town or Johannesburg. In Cape Town there tend to be more overlanders wanting to sell their cars than in Johannesburg. Recommended places to look are guesthouses, garages/dealers, special overland equippers, private persons, internet: www.autotrader.co.za.

If you want to be sure that you are buying a good car, you can do a Test & Drive check at one of the AA test stations (*www.aa.co.za*). The AA test is very thorough.

Money and paperwork When you have decided which car to buy, it's a matter of paying for it and getting the paperwork done. Getting money transferred to a South African bank account can be quite a hassle. In 2003 we couldn't easily transfer money from Holland to South Africa through our internet bank accounts. So we withdrew money with our credit cards (maximum €7,500 per card) and paid for our car in cash. This was not the safest option, and we were really glad our backpack full of R100 notes arrived safely at Johannesburg to pay for our Land Rover.

Getting the paperwork done is not too difficult. The following steps must be completed:

1. The seller needs to get the car through a roadworthiness test.
2. The buyer and seller need to fill in two copies of the selling papers, which the seller sends off to get the car de-registered from his name. The buyer needs to go to a local municipality office with one copy to buy a licence disc, and to register the car in his/her name. Total costs are less than €100, but you need an address in South Africa to be registered as a South African road user. Ask the guesthouse where you stay if they will support you. We used the address of friends with whom we were staying.
3. You obtain a *carnet de passage*. This is not necessary if you stay in southern Africa (Mozambique, Namibia, Botswana, Zimbabwe, Zambia, Malawi). If you plan to go to other countries, it's mandatory. Make sure Egypt, Jordan and Syria are on the *carnet* as you might need to cross these countries, and many AAs tend to exclude those countries.

Insurance Normally when you try to insure your car for an overland trip, you need only third party insurance. If something happens, however, for example if you hit a child in Ethiopia, your third party insurance won't help you much. Whether you are insured or not, you have to pay for the costs (typically in cash US$).

If you want comprehensive insurance, try Cross Country Consultants (*www.allterrain.co.za*). They have a modestly priced (€60 per month) comprehensive insurance for southern Africa, Kenya, Tanzania and Uganda.

If you are crossing Africa (across the east) all the way from/to Europe, you need roughly the following insurance:

- Green Card for Europe as far as Morocco, Tunisia and Turkey.
- COMESA/Yellow Card: one policy covering third party insurance for Burundi, Djibouti, DRC, Eritrea, Ethiopia, Kenya, Malawi, Rwanda, Sudan, Tanzania, Uganda, Zambia and Zimbabwe.
- Third party insurance at all other borders.

Preparing the car In South Africa you can find a good selection of spares, tools, accessories, camping equipment and skilled mechanics.

Tools and spares Tools are readily available at every hardware store. Spares like oil filters, air filters, points, etc, can be found around the country at Midas. For more specialised Land Rover spares in the Gauteng area, you can visit Leimer's Land Rovers.

Camping equipment South Africa has probably the best selection of outdoor and camping equipment in the world and prices are considerably lower than Europe. You can find the world's best portable fridges (National Luna, Engel), and many rooftop tents originate from South Africa (Eezi Awn, Echo, Howling Moon, Hannibal). Just visit an outdoor store and you will get an idea. When buying equipment, make sure you haggle about the prices (you will get at least 10% discount for paying cash). Rooftop tents can also be bought directly at the factory for great prices.

Some useful outdoor stores

Camp World www.campworld.co.za **Makro** www.makro.co.za
Outdoor Warehouse www.outdoorwarehouse.co.za

One great thing to keep in mind when you go shopping for outdoor equipment is the following: when you leave South Africa and don't intend to return, you can get reimbursed for the VAT paid on all stuff that is not permanently attached to the car and is not consumed (eg: your rooftop tent). All you have to do is keep the original receipt and fill out the forms at the border when you leave South Africa. You must do this within three months of purchasing the goods.

Accessories South Africa is also the ideal place for buying car accessories. Hi-lift jack, winch, tyres, fuel jerrycans, long-range fuel tank; you name it, everything is for sale and most of the time the seller will be happy to install it free of charge for you.

Mechanics If you need to get some work done on your car, there are many options. In general the mechanics in South Africa are skilled and the labour is cheap compared with Europe. A recommended Toyota mechanic and safari outfitter is Baillies Off-Road (*www.baillies.co.za*).

Our own experience We arrived in South Africa on a one-way ticket with only our backpacks. We stayed for two weeks with friends in Johannesburg. In that period of time, we bought a car (which took two days), built in a long-range tank, rooftop tent and fridge, and bought all our camping equipment (chairs, table, plates, cutlery, boxes, braai), tools and spares.

We paid R50,000 for the vehicle (1984 Land Rover Series III, LWB, with a new 3.5L V8 petrol engine). We bought it through *Autotrader* from a private person. We spent another R20,000 on all the equipment. Altogether it cost us about R70,000. We rented a car and mobile phone for the first ten days, to make it easy to look for a car and do the shopping while we were preparing our Land Rover.

Next time we would do it the same way, with the one exception that we would buy a diesel-powered car instead of petrol, as diesel fuel is generally cheaper, easier to handle and the engine needs less maintenance.

PLANNING A MOTORBIKE TRIP

See also *Motorbike preparation*, page 83.

Much of the planning for a motorbike trip can be based on the above details. The major differences will be in costs, which will be significantly lower. The other main difference concerns route planning. The chosen itinerary will to some extent depend on the quantity of fuel and water your motorbike can carry and how far off the beaten track you feel confident to go. That said, motorbikes are much easier to handle in many situations. They can be carried across rivers on canoes, and put on trucks, buses and even planes. They offer a greater degree of freedom in many respects and generally are less worry if they go wrong. They also do not look extravagant and desirable.

See also *Bicycle preparation*, page 87.

Those thinking of driving across Africa might be surprised to learn there is an even more adventuresome bunch planning the trip on a bicycle. If you have plenty of time and do not mind the hardship and physical effort, cycling when done intelligently can be a very rewarding way to see the continent. It certainly brings you into closer contact with both the people and the environment than most other methods. But honour the caveat – this means taking into account the geography, weather patterns, political reality, culture, and availability of food and water, as well as being prepared and having the proper equipment.

Just as in Western countries, there is something nicely different, and sometimes inspirational, about arriving almost anywhere in Africa by bicycle. In the cities, bicycles are efficient – even in Africa streets are congested and parking spaces few, which is not a problem with a bicycle.

In the countryside the bicycle is liberating. It reduces your dependency on mechanically questionable, overcrowded and unpredictable public transport. It expands your range over those who walk and it creates more social interaction than is possible from a tourist van or overland truck. As you cycle you are certain to meet people whom you would not meet any other way, generating rich experiences. The physical activity benefits your health and fitness, and the unrestricted access to the environment puts you into the middle of an exciting world that begs exploration.

Even if you don't like a lot of extreme hardship and can settle for seeing a carefully selected area of the continent, you can get the people-to-people benefits of a bike tour in Africa. Because of the flexibility of a bike and the ease with which it integrates with planes, trains, buses and boats, you can start and stop your road adventure almost anywhere you want.

If you are riding coast to coast, it goes without saying that you should not dream of such a trip unless you are in good health – cycling across the sands of the Sahara or through muddy forest trails can be extremely hard work. Some previous experience of long-distance cycling is vital before setting out. On the other hand, if your interests are for a more modest cycling tour on some of the thousands of miles of sealed roads in Africa, your preparation is similar to that which you would need for a similar tour in Europe or North America: a basic level of physical activity in your life, and proper equipment. Of course there are no written rules and attitude can prevail over all else; Christian and Gilly Lee, who contributed to earlier editions of this book, didn't do any cycling at all before they set off on their successful trip from Victoria station to Victoria Falls.

Bicycle Africa Tours report that they regularly have complete bicycle touring novices and African travel novices on their programmes, who do very well because they have so much enthusiasm for exploring Africa.

In most ways, the fundamentals of long-distance cycling in Africa differ very little from those of long-distance summer cycling in North America or Europe: the hills go up and down; the weather can be wet and dry; the temperature is hot and cold; the humidity varies from high to low; and it seems that regardless of which direction you are going there is a head wind at least part of the time. But, there are also differences to keep in mind:

- Repair facilities are fewer and farther between, so that the initial quality, ongoing upkeep of your bike and your general self-sufficiency need to be more of a concern. This is covered in the sections on selecting and preparing a bike for travel in remote areas and the bike tools section of the packing list (pages 87 and 98).

- Although there are tens of thousands of kilometres of paved roads in Africa, the proportion of major roads which are unpaved is much higher than in most industrialised countries, and many of the paved roads are deteriorating. The rotating joke for countries that have fallen on hard times is, 'What do you call a driver going in a straight line?' Answer: 'Drunk.' On the other hand, new stretches of roads are being paved each year and the dust is gradually disappearing.
- Cycling in Africa can easily be made more rigorous than is typical of touring in Europe and north America, especially if you are motivated to get off the highways and off the beaten track into the villages. It is there that you will find some of the most interesting scenes the continent has to offer. On any long-distance tour in Africa it is likely that you will find a mix of riding conditions. You will enjoy it a lot more if you prepare appropriately. Important points on this are covered in the relevant sections of this guide.
- Don't expect generic highway McFood. The food will be different. If you keep your expectations of the variety of food modest and learn to like Africa's cuisine, you will find plenty to eat in most areas. Cuisine in Africa is not homogeneous; some is more elaborate than others. If you are willing to explore, the chances are that you will find some excellent hole-in-the-wall restaurants and great local cooks and dishes. Unless you have heard that a specific area is suffering from famine it probably has adequate, if not abundant, food supplies.
- Quiet and personal privacy may become a luxury. Personal space, private property and 'the individual' have very different implications and associations in African culture. Even where the general population density is sparse, where people are living can be crowded, active and communal. Many Westerners find the gregariousness of African culture a challenge.
- Things that we take for granted, like water acquisition, may need to be carefully planned. Bottled water, carbonated drinks and beer are not always available in grocery stores, restaurants or bars. When they are, they probably won't be as cold as you would like and the choice will be limited, with a different selection from that in the last town. Even coffee, in countries that export tonnes of it each year, may not be brewed and sold outside the major cities. If you are drinking water from other sources it may need to be boiled, filtered or treated so that it is a blessing and not a curse.
- There is also an element of truth to some of the myths: toilet facilities may not meet the standards of cleanliness and freshness of the Western service station or may be absent altogether. Smells engulf markets, towns, people and all aspects of life more than in the West.
- Lastly, unless your initial cycling is in Burkina Faso, or a few other select spots where cycling is a popular mass activity, you will quickly note that cycling does not command the status in Africa that it does in China, much of the rest of Asia, or even Europe and North America. This is not a point of concern per se, but may explain some bewildering looks and questions of disbelief. Hold your ground. Cyclists may be in the minority, but Africans are used to minorities and they are willing to bestow respect on deserving innovators.

The watchwords are 'plan well, be flexible, be tolerant'.

Bicycle touring may be one of the hardest, but it also is one of the most economical means of travel. The main costs you need to incur are on your bike, visas, food and accommodation. If you eat the local cuisine and camp or stay in rock-bottom guesthouses, you can keep expenses to the absolute minimum. Even at the end of your trip, many airlines will ship your bike back free as part of your luggage (but not all of them, so shop around – see www.ibike.org/encouragement/travel/bagregs.htm).

If the idea appeals to you, a good first stop would be to contact the Internet Guide to Travel in Africa by Bicycle, www.ibike.org/africaguide, or the Cyclists' Touring Club (CTC) in the UK (*Cotterell Hse, 69 Meadrow, Godalming, Surrey GU7 3HS;* ✆ *01483 417217;* f *01483 426994;* e *cycling@ctc.org.uk*).

Once you join the CTC, you get a wide range of services – insurance, technical advice, touring itineraries and travel information. Information sheets are published by the CTC on various aspects of travelling with a bicycle and on specific countries and areas in Africa – including west Africa, South Africa, Seychelles, Malawi, Gambia, Zambia, Zimbabwe, Algeria and Tunisia, Egypt and Sudan, Morocco, and the Sahara. Information is also available for trans-African journeys and those planning round-the-world trips.

No guide to overland travel in Africa would be complete without such reference to cycling – a mode of transport that is more popular than you might imagine. But there are plenty of practical questions that need to be addressed by anyone who has plans for such a trip. So that you learn a minimum of the lessons the hard way, here are some general aspects that are worth considering.

CONSTRUCTING THE ITINERARY Constructing an itinerary, especially for a bike tour, is a multi-faceted project; the desire to see what you want to see, the limitations of daily range, the need for food and lodging and the complications of weather and topography can make it seem like solving Rubik's cube. Here are some of my approaches and considerations.

Mileage Experienced international bicycle travellers find that for a variety of reasons their daily mileage in foreign countries is less than they would typically ride at home. For starters there is a lot to see, and because everything is so different you will want to leave extra time just to look around. Second, it also tends to be the case that everyday chores, small business matters (ie: banking, posting mail and buying supplies), transportation and unfamiliar procedures in a foreign culture generally take longer than similar tasks at home. If you are travelling in a less developed country, you might need double, triple or quadruple the amount of time you would regularly set aside for these matters.

As a practical tip, it is more comfortable and easier on your health to plan your itinerary with conservative estimates of daily distance, so that most of the bicycling can be done in the morning or late afternoon if necessary. Since this is likely to be a once-in-a-lifetime opportunity, you want to enjoy the places you go, not merely pass through. Don't overestimate the daily distance you will cover.

Planning for daylight Because Africa straddles the Equator, in most of the continent the sun rises at about 06.00 and sets around 18.00 (natural time), plus or minus half an hour, all year round. An excellent, practical and recommended routine on cycling days is to live by the sun. Mostly pack the night before, get up at 06.00, eat breakfast around 06.30 and try to be on the road by 07.00. For the next few hours bicycle, sightsee and stop as necessary to eat and drink. If you don't reach your destination before the midday heat hits, stop from 12.30 to 15.30, eat a good meal, take a siesta, read, write and/or watch the local life. When it starts cooling down, saddle up and finish the day's ride. If you are staying in villages where there is no electricity, there is all the more reason to get in, washed, fed and set up for the night early; then it is easy to be in bed by 20.00. You will then get a good ten hours' sleep before you have to confront the journey again.

Route One approach is to push pins for the places you want to see into a map and then cogitate on how to connect the dots. There are now thousands of kilometres of excellent paved roads in developing countries. As modernisation continues, new stretches are paved every year. Even unpaved, the laterite (clay) and black cotton soil roads, common in Africa, can be nearly as smooth to ride on as paved roads – when they are dry. When wet, laterite and black cotton soil roads are viscous and virtually impossible to ride on. Depending on the situation, they may take from a few hours to several weeks to dry out after the last rains. Washboard, rocky and rutted dirt roads create their own discomfort and fall somewhere between dry and wet laterite roads in difficulty. It is on the unpaved roads that you tend to find a much more traditional and interesting side of Africa. To best enjoy these areas you need to schedule your visit to correspond with the dry season – though nature always reserves the right to be spontaneous. Even where the roads have good, all-weather surfaces, you should take note of the prevailing winds for the time of year you plan to travel. The wind can determine the direction of travel. If the route is a loop – *c'est la vie*. If your itinerary involves large changes in elevation, the geography may also be a major influence on your choice of starting and finishing points and your direction of travel.

Climate The weather can be a giant determinant for the ease and enjoyment of bicycling, especially in less-developed areas. If you have a choice, schedule your travels for the cool part of the dry season. This varies from month to month and place to place and is further complicated by the fact that the lowest temperatures and lowest humidity do not always occur at the same time. In general, the best time for cycling is usually near the beginning of the dry season, just after the end of the rains. This period has the added advantage that the dirt roads are packed and the dust is relatively low, though the high-altitude *harmattan* dust affects west Africa a couple of months into the dry season. In addition to moisture and heat another important factor can be wind – try to keep it on your back.

2

Routes

The following section has been greatly expanded since the last edition, to examine many more of the routes that are now possible for vehicles and motorcycles. There's information for cyclists in *Planning a bicycle trip, Chapter 1*, page 17.

Since the last edition, it's fair to say that, despite ever-increasing high-tech mobile communications, some new roads and plenty of travel information on the internet, things are actually becoming harder for overlanding, with security issues, sometimes overwhelming bureaucracy concerning visas, vehicle paperwork and import regulations.

With the complete trans-Africa trip sometimes unlikely and only just possible at times, some may wish to plan a shorter overland journey in west, east or southern Africa. Since the last edition was published, getting so many visas for very long trips is more problematic. Obtaining visas for countries like Nigeria, Cameroon, Angola and Sudan can be very sticky, although in the end there usually seems to be a way through the bureaucracy, like any mud hole *en route*.

Having said that, on our most recent trip we failed to get through from the UK to South Africa because of Angolan visas being refused at all west African Angolan embassies. We turned around in Lomé, and, with Niger and Algeria unsafe, that meant almost exactly the same route back for 6,000 miles.

For those planning the big overland trip all the way down to Cape Town, the best route today is probably down the Nile. Any other route may result in disappointment, having either to turn around and drive the vehicle back for thousands of miles, or ship the vehicle out of a dodgy African port. Both of these are rather dreadful prospects, as we can say from personal experience.

That said, it's just possible that Angola will improve regarding visas (and roads) soon, making the west coast route a serious contender for a great trans-Africa expedition. We wait with anticipation!

GETTING TO AFRICA

For information on ferries see *Ferry routes* in *Chapter 1*, page 10.

Many roads cross France and Spain to Algeciras for Morocco, but remember France and central Spain will be cold in winter. At that time of year, open campsites are difficult to find in France, so try the F1 hotel chain www.hotelformule1.com for the cheapest available lodgings. One or two campsites are open in central Spain in winter. Look out for Santa Elena near La Carolina, south of Madrid on the A4/E5 and La Cabrera, north of Madrid on the A1/E5.

For Tunisia, Libya and Egypt, head south from Italy, preferably by ferry from Genoa to Tunis. Cross the Alps during the daytime, as January temperatures in Chamonix can be more than ten degrees below zero! It is also possible, though more expensive, to get a ferry from Marseille to Tunis.

Don't discount the great options through the Middle East either, despite the media hype. See the trans-Sahara route map on page 24 for details on routes NA, ME1 and ME2.

ROUTE NA: EUROPE, TUNISIA AND LIBYA TO EGYPT

The quickest route to Egypt from Europe is from Genoa to Tunis and along the Libyan coast to Cairo. These roads are excellent. Formalities at the Libyan border have to be handled by a local agent and you must travel with a Libyan guide in your own vehicle, or accompanying you in his own car. At the moment this cannot be avoided, but at least you can learn more about the country and you have someone to read the Arabic road signs. Along the way, the old part of Tripoli, the Roman ruins at Sabratha and Leptis Magna and the solemn war graves at Tobruk are the main attractions. Those with bags of time can head south to the Dune Lakes circuit near Awbari and on to the Akakus near Ghat.

Entering Egypt and dealing with the bureaucracy is a minefield, but everyone will be at pains to welcome you and take a little reward for services rendered. The road to El Alamein, Alexandria and on to Cairo is excellent, if a little busy nearer the capital. It's possible to drive around the oasis route via Siwa, Farafra, Dakhla Oasis, El Kharga and even to the Gilf Kabir Plateau, but probably only in the company of an Egyptian guide/vehicle.

ROUTE MEI: EUROPE, TURKEY, SYRIA AND JORDAN TO EGYPT

Using this route via the Middle East will take a little longer to reach Egypt than going directly via Tunisia and Libya, but it offers a whole new world of historical attractions, varied scenery and hospitable people. Coming from Europe, you will need a visa for Syria in advance, but Turkey and Jordan issue them at the borders. Going northbound, Syrian visas are easily obtained in Amman. Other considerations are the vehicle taxes charged on the borders of both Syria and Jordan, which can be significant amounts. Fuel, though, is cheap, which makes up for some of these charges. Campsites do exist and some hotels will allow parking/camping in their grounds.

From Istanbul any number of excellent roads head to Syria and, with time, a fascinating trip can be made along the southwest Turkish coast. Here are many ancient Greek and Roman attractions, as well as fine beaches and rugged mountains. In central Turkey, not far off the direct route from Ankara to Aleppo in Syria, are the amazing underground churches, settlements and volcanic chimneys of the Cappadoccia area near Göreme. In Syria one of the highlights is the city of Aleppo, with its bazaars and ancient citadel. Crusader castles dot the country, the best preserved being Krak des Chevaliers. The aromatic bazaars of Damascus are atmospheric and, a little off the route to the east, are the ruins of Palmyra in the desert. Jordan has some great attractions too, with the Roman ruins at Jerash, world-famous Nabataen Petra and the wonderful desert canyons at Wadi Rum at the top of the list. A ferry links Aqaba in Jordan to the Sinai peninsula in Egypt. All the roads on the way are good throughout.

ROUTE ME2: SAUDI ARABIA TO JORDAN

We will make just a quick mention here for those heading northbound from Sudan to Europe or the Middle East. A ferry operates between Port Sudan and Jeddah across the Red Sea and, if you are lucky enough to get a three-day transit visa for Saudi Arabia, this could enable you to bypass a lot of the famed Egyptian border/customs/Lake Nasser bureaucracy! Roads in Saudi Arabia are superb and heading north to Aqaba in Jordan is quick and generally safe.

The main road goes via Medina, the second holy city of Islam, which foreigners must bypass, and then to Tabuk. The scenery from here to the Aqaba border of Jordan is superb, reminiscent of southern Jordan's Wadi Rum with red craggy canyons. A new road along the coast is another option, but we have not done that. In any case, three days is easily enough time for this sector.

We have not heard of anyone being able to do this route in the opposite direction, because it is difficult to get a Saudi transit visa to go south. This may be because the ferry schedules are uncertain.

AFRICAN ROUTES

NORTH AFRICA AND THE SAHARA North Africa and the Sahara includes the following countries: Morocco, Algeria, Tunisia, Libya, Western Sahara, Mauritania, Mali, Niger, Chad, Egypt and Sudan. You should plan to cross the Sahara between October and March, when there is less danger from the heat.

Route SI: Morocco to Mauritania This route remains the most popular trans-
Saharan route at the moment. The road all the way through Morocco, Western Sahara and on to Nouakchott is tarmac. Within Morocco, main roads are excellent, with Fès, Marrakech, Todra Gorge and the Road of the Kasbahs being some of the highlights. Going south, you enter Western Sahara, which is currently administered by Morocco and awaiting a referendum on its status. Laayoune is the nominal capital of Western Sahara and it is possible to camp along the coast. Be sure to carry enough fuel, as there are long stretches of uninhabited desert.

The Morocco/Mauritania border immigration and customs are at Fort Guergarat. There is a 5km rough sandy/stony track between the two border posts. The Mauritanian and Moroccan governments have normalised all overland travel northbound into Morocco now. The border area was heavily mined in the past, so you should keep to any marked tracks until the road is completed.

A word of warning though – in early 2008 the Mauritanian government imposed new visa rules stopping the issue of visas at the borders. This followed the French ban on their tour groups visiting the country after the cancelling of the Paris–Dakar rally. It would be very wise to get the visa in Rabat (or Bamako for those heading north). In March 2008 this was a quick procedure. Some extremely unfortunate people who did not have visas were sent on a 700-mile return trip back to Bamako from the border near Ayoun el Atrous/Nioro at that time.

Once in Mauritania, the new super-highway from Nouadhibou to Nouakchott is open, thus avoiding the beach road of the past. (There are still plenty of guides who will take you along the beach road if you wish, through the Parc National du Banc d'Arguin. Prices quoted were from €10 per day plus guide's expenses.)

With so many new tarmac roads, it's currently harder to make use of your 4x4. Until the over-hype regarding the cancellation of the 2008 Paris–Dakar rally, the desert areas of Mauritania offered the best opportunity. Things are uncertain as we go to press, but the following options should be possible. You can take the piste from Nouadhibou to Choum and Atar beside the railway line. Allow two to three days and keep on the south side of the tracks to avoid the possibility of hitting any old landmines. Close to Atar are the oases of Chinguetti and Ouadâne. The routes between Chinguetti, Ouadâne and Guelb Richat are enough fun for any desert addict. For serious desert motoring and a big challenge, the route between Chinguetti and Tidjikja to the south is a serious affair – guides are recommended.

The ancient camel caravan routes from Tidjikja to Tichit, and particularly on to Oualata, are also exciting desert options for experienced Saharan drivers. Taking a guide is the sensible option. A good road heads east of Nouakchott towards Nema and Mali (*Route W2*; see page 34). A new sealed road now heads from Ayoun el Atrous south into Mali via Nioro to Bamako, and the stretch to Tidjikja via Moudjeria is also sealed.

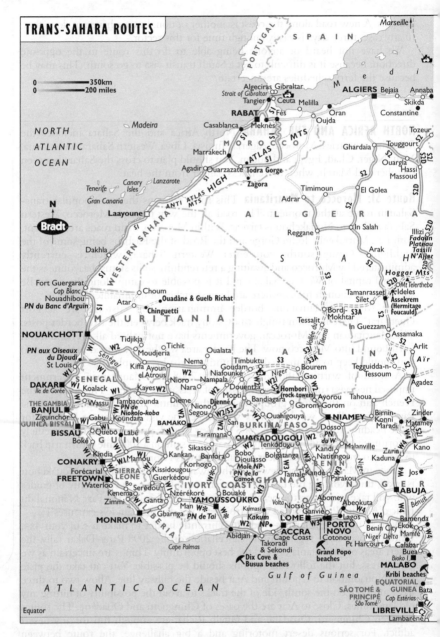

TRANS-SAHARA ROUTES

| 0 | 350km |
| 0 | 200 miles |

NORTH ATLANTIC OCEAN

N

Bradt

Marseille

SPAIN

PORTUGAL

Algeciras Gibraltar
Strait of Gibraltar
Tangier Ceuta Melilla
RABAT Fès
Casablanca Meknès
Oran Oujda
ALGIERS Bejaia Annaba
Skikda
Constantine
Tozeur
Ghardaia Touggourt
Marrakech
Agadir Ouarzazate Todra Gorge
Zagora
Ouargla
Hassi Massoud
Timimoun El Golea
Adrar
Laayoune
ALGERIA
SAHARA
Reggane In Salah
Arak Illizi
Fadoun Plateau Tassili H'N'Ajjer
Hoggar Mts
Mt Telertheba
Idéles
Tamanrasset Silet Assekrem (Hermitage Foucauld)
Bordj-Mokhtar
In Guezzam Assamaka
Madeira

Canary Lanzarote
Isles
Tenerife
Gran Canaria

ANTI ATLAS MTS HIGH ATLAS

WESTERN SAHARA

Dakhla

Fort Guergarat
Cap Blanc
Nouadhibou
PN du Banc d'Arguin
Atar Choum
Ouadâne & Guelb Richat
Chinguetti
MAURITANIA

NOUAKCHOTT
Tidjikja
Tichit
PN aux Oiseaux du Djoudi
St Louis Moudjeria Nema Oualata
Kiffa Ayoun el Atrous
Goudam Timbuktu Bourem Gao
Tessalit Arlit Aïr
Agadez Assamaka
Tegguidda-n-Tessoum

DAKAR Koalack
Kayes
Nioro Nara Nampala
Douentza Hombori (rock towers)
Ayorou Tahoua
Birnin-Konni
Zinder
SENEGAL
Sénégal
THE GAMBIA
BANJUL
BISSAU
GUINEA BISSAU
Ziguinchor
Quebo Labé
Boké Gabu
Kindia
CONAKRY
Forécariah
FREETOWN
Waterloo
Bo Serédou
Kenema
Zimmi
MONROVIA

Tambacounda
PN de Niokolo-koba
Koundara
BAMAKO
Faramana
Sikasso
Banfora
Kankan Bobo Dioulasso
Korhogo Bolgatanga
PN de la Comoé
Kissidougou
Guerkédou
Nzérékoré Bouaké
Ganta Man
Gbarnga
PN de Tai
Abidjan Cape Coast
Cape Palmas

Dieme
Niono
Segou
Djenné
Bandiagara
Mopti
Gorom-Gorom
Ouahigouya
BURKINA FASO
OUAGADOUGOU
Tenkodogo
Mole NP
GHANA
Kumasi
Kakum NP
Takoradi & Sekondi
Dix Cove & Busua beaches

Dosso
PN du W
Kandi Malanville
Natitingou
Kandé Parakou
BENIN
Tamale
Kara Zaria Kano
Kaduna
Jos
ABUJA
Bamenda
Ekok
Calabar
Buea
MALABO
Kribi beaches
EQUATORIAL GUINEA Bata
Cap Estérias
LIBREVILLE
Lambaréné

NIAMEY
Gorom-Gorom
Notsé
Abomey
Abeokuta
Ganvié
LOME
Cotonou
PORTO NOVO
Lagos
Benin City
Niger Delta
Pt Harcourt
Grand Popo beaches
SÃO TOMÉ & PRINCIPE
São Tomé
Bioko I
Gulf of Guinea

ATLANTIC OCEAN

Equator

IVORY COAST
LIBERIA
GUINEA
MALI
NIGER
NIGERIA
CAMEROON

Beware of occasional problems with bandits on the stretch of road from Nema further east into Mali.

Route S2: Tunisia to Nigeria

☞ **WARNING!** At the time of publication Niger is experiencing a very serious and distressing rebellion. Many nomads and villagers have had to leave their homes in

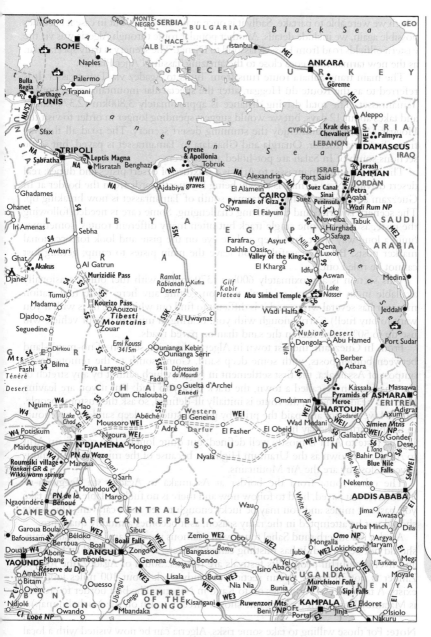

the Aïr Mountains and mines have been laid. According to one disillusioned aid worker, some of the problems relate to oil exploration of the Tuareg regions, principally by the Chinese.

This used to be the main Sahara overland route until early 1993. By 1999 a few intrepid travellers were starting to take it again. Until the kidnapping of 32 Westerners in their vehicles in 2003, the route was experiencing a great revival, in which we were able to partake. Sadly it is once again off-limits, but in case it becomes possible again, we include details. Another popular route through Algeria was via the eastern oilfields road from Hassi Massoud to Djanet. The scenery is truly spectacular, as the new tarmac road goes close to the amazing Tassili N'Ajjer Plateau.

The main trans-Sahara route runs from Tunis to Agadez via Tamanrasset. It is referred to as the Route du Hoggar, after the spectacular mountain range outside Tamanrasset. The total driving distance is approximately 3,800km (2,370 miles) and takes about 12 days, but we would suggest spending longer in order to visit the Hoggar Mountains and enjoy the stunning desert scenery. The road all the way from Tunis via Tozeur, Ouargla and Ghardaia to Tamanrasset is paved, but some sections south of In Salah are pot-holed and uneven.

The road from Tamanrasset to Arlit is a mixture of desert pistes and dunes; real desert driving. New tarmac is slowly being laid northwards from the border at In Guezzam and a short section of tarmac south of Tamanrasset is now breaking up. The scenery is varied and the driving challenging. Some care is needed following the piste, as it is not one single track but often many different routes, sometimes quite a long way apart. Just keep a close eye on the piste and look for occasional marker posts. Be very careful if you leave the main pistes to camp; getting lost cannot be ruled out.

This section is approximately 600km (370 miles) with fuel only occasionally available in In Guezzam, so don't plan on getting any here. (The fuel station manager has several wives, and it is difficult to find out which one he is with if you want to buy fuel!) Carry enough with you, bearing in mind that your vehicle will use up to 50% more fuel in the sand than on paved roads.

From In Guezzam, the last town in Algeria, there is a section of no-man's-land between border posts, with some deep sand. Going south to the remote desert outpost of Assamaka, the first settlement in Niger, which cannot by any stretch of the imagination be called a town, the track is easy to find. But if you are leaving here and heading north, the route is initially ill-defined, so ask the customs people. In 2004 we did not and paid the price by getting stuck in deep sand for two hours in the blistering midday heat.

The piste to Arlit is mostly well defined, but quite lonely. The road from Arlit to Agadez is known as the Uranium Highway, because of the mines at Arlit, and is paved. Close by are the Aïr Mountains.

The other route from the border at Assamaka to Agadez via Tegguida-n-Tessoum is not paved, hard to follow now and there is no fuel available. It does take you past salt mines and you may be lucky enough to see a salt caravan. This route should not be attempted in the rainy season, as it becomes a muddy quagmire.

Agadez is a superb mud Sahel town with a famous mosque and, when safe again, should not be missed. It has bustling camel markets, traditional mud architecture and lively colourful people. Its festivals are riotous. South of Agadez, the road to Zinder is not all paved. A fun section of sandy track about 100 miles long still exists. A tarmac road continues on to Kano in Nigeria. The best border to cross at is Matamey/Kongolam (not the one shown directly south on the Michelin map).

Note: For those willing to take some risks, Algeria can be now visited with a local guide. How much security this adds to the trip is debatable.

Route S2D: Algeria to Niger via Djanet
We will make a brief comment about this alternative route from Tunisia to Niger, a route currently not advisable but which may be possible soon.

From Touggourt a good sealed road runs through the oilfields via Hassi Massoud and Ohanet to In Amenas. After Illizi the road climbs on to the Fadnoun

Plateau, once a rough area and now crossed easily. A detour to the lost canyon of Iherir is a must before the truly spectacular drive along the foot of the Tassili N'Ajjer Plateau to Djanet. Leave your vehicle in the campsite in Djanet and go trekking on the plateau; it's a superb experience.

From Djanet the route is almost all piste to Tamanrasset. Fuel must be carried; don't forget to allow extra for some stretches of soft sand that will devour it. Ideally you should travel with more than one vehicle. GPS is advised if you are not with a local guide. This route is not always well defined, with many tracks once you are off the main road north of Djanet from Bordj el Haoues. The military have reoccupied the lonely fort at Serouenout and nearby Mount Telertheba acts as a prominent waymark. Once past here, the piste is more clearly defined to Ideles and Hirafok. Note that some local drivers use a sandier route further north from near Bome to east of Ideles, avoiding Serouenout, but route finding is more difficult.

From Hirafok a well-defined but extremely rocky, and in one place extremely steep, track climbs into the Hoggar Mountains to the hermitage of Assekrem. A better way is to continue west to the main road, follow it towards Tamanrasset and then go to the Hoggar from there. It will save your vehicle as well as your nerves and is strongly recommended. The better track of the two from Tamanrasset to the Hermitage Foucauld and the viewpoint at Assekrem is the eastern one. From Tamanrasset the route to Niger is the same as route S2.

Routes S3 and S3A: Algeria to Mali

☞ *WARNING!* Again, because of the kidnapping of 32 Westerners in their vehicles in 2003, this route is currently not very safe. That said, in 2008 we did meet some intrepid (and quite old) French overlanders, who had crossed Algeria to Tamanrasset, then followed the old route through Silet to Bordj Mokhtar and then south through Tessalit to Gao. They required guides for Algeria, charged at €50 for the guide or €100 for a guide in a car. In Mali they ran the gauntlet to Gao as fast as possible. Hats off to these trail-blazing adventurers! See route S3A on the maps, page 24.

In case the route between Reggane and Gao becomes possible with improved security, it is included here. Known as the Tanezrouft, it was always less popular than the S2 route above, mainly because the distance between water and fuel stops was much larger – Adrar to Gao is approximately 1,500km (930 miles) and the unpaved section is 1,320km (820 miles). Fuel is generally available in Reggane, but again don't count on it.

In the past this route was often preferred by those travellers using VW Combis, Citroen 2CVs and motorcycles, as its surface tended to be harder. The road is paved from Adrar to Reggane. South of Reggane there is new tar, then the piste is mostly hard-packed sand and quite fast, with only a few softer spots. The terrain is flat and less varied than the Hoggar route, but nonetheless has a certain remote feel. The Algerian border post is at Bordj Mokhtar and the Malian customs is at Tessalit. There was a well here for water.

The last section from Tessalit to Gao along the Vallée du Tilemsi is the hardest section, with areas of soft sand. It too can be confusing, with a number of tracks, but there are some wells and settlements *en route*. It's often impassable during the wet season.

Once in Gao, you can continue on to the Malian capital, Bamako, on a paved road. This route offers some fascinating destinations, such as the Hombori rock towers, the Dogon villages and the mud mosques at Mopti and Djenné. Heading southeast from Gao, you can follow the River Niger along a scenic route to Niamey, the capital of Niger (see route W2). This route is at times very sandy, but has now been tarred on the Niger side after Ayorou. A very sandy track also heads west from Bourem, crossing dunes in places, to Timbuktu. Allow two days for this trip.

The total driving time from Adrar to Gao is approximately six to seven days. As with the S2 route, there has been continuing political unrest in the area, particularly in northern Mali, so seek advice before you set out.

Route S4: Libya to Niger

☞ **WARNING!** This route is not advised at present due to the latest Niger rebellion, which started in 2007. Information from previous years is included.

Travelling in convoy with at least one other vehicle is essential, and taking a guide from Al Gatrun to the border is both advisable and currently required by the Libyan government throughout the country, even in the north. Guides with vehicles are required in Niger as far as Agadez. Remember not to take alcohol into Libya. To get a Libyan visa, you need to have your passport officially translated into Arabic and you also need an invitation letter from a Libyan agency. (See page 254.)

In May 1995 a peace accord with the Tuaregs in Niger came into effect and the situation in northern Niger improved markedly. Isolated banditry is still a possibility, though, and you are advised to enlist the help of, and indeed required by law to link up with, a local tour operator for safety and security reasons. A number of agencies in Agadez operate trips to Bilma, Djado and the Aïr Mountains; contact www.expeditionworld.com or do an internet search.

In Libya, roads south from Tripoli are excellent. A diversion to the Akakus Mountains near Ghat and the dune lakes near Awbari is well worthwhile. The dune lakes must be visited with at least one other vehicle and are only for the experienced; the dunes are seriously big here and potentially extremely dangerous. At the campsite it is possible to hire a 4x4 with driver for the day trip to the lakes if you don't want to risk it yourself.

From Ghat there is a route through to Djanet in Algeria, but this is not always open and is said to be very wild and sandy. From Sebha, paved roads lead to Al Gatrun and then it is piste to the border at Tumu.

When possible, the most common route in Niger is from Tumu to Madama, Seguedine, Dirkou and through the Ténéré Desert direct to Agadez. The route via Bilma and Fashi is serious dune driving and potentially extremely dangerous for the inexperienced. It is therefore not recommended except with a local operator. The total distance is about 1,500km (930 miles), with fuel available at Sebha, Dirkou (mostly) and Agadez. You will need to carry fuel for approximately 1,200km (745 miles). It is easy to lose your way on this route and there are some difficult sandy sections.

From Agadez allow a day and a half to reach Zinder (see route S2). Otherwise the roads west in Niger to Tahoua, Maradi and Niamey are pretty good, with the odd pot-hole: beware!

Route S5: Libya to Chad via the Tibesti Mountains

☞ **WARNING!** This route is currently unsafe due to political problems in Chad.

In case things change, details are included. The Libya-to-Chad routes are not for the inexperienced. The Tibesti area of northern Chad is very remote and renowned for its landmines and bandits. Routes through the Tibesti are rough, rocky and severely punishing, but it is one of the most spectacular areas of the

Sahara, with volcanoes, hot springs, crater lakes (Trou du Natron) and mountains (Emi Koussi) up to 3,415m (11, 000ft) high. Sadly it is currently off-limits. The main routes were either Al Gatrun – Murizidié Pass – Kourizo Pass – Zouar to Faya Largeau or, longer but more scenic, Al Gatrun – Murizidié Pass – Aouzou – Zouar to Faya Largeau.

From Faya to N'djamena, the piste is reasonably easy to follow, but is quite sandy. Fuel is generally available in Faya. Some small settlements such as Moussoro might have diesel drum supplies, but this cannot be guaranteed. It is possible to do these routes in either direction, but getting permission from the Chadians to head north was harder than heading south from Libya. The crossing is about 1,250km (775 miles) via Zouar and an extra 300km (185 miles) if you go via Aouzou. Fuel is extremely cheap in Libya, so fill up regularly and particularly in Al Gatrun.

This route, should it become possible, is not for the faint-hearted. You must be very well equipped, research all the latest information and travel with at least two vehicles. We recommend that you take a local guide, despite the costs. In fact you will probably be obliged to take a guide anyway, to satisfy local etiquette and contribute to the local economy. Even agents in N'djamena do this.

Route S5K: Libya to Chad via Kufra

☞ **WARNING!** This route is currently unsafe due to political problems in Chad.

Another perhaps more feasible option to cross the Sahara if Chad settles is this exciting route. It is, however, only a possibility for very experienced Saharan travellers. It crosses eastern Libya from Ajdabiya to Kufra (Al Khofra) close to the Egyptian/Sudanese border (Route S5K on the map). A minimum of two vehicles is essential and you will need to be accompanied by a Libyan guide in his own car. This would also be advisable in Chad because of mines. The remote and little-used piste from Kufra heads around the Ramlat Rabianah sand desert and crosses into Chad north of the outstandingly beautiful Ounianga Kebir and Ounianga Serir lakes. Mines are said to be a serious issue on this route near the border area, and normal border formalities do not exist.

From Ounianga Serir, an ill-defined piste goes to Fada, passing some smaller lakes. From an isolated settlement at Demi, whose inhabitants do not appreciate visitors, a treacherous piste continues adjacent to the Dépression du Mourdi and through some amazing rock formations in the northern Ennedi. Gigantic rock arches and the famed Guelta d'Archei with its colony of rare dwarf crocodiles are the highlights here. After Fada the route via Oum Chalouba to Abéché is fairly obvious. Taking a local guide is essential, though, to smooth a path through the larger settlements. We have met only one couple who have done this complete route; a remarkable achievement, and they were not so young either.

Route S6: Egypt to Sudan and Ethiopia
This route is currently the best option for a complete trans-Africa trip by road, avoiding major political hotspots. Sudanese visas are available in Cairo in a few days and are possible to obtain in London, allowing up to two months for the process. Bear in mind that evidence of having been in Israel renders your passport useless for travel in any other Arab countries. Some travellers who have crossed from Israel into Egypt and onwards have carried two passports, but be careful about this. The expensive *carnet* bond for Egypt is the main obstacle on this route.

Currently the Egyptian authorities require all tourist vehicles, including tourist coaches and private cars, to run in daily convoys from the Red Sea resorts of Hurghada or Safaga to Luxor and south to Aswan. You may stop to stretch your legs and visit the antiquities of Kom Ombo and Idfu within this convoy system. Tourists can also drive to Abu Simbel in daily convoys with pre-arranged permits.

It was occasionally possible some years ago to drive to Abu Simbel and catch a pontoon ferry across to Wadi Halfa, but this whole area is run by the military and is effectively off-limits at present. It was suggested that tourists might be allowed to drive directly to Wadi Halfa in future, but that is perhaps hard to imagine when certain vested interests are understandably doing very nicely at present from the ferry arrangements. The route shown on the maps along the Red Sea south from Safaga to Port Sudan is currently not an option, but things could change.

The normal route south from Aswan to Wadi Halfa is via the ferry, which runs once a week each way. Recently this was on Mondays heading south and Wednesdays heading north. The ferry is quite expensive (extortionate if you are the only vehicle wishing to travel) and can be a great deal of hassle. Prices might be 'fixed', but it is more likely that it is you who will be in a fix as you try to negotiate. Patience, tact, restraint and a sense of humour are needed to deal with Egyptian officials, who know that there is no other route south at present. Sometimes a different barge is used if there are a number of vehicles waiting, but that is rare. Heading north, the ferry can also be expensive and difficult to get onto at Wadi Halfa, but at least the Sudanese are super-friendly as they extract your money.

In Wadi Halfa, be sure to get an alien's registration stamp added to your visa stamp. This is a time-consuming mystery tour and will cost around US$20 per person. (A bank nearby changes cash. Travellers' cheques are not usable in Sudan at present.) From Wadi Halfa to Khartoum there are two routes, following either the Nile or the railway line. The Nile route is now used by all local vehicles, but is initially rough and then sandy. It is said to be hard to follow, particularly near settlements. Once you reach Dongola, where fuel should be available, a new super-highway leads to Omdurman and Khartoum. Allow three days at least.

The route beside the railway is surprisingly isolated and the train only runs slowly once a week in each direction. You must follow the railway or watch for the telegraph poles at all times, otherwise getting lost is a serious possibility. Because there is a lot of very soft sand close to the tracks and even nearby, you might be forced in some sections to drive with your wheels astride the railway lines. We don't imagine the Sudanese railway company approves of this, so try not to be seen doing it near a station. A couple of stations are manned; do remember what day a train is scheduled. Driving on the line is hard but not bumpy, as the line is submerged in hard-packed sand. For your safety, though, try to use the line only as a last resort, and be very careful not to hit the rails with the sidewalls of your tyres.

Allow almost two days to reach Abu Hamed, and don't expect much when you get there. From there another lonely piste, which is indicated by tall, metal kilometre markers, leads to Berber, where a tarmac road begins. Fuel can be obtained here and at Atbara. A new desert highway runs to Khartoum east of the Nile and passes close to the famous Pyramids of Meroe, not to be missed. You can camp nearby in the bush; the local people were very friendly to us and got down off their camels to help us change a wheel. Their camels needed no maintenance! Other antiquities along here are hard to find without some local help.

From Khartoum an excellent new tarmac road runs south through the Gezira cotton fields to Wad Medani and on to Gedaref (and to Port Sudan). From Gedaref the once ghastly weather-dependent track to Gallabat and the Ethiopian border is now a rough but all-weather gravel road. On the Ethiopian side there is a reasonable gravel road from Metema to Gonder, a scenic and spectacular drive. From Gonder, unbelievably rough gravel roads lead north to Axum, east and then north to Lalibela and south, with some tarmac later, to Addis Ababa.

WEST AFRICAN ROUTES West Africa includes southern Mauritania, Senegal, Gambia, Guinea, Guinea Bissau, Sierra Leone, Liberia, Ivory Coast, Ghana, Mali, Burkina Faso, Niger, Nigeria, Togo and Benin.

With ever-improving roads, west Africa is a great region for some exciting new non-trans-Africa options, especially as Sierra Leone and Liberia are just on the list again. In the whole region, only Ivory Coast remains an unknown option at present. In Senegal, Gambia, Guinea, Mali, Burkina Faso, Ghana, Benin, Togo, Niger and Nigeria, main roads are generally good paved routes, but pot-holes soon appear when away from these. Traditional routes in Mali and Burkina remain as popular as ever and can be linked into the coastal route for a complete trip around west Africa. Further east is the coastal route between Ivory Coast (maybe), Ghana, Nigeria and on into Cameroon, as well as options into Benin and Togo from the Sahel regions of Burkina Faso and Niger. Two major routes lead across Nigeria into Cameroon and hopefully Chad for those heading to central Africa.

With possible visa turmoil to the south of Cameroon, taking a trip around west Africa has become the main option for a more stress-free, two–three-month trip.

Route W1: Mauritania to Senegal, Guinea, Sierra Leone, Liberia and Mali

A fairly good paved road leads due south from Nouakchott to St Louis and Dakar. Crossing the border into Senegal is better (and currently cheaper in 'non-value added taxes') at Diama and gives a taste of dry dirt-road driving. Senegal has some of the best roads in west Africa, with the notorious exception of the road to Tambacounda from east of Koalack. In early 2008 it was perhaps the most ghastly pot-holed main road in west Africa, with holes every few seconds. Rumour has it that it may be improved at some point, but there is no way to avoid this aberration at present when heading to Mali or Guinea via Senegal. Variations across Senegal could involve the Senegal River route, another poor road, or through the central baobab tree-covered countryside via Touba, a religious centre. Super new empty roads link this pilgrimage town with Keberma on the main St Louis–Dakar highway and with Kafferine on the road east of Koalack. Another new route in Senegal involves a visit to the Parc National du Niokolo-Koba where some of the animals lurking include lions and elephants.

Many people of course follow the coast from St Louis to Dakar and then into Gambia on good roads. Routes beside the Gambia River are bad, but the coastal roads are good. Find out about the security issues in the Casamance region around Ziguinchor before visiting.

Guinea Bissau If you are continuing from Gambia/Senegal and into Guinea Bissau, the roads are steadily improving but have some testing stretches inland. The main route between Guinea Bissau and Guinea is from Bissau to Gabu, then from the border to Koundara in Guinea. Another route into Guinea is the dreadful road from Quebo to Boké in Guinea. This is a dry season option only. Check the road conditions, whether local transport is going and that any ferries *en route* are working before heading this way.

Guinea Heading into Guinea from Tambacounda in Senegal, there are two routes. The dangerous rocky one via the Parc National du Niokolo-Koba and Maliville in the mountainous Massif du Tamgue is not recommended if you want to keep your vehicle in shape.The preferred route into Guinea is the dry-weather-only road through Koundara. This is initially a fun road with reasonable dirt, but soon becomes a big mud-hole roller coaster, which is still fun in the dry but abysmal after rain. Koundara has a couple of extremely basic but friendly places to stay, though you will probably want to sleep in your vehicle even if you do pay for a

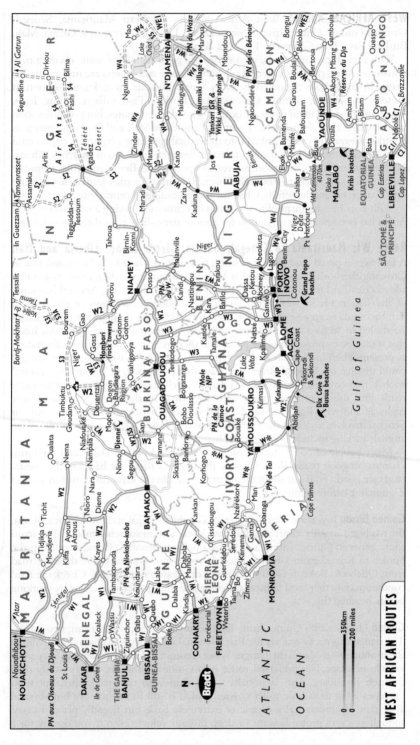

WEST AFRICAN ROUTES

N

Bradt

0 — 350km
0 — 200 miles

room. From Koundara, the road winds its way over hills, through thick pleasant Sahelian bush and between isolated friendly villages. There are no other places to stay except the bush if you plan to do it in two easy days from Tambacounda to Labé. One good spot could be south of Koundara, where termite hills dot the plains and few villages are found.

There is a junction at about 50 miles where you go left (Labé is 158km from here). A ferry interrupts your drive and the operators work by hand to take you across. We paid US$8 with tips, but there was no hassle. The route heads through Bori and Poopodara, which makes you think you are nearly there, but shocking roads mark the entry into Labé. (Allow nine to ten hours for this stretch between Koundara and Labé in one shot.)

Once in central Guinea, the main roads close to the capital Conakry are quite good. In the Fouta Djalon region, Labé and Dalaba via Mamou and Kindia are serviced by good but twisting roads. Watch out for other vehicles on blind bends. Heading inland after Dabola to Kankan, the roads are reasonable, with some occasionally pot-holed sections. The Kankan to Bamako road is now almost complete, a breeze to drive on and not busy. Further south and east of Kankan, the condition of the roads is variable.

Coming **into Guinea from Liberia**, the first section of the route from the Ganta border to Nzérékoré is another fun road through some sections of exotic dense forest. It's extremely isolated, though, with a few villages but no facilities. Allow three hours for this route via Diéké. From Nzérékoré to near Serédou, a brand-new highway has been completed (it comes to a sudden end at 103km) but then the section on through Macenta to Kissidougou is appalling in many places and mainly dirt. Follow the route through Guerkédou, not the 'lane' suggested at a signpost. This is another slow-going, rough section.

From Kissidougou, the road out of town is diverted on a small dirt lane beside a fuel station/central roundabout and is appalling for 96km (60 miles). This road is not pot-holed but effectively 'deceased' as a 'proper' road. After that, improvements make it faster to Kankan at around the half-way point. Beware, though, of isolated holes and enjoy the last 30km, which are nearly perfect. Hooray!

Sierra Leone and Liberia The main highway road from Conakry to Freetown is 'expected to be completed one day'. In fact the Guinea section has been done via Forécarial where the road is not obvious; take the right fork at the town roundabout and head initially south. After a three-hour drive, as you get close to the border, the last five miles of road is bumpy dirt. Things don't improve in Sierra Leone either, with 15 miles more slow dirt. Don't expect a super-highway from Kambia to Freetown – work seems to have stopped and the road is deteriorating already. It is wide, though. The road from the Makeni turn-off is, however, glorious new tarmac into the capital. There is a choice of roads into Freetown, either on the main road or via the much slower, mostly unsealed and longer coastal route.

Very surprisingly, the road along the beautiful coastline south of Freetown is not all sealed. We came around the coast from Waterloo via Kent and the super road comes to an abrupt end at Tokeh. A narrow, almost overgrown, rocky lane continues on to River Number 2 beach and all the way into Lumley Beach at Freetown. This is one of the worst 'roads' in west Africa, despite all the nice unspoilt beaches along the route. Rumours suggest that it has all been bought by China for development.

The horrors of driving around Freetown are a shock. The streets are crowded, the markets tumble on to the highways; nudging your way out of here takes hours and that's once you've found the road out (Kissy Road) from the clock tower beyond the massive and notoriously unsafe 'Eastenders' market. As for the rest of

Sierra Leone, the road to Bo is fairly good and being worked on in sections. It's complete after Taima. From Bo a good road leads east for 45km to Kenema. Just before town is the junction for Zimmi and the route into Liberia. The direct secondary route on the Michelin map from Bo to Zimmi was not recommended in case of problems at the ferry across the Mole River.

From Kenema, the main 'international highway' is a fair dirt road and it takes an hour to cover the 18 miles to Joru. This road now becomes a narrow lane and passes through friendly villages south for 36 miles (2hrs) to Zimmi. One could call this a fun road in the dry; nonetheless this is very remote countryside with almost no traffic – it was previously RUF (Revolutionary United Front – former rebels) territory. The road naturally deteriorates more close to the border – another grinding 30 miles in 2 hours – and gets worse. The forest is beautiful, though, as the area near the border is the Gola reserve. The Morro River designates the border. There are a lot of 'checkings' of papers, but it's a relaxed place.

Currently all arrivals on the Liberian side of the river are greeted by UN Pakistani soldiers. The Bangladeshi UN contingent take over at Bong district checkpoint near Gbarnga. It's obviously a rarity for these fellows to see a foreigner, but traditional Pakistani hospitality is, as always, welcoming and pleasant.

Once in Liberia, the road from the Bo Waterside border post to Monrovia is sealed and reasonable all the way. Heading up country through Gbarnga and on to Ganta is also mostly OK, but a few sections slow the pace here and there. The road from Ganta to Ivory Coast is a dirt route and initially fair. We did not explore further, because of political problems in Ivory Coast. The route into Guinea from Ganta is remote and little more than a lane out of Ganta. The Liberian side of this border was relaxed.

☞ **WARNING!** If you are contemplating continuing east to Ghana, the insecurity obstacles of travel in Ivory Coast need to be checked. Roads were formerly in a good state of repair, but they are probably now full of pot-holes.

Route W2: Mauritania to Mali, Burkina Faso and Niger There are two main routes south into Mali from the Mauritanian highway between Nouakchott and Nema. These are from Ayoun el Atrous and Nema. The best and safer route is from Ayoun el Atrous south through the Sahel bush to Nioro. This is a new sealed road. It's just one day's drive on to Bamako now. The road west from Dieme, south of Nioro, is also a new, sealed option leading to Kayes and the Senegal border.

From Bamako, the most popular route involves heading through Segou, San, Djenné and Mopti to Hombori, Gao or Timbuktu. Beware – there are almost as many 'sleeping policemen' built into the roads near villages on this main route as there are sleeping policemen in Mali, and luckily in this heat, there are lots of those.

For Timbuktu, the best route is from Douentza, although the road is quite badly corrugated on the middle section around Bambara-Maoundé. Route-finding is easy and the first section is a fun road, but with many small creek beds to watch out for. The scenery is stunning for much of the way. Despite rumours of rogues at the ferry *en route* across the River Niger to Kabara/Timbuktu, we had no such problems. All the ferry staff were pleasant and welcoming. Allow plenty of time, though, for the crossing, as the ferry has to head up or downstream some distance to cross the river. Leaving Timbuktu in the morning, you may have to wait a few hours in a queue before you can even get on the ferry.

Heading from Segou via Nampala to Timbuktu, the roads are improving as well, but security issues need to be checked before taking this adventurous route. Also the Niger swamp route between Mopti and Timbuktu via Korientze, Niafounké and Goudam is not advised due to unreliable ferry connections. Timbuktu remains the enigmatic city that its fame suggests and did not disappoint us even after 30 years.

After taking in the cultural sites of the Dogon region around Bandiagara, good, well-used routes now head to Burkina Faso from Bankass or Bandiagara through Koro and Ouahigouya to Ouagadougou. A fairly good but not all smooth road runs from Segou or Sevare via San to Bobo Dioulasso. At least 96km (60 miles) of this route is bad at present, from Kimparana to Kouro. After the border at Faramana, it's a super-highway to Bobo.

From Mopti via Hombori and Gossi, the fair sealed road also makes for Gao and then along the Niger River on varied, bad and OK road surfaces to Niamey. The main roads in Burkina Faso – Bobo to Ouaga, Ouaga to Niger and Ouaga to Togo are very well-made new roads. Burkina is very pleasant with welcoming people everywhere – your arms will get plenty of waving exercise here.

Note: Linking routes W1 and W2 currently involves following the road in Guinea from Conakry through Kankan to Bamako. If things improve, another route is possible from Liberia via Ivory Coast from Ganta to Sanniquellie, Man, Yamoussoukro then north to Bobo Dioulasso. Heading east, the route goes via Yamoussoukro to Abidjan and on to Accra in Ghana via Sekondi and Takoradi (routes W★).

Routes W3: Burkina Faso, Niger, Ghana, Togo and Benin
Three good options link Burkina Faso and Niger with the coastal roads of Ghana, Benin and Togo. Heading from Ouagadougou south via Bolgatanga in Ghana, the countryside is the typical Sahel of dry scrub at first then slowly transforms into denser forest. Few traces of the rainforest remain in Ghana but, along the coast, interest lies in the slave ports of Elmina and Cape Coast as well as good beaches. Traffic is hectic in Accra and Kumasi, but the condition of the roads will not need as much patience.

From Ouagadougou into Togo the main highway is mostly fine through Tenkodogo. Once in Togo, some sections are a bit scrappy.

The Tamberma villages should not be missed; these can be visited from Kante (Kandé) by a reasonable dirt link road that is controlled by guides just out of town. All visitors to the area are expected to take a guide, mainly to prevent offending local tribal people and contribute to the economy.

Potential visa issues aside, it's possible to divert into Benin near Kara through the Tamberma and Somba villages.

The road south to Lomé should not present any surprises, but watch out on a couple of hilly sections for huge numbers of very slow or broken-down trucks. There may be a diversion on this road around a government installation, which is confusing, but keep asking and they will tell you which way to go. Just near Bafilo is an amazing cutting on the southbound lane! It may be possible to get into Benin from Notsé in Togo to Abomey, but Benin 48-hour transit visas may not be available at the border. Heading south, watch for a few poor road sections. Once in the city of Lomé, the traffic, and in particular lack of any signposting, will test the most patient of drivers.

We believe the road east from Lomé Airport will take you around the worst of the traffic to reach Benin and Grand Popo. The coastal road east of Cotonou is very busy and best avoided for those wanting a quieter introduction to Nigeria, or who want to put off the inevitable. A border exists at Ketou, from where the road heads into Nigeria around the north of Lagos via Abeokuta.

From Niamey in Niger, once you've done the rough section to Dosso, a good road heads south to Benin. The border is across the Niger River, where you reach Malanville. After Kandi, south and west of the main road, a visit to the Somba people around Natitingou is a must. Parakou and Dassa are the main overnight options heading south. Don't forget to visit Abomey for Benin culture at its best. A boat trip on the lagoons at Ganvié just before Cotonou is another unmissable but touristy sight. Cotonou is best avoided, with much-discussed crime statistics.

Route W4: Nigeria to Cameroon and Chad
All roads to central Africa lead through Nigeria, except the long, lonely, sandy and insecure option around Lake Chad via Nguigmi in eastern Niger and Mao to N'djamena. So, at present, Nigeria it has to be!

Most main roads in Nigeria are good and looked after 'lovingly' by police at many checkpoints. Coming from the north via Zinder in Niger to Kano, cross at the Matamey/Kongolam border. The road from Kano, a pleasant place with some old Hausa buildings, is good, heading east via Potiskum to northern Cameroon. In central Nigeria, the new capital Abuja is linked by motorway through Kaduna (civil inter-communal disturbances possible here) to Kano. Various good roads link Abuja with Ekok, the border town with Cameroon, in the south.

Those who have avoided Lagos or braved its horrendous traffic, crime and general hullabaloo can relax as they head east through Benin City. Give the Niger delta around Port Harcourt a wide berth and head further east. Calabar is a pleasant place, though, and there is a Cameroon consulate here that issues visas. From Calabar the border is northeast at Ekok.

Cameroon has some excellent roads and some dreadful ones. Those in the north are generally tarred and fairly OK. The road from Ngaoundéré to Yaoundé is a typical example of a route that springs a surprise. South of Ngaoundéré is a relatively good dirt road to Garoua Boulai, which then becomes an amazing but empty (a telltale sign) super-highway to Bertoua. Then suddenly the tarmac ends and a dreadfully corrugated section of 200 miles follows, only improving just before Yaoundé. The Michelin map indicates that a road via Abong Mbang is a better option, and this is now true.

The road from southern Nigeria via the Ekok border into Cameroon has some bad truck-swallowing sections. It is OK in dry weather only after the border to Mamfe and south to Buea (for Mount Cameroon's cool retreats). Further south on the coast is the beach resort of Limbé, from where the road goes on to Douala then Yaoundé.

Those heading to Bamenda from Mamfé to escape the heat in the cool high country and travelling on to Yaoundé should check conditions in Mamfé before heading up. There were also civil disturbances in March 2008 in Cameroon, with this region being particularly vocal – that's a polite way of saying it. Private cars and foreign vehicles were apparently targeted by mobs.

Heading into Chad at present is subject to security improvements. Roads in some areas of southwestern Chad have improved, now that oil has been found. These run close to the new oil pipeline from Chad into Cameroon through Moundou.

CENTRAL AFRICA
Central Africa comprises southern Chad, Cameroon, Gabon, Central African Republic (CAR), Congo, Democratic Republic of the Congo (DRC) and Angola.

Central Africa has plenty of rain and mud to slow you down; this is where 4x4 really comes into its own. The easiest time to cross east–west (or vice versa) is in the drier season from about December to February. There is also a 'less wet' season in June/July. The 'rain barriers' set up on roads in CAR during the rainy season could cause you considerable delays. These routes have been closed to travellers since June 1998, but, with the changing political climate in Africa, these challenging routes might become accessible once again to overland travel.

Central African north-south routes
Route C1: Gabon via Congos and Angola to Namibia

☞ **WARNING!** Although the security issues on this route have improved, the bureaucratic obstacles have increased. Avoid the Poul region west of Brazzaville. On the road between Brazzaville and Pointe Noire robberies were occurring as recently as March 2008. Consider the route via Franceville to reach Brazzaville, but be prepared for bridge building and delays. Foreign Office advice currently says don't go this way either, so be prepared to keep up to date with the latest situation.

Since the last edition, when we mentioned a handful of brave or perhaps foolhardy travellers trying routes via Kinshasa in the DRC, more travellers with vehicles have used or attempted to use this route. Oasis, one of the leading overland truck operators, still runs trips on this route, although their early 2008 trip did have visa problems with Angola and DRC, as did everyone else in that spring period. It is to be hoped that the authorities will clarify the situation in order to stop putting black holes on the map and to encourage overlanders into areas of outstanding natural beauty.

That said, it is likely you will still encounter some gun-toting soldiers, difficult bureaucracy and bad roads – the worst countries being the two Congos. Cameroon and Gabon are fairly stable at the time of writing and thus reasonably safe. Visas for the region are increasingly expensive, though.

Gabon Heading south from Yaoundé, the road is good but hilly tarmac and very pretty, with dense jungle and occasional distant mountain ridges. From Ambam there are two routes. The main one heads south from town to the Ntem River, where a new bridge must surely be finished. Then a wide road heads towards Equatorial Guinea. East of the border post of Meyo, this soon becomes a dirt track to Bitam in Gabon. The other route heads east from Ambam on a very narrow muddy track with ageing log bridges. A friendly ferry crosses the river here to Gabon. Most formalities are carried out at Bitam.

Going south in Gabon, the road is virtually all finished with new tarmac. Again the scenery is spectacular. Before Ndjolé the road is badly pot-holed, but then to Libreville (and Lambaréné) it is good.

The road from Ndjolé to Lopé National Park is little more than a country lane and very hilly. One section of 30 miles could take two hours or more. The road has deteriorated in the last few years, but if you have plenty of time it should be OK, though slow and isolated. Fortunately, after Lopé the road improves, with more hilly sections but a better road surface. It should, under normal circumstances, be possible to drive from Lopé to Lastoursville in a comfortable six-hour day. The route improves between Lastoursville and Franceville and may take only three to four hours.

Congo Brazzaville There seem to be two potential routes from Franceville around the Congo border area. According to Paul Telfer of WCS (Wildlife Conservation Society) in Franceville, a small sandy track leads from the Batéké Plateau into Congo and on to Lékana, where roads of a sort lead to the newish main Owando to Brazzaville road. We have only sketchy information about this route, so you will have to ask around in Franceville about its viability.

Others have reported heading due east from Franceville to Lekoni (Leconi), where some canyons make a good if hairy diversion. A short new section of Chinese-built tarmac exists here. The border of Congo is 30km further east (marked as Akou on the Michelin map). Immigration is done in Mbie. It's around 125km between Lekoni and Okoyo, the first settlement of any size in Congo, but you might do it in one day. It just depends on the weather, the rivers and the

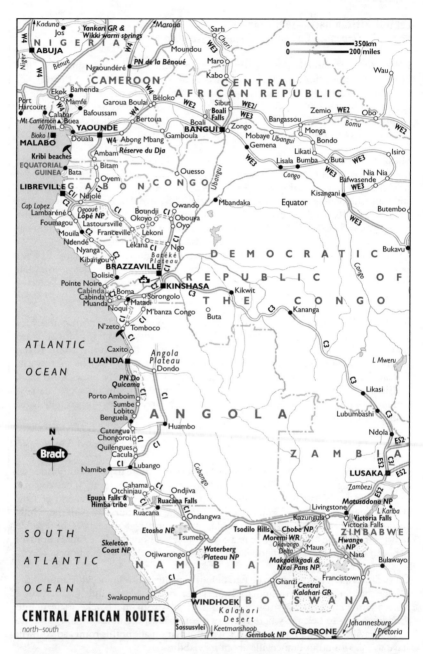

CENTRAL AFRICAN ROUTES
north–south

bridges along the way. A sandy and then rough track leads on for more than 100km via Boundji to the towns of Obouya and Oyo on the main road.

Heading south now on a mostly good tarmac road, you come in 160km to Ngo, where the other route from Lékana meets the main road. Another much easier day heading south along the main road leads to Brazzaville, but beware of pot-holes all the same.

DRC From Brazzaville you have to cross the river to Kinshasa. The actual ferry takes little time, but formalities make this an all-day affair. Expect to bargain for the ferry tickets. Do NOT take any photos of the Congo River from anywhere, or get cameras out either anywhere near it. They will confiscate the lot.

From Kinshasa to Matadi, the road is in a variable state. In future it may be possible to head directly from Matadi into Angola, but for now this is merely a rumour. If you have been lucky enough to get your visa in advance, you will not actually need to go as far as Matadi. Currently the turn-off for Angola is in the small crossroads town of Sorongolo/Songololo, 81km east of Matadi. Be sure to get your *carnet* stamped here. Then head south on a poor dirt road to Luvo, with DRC immigration 11km from the turn-off. The Angola border at Noqui, close to Matadi was also used by Oasis Overland in the summer of 2008. A pretty awful stretch of dirt then leads to Tomboco.

Angola After another 3km from the last check-post you reach the Angolan immigration. The infrastructure in much of Angola is still in a bad way; mines are still a big hazard away from the main routes. Possibly impassable in the wet, the next 75km is a single-track route on to M'banza Congo.

In very good weather conditions, you might get as far as the delightful beaches south of N'zeto. The road surface, though, changes a lot, from broken tarmac to sand or gravel. The distance is around 300km from the border to N'zeto, but in bad, wet conditions it is a long rough drive through Tomboco that could take up to 14 hours in all.

Don't expect any good road to the capital from N'zeto. The coastal road is no better, taking 11 more hours to reach Caxito. The road from Caxito on to Luanda is much better, but there could be endless check-posts on the way.

Latest reports (2008) suggest that the average speed along this section will rarely exceed 35km/h for half of the day. Improvements towards Luanda are likely to be done by the time this edition is out though – but how many times have we said that before!

Once in Luanda, beware of theft and street crime. Luanda is also one of the most expensive cities in Africa.

The choice of route to the south has now changed. Latest reports from travellers who have made it into Angola suggest that some Chinese-built new roads are now completed. From Luanda to Lubango via Huambo can probably be done in just two long days on good surfaced roads. The entire 640km to Huambo can be navigated in one very long day. The first section of good road goes to Dondo. The scenery is more varied from here on and the road newly rebuilt all the way to Huambo. From here the next 400km or so to Lubango is also new tarmac road.

If you still want to follow the previous option along the coast, and have a visa giving you sufficient time, the following rather dated notes are included. Heading south from Luanda along the coast to the Parque Nacional Do Quicama will take a couple of hours. With interesting and varied scenery and slightly better pot-holed roads, the trip down to Benguela could take two days, allowing for a side trip to the Quedas de Agua da Binga waterfalls.

In 2007 Jeff's Oasis Overland group took the road from Luanda down the coast road through Porto Amboim and Sumbe to Lobito: 'The road from Luanda to Sumbe is all pretty good – mainly new tarmac except for a few patches of old road.' The route from Sumbe to Lobito and Benguela is being rebuilt by the Chinese and work should be completed by the time this edition is printed.

Continuing along the dreadful coastal route through Santa Maria and on to Lucira is not recommended by anyone now that the inland road is much better. Take the route from Benguela inland via Quilengues to Lubango. Expect diversions and roadworks *en route* to Quilengues and watch out for mines. Jeff continues, 'From Catengue it was all churned up muddy and ruts – a lot of corrugations. From Chongoroi the road is still slow going – mostly pot-holed earth roads – some good patches of tarmac but nothing to get excited about.' The main road from Cacula through Toco to Lubango should be sealed by now. Expect to take three and a half days to do Luanda to Lubango on this route.

There is also now a brand-new sealed section between Namibe and Lubango, which climbs into high country with great views.

On the road south from Lubango to Namibia, things still take time. The first 100km or so of the road is good tarmac, but as you head south things gradually deteriorate. Closer to the border things improve again. It is possible to travel the entire distance from Lubango to Ondangwa in Namibia in one very long push, but if you are in no hurry you can stop in Cahama and then continue on the next. The main border crossing from Angola to Namibia near Ondjiva is reported to be rather slow. Another possibility is the small road leading south of Cahama, through Otchinjau, direct to the Ruacana Falls border with Namibia.

Namibia Once in Namibia the roads are a joy and so is the Etosha National Park. It's one big holiday from here on, whether down to the Cape or up to Nairobi.

Route C2: Gabon to Angola via Cabinda Should the route above (C1) via Franceville prove better, the following section of the route via Cabinda may not need to be endured. Notes are included in case, though. Heading south into Angola was tried by at least one group in 2004–05, but they were unable to get visas for Angola. They (Debs and her Overland Club truckful) got as far as Pointe Noire in Congo Brazzaville. From then until spring 2008, a few parties followed the route successfully.

From Libreville the road is very good through Lambaréné and on to Fougamou. A side trip to the old abandoned missions at Sindara village and the rapids on the River Ngouniets is worthwhile; it should be possible to camp in the bush there. Once across the Ogooué River the road is reasonable through Mouila and Ndendé to the border. Gabon exit procedures start at Ndendé and, after a final check *en route*, it's across the bridge and on to a far worse road in Congo.

This was as far as we got in 2003, when an Ebola virus outbreak and political unrest blocked the way. In any case travelling alone on this route is not recommended for quite some time into the future. Rebel activity has not completely disappeared around Dolisie. We had hoped to report on a new route through Gabon, but the Angola visa problems of spring 2008 stopped us in our tracks.

The Congo border formalities start at Moussogo; further checks are normally done at Nyanga an hour or so south. The route emerges from the forest into more open grassy savanna. Watch out for deep ditches on the side of the road and try using old quarries for bush camping. Expect lots of road barrier checks along the way throughout Congo.

The Cabinda Angola border is about an hour's drive south. The nice road marked on the Michelin map might as well be an apparition, for the next 100km could take six hours, half of it being particularly memorable. It's not far from Cabinda town to the border, less than an hour, but remember the border with DRC could be shut on Sundays and public holidays. Expect a thorough search here before continuing to Muanda. Welcome to the DRC – it's only 300km to Angola and it's all one big, exciting, grinding wonderland of delay. Still sure you wanted to come to this final African frontier? No? Well, there's no going back now!

From here to Boma are some of the worst roads imaginable, with truck-swallowing holes. It could take seven hours to go just 105km (65 miles). In the wet you can't even start out, as it is completely impassable. Don't expect things to get much better between Boma to Matadi either, with check-posts as well as poor road conditions. It may take another whole day at about 14kph.

As above, do not take any photos of the Congo River bridge from anywhere or get cameras out either anywhere near it. They will confiscate the lot.

From Matadi the road is – surprise, surprise – good for 81km to Sorongolo/Songololo. The route described above, via Franceville, Brazzaville and Kinshasa, joins here. (See *Route C1*, page 37.)

Route C3: DRC to Zambia

☞ *WARNING!* Travel within the DRC from Kinshasa to Zambia is a completely unknown option at present and has been for many years. From Kinshasa, roads of an unknown nature head southwest towards Lubumbashi via Kikwit, Kananga and Likasi. Many years ago you had to obtain permits in Kinshasa to cross the mining region. It may also be possible to put your vehicle on the train at Kananga.

Note: The information given in the paragraph above is not firsthand and is included only as an outline. Some overland companies used this route a long time ago, before the troubles.

Central African west–east routes

☞ *WARNING!* The three routes described here are all currently off-limits, although there is always hope if the political situations improve.

Avoid the African rains. These tend to start around May and last throughout the summer months. They start slightly later the further north you go.

Route WE1: Chad to Sudan to Ethiopia Although this route is at present not possible due to the conflict in the western Darfur region of Sudan adjacent to the Chad border, the information collected by the previous authors (of the third edition), Charlie and Illya, is included here in case things improve.

The main route is from N'djamena to Abéché near the Chad border at Adré then to El Geneina (Sudanese border), Nyala, or El Fasher, El Obeid, Kosti and Khartoum.

Leaving from N'djamena and heading to Khartoum will take ten days of solid driving during the dry season. The route via Ngoura and Mongo is said to be better than the main route to Abéché from N'djamena.

The route in Sudan is uncomplicated and the tracks are mostly hard-packed sand. There are usually two tracks, one for the Bedford trucks acting as the local taxi service and another for cars. The deep ruts left behind by the Bedfords are trying at times for smaller vehicles to navigate through.

It is hard to lose your way later on, but if in doubt, just follow the railway line or drive on it (oh no, not again!). A few police checks are evident along the way, but if your paperwork is in order, it's an absolute breeze. 'More often than not we politely had to decline the invitation to lunch at most police check-posts! The hospitality in Sudan is extraordinary.'

Make sure you get your Sudan visa before entering (either in Ivory Coast, Chad, Ethiopia or Kenya) and check whether you need a travel permit stating your route. (See also *Red tape* under *Sudan* in *Chapter 9*, page 291.)

From Khartoum it is possible to get to Ethiopia via Gedaref (Sudanese border), through Metema and Gonder to Addis Ababa. Currently you cannot go via Eritrea,

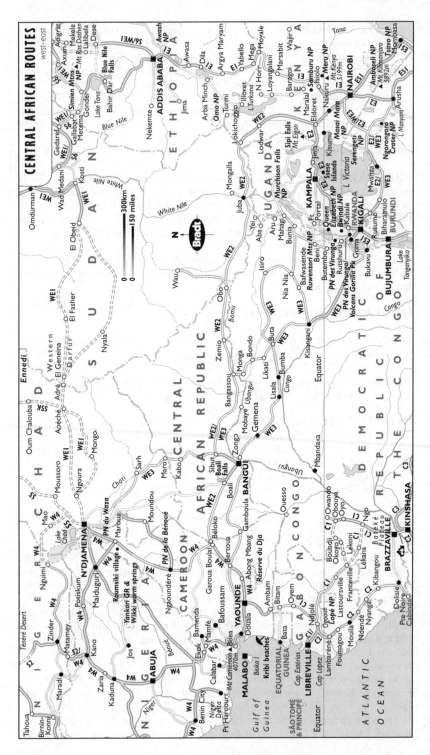

CENTRAL AFRICAN ROUTES
west–east

as the border with Ethiopia is closed, and going from Assab south to Djibouti is not advisable without local assistance, if at all.

Route WE2: Central African Republic to Sudan and Kenya With a few years of tentative peace in southern Sudan, the old route from Bangui in CAR to Nairobi via Juba might reopen. If you take the various government warnings about the situation in the CAR as gospel, this route is not to be trifled with yet. However, it is in fact quite hard to verify how bad it really is. Any news on this route would be particularly welcome.

A none-too-comfortable unsealed road used to run through dense savanna forest over rolling hills from the Cameroon/CAR border at Garoua Boulai/Béloko to Boali Falls – an amazing spectacle when in full flow. A sealed road then continued to the capital, Bangui. When 'Emperor' Jean Bedel Bokassa ruled the roost here, things were unpredictable and there is little hard evidence to indicate that things are much different today. The road to Sibut was good before, but it's likely the stretch to Bangassou is badly pot-holed by now

From Bangassou the route, formerly a rather dreadful narrow track through quite dense dry forest, runs east through Zemio and on to Obo. A number of ferry crossings also made this route slow going. Things were little better in the Sudan between the border and Juba. A rough track leads north to a place called Wau, an apt name for it! After Juba this was a superb but isolated route with varied mountain scenery, acacia scrub inhabited by the interesting Turkana people and friendly villages in the Sudan. The road surface was not superb, though. Once in Kenya, improved roads via Lokichoggio and Lodwar lead on to Nairobi.

Route WE3: Cameroon via CAR, DRC, Uganda, Rwanda to Kenya This was the classic trans-African route, renowned for broken bridges and enormous bog holes. It may be the only time you need your winch, snatch blocks and full capacity of fuel, not to mention your reserves of inner strength and patience. Ferry river crossings can be a big headache. Operators may need to use your battery to start the ferry, your diesel to run the ferry and your donation in order to begin the process. But remember, this is why you planned to see Africa in the first place.

Entry to the Central African Republic is from Cameroon or Chad – south of Sarh at Maro and Kabo – but it's unlikely that anyone has done this for years. Once in the CAR, things deteriorate. Bridges can be down and rain barriers are set up during the wet season to stop vehicles using and damaging the roads. The road used to improve the closer you got to the capital as detailed above. At present Bangui may not be safe for tourists.

There were two routes across Zaire, now the Democratic Republic of the Congo (DRC). One crossed the Ubangui River directly from Bangui to Zongo and then slipped and slid its muddy way via Gemena, Lisala, Bumba and Buta to Kisangani. Problems concerning security in Zongo used to be avoided by making sure you crossed early in the day and carried on for at least 50km (30 miles) from Zongo before stopping.

The other route involved driving east from Bangui via Sibut and Bambari to Bangassou. Once across the river from Bangassou, a fairly narrow and overgrown road used to head south via Monga, Bondo, Likati and Buta to Kisangani. This route is apparently now much the worse for wear, but might still be preferable to the other one. Another crossing of the Ubangui was at Mobaye, but we have no personal experience of this. Should these routes open in the near future, try (difficult unless you meet others coming north) to get an accurate picture beforehand in Bangui.

After Kisangani the route used to head east through Bafwasende and Nia Nia into Pygmy territory around Ipulu. Overland parties used to go into the forest with

2

the Pygmies on hunts and also visit the rare okapi reserve – it may not exist now. The rainforest continued until Komanda and nearby Mount Hoya. Here the route headed along a ridge with spectacular views, south to Beni, Butembo and on to Goma via the Virunga National Park. Another little-used and currently very unsafe bad road went north through some grassy, rolling hills around Bunia to Aru and Aba. Some dreadful bridges caused heart-stopping moments before the route crossed into southern Sudan near Yei. A better track continued through superb scenic boulder areas to Juba.

A new road shown on the Michelin map goes southeast from Kisangani to Bukavu and the Rwanda border near Goma. Until the political situation improves in the eastern DRC, we can only speculate about this future option. It was also possible to cross into Uganda from Beni some years ago before the troubles. Once in Rwanda the roads are better, but slow going and hilly. Some paved road was built in the late 1980s from the Rusumo Falls border into Tanzania around Biharamulo, well before reaching Lake Victoria. The classic route then went through the Serengeti, up onto the Ngorongoro Crater and Arusha before reaching Nairobi.

EAST AFRICA East Africa includes southern Ethiopia, Djibouti, Kenya, Tanzania, Uganda, Rwanda and Burundi. Somalia is off the planet at present.

Hitting the wrong climate in eastern (and southern areas) is more likely to be a nuisance than a disaster, as the roads tend not to be so bad. Most rain in the east falls between March and June and October to December.

Route E1: Ethiopia to Kenya

The simplest and currently most-used route from Ethiopia into Kenya or vice versa is the Moyale to Isiolo road, if it can be described as a road. From Addis Ababa a good sealed road goes via Awasa as far south as Dila before becoming pot-holed, very hilly and slow. After Argya Maryam it improves and is generally good through Yabello and Mega to the border at Moyale.

Once in northern Kenya the road is soon shocking and security concerns mean you are advised at the border to take an armed guard. A convoy system seems to be in use periodically due to isolated banditry. Check at the border for the latest advice.

Before Marsabit the road is dreadful, allowing speeds of no more than 10–15mph. After Marsabit, a veritable haven of civilisation and good food, the road is patchy. Allow nearly two days to get to Isiolo from Moyale.

Local trucks from Moyale now appear to be taking a better, sandier track via Wajir to Nairobi, but this also heads through bandit areas. Local advice must be sought due to its proximity to the Somali conflict.

Some travellers were going via the Omo region around Arba Minch *en route* from Addis Ababa to Moyale. On the Kenyan side, going via Lake Turkana might be a possibility, but security concerns often prevent this option. Local advice must also be sought here.

The road from Addis Ababa to Djibouti is good, and Djibouti is an exciting country.

Route E2: Kenya, Tanzania, Rwanda and Uganda loop

For a shorter trip around the classic east African region, this loop is a superb choice, taking in some of the most famous game parks, Lake Victoria, gorilla tracking in Rwanda, the Mountains of the Moon and the highlights of Kenya such as Lake Nakuru. Burundi is still a bit iffy.

Those with their own vehicles can enjoy the comforts of travel here, while those looking for an organised trip by truck or safari vehicles can look forward to a great experience in some of the most varied terrain of Africa. Try not to time your visit here during the rainy season, as some black *murram* (mud) park roads become boggy or very slippery.

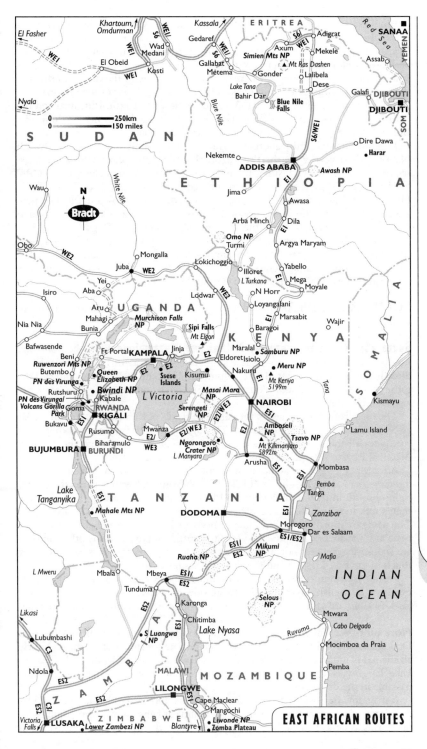

EAST AFRICAN ROUTES

From Nairobi a good road runs to Arusha. Then, as you pass Lake Manyara and climb through Karatu, the dirt road is fine in the dry but awful in the wet. Ngorongoro Crater National Park and the open plains of the Serengeti National Park are magical places where even the most 'natural world-challenged' visitors will be converted. Heading for Lake Victoria is a breeze in the dry, but fearful in the wet. The countryside around Lake Victoria is reminiscent of the savanna.

At Rusumo you enter Rwanda. A good road leads to Kigali, Rutshuru and the Parc National des Virunga/Volcans Gorilla Park. It would be nice to think that Burundi could be added to this great circular route soon.

Heading into Uganda, another gorilla-tracking option is possible in Bwindi National Park; nearby are the Ruwenzori cloud-hugging peaks. Check the latest security concerns when visiting Bwindi National Park, as it is close to the DRC border. Across Uganda, most of the main roads are now in good condition. When Idi Amin held sway, no-one dared to stop even at a broken-down traffic light here – we speak from personal memory of this. No such fears today as you continue to Jinja, for some rafting perhaps, then into the high country of Kenya.

North of the main road are the picturesque lakes of Baringo and Bogoria, with flamingos and hot springs. The more famous flamingos at Lake Nakuru are the last attraction before reaching Nairobi and its famous Carnivore restaurant. Kenya has returned to normal after the election riots in 2007–08.

EAST AFRICA TO SOUTHERN AFRICA ES routes are covered on the Southern African Routes map (page 47) and the East African Routes map (page 45).

Route ESI: Kenya to Tanzania, Malawi and Mozambique From Nairobi, any number of good roads and routes lead south into Tanzania, the most popular being directly south to Arusha. Heading to Mombasa and south to Tanga, or going via the game parks circuit, including Masai Mara, Serengeti and Ngorongoro Crater, are also possible routes.

The road from Arusha, below the southern flanks of Kilimanjaro, and on to Dar es Salaam makes for easy motoring. Through southern Tanzania, another good road goes all the way from Dar es Salaam through Morogoro and the Mikumi National Park to Mbeya, then on into either Zambia or Malawi.

After Mbeya, a good road heads south into northern Malawi and then passes the 'beach resorts' along the shores of Lake Nyasa. From Malawi it is perfectly feasible to head south into Mozambique from Blantyre across the Zambezi River to Tete, then south to Chimoio, in a scenic area near the Parque Nacional da Gorongosa. The roads are mostly good, but some sections are breaking up and pot-holes are an issue in some areas. The route has very little traffic, and fuel and any other supplies are sparse, particularly north of Vilanculos. Be prepared for an isolated journey much of the way. Hassle from traffic police has lessened.

From Maputo into Swaziland and on into South Africa, the roads are generally excellent. Be vigilant on the South African side of the Swazi border, though, where car hijackings are said to be a hazard. Signs around here recommend no stopping!

Note on other Tanzanian routes: The road from Arusha south to Mbeya via Dodoma is said to be very rough and quite remote for much of the time. Nearly all the roads in the western part of the country leave a lot to be desired. Close to Lake Tanganyika, the road from Rwanda or Burundi down to Mbala is only really passable in the dry season.

It may now be possible to cross from Tanzania into Mozambique south of Dar es Salaam, as a new bridge over the Rio Ruvuma at Mtwara was being built, with new roads as far as Pemba. But with periodic heavy floods, the status of roads and

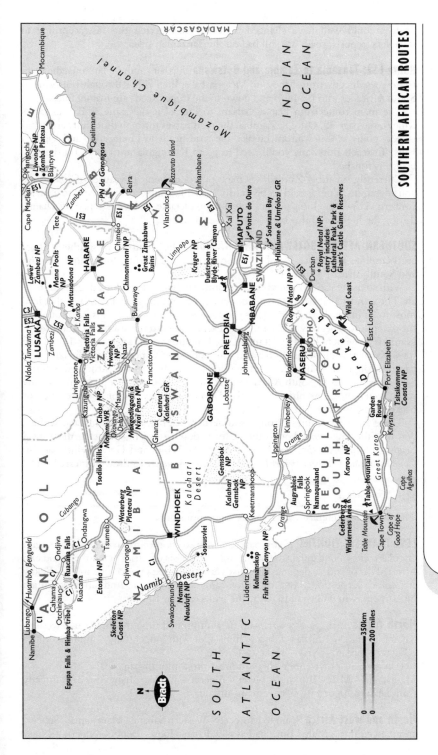

SOUTHERN AFRICAN ROUTES

MADAGASCAR

INDIAN OCEAN

Mozambique Channel

SOUTH ATLANTIC OCEAN

Mocambique
Mangochi
Liwonde NP
Zomba Plateau
Blantyre
Cape Maclear
ES1
Quelimane
Zambezi
Tete
IS3
PN da Gorongosa
Beira
Chimoio
Chimanimani NP
Great Zimbabwe Ruins
Vilanculos
Bazaruto Island
Inhambane

Lower Zambezi NP
Mana Pools NP
HARARE
Matusadona NP
L Kariba
ZIMBABWE
Bulawayo
Limpopo
Kruger NP
Dulstroom & Blyde River Canyon
Xai Xai
MAPUTO
Ponta do Ouro

Ndola, Tunduma
LUSAKA
C3/
ES2
ES2
Zambezi
Victoria Falls
Victoria Falls
Livingstone
Kazungula
HWANGE NP
Nata
Francistown
Hwange NP

SWAZILAND
MBABANE
PRETORIA
Royal Natal NP *
Johannesburg
Durban
Sodwana Bay
Hluhluwe & Umfolozi GR
* Royal Natal NP: entry includes Cathedral Peak Park & Giant's Castle Game Reserves

Chobe NP
Moremi WR
Makgadikgadi & Nxai Pans NP
Okavango Delta
Maun
Ghanzi
Central Kalahari GR
BOTSWANA
GABORONE
Lobatse
LESOTHO
MASERU
Bloemfontein
Wild Coast
East London

Tsodilo Hills
Kalahari Desert
Kimberley
Uppington
Orange
REPUBLIC OF SOUTH AFRICA
Garden Route
Great Karoo
Port Elizabeth
Tsitsikamma Coastal NP
Knysna

Waterberg Plateau NP
Otjiwarongo
Tsumeb
WINDHOEK
Gemsbok NP
Kalahari Gemsbok NP
Keetmanshoop
Augrabies Falls
Springbok
Namaqualand
Karoo NP

ANGOLA
Huambo, Benguela
Lubango
Namibe
Cahama
Ondjiva
Orchinjau
Ruacana Falls
C1
Ruacana
Himba tribe
Epupa Falls &
Etosha NP
Ondangwa
NAMIBIA
Cubango
Cunene
Skeleton Coast NP

Swakopmund
Namib Naukluft NP
Namib Desert
Sossusvlei
Lüderitz
Kolmanskop
Fish River Canyon NP
Orange
Cederberg Wilderness Area
Table Mountain NP
Cape Town
Cape of Good Hope
Cape Agulhas
Drakensberg

N
Bradt

0   350km
0   200 miles

47

bridges could well have changed. Check before trying this, as, according to travellers' reports, roads are still bad on the Tanzanian side.

Route ES2: Tanzania to Zambia and Botswana Further south of Tanzania, the main route goes directly from Mbeya to Victoria Falls, then either through Botswana to South Africa, or into Namibia and down to the Cape. Roads are mainly fine.

The main route from Dar es Salaam to Lusaka is the same as ES1 as far as Mbeya, see page 45. Once in Zambia, the road passes through quite hilly areas and is slow going at times. From Lusaka, the road heads to Livingstone and Victoria Falls. To reach Botswana you'll need to go to Kazungula until work on the new bridge is finished.

Currently, visiting Zimbabwe may prove difficult, because of economic considerations. Fuel is said to be hardly available and security issues are a major concern. However, local politics are not predictable and will hopefully change during the lifetime of this book.

SOUTHERN AFRICA, BOTSWANA AND NAMIBIA The countries of southern Africa are Namibia, Botswana, Zambia, Zimbabwe, Mozambique, Swaziland, Lesotho and South Africa.

With so many varied routes through southern Africa, it is impossible to list them all. The standard of roads is excellent compared with the rest of Africa, and indeed most roads in southern Africa are as good as those in Europe. Roads in Lesotho are the exception, especially in the mountain areas away from Maseru. Gravel roads in Namibia are generally very well maintained and offer some spectacular drives. The trans-Kalahari route across Botswana from Lobatse to Windhoek via Ghanzi is now paved throughout (Michelin is wrong here), as is the Caprivi Strip in the north. Security concerns in South Africa are, perhaps, sadly, more of a problem than any road, route or geographical obstacle. Don't camp away from secure sites or backpackers' hostels.

There are a few routes through southern Africa that are 4x4 only and will get you into the unknown. For further information on 4x4 in southern Africa, read *Southern Africa 4X4 Trails* by Andrew St Pierre White and Gwyn White, or *The Complete Guide to a Four Wheel Drive in Southern Africa* by Andrew St Pierre White.

SUGGESTED ITINERARIES

The following itineraries are listed as suggestions only.

LESS THAN SIX MONTHS If you have only up to six months available, we suggest circular routes along either the north and west coasts of Africa or southern and east Africa. This of course depends on what you want to experience, see and do. Below are some suggestions, but the timescales are limitless. And after so much investment, you will want to enjoy the fruits of your labours.

North Africa Perhaps as a warm-up or with limited time: Morocco and Western Sahara; or Italy – Tunisia – Libya – Tunisia; or with longer, Italy – Tunisia – Libya – Egypt – Jordan – Syria – Turkey – Greece.

If Algeria improves, then this is a great three-month trip: Spain – Morocco – Mauritania – Mali – Burkina – Niger – Algeria – Tunisia – Italy. Also back directly from Mali to Algeria if Niger remains unsafe.

North and west Africa Spain to Morocco – Western Sahara – Mauritania – Senegal and the Gambia – Mali – Burkina Faso – Ghana – Togo – Benin – Nigeria – Niger

– Algeria or Libya – Tunisia and back to Italy. Niger is currently off-limits. With longer time and improving security, possibly from Nigeria into Cameroon, then across to Chad and Sudan. Then Egypt or Saudi Arabia to Jordan.

West Africa Mauritania – Senegal – Gambia – Guinea – Sierra Leone – Liberia – Guinea – Mali, or Ivory Coast when safe – Burkina – Togo – Benin – Nigeria – Western Niger – Mali – Mauritania or any shorter versions.

With visa difficulties further south, many overlanders are planning trips around west Africa, accessed from Morocco and Western Sahara. The downside at present is having to repeat the Atlantic coast, unless Algeria and northern Mali become safer.

Central Africa Cameroon – Gabon – Congo – Congo DRC to Angola. This route will surely become easier within the lifetime of this guide. Good luck!

East Africa Ethiopia – Kenya – Tanzania – Malawi or Zambia – Mozambique or Botswana to South Africa.

Plus, in addition the varied and exciting options, Kenya – Uganda – Rwanda – Tanzania, with Burundi maybe getting in on the act soon.

Southern and east Africa Cape Town – Namibia – Botswana – Zambia – Zimbabwe – Malawi – Mozambique – Swaziland – Cape Town.

TRANS-AFRICAN LONGER ROUTES The routes we have suggested are completely dependent on the political situation at the time. A full overland trip from London to Cape Town or vice versa can be done in as little as four months, but taking at least six to eight months would be more relaxing. Of course a year would not be too long either; there are always plenty of options to fill your time.

Currently feasible are: Turkey – Syria – Jordan – Egypt; or Tunisia – Libya – Egypt; then Sudan – Ethiopia – Djibouti – Kenya – Tanzania – Zambia – Namibia – South Africa; or Tanzania – Malawi – Mozambique – Swaziland – South Africa – Lesotho plus Botswana and Namibia.

Currently the following is not a reliable option, and success will depend on the situation in DRC and Angola: Morocco – Western Sahara – Mauritania – Senegal – Gambia – Senegal – Guinea – Sierra Leone – Liberia – Guinea – Mali – Burkina Faso– Ghana – Togo – Benin – Nigeria – Cameroon – Gabon – Congo – DRC – Angola – Namibia – South Africa.

In future, when Darfur is safe perhaps, as above, then from Mali to Niger – Chad – Sudan – Ethiopia – Kenya – Uganda – Tanzania – Malawi – Zambia – Botswana – Zimbabwe – Mozambique – South Africa.

3

Vehicle Selection and Preparation

Your budget is assessed and you have outlined a route, so now you can think about your biggest expense of all: the vehicle. Don't rush off without careful preparation; it could be a fatal mistake. An eye for detail will make your trip much more enjoyable and help you to avoid some potential pitfalls later on. Planning and preparation is half the fun.

If you are taking your own vehicle, we would recommend a planning period of about a year. You should have your vehicle for at least six months or more before you leave, especially if you are doing the preparation work yourself in your spare time. It may sound like a long time, but you will be amazed at just how much preparation is necessary and how many things there are to consider. Don't be put off, though.

We have divided the chapter into vehicle, motorbike and bicycle sections, detailing every requirement before and during your trip.

At the end of the book (*Appendix 3*, page 317) we have included a checklist to help you with your planning decisions.

SELECTING YOUR VEHICLE

Travelling in a vehicle might distance you from the environment you are visiting, cocooning you in a self-contained world. However, this is true only if you allow it to be. The major advantage is that you are free to go more or less anywhere, stopping for tea or a snooze anytime. With relative comfort and the capacity to carry a fair amount of supplies, this is the best option. The biggest decision is what type of vehicle to choose. Of course all have their advantages and disadvantages.

4X4 This is the best option if you can afford it. The range of 4x4s is quite varied now, but most are being used on the school run. Of the more suitable models, there is a choice of permanent or part-time 4x4 and, more useful, low and high (normal) ratios for all gears. Some have diff lock and others have varying degrees of automation. Diff lock is when all four wheels are able to rotate without the loss of traction that normally occurs if one wheel is spinning. Diff lock should never be used for normal driving any longer than necessary, as the gears will 'wind up' and create excessive stress on gear components. The other significant factor when choosing a 4x4 is the type of suspension it has. Some have leaf springs, others have coil springs and some have a mix. Coil springs rarely give trouble but can induce a rolling effect. Leaf springs are more stable, but prone to breaking. Is there ever a perfect answer?

Petrol or diesel? It's hard to see any advantages in taking petrol, so we recommend you to stick with diesel. Diesel engines usually offer superior fuel consumption. Diesel is also safer to carry, unlike petrol, which is lethal once it has been shaken about in hot jerrycans. Diesel engines are also simpler in that they have no points, coils, condensers or distributors, though they do have more complex fuel systems. Make sure your injector pump and injectors have been professionally serviced before you leave. Diesel engines produce high torque at low revs, whereas petrol engines tend to produce maximum torque at high revs, which can be a disadvantage in difficult conditions where wheelspin is a problem.

Most of the 4x4 manufacturers have now moved on to diesel engines that are turbo-charged. To gain more power, some have inter-coolers. These two systems basically make use of exhaust gases and colder air to boost power levels. Being more complicated, they have some disadvantages. Buying such models secondhand can have risks. Ideally you should ask for the servicing record of the vehicle. Wear rates can be higher with the faster motion and greater heat generated by these models. Of course the power gains are significant and undoubtedly an advantage in deep sand.

Fuel availability (either diesel or petrol) varies from country to country. As a general rule, however, diesel is cheaper throughout Africa and more readily available than petrol. Vehicles that use unleaded petrol have a definite problem, since such petrol is not available in many countries.

Short or long wheelbase? A long wheelbase has the obvious advantage of space. Remember you are most likely planning to live in and on your vehicle for long periods. It will be a close companion, and so will the person you share it with, so you might as well start out with the idea of making it comfortable. Having more space means more flexibility; more equipment can be stored inside and out of sight. Pick-up versions of long-wheelbase vehicles with added rear box units are extremely good for storage capacity. Rear box shells are available; some are rather low. Otherwise, if you are lucky enough to have access to welding and fabricating equipment, you can make your own metal- and aluminium-clad box. Some people put custom-made caravan-style boxes onto pick-ups. Some are quite good; others look unstable and are not ideal in sand dunes.

A short-wheelbase vehicle does not really have the capacity or the convenience. Attaching a trailer to a short wheelbase for extra storage space is a possibility, but we don't recommend it. Towing a trailer can be a severe hindrance in some terrain, particularly sand or mud and over loose, uneven or sloping surfaces. There is potentially some danger when manoeuvring trailers at difficult angles or on sloping muddy roads. A badly loaded trailer can cause instability when cornering and braking. Trailers do spread the load better, but overall are best not considered.

Further information on storage and driving techniques regarding a short-wheelbase vehicle with trailer can be obtained from major 4x4 or trailer outlets. Companies offering 4x4 courses will also be able to assist. For a list of 4x4 clubs, research website: www.fourwheeler.com/facts/clublist.html.

Age and value Buying the latest model or the most expensive vehicle might be desirable ordinarily, but there is one important factor to consider. Remember that the level and cost of your customs document for the vehicle, the *carnet de passage*, is related to the value of your vehicle. The bond or insurance-cover fees you must arrange before leaving your home country will depend on the value of the vehicle you choose, its age and in some circumstances its initial cost when new. When a country like Egypt charges a 800% mark-up on the assessed value of your vehicle, new or old, it can be a seriously daunting amount to put up as collateral. If you are planning a limited trip and to travel in countries that do not require a *carnet*, the problem is not an issue.

See *Paperwork* in *Chapter 5*, page 107 about this **before** deciding on the vehicle. Unless you have inherited a lot of money, this effectively means buying an older model, preferably in good condition, and spending some considerable time fixing it up. How old it is depends on your mechanical ability, the time and enthusiasm you have, and the depth of your pocket.

Vehicle makes By far the most common 4x4s in Africa are the Land Rover, Toyota Land Cruiser, Toyota Hilux (4x4) and the Nissan Patrol in southern Africa. You are more likely to find spares and experienced mechanics for these vehicles than any other.

The older models are more common, such as the Land Rover Series III, 90, 110 and Defender, and the 60, 70 and some 80 series of the Land Cruiser and mid-1980s Hilux. There aren't so many spares for much older models now. You will also find Land Rover and Toyota dealers in most capital and larger cities, although the stock of spares varies greatly from dealer to dealer. They will sometimes only stock spares for the newer models.

Unless you are a very experienced mechanic, have a very reliable vehicle or can afford to have spares sent out to you, avoid the seriously overcomplicated computerised newer models for which bush mechanics will not have the tools or know-how. Go for an older Land Rover, Land Cruiser or Hilux.

The following is a brief rundown of the vehicles available and a few of their advantages and disadvantages.

Land Rover (*www.landrover.com*) It is often lamented that 'a Land Rover is always sick but never dead!' That said, there are still more overlanders using Land Rovers than Toyotas, thus defying logic, but then so is crossing Africa these days!

The ageing Land Rover Series III's are probably a bit long in the tooth regarding chassis rust and suspension when buying secondhand, so are not advised. Favourites now include the 110 and Defender Land Rover series, which are the most suitable for African roads. Their fairly simple and robust design makes them ideal for the wide variety of difficult conditions. They are available in long or short wheelbase, with six-cylinder petrol or four-cylinder diesel engines. The smaller 2,286cc engine is too underpowered. The 2.5 engines are normally aspirated or with turbo-charging and injection – the Tdi series. The later models are more powerful but more complicated. The early 2.5 turbo is best avoided, but the following 200 Tdi-engine models are quite popular. The later 300 Tdi originally had some timing-belt problems but is now considered to be the best engine. The very latest Td5 is more sophisticated; some servicing is probably best done by main dealers in African capitals.

The 110 and Defenders have permanent 4x4. With coil springs, they are a joy to drive on rough terrain. This is not to say that even Land Rovers are sufficiently robust to ignore bad conditions. They actually need constant attention and nurturing throughout the journey. Land Rover fans are a very caring, enthusiastic lot, spending happy hours underneath, admiring their steeds and keeping an eye out for oil leaks and loose bolts.

Range Rover (*www.landrover.com/RangeRover*) This vehicle was designed to bridge the gap between off- and on-road driving. It offers greater comfort than the Land Rover and is an excellent vehicle, but for a trans-African journey it is of fairly limited use. It does not have much in the way of storage capacity and the compensating advantages of its powerful engine and comfortable interior can now be found in the newer Land Rovers.

Land Rover Discovery (*www.landrover.com*) Although it has virtually the same engine, gearbox and axle specifications as the Land Rover Defenders, it has fewer practical advantages. It does have greater comfort, though. It is not common outside southern and eastern Africa. This vehicle has the 200 or 300 Tdi engines, which are now fairly reliable. The gearboxes are still liable to early wear and the shape is not ideal for tinkering with or living in for long periods.

Toyota Land Cruiser (*www.toyota.com/landcruiser*) The Land Cruiser's design is rugged and very reliable, and spare parts are readily available throughout Africa. Toyota is rapidly taking over Africa! Toyota have a rather confusing numbering system for their various Land Cruiser models. To put it simply, they started with the 40 series and worked up to the 80 series in the early 1990s. The FJ prefix denotes a petrol engine and the HJ series diesel engines. Just to confuse you further, BJ refers to the short wheelbase. The engines tend to be large but very reliable and, in particular, the H2 engine (fitted in the HJ 60 series) will go on forever if looked after. The suspension is by solid axle and leaf springs, and the older models are all part-time 4x4 with a two-ratio transfer gearbox. Watch out for chassis rust when buying older secondhand models.

In 1984 Toyota introduced the 70 series. The HJZ75 and HJZ78 are still probably the best models for the Sahara and Africa. The 78 had coil springs fitted to the front and retained leaf springs on the rear, which can mean broken springs if you drive too fast. Toyota's 4-cylinder 3.5 and 6-cylinder 4.2 engines are still reliable workhorse power units. The 80 series came along in 1990 with all coil springs, and the VX models have permanent 4x4. It may be better perhaps to look out for the GX models, which do not have permanent 4x4. Local mechanics tend to be more familiar with these earlier vehicles. The later Toyota 100 series are a step backwards for overlanding – far too complex and an impractical shape. Toyotas are now made in South Africa, but specifications can vary.

Toyota Hilux (*www.toyota.com*) The Hilux is available as a double or single cab with either a 2.2-litre petrol or 2.4/2.8-litre diesel engine. The engines are fine unless you expect to be dune-bashing for most of your trip. It also has part-time 4x4 with a two-ratio transfer gearbox. They are quite popular vehicles in Africa and nearly rate up there with Land Cruiser and Land Rover. They are a little easier to roll over onto their roofs if you are not careful, so take particular care when crossing slopes and cornering at speed. If you are considering buying a Hilux pick-up, be sure to keep the height as low as possible when designing the rear living/storage area.

Following on from the Hilux are the 4Runners. These have part-time 4x4 and a 3-litre turbo diesel engine. The Hilux is still more common at the moment in Africa.

Nissan Patrol (*www.nissanuk.com and www.nissanusa.com*) These vehicles have a good reputation in Australia and South Africa and are reported to be very reliable. They are increasingly seen in southern Africa, where spares seem to be available in larger towns. They have coil-spring suspension and part-time 4x4. The later Patrol GR had a 6-cylinder 2.8 turbo diesel engine. The TD42 models have a larger engine. These two versions kept the part-time 4x4. We do not have any direct experience of these vehicles, but their shape and size certainly have no apparent disadvantages.

Jeep (*www.jeep.com*) The Jeep Wrangler is probably a bit small for all the equipment you'll be taking, and the Cherokee range tend to be gas-guzzlers. We met one Dutch couple with a Jeep and, although new, it suffered from suspension problems. Again it is virtually impossible to find even basic spares and is not recommended.

Mercedes Unimog (*www.unimog.net*) The Unimog is popular with some German travellers and it is indeed a wonderful vehicle. It is a powerful 4x4 truck with very high ground clearance and offers a lot of storage space. The living quarters are separate from the driving cab. Although you can buy Unimogs quite cheaply at auction in Germany, costs can really start to mount on the road. The fuel consumption can be very high indeed, and some are petrol. You should test drive the Unimog in various conditions, as it can easily tip over in soft sand.

Bedford and other trucks Bedford 4x4 trucks, especially ex-British army models, were much favoured by British-based trans-Africa overland tour companies such as Exodus and Encounter Overland. Bedfords are seriously old and outdated these days. It's not the most suitable vehicle to invest in, unless there are quite a few of you. You would need to carry most parts, spares and tools with you, preferably taking a Bedford expert along too. Very old J6 Bedfords are still used along the desert tracks of the Sudan as transport for the locals (and hardy travellers) who have to sit on top of the loads. In much of the rest of Africa they have now all but disappeared.

Although only suitable in general for larger parties, some Europeans have converted small trucks into quite spacious mobile homes. Both Mercedes and MAN have 4x4 versions, but preparation costs are high. MAN has the smaller models. Trucks are a pain when stuck in sand, though.

Top of the range These models are best avoided. That said, for a go-anywhere vehicle there is the Austrian Pinzgauer, which is available in either 4x4 or 6WD – this is a phenomenal vehicle at a phenomenal price. Others include the Land Cruiser Prado models, Isuzu Trooper and Mitsubishi Pajero. You are more likely to find these in supermarket car parks or outside schools in the smart suburbs of London or Sydney than you are crossing Africa. That may be more to do with their price than their off-road ability. More seriously, you will struggle to find a mechanic who can fix them, or any spares outside Europe or South Africa.

Isuzu Trooper (*www.isuzu.com*) This is one of the top-of-the-range, undoubtedly comfortable, vehicles. It is reported to suffer from a very sensitive accelerator that may cause difficulty when delicate accelerator work is required. It may also cause excessive wheelspin in sandy and muddy conditions. Some are seen in east and south Africa, but further north it is probably an unwise choice.

Mitsubishi Pajero (*www.mitsubishi.com*) The Pajero is reportedly one of the better top-spec vehicles when it comes to off-road ability, but its front suspension is said to let it down.

Mitsubishi Colt (*www.mitsubishi.com*) The Colt is another vehicle in the same vein as the Hilux. It has part-time 4x4 with automatic free-wheel hubs.

TWO-WHEEL DRIVES Although not really suitable for more adventurous, full-blooded trans-African trips, 2WD vehicles can be used quite happily if you plan your route with care or will be travelling in areas with better roads. Some actually have definite advantages, because of either their comfort or their light weight – the lighter the vehicle, the less power you need to get it through difficult conditions.

It is possible to drive across the Sahara, and even right across Africa, in a vehicle like a VW Combi. Twenty years ago quite a lot of overlanders used these air-cooled models. They provide far more comfort than most 4x4 vehicles. But you have to time the seasons precisely and definitely be prepared to get stuck more often than with a 4x4. Combis are not so good in seriously thick mud, but in harder-packed

Your vehicle timing chain or belt, where there is no reliable service record, should be replaced before departure. Even if it is not causing you any problems before you set off, you could get into big trouble if it were to break while you were on the road.

sand they can be surprisingly effective. However, travelling with another vehicle is highly desirable.

Some smaller 2WD cars can be surprisingly good in all but the muddier sections of central Africa. Citroen 2CVs and Renault 4s are economical on fuel and capable of desert crossings on main tracks with some pushing and cursing. Their lack of ground clearance is a limitation and is a particular problem where rocks poke out of sand – south of Tamanrasset in places, for example, but not so bad south of Reggane on the Tanezrouft route. If you don't mind the lack of space, they could prove a low-cost option for much of the continent where roads are reasonable. Charlie and Illya met someone who had converted a 2CV to adapt to the harsh African conditions and had travelled not only most of the Sahara, but also Zaire as it was then known. It is advisable to go with a convoy if you are travelling in a 2WD and wanting to cross the Sahara or any other difficult sections.

CAR HIRE There is no need to drive all the way if you are short of time or do not fancy a complete trans-African trip. Much of southern Africa and parts of the east and west are perfectly accessible by 2WD vehicles that can be hired locally. If you want to get off the beaten track once you arrive, you should be able to find more substantial vehicles for hire in some of the major tourist centres. In cities like Windhoek and to some degree Nairobi, for example, it is possible to hire 4x4 vehicles such as Suzuki, Isuzu Troopers and Land Rovers, already kitted out with camping gear, cooking equipment, water containers, etc. Hire can be arranged in advance through the Africa Travel Centre.

Africa Travel Centre UK 21 Leigh St, London WC1H 9EW; ☎ 0845 450 1520 & 020 7387 1211; f 020 7383 7512; e info@africatravel.co.uk; www.africatravel.co.uk; *South Africa:* PO Box 772, Hurlingham View, 2070 Johannesburg; ☎ +27 (0) 11 880 5108; f 011 880 5655; e webmaster@backpackafrica.com; www.backpack.co.za

VEHICLE PREPARATION

The range of possibilities for vehicle preparation is obviously enormous – from paying someone else to do the job for you, to having the fun of tackling most of it yourself.

Varying degrees of help are available. Some companies can provide a vehicle completely customised to your own requirements, while others will give advice and help so that you can prepare your own vehicle. Keeping the vehicle close to the standard is best. Try not to overload it.

Whatever model you have, it is crucial that you should know your vehicle well. This is extremely important if you have not had a hand in getting it ready to leave. Take time to become totally familiar with it before setting off.

What follows is a guide to some of the more important issues to bear in mind. You will all have your own ideas about what is essential and what optional extras are necessary.

The first and most important part of vehicle preparation is to ensure that the basic vehicle is in sound mechanical order. That is before you add on any extras. If you are not a mechanic, you will soon become one! In the meantime, it would be advisable to take it to a garage for a major check/overhaul. This should include the engine, cooling system, fuel system, suspension, gearbox, transfer box, clutch, differentials, brakes, electrics and chassis condition.

Initially take the vehicle on some test drives, then some longer day trips. It is really preferable to take it on a more extended drive, a trip around your own country or further afield, before going to Africa. This applies whether or not you have some mechanical knowledge. If you are already in southern Africa, you will be well ahead of the game. Teething troubles are most likely to occur earlier on and many can be ironed out over these initial forays. Try to identify any problems and get them fixed while you still have access to good mechanics. With thorough and conscientious preparation beforehand, the number of problems, and hence headaches, will most probably be limited later to the effects of African conditions.

Make sure as many nuts and threads as possible have been greased before you go; there is nothing worse than rusty nuts on the side of the road.

Once you have the basic vehicle in good working order, you can start to fit it out for overland travel. From a security angle, it is desirable to limit the amount of equipment placed on or around the vehicle. With gear all over, it can look a bit pretentious; it certainly shows a level of wealth undreamed of by most Africans. This in turn might attract petty thieves. The more you keep hidden, the more you blend into the local ambience. Or maybe that is wishful thinking.

FACTORS TO CONSIDER The following section details some of the main factors to consider. Again some personal preferences will come into play.

Sleeping options You have the following choices: a rooftop tent, sleeping space inside the vehicle, a tent or hotel accommodation. The ultimate choice is obviously dependent on where and for how long you intend to travel.

The option of hotels every night is only a consideration if you are travelling in places like Morocco, Tunisia, Egypt and southern Africa, where towns are frequent and roads good. Although you will find hotels in some places in all countries, you should always be prepared to camp out, as you never know where you might end up.

Tents Pitching a tent with a sewn-in mosquito net and groundsheet is the cheapest option, but invariably not convenient. When sleeping on the ground in Africa you will not be alone, as all manner of bugs will find your presence attractive; a camp bed helps, but takes time to set up. Getting tent pegs in can be a bind; sand is too soft, mud too sticky and the Sahel too hard. Aren't holidays a hassle! Pitching a tent daily can be a nuisance when driving for long stretches over a long period. Finding suitable rough camps is not so easy in a continent with a rapidly increasing population. Dome tents (requiring fewer pegs) are better in any event, except in tropical downpours. Things do dry fast, though.

Rooftop tents Most overland vehicles that you see throughout Africa have rooftop tents of various designs. They are the most convenient option. They do not require much space, are quick and easy to put up, and keep you away from people as well as from large and small wildlife. Being well above ground, they afford good ventilation. There is the standard air camper, the folding roof-rack tent or the pop-up variety. Any one of these can usually take a double mattress, which stays in the tent as it is folded up and can be fitted to most vehicles. With a little ingenuity, it is possible to pitch any normal robust tent on the roof rack, assuming your rack has a plywood base. This is a cheaper option if you already have a good tent stored away.

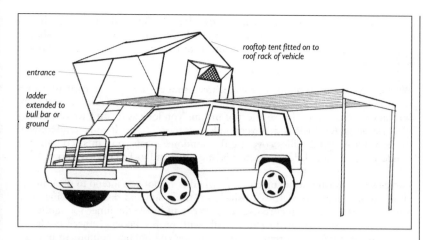

entrance

ladder
extended to
bull bar or
ground

rooftop tent fitted on to
roof rack of vehicle

Sleeping inside the vehicle Even if you have a roof tent, it is a good idea to plan some way of sleeping inside. This can be handy in certain situations, foul wet weather, sandstorms, borders and some rather public places. If you intend to sleep inside the vehicle a lot, try to devise a system that minimises the number of things you need to move when you go to bed. Sleeping inside can sometimes be too hot and ventilation needs to be considered. It is useful to have a multi-purpose platform that can slide in and out, and which lies above the equipment. Part of the platform can double up as a table by attaching legs to it. Sleeping in the vehicle is clearly the most secure option for both you and your belongings. See the *Suggestions for vehicle layout* diagrams on pages 63–4 for options.

Roof rack Roof racks are available in all shapes and sizes. They can be used as a low-cost alternative to a rooftop tent by simply adding a sheet of plywood so you can sleep under the stars. If you are adding a plywood sheet, you might consider ways of extending it over the windscreen. The shade offered by this will be seriously appreciated under the burning hot African sun. This will be perfectly adequate in many situations, but is far from offering a comprehensive solution. Do not overload a roof rack. Most 4x4 vehicles are not built for heavy loads on the roof. Structural parts, like windscreens, also have a habit of cracking under the strain if overloaded. Roof racks should only be used to store light equipment like sand ladders and empty jerrycans. Try to devise a system in the rear of your vehicle that can take as much equipment as possible inside and out of sight. Overloading the roof increases the risk of tipping over on uneven or sandy roads.

Security It is surprisingly hard to find good places to camp wild, as much of Africa is populated. That idyllic spot you found may prove to be a much-used track between the local village and its distant well. One hundred per cent security is impossible to achieve, but every effort you make is worthwhile. The most important security system will ultimately be your own vigilance. It is worth mentioning here that security concerns and how you plan to camp are linked.

More about this later under *Accommodation* in *Chapter 5,* page 135.

Padlocks and hasps Padlocks should be put on any items mounted outside the vehicle, and may be put on some doors. Avoid any delicate mechanisms such as combination locks, which will very quickly become clogged by the thick dust that will cover your vehicle once it hits the African roads. Also try to buy a set of padlocks with a common key, or it will take forever to find the right one. If you can't do this, paint them different colours. Hasps can be forced, so you should consider some form of internal mechanism to back them up, such as additional locks or bolts.

Windows Windows are another problem area. Rubber surrounds in particular are a security hazard, as they can easily be cut away. Metal grilles on windows will help, but they also have the adverse effect of making you look as if you have something worth stealing. A vehicle with fewer windows is more secure. If you intend to sleep in the vehicle, metal grilles covering the windows mean you can sleep with the windows open. Sand ladders can also be mounted and locked over windows.

Curtains It is worth putting up curtains, whether or not you intend to sleep inside all the time. They provide instant shade in strong sun and dissuade prying eyes. Simple strips of fabric on curtain stretchers can fit inside the inner roof gulley of most vehicles, or you can fit curtain rails with proper hooks. Bungee cords are useful for many things: curtains, drying washing and holding equipment in place for starters.

Valuables – safety box This is tricky. You don't want to be with your vehicle all the time, and carrying vital documents, passport, *carnet* and cash on your person all the time is not ideal. But leaving them in the vehicle is not ideal either. Bolting in a safe box is one possibility, but don't keep everything in it, just in case the worst happens. It is best to have a few hiding places around the vehicle for spare emergency cash; carry the rest with you in a moneybelt along with your passport. Travellers' cheques are less of a risk, but be extra careful about the *carnet*. Carrying this around is not great; they are bulky. We tried to find a hiding place behind the spares, but anywhere secure is fine as long as you remember where it is.

It is also advisable to hide copies of documents, as well as travellers' cheque numbers and purchase receipts, in some other area of the vehicle. If staying overnight in a hotel, whether cheap or expensive, take the *carnet* and main valuables with you before retiring.

Another good idea is to scan all valuable documents – passports, driving licences, *carnet* and other vehicle papers, yellow fever certificates, travellers' cheque receipts, insurance policies, credit card numbers and other important documents etc – and store them in a folder in your email account. That way, even if you lose everything, you can print off a copy in the nearest internet café, which will not be so far away.

Alarm systems Some form of alarm system will undoubtedly help, as it should deter a thief from continuing with a break-in. But do not depend on it to safeguard your gear. There is a wide selection of alarm systems available from all accessory shops.

Bull bars These are designed to protect the lights and radiator from anything you may hit. Bull bars are optional. However, bearing in mind the amount of general debris on the roads, it may be advisable to fit one. Cows, goats and other animals, including camels in particular, will often stroll out nonchalantly into the middle of the road just as you are passing. The bars can also be used to install mesh to prevent stones breaking your headlights. Additional lights are best placed higher.

Baffle/bash plate A baffle plate is a steel plate fitted beneath the vehicle, helping to protect its vulnerable underside from rocks. They can, however, make routine maintenance considerably more awkward. You should consider covering the tie rods on your vehicle, as these are vulnerable. An old tie rod can be bolted on in front of them with a little thought and can even be designed to act as a tow bar. Putting baffle plates under the sump and gearbox is only really worthwhile if you are heading off into the remoter pistes in the Sahara, where rocks are hidden in sand. It is better to drive with caution where potential obstacles exist; get out and check first if in doubt.

Suspension The biggest enemy for vehicles in Africa is the state of the roads. That means your suspension is more at risk than anything else. There is a great deal to be said for fitting new springs and shock absorbers all round before setting off. Some people even strengthen the chassis – only a good idea if you are likely to be carrying heavy loads.

Opinion is divided as to which springs are the best. Fitting heavy-duty springs for the additional strains of African roads might sound fine, but African mechanics will often tell you that lighter springs are more supple and less likely to break under the strain. The chassis will be under less vibration too.

If you can afford it, Old Man Emu shock absorbers and springs still have the best reputation throughout Africa. Take plenty of spare rubber bushes, as they will disintegrate with great rapidity on some road surfaces. Some people take poly bushes, but, being less supple than rubber, they can induce more vibration. By driving carefully, you can reduce the worst effects of rough roads. Old car tyres are cut up and made into bushes in Africa. They usually last much longer than any spares you might buy from the manufacturer, though they probably won't pass any vehicle road-worthiness test such as the British MOT!

Spare battery and split-charge system Carrying two batteries is definitely a good idea, especially if you are intending to be out in the wild for long periods. Batteries can fail without warning. The cheapest option is to change the batteries periodically to keep them charged. It is a bit of a bind, however, and, in storing the second battery, you must ensure it cannot tip over. If you are intending to run other electrical items, like a refrigerator, off your battery, we would suggest a dual battery and split-charge system. This enables the second battery to run other electrical items while the vehicle's main battery stays unaffected.

Fashions change over the best set-up for batteries and charging them. Many campervans have a deep-cycle-type second battery like the Willard 722 Pleasure Master (available in South Africa). This is designed to cope with charge and recharge. These batteries are not ideal for starting, though. You might consider having a dry cell, sealed battery as the second battery. A split-charging system ensures both batteries remain charged. Since these need to be in good order, we strongly suggest you seek appropriate advice. As with all things, the more complicated the more risk of problems. Maybe it's easier to change the batteries over manually after all. Don't forget to take some good-quality jump leads anyway.

Oil cooler Recommended by many, ignored by many others. Probably a good idea if you are likely to take full advantage of fast roads in the hottest conditions. Less useful if you are in an older vehicle.

Raised air intake This is standard on many African 4x4 vehicles, reducing the intake of large quantities of dust and acting as a safeguard if you intend to drive through deep water. It will certainly do no harm to fit one and might help to save your engine from damage. The Australian Safari Snorkel is the most popular and is available at most off-road outlets.

3

Axle breathers Another tip, if you think you are likely to do some deep wading, is to extend your gearbox and axle breathers. These are small air valves, mounted on the top of the axles and gearbox, which allow air to be drawn in or out as the parts heat up and cool down. The problem is that, when you go into deep water, the axles cool quickly and suck in water through the breathers. The easiest way to deal with this is to fix a length of plastic tube over the breather and thread it up into the vehicle.

Wheel rims Riveted steel rims should be selected for tougher terrain, as they are more reliable. Magnesium alloy rims are not very convenient because the bead, the part of the rim most often damaged in tougher terrain, cannot be hammered back into place like a steel rim. If you have a puncture repaired by an African, he will usually use a very heavy hammer, often skilfully, to break the bead; that is, to separate the tyre from the rim. Sometimes it's best not to look!

Some older cars are fitted with split rims, which are very convenient when you are repairing your own tyre. Ensure that the tyre is properly deflated before splitting the rim, as air pressure remaining in the tyre could cause an explosion and serious injury. Some people fit a ring of shaped rubber around the inner wheel rim to stop the tube wearing and ripping.

Tyres Set off with a completely new set of tyres, including two spares, if you are planning a long trip. Aim to fit the best you can. It will be well worth the extra expense. You will be facing a wide variety of terrain – sand, mud, laterite, rocks and tarmac roads. Good-quality, all-terrain tyres are the best bet. The brand you use is often a very personal choice. Many people opt for Michelin or the Continental Super All Grips. BF Goodrich tyres are significantly cheaper than Michelin. There is no way of saying which manufacturer is the best. Tyres need to be suitable for mixed terrain on a general African trip. Seek advice from experienced enthusiasts if you can.

If you are going only to the Sahara, you may decide to take specialist sand tyres. But nowadays some of the newer tyres are multi-purpose anyway and will be good on sand as well as tarmac and mud. In any case, you can do a great deal to cope with sandy conditions by reducing tyre pressures until you get back on firmer roads.

Keep the least-worn tyre from the old set as an extra spare. The main spare wheel is sometimes fitted on the rear doors; if so, the hinges and clamps should be periodically checked and tightened. Sometimes it is fitted under the rear below the fuel tank, which reduces ground clearance, or on the bonnet. Those fitted to the bonnet can be a real nuisance, making the bonnet very heavy to lift and restricting the view. The second spare may well have to be fitted on the roof. In our case we fitted the two spares inside; much better if you have the space.

Tubed or tubeless tyres? Tubed tyres are generally easier to remove from the rim, as the bead does not need to be so tight, but it is possible to fix a puncture in a tubeless tyre without removing it from the rim. We have always used tubed tyres, but many people take tubeless and have no problems. Tubeless tyres can be repaired from the outside using the 'gluey plug', but, since this method is outlawed in Europe now, getting the kits could be a problem. Surprisingly perhaps, tubeless tyres can be run with low air pressures in sand without many snags. There are pros and cons to each type, but in the end it comes down to personal preference.

Inner tubes It is important to carry two or three spare inner tubes, particularly if you are visiting isolated areas where tubes can be found but not necessarily in the correct size or make. It is also preferable to inflate, deflate and re-inflate the tyre once the new tube has been fitted. This will remove twists in the tube, which can cause splits and major blow-outs while driving. This takes a lot of effort in some circumstances so try to be careful, inflating slowly if you do it once only.

Valves It is better to fit your tyre with a short-stemmed valve rather than the longer one often stocked by African parts shops and garages. Longer valve stems are more susceptible to breakage, particularly in tough terrain. Always carry some extra valve cores with you. Valves have a habit of flying off into the sunset when being removed to let air out, so beware!

Extra fuel and water tanks

Fuel In most parts of Africa fuel is actually more readily available than you might think. Unless you aim to go deep into the Sahara or get right away from the normal routes, you should not experience many problems. There are not many places where you will need to go more than 640km (400 miles) without supplies. But you can't always guarantee to get fuel when you expect to, and you may want to take full advantage of cheaper supplies when you have the chance. The final judgement on how much you should carry is always likely to be something of a balancing act. We would recommend a 1,000km (620 miles) capacity. Work out your fuel consumption to determine your desired capacity.

Keep things as simple as possible. The more complex the system, the more things can go wrong. African roads will constantly cause things to shake loose, leak and wear away. Fuel pipes are notorious for shaving and becoming holed, and it's very difficult to find such leaks. The cheapest and simplest option is to take metal jerrycans, available in many places. Unless you are going into remote desert, four will probably suffice, except if your vehicle has a high fuel consumption.

If you really want to avoid filling your vehicle with jerrycans, then you may consider fitting extra tanks, particularly for older models with higher fuel consumption. Land Rovers can be modified to add an extra tank. Be aware, though, that you will need to have either an electric pump to transfer the fuel from the extra tank to the main one, or have a two-way fuel valve. Both options add to the list of things that can go wrong.

You can supplement the standard long-wheelbase, 15-gallon, rear-mounted fuel tank with short-wheelbase 10-gallon tanks under each front seat. That's a total of 35 gallons. Customised tanks with even larger capacities for both fuel and water are also available and can be fitted to most vehicles. Plan to carry as much fuel as possible, but always bear in mind weight restrictions. Fuel and water are the two most important items you need, but they are also incredibly heavy. There is little point in being well prepared if you destroy your suspension or even break your chassis in the process.

Water Make sure you carry enough, but beware of overloading. The cheapest option is to take good-quality plastic jerrycans. These containers also enable you to see quickly how much water is left. You should aim to carry at least 40 to 50 litres, preferably in two or three containers in case one of them leaks. Keep one untreated water can for boiling and cooking, one for treated cleaner water and keep some extra plastic bottled water for drinking as well. Make sure all jerrycans stored inside are held in place securely. These containers can be worked into your general interior plan. Of course there is always something in the way inside; that's life.

A built-in water tank can be more convenient than a vehicle full of jerrycans. However, filling the tank can sometimes be quite awkward. You will need a hose where taps are inconveniently located. And filling tanks from wells is not always plain sailing. Also, tanks need to be drained periodically, as sludge can build up and, with it, contamination. Keep it simple. All jerrycans can be stored between inside lockers below a sleeping platform, keeping them secured. See *Suggestions for vehicle layout* diagrams, pages 63–4.

If you do use jerrycans, don't put them on the roof when full (**never** overload your roofrack with heavy items). **Never** have petrol in jerrycans on the roof; it spells double trouble, as the sun will soon make it hot and very dangerous.

Jerrycans You *must* use metal ones for fuel; we repeat, storing petrol in plastic jerrycans is dangerous as it could explode. Do not store water in jerrycans that were previously used for fuel, as the taste never disappears. The number you take will depend on fuel consumption, tank capacity, route, load and how much you plan to take advantage of cheaper fuel supplies when you find them. For water, your route is the most important factor. Long stretches in the open desert will mean you need to carry substantially more.

Oils You are likely to get through more oil than in normal conditions, so be prepared. Engine oil is generally available, but some specialised gear oils, brake and clutch fluid are more difficult to locate. You will find everything you need in the bigger cities like Accra or Nairobi, but don't count on it elsewhere. We carried 25 litres of engine oil, in different containers, which gave us two oil changes, ie: one emergency change (broken sump) and one regular change. Try to buy internationally recognised brands of oil, as some local supplies may be substandard.

Storage Careful planning of your storage facilities can make all the difference between ease of access, general comfort or a permanent nightmare. Try to achieve a closely packed but accessible arrangement. At all costs avoid having anything loose that can be thrown about in the back. Fitted cupboards and storage space can be built by customising companies, or, if you feel confident, you can do the job yourself. Remember the whole thing can easily get shaken to bits unless it has been well made.

You need to be able to pull things out quickly, find what you are looking for and repack into the same space you started with. This process is generally a lot harder than it sounds. It can be very useful to split your storage space into compartments and within this into a series of rigid sections or boxes.

Over the years we have found that a locker system works quite well. You can build in sections for spare parts, food supplies, oils, grease, etc, spare battery, even valuables. The ways are infinite. Try to keep your toolbox safe but accessible – you'll need it daily for maintenance checks. To make simple lockers you need only a drill, saw and energy, or get the plywood cut by your friendly wood merchant. Before you start, though, consider the width and size of any jerrycans. You will need to work out a basic design first and calculate the sizes. It should be possible to keep the jerrycans in place between the lockers. Further wooden sheets can be cut to fit between the two lockers to separate fuel and water cans if necessary. It can be fun devising such units.

Using 11mm plywood cut and bolted together with metal angle pieces from a hardware store, one can make a series of compartmentalised lockers. These can have hinged lids attached. Use spring washers on all bolts or they will shake loose quickly. Make two long lockers and fit them in each side of the rear part of the vehicle. The jerrycans need to have good seals as they may need to be lying down. Two or three central plywood sheets can then be put between the two lockers and above the cans. One might be a table and all together can provide a platform on which to sleep.

If you don't have the time or inclination to do the above, then use rigid plastic storage boxes, or even metal flight cases if you can afford them. Elastic bungee

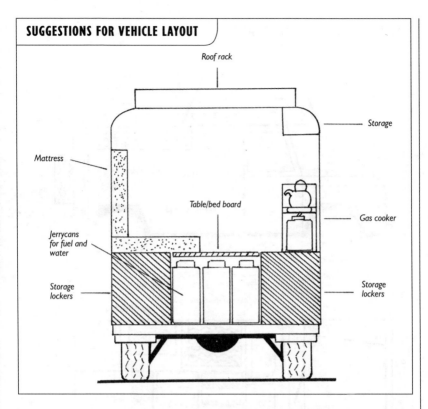

SUGGESTIONS FOR VEHICLE LAYOUT

Roof rack

Storage

Mattress

Table/bed board

Gas cooker

Jerrycans for fuel and water

Storage lockers

Storage lockers

cords and canvas or webbing belts are useful for lashing things down. Anything removable on your roof rack should be secured with padlocks. Whatever system you adopt, something that you need will always be at the bottom or in 'the bl...dy locker'!

Comfort

Seat covers The choice of seat covers depends on the seats in the vehicle. If they are plastic, they will be very uncomfortable in the hot sun. Towelling is ideal. With removable covers you have the added advantage of being able to wash out the grime that will inevitably build up. Even if you have fabric-covered seats already, you will appreciate washable covers – you will pick up more dust and grime than you could believe possible!

A set of beaded seat covers is a good option; they help in extreme heat when long hours behind the wheel cause sweat and sores. They also ease your back over long distances.

Steering-wheel cover Standard black plastic steering wheels can become extremely hot in direct sunlight and your hands can easily slip. It is advisable to fit some type of non-slip cover before you leave.

Music Install a standard hifi deck and radio, mounted securely, and bring a selection of tapes/CDs. When driving long distances in a country where you may not understand the local language, a variety of music is irreplaceable. It's a good idea to mount the stereo in the glove compartment and keep tapes in a dustproof box. You

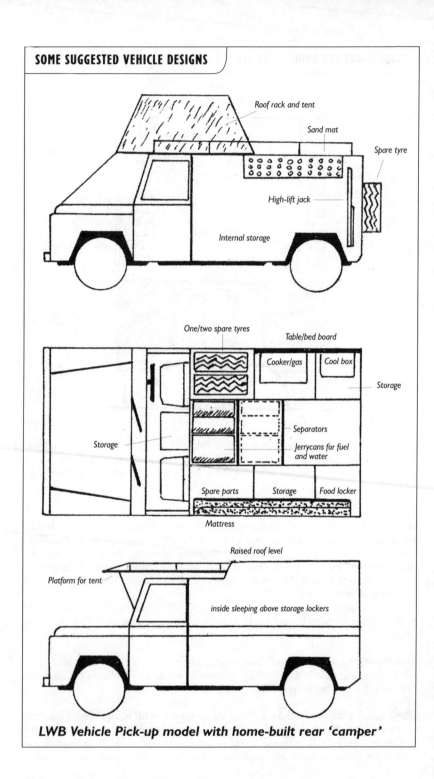

SOME SUGGESTED VEHICLE DESIGNS

Roof rack and tent

Sand mat

Spare tyre

High-lift jack

Internal storage

One/two spare tyres

Table/bed board

Cooker/gas

Cool box

Storage

Storage

Separators

Jerrycans for fuel and water

Spare parts

Storage

Food locker

Mattress

Raised roof level

Platform for tent

inside sleeping above storage lockers

LWB Vehicle Pick-up model with home-built rear 'camper'

may not be able to hear anything over the engine and road noise, but at least when you stop you can relax to your favourite tunes.

We also recommend a shortwave radio, to tune in to the BBC or similar and keep up to date with what is going on around you or further down the line.

Canopy Just an optional extra. A canopy will keep you dry during the wet season, and it will also offer shade and a certain amount of privacy. You can either make up your own canopy with strong canvas or vinyl-based material, or have one fitted to your vehicle.

VEHICLE EQUIPMENT

We all have our own priorities. Deciding what to take and what to leave behind is difficult. Ask yourself if you really need it. When your springs sag, or break, you'll regret every kilo of unnecessary weight. With four wheels you will be nothing like as restricted as with a motorbike or bicycle in terms of what you can carry.

If you are carrying a cooker with a gas cylinder, always ensure that it is tightly secured, that both are locked into a base, and that both have been turned off when leaving the vehicle for long periods of time or while driving. Refrigerators should also be secured tightly with straps, but can be kept switched on while driving.

You should have a **fire extinguisher** with you. It is not only compulsory in many countries, but might very well be needed at some point. If your vehicle already has one, make sure that it works properly.

Here are a few of the most important items of equipment you will need to consider.

RECOVERY GEAR Recovery gear is defined as anything you might need when trying to get yourself out of a difficult situation or rescuing another vehicle.

Electronic or manual winches Winches are of limited use and possibly not worth the expense or extra weight. In practically every situation it is easier to be towed out of trouble.

A winch may give you the confidence to explore further off the beaten track, away from roads and tracks used by other vehicles. However if you plan to be that adventurous, it would be wiser to team up with at least one other vehicle anyway.

A sensible compromise could be a good hand winch; the best is probably made by Tirfor. Another simple winching technique is to make use of a high-lift jack. If this is chained to the vehicle at one end and to a winching point, such as a tree trunk, at the other, you can slowly pull the vehicle out of trouble. The only drawback with this technique is that you can only winch the length of the jack (1m/3ft) at a time. If you are using a tree as an anchor, use canvas, or the purpose-made anchor straps available at most major equipment outlets, to protect the tree. In general, a winch is not your highest priority. See also *Winching* in *Chapter 6*, page 146.

High-lift jack The high-lift jack could be one of the most useful tools that you will carry with you. It is highly versatile. The classic high-lift jack is the red American-made one,

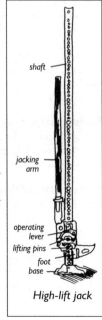

shaft

jacking arm

operating lever

lifting pins

foot base

High-lift jack

which is simple and reliable. However, there are now numerous other makes on the market that are modelled on the original version and are just as good. Remember to use wooden blocks or some sort of base when jacking the vehicle up. Also ensure that your vehicle is in gear and that the handbrake is on. Older vehicles with heavy-duty bumpers make good jacking points, but you will find that a jacking point may need to be fitted to your vehicle if you have a newer model. If you have to store the jack outside, ensure regular cleaning, as dust can get trapped in the oil. Cover the jack with canvas for further protection. See also *High-lift jack* in *Chapter 6*, page 145.

Hydraulic jack You will need a hydraulic jack for punctures, changing springs or lifting the engine to change engine mountings, for example. Make sure you have an assortment of flat and chunky wooden blocks for jacking. Old-style hydraulic jacks are hard to find now, because trolley jacks are the latest preference. These are too bulky and not very good on sand and mud. Hydraulic jacks, made in the Far East, can be bought in many places in Africa, but you might need one before you get there.

Sand ladders (sand mats) With luck and careful driving you may not need sand ladders at all, but it would be crazy to leave home without them. As well as getting you out of soft sand, they can have other uses, for example on broken bridges and, with extra support, for bridging some holes. Various types of ladders and planks are available, including some made from lightweight alloys. Aluminium alloy ladders are expensive but easier to use. Perforated steel sand ladders are just as good, although a little heavier.

perforated steel planks

flexible tank tracks

Sand ladders

Another type is the flexible variety that look a little like the tracks from a tank. These do not have to be laid flat like sand mats, so you can save yourself some digging.

DIY fans with welding equipment can make ladders from square or round metal tubing. These can be just as effective and are much cheaper. See also *Sand ladders* in *Chapter 6*, page 145.

Towing points Ensure you have adequate towing points on your vehicle, usually mounted below the vehicle at the back and front, making sure that they are easily accessible.

Towing straps/short cable Kinetic straps are slightly elastic, flat towing straps, known as snatch straps. A popular brand is Tuggum. These are specifically designed for pulling other vehicles out of a difficult situation. Snatch straps have a limited life of about 20 tugs as the line becomes static. A short cable of sufficient strength can also be used with care. You should carry at least two towing straps of either type with sufficient **shackles** to connect them.

'D' shackles

bow shackles

Shackles – the only types that should be used on a vehicle

Shovels A small shovel may be useful as a companion to the sand ladders. Failing to scoop out sand or dig out mud from around your tyres will result in more strain. Sand can be cleared by hand, but mud is a different kettle of fish. Clearing mud by hand may be fun for five minutes but not for hours.

For sand, a shovel with a concave blade is better. In mud, a flatter angle is better. Compromise, but take only one. A shovel can be used for rubbish; always burn or bury anything you are planning to leave behind. Be careful not to bury jagged cans or broken glass in game parks where animals may dig up your rubbish and injure themselves. Also be aware that locals can use empty cans for water storage if they are cleanly cut with a tin opener. A garden trowel is useful for toilet trips.

SLEEPING GEAR You will need a mattress, pillows, duvet or sleeping bag and sheets. A covered duvet or quilt is much more comfortable than a sleeping bag, which over long periods can feel restricted, and proper pillows will make you feel much more at home. If you have limited space use a roll-up mattress, fold-up pillow and a sleeping bag. A washable, three-season bag should be adequate, but some parts of Africa can be very cold. For the cover of your mattress and pillows, use some thick cotton material. A darker colour helps to avoid having to see every speck of the grime you will accumulate! Also see *Hammock*, page 73.

Mosquito nets A mosquito net is not an optional item; it could be a lifesaver. Whatever type of sleeping arrangement you have, it is very important that you equip your tent, rooftop tent or sleeping space inside the vehicle with a net. Even if you opt to find local accommodation, it is advisable to carry your own mosquito net. Some places in Africa do provide them, but they are not always in the best condition. Nets can be bought in specialist shops. It is not always easy to find them abroad and/or the choice is limited.

LIGHTING Fluorescent strip lighting is bright, convenient and doesn't put too much strain on the battery. Festoon bulb lights also use little power, but are less bright. Bring some electrical wire in case you need to adapt things, or have a mobile lighting strip as well as normal internal lights. Camping Gaz lights are not a good idea, as the canisters are almost impossible to find and are extremely expensive. Whatever you do, remember to bring a torch with spare bulbs and batteries.

Map light Standard map lights that can be attached to the car lighter are available for reading maps at night. A torch would do as well, or a mobile camera phone with a light. Avoid night driving in general, though.

WASHING GEAR

Portable shower Not really essential, although a pleasant luxury. Various devices are available: a plastic bottle, pump-action shower which holds enough water for a seven-minute shower, heating water on the stove to take the chill off in cooler weather; a solar-heated shower which heats four litres in about an hour; or a simple plastic tub with holes and filled with hot water from the kettle or a plastic bucket.

Of course, unless you are showering fully clothed, you risk providing amusement for the locals or causing some offence; be discreet.

Portable washing machine (ie: a bucket!) This idea was suggested by Sue and Steve Marshall, who did a trans-Africa trip in 1996. Use a bucket with a lid as a portable washing machine. Before driving off, fill the bucket with washing detergent, water and dirty clothes and strap it firmly in the vehicle. Remember to put the lid on and make sure it fits securely. The motion of the vehicle will act as a washing machine, leaving you to rinse and hang up the clothes once you've reached your destination. Take a washing line and clothes pegs. A plastic bucket will also have many other uses (like draining the oil or radiator too, but don't tell your better half).

TABLE AND CHAIRS These might seem like a luxury, but, depending on how long you intend to travel for, folding chairs and a table are a very good idea. When choosing, remember that they need to last for as long as you need them and will be used on a daily basis. Canvas-covered chairs (some are like director's chairs) have a much longer life and can also be washed regularly.

COMPASS AND/OR GLOBAL POSITIONING SYSTEM (GPS) Many travellers today use GPS as a navigational aid. GPS is essential and fun if you are going into really isolated areas like the Sahara, and you can set your co-ordinates accordingly. Most guidebooks specifically relevant to the Sahara and southern Africa have recorded co-ordinates of an area.

It is best to hide your GPS when crossing borders. It could be misconstrued as a transmitter and get you into trouble with the security forces. In general you will be quite surprised by how little you actually use either the GPS or a compass.

Remember that the electrics will throw off a normal compass so if you have a hand-held type, stop and walk off a few paces for an accurate reading. Also remember that, without a good map, a GPS or compass is often useless.

MOBILE PHONE With ever more sophisticated mobile phone systems, you may well consider taking a satellite phone or normal mobile phone for peace of mind. See www.thuraya.com and all the mobile phone operators' websites for details of coverage. You can of course also use other features like a camera, light, radio, music player, alarm clock...

OTHER ESSENTIAL EQUIPMENT

Axe or machete Very useful for chopping wood and hacking through vegetation.

Warning triangles/jackets In many African countries it is compulsory to carry two warning triangles. Some European countries now require a fluorescent jacket for each passenger in the vehicle.

Foot or electric tyre pump This is an essential item when repairing tyres on the side of the road, or pumping up an airbed. Try using a foot pump in the heat of the African day and you will wish you had purchased a cheap electric pump. They have crocodile clips to attach to your battery. Extra wire may be required with some models.

Tyre repair kit Getting normal tube patches is increasingly difficult in Europe, but once in Africa patches or something usable can be found. Chris Scott suggests in his excellent *Sahara Handbook* (see *Appendix 5*, page 332) taking a bicycle tube to assist when pumping up tubeless tyres in the desert after a puncture. It is used to fill the gap between the tyre and rim before a seal is made under pressure. It should be the same size as the tyre rim.

Pressure gauge A good pressure gauge is particularly useful in the desert, where you will be deflating and re-inflating tyres continually.

Assorted wooden blocks As mentioned above, these are essential to place under a jack in soft sand or mud.

FOOD AND COOKING
Water and water purification methods As discussed under *Storage* in this chapter, page 62, your best bet for carrying water is in 20-litre jerrycans. One of these should be accessible at all times to be easily filled with water. Some plastic containers have a tap, but it may leak. Any major outdoor equipment retailer can supply them. Traditional nomads carry water in goatskin sacks called *guerbas*. These keep the water remarkably cool, as the skin allows for slow evaporation.

In many parts of the Sahara and wilder regions, you may have to obtain water from local wells. You should be careful not to contaminate them. Wells in places like Niger are often the only source of water and it can be very pure. Getting such water up is an art form in itself. It may sound easy, but have you ever tried throwing an empty bucket 50ft down a well so that it lands upside down? You will certainly create some amusement for the nomads at these wells. It is very likely that they will give you a lesson in the art of extracting well water. Wells in the Sahel are a pivotal point for the community and are places of social interaction for all: local villagers, nomads, long-horned cows, goats and occasional tourists. Some wells are astonishingly deep. The water is raised in containers attached to exceedingly long ropes and hauled by recalcitrant camels.

Unless you are certain the water is safe, you will need to purify it. The simplest, cheapest and safest option is to boil it. Another popular option is Chloromyn-T. You need only an amount equal to the tip of a matchstick to purify 25 litres. Allow it to work for one or two hours, until the Chloromyn-T has settled. Micropur, Puritabs and iodine are other purification methods. Iodine is an effective purifier but shouldn't be used on a long-term basis, as your body absorbs it (see *Health* in *Chapter 5*). Some people use 'filter socks', but no method completely guarantees the killing of all evils that may lurk in the water.

Ideally, you should take a water filter with you, particularly if you are going to be travelling in more remote areas. Cyclists should definitely have one. There are many filters on the market. Top of the range are the Katadyne filters used by the Red Cross throughout Africa; though excellent, they are expensive. Mountain Safety Research (MSR) also make a range of filters and Charlie and Illya used the MSR MiniWorks, for which you can also purchase an additional virus filter.

Suppliers in the UK, South Africa and Australia include:

First Ascent Units 4 & 5, Limetree Business Pk, Matlock, Derbyshire DE4 3EJ; ☏ 01629 580484; f 01629 580275; www.firstascent.co.uk
Outward Ventures 14 Second Av, Claremont, 7700 Cape Town; ☏ +27 21 683 3638

Grant Minervini Agencies 1 Quinlan Av, St Mary's, South Australia 5042; ☏ +61 8 275 1555; f +61 8 275 1556; e info@gmagencies.com.au; www.gmagencies.com.au

Refrigeration Refrigerators for vehicles run on either 12V DC, 240V AC or gas; some refrigerators are built to run on all three. If you have the space a small fridge might be one of the first luxuries to take. Whether the added cost and space it takes are justified by the cool film and cold drinks it provides is a matter of debate. It is surprising how cold things can keep when buried in the depths of a good locker after a cool night.

Ordinary camping shops can be a good source. The Engel fridge has been recommended as an efficient but expensive option.

The simpler option is to have an insulation box. We have managed like this every time; cold drinks can be found in many places along the way. Keeping margarine and yoghurt is a little more difficult. The traditional bush method of wet towels draped over boxes and even bottles is very effective at keeping things cool.

Cooking equipment When it comes to cooking, your choice of fuel and equipment depends on how long you intend to be on the road. Bringing vegetables etc to the boil and then leaving them to cook in the hot water will save your valuable fuel, whichever you choose.

Gas stoves Gas stoves are the easiest, cleanest and most reliable option. We have always used Camping Gaz, but it is not a complete answer. The bottles are quite small, so we have had to carry at least four. A Camping Gaz (size 907) bottle can be made to last about three to four weeks with very careful usage and easy-to-cook food supplies. We have used a standard Camping Gaz cooker mounted inside a riveted, aluminium box structure that offers windbreaks around three sides. Underneath, in the enclosed area below the cooking level were the gas bottle, pots, pans, etc. It can be used inside or out but needs securing properly.

Many local families cook with gas (particularly in the Sahara) and most gas stoves have a choice of regulators to cover a range of gas fuels. The larger gas bottles can be filled in some of the larger towns. Perhaps taking two Camping Gaz bottles and later buying a larger refillable butane bottle in Africa might be better. On a very long trip, using a purely gas system might have its limitations, but its simplicity is a prime factor. It invariably comes down to personal choice and the routes chosen in the end.

Petrol stoves The wide variety of camping stoves available means you can exercise a fair degree of choice, though bikers and cyclists tend to opt for small, lightweight petrol stoves or burners. These can be fussy to light but are fairly reliable, though even expensive models can let you down. Several people have recommended Coleman petrol stoves (one, two or three burners) as very reliable, though they are rather bulky and so not suitable for bikers or cyclists.

Disadvantages of petrol ovens are the blackening of pots (though the soot does rub off much more easily if you smear the outside of your pans liberally with soap or washing up liquid before you cook) and smoking when you first light them.

Kerosene stoves The Chinese-made kerosene wick stoves can be found almost everywhere in Africa. There is virtually nothing that can go wrong with them, and the small amount of fuel they burn means you can easily carry enough to last until the next source of kerosene. They can be a bit messy to operate.

Open fires Although open fires are harder to control for cooking, they are an instant focus when camping, particularly when it gets cold at night. Take a small fire grille, self-supporting preferably. Otherwise you can do it 'nomad-style' with a few strategically placed rocks. Nomads use very little wood by using the burnt ends of small branches or the charcoal remnants. It's a bit slow, though. And remember that rocks aren't available everywhere!

Potatoes and other vegetables, wrapped in foil with a few herbs or spices for extra flavour, can be roasted in no time on an open fire. If you do build a fire, be sensible in dry areas where sparks may set grass or scrub alight. And never cut green wood for a fire, particularly in the desert and Sahel areas or game parks. Africa has enough deforestation problems of its own without you adding to them. If your transport allows you to carry firewood as you go, you can dry it out by lashing it to the roof rack of your vehicle.

Remember from a security point of view that an open fire may be visible for miles.

Matches/lighter Matches are available almost everywhere, but it is a good idea to carry a spare box. A couple of lighters are advisable too.

Even if you only have one burner, you don't need to restrict yourself to one-pot meals. Bring your rice or pasta to the boil for a few minutes, then leave to continue cooking in its own heat. You can then make up a basic vegetable sauce, or heat a tin of chicken curry. If you are cooking with meat or beans, start off your rice or pasta about half an hour before you plan to eat and set it aside while you finish off your other dish. Always bring rice or pasta back to the boil and check it is thoroughly cooked before straining.

If you are cooking two dishes, you can always prepare them separately and heat them up just before you eat. In time you will get more than skilled at juggling pots. If you find yourself travelling in convoy, meeting up with other travellers in campsites or free camping, you can pool resources and end up with some really adventurous meals. Four one-burner stoves means four hot dishes to share.

Cooking utensils Like everything else, it is best to keep these to a minimum. You will quickly learn to adapt what you have for a whole range of purposes, and cooking on the road is all about using your imagination. We have used two small stainless-steel cooking pots, which fit inside each other and have flat lids, plus a small non-stick frying pan and kettle. Our food has tended to be simple, though. Charlie and Illya used a two-tier steamer. You might want to be more creative on a long trip. It's a matter of personal expectations, personal requirements and dietary variations. Other favourites are pressure cookers, woks and, particularly if you are in a reasonably sized group, cast-iron pots for fires. Pots can be left sitting on an open fire to stew away for hours.

A small Thermos flask is a good idea for easy hot drinks on the way or at borders. Other items needed are a decent sharp knife, a wooden spoon, something to strain boiled pasta or vegetables (unless you have a saucepan and lid that are suitable), a tin opener, a bottle opener, Swiss army knife or Leatherman's knife, vegetable peeler, bread knife and a small chopping board.

Go for enamel or plastic plates and bowls, but plastic or melamine mugs for tea and coffee, as enamel gets frustratingly hot. Plates are best with raised edges, bowls are easier to eat from without a table and safer for runny dishes. Take a plastic box for the cutlery; teaspoons love inaccessible corners in a vehicle. Don't lose the lighter!

Food to take with you It is surprising how your taste buds change in Africa. That bottle of salad cream or ketchup you never finish at home might suddenly seem the missing ingredient you are craving. You will not be able to take everything you are going to eat, but it is a good idea to assemble a store of basics and emergency supplies before you go. As a rough guide, the following food items are mostly available on the road: bottled water, bread, tomatoes, bananas, carrots, garlic, tinned fish, potatoes, eggs, rice, pasta, couscous, cooking oil, spices and dodgy meat as well as good fresh meat. Items like margarine, yoghurt, other fruits and vegetables can be found, depending on location and climatic zone. Across north Africa, some towns have reasonable supermarkets with a limited choice. In west Africa you will find expensive French supermarkets in all the capitals; these have a good but expensive selection. Nairobi has large supermarkets and further south things are mostly as good in the capitals and larger cities. What you don't find are tinned curries, assorted tinned meats, puddings and standby dehydrated meals.

Good basic supplies to take with you include plenty of salt for the extra fluid loss; sugar (even if you do not normally use it – sweet tea is great if you are ill and cannot face food); herbs and spices to liven up vegetables; tea and coffee. Take some cereals and muesli for an easy breakfast when bread is not available. Some boil-in-the-bag rice, instant mash and pasta are easy and quick to cook. Tomato purée in tubes, stock cubes, oil in plastic screw-top bottles, cornflour for thickening, dried milk. Small packets of Parmesan cheese are a wonderful addition to basic pastas.

Make sure you always have a few days' supply of emergency rations. You never know if you are going to be unavoidably delayed along the way, and you may not find any food *en route*. We always had enough meals for a week, just in case. Good standby meals are instant potato, dried vegetables/fruit, tinned tuna, tins of meat, peas or beans, long-life cakes, peanut butter, Marmite (said to keep the mosquitoes at bay), Vegemite, jam and/or marmalade, instant desserts, etc. The list goes on: mustard, dried mushrooms or onions to liven up pasta or rice dishes, lemon juice in plastic bottles, custard, biscuits or crackers. Boiled sweets are good for when you need a burst of energy, and Kendal Mint Cake when you are flagging (it's a high-glucose bar that goes into the supplies for every major expedition). An indispensable item on all our expeditions has been a homemade Christmas cake, always delicious at any time of year!

Unless you are extremely lucky, there will be times when you will be unable to cook anything hot because the weather, circumstances or fate conspire against you. On these occasions you will feel a lot better for having some provisions that can be turned into a cold meal. For example, a refreshing salad can be made from a tin of tuna in oil, with beans in lemon juice and a freshly chopped onion or tomato.

With a vehicle you can afford to carry quite a number of tins, some as standby. Sadly, your chocolate won't go far. Take the odd luxurious items such as a bottle of wine, sweets, Christmas pudding and other goodies, specifically for those arduous days when you need to spoil yourself. You can always live on bread and generally bananas. And don't forget those plastic bottles of mayonnaise, ketchup and Branston.

Obviously food that requires longer cooking times will use more fuel, so use open fires if possible when you plan a hearty meal.

Storing food We kept our food reserves in a locker, but any vermin and bug-proof containers would do. Food storage boxes need to be kept reasonably clean. Choose storage containers with care. Square ones pack better. Rough driving conditions will shake things around so much that jars will literally unscrew themselves, plastic lids will pop off, and tubes of tomato purée will puncture. You can minimise these nightmares by having the right containers in the first place. Pack loose spaces with towels and toilet rolls, etc, so that things do not jump around too much.

Plastic jars and bottles with deep screw tops are best used for storing things like sugar, tea and coffee. Tupperware-style boxes should have very tight seals. Be sure to keep cooking oil in a container with a screw top! You are only likely to forget this once! An open cardboard box is a good idea for fresh vegetables, or tie them up in a cloth local-style to keep them as dry as you can.

Washing up A plastic bowl, which can double up as your personal washbasin is fine. Washing-up liquid, a cloth and a scourer are the essentials. Some travellers wash their dishes in Milton (a gentle disinfectant). Giving all your dishes, cutlery and pots a good clean when hot water becomes available should be sufficient to keep the germs at bay. If you are struggling to clean that burned-on mess at the bottom of the pan, use sand or gritty mud – the best scourers you could ever find.

A few tea towels are useful, but they do need frequent washing. Some travellers either leave their dishes to dry or flap them vigorously to dry them off. You will see a lot of overland tours doing this, usually to the amusement of onlookers.

PERSONAL EQUIPMENT/ITEMS We have listed here a few personal items that we found useful.

Clothes Take as few as possible; you will not need much once you are on the road. You'll need warm clothing for nights in the desert and in the highlands, and something to keep the rain out is also useful. Otherwise, lightweight cotton is the general rule. Dark and patterned fabrics don't show stains and rips, but can be hotter to wear.

You should also be aware of local dress customs. In Islamic countries women in particular should take care; even the tops of your arms can be regarded as offensive. Men also should wear long trousers and long-sleeved shirts. To make sure you are not upsetting anyone, look at what local people are wearing. Their reactions will soon let you know if you have crossed acceptable levels of modesty.

Taking one 'smart' item of clothing helps when having to deal with a recalcitrant embassy or border crossing. Besides, you never know who you might meet on the way!

Shortwave radio A shortwave radio with plenty of bands is great for picking up news from home and information about conditions in the countries you may be visiting. We sat alone in the silent vastness of the Sudanese desert listening to news about the conflict in Darfur. It is a good idea to take something that is not fixed to the vehicle, for both security and portability.

Camera Although such cameras are out of fashion, people in Africa still ask for Polaroid pictures. A Polaroid camera can be of real help when wanting to take photos of people. If you first give them a Polaroid picture they may be happy for you to take as many pictures as you wish with your usual camera.

Fun and games We found it useful to carry a pack of cards or backgammon, for those lonely nights in the middle of nowhere. The most popular game throughout Africa, played on street corners, is a kind of backgammon, most commonly known as *woaley*. It changes its name and rules slightly from country to country. It goes by *awalé* in the Ivory Coast, *ayo* in Nigeria, *aju* in Togo and Benin, *ouri* in Senegal, and *aware* in Ghana.

Pocket calculator One of these is useful for working out fuel consumption and exchange rates.

Hammock This is a non-essential item, but one that people on long trips recommend. After a hard day's driving, if you are intending to stay a few days, there is nothing like stringing up the hammock and relaxing under the African sun.

Gifts It is quite amazing just how important a small supply of inexpensive gifts can be, particularly for children who are desperate to help you fill your jerrycans at wells, guard your vehicle or give directions. On the other hand, you should never hand out gifts just for the sake of it. Constant handouts can mean that the local economy comes to depend on them, and later travellers will suffer because the same will be expected of them.

There will, however, be occasions when people have greatly helped you. Generosity can be thanked with a simple gift. Pens and postcards of your home country are always welcomed. Other items asked for were magazines or newspapers, cotton and needles (particularly in the Sahara for the local nomadic women), and recycled goods from your own supplies. Empty containers of any

3

kind that can be used to carry water are highly sought after in many areas. You don't need to bring everything with you from home – you can top up your supplies at local markets, thereby helping the local economy, too.

Also see *Giving something back to Africa* in *Chapter 8*, page 195.

SPARES AND TOOLS

Working on your vehicle before you leave will give you some idea of what you are likely to need. Check through your workshop manual or talk to an off-road enthusiast to find out if you are missing something essential regarding spares and tools. In many cases you will be able to limp along to the next big town where spares are available. In general, labour is cheap but parts are expensive. It pays to be as well equipped as possible.

Some places in Africa are better than others for picking up spares. The high cost of imported parts means old spares may be the only viable option. Even official dealers for your vehicle may not have what you need, although they will generally direct you to the best secondhand source. The hammering a vehicle takes on African roads means that in most sizeable towns something can be found to fix the job.

Having worked for various overland companies for many years with often 'knackered' trucks has given us an insight into just how many things can go wrong. Perhaps our list of spare parts reflects this expectation and is more comprehensive than most. You make your own choices.

SPARE PARTS Deciding what spares to take with you is a bit of a guessing game. It's Murphy's Law: it's always the one bit you didn't include a spare for that fails. Too many heavy parts are likely to damage your suspension, but not taking sensible items isn't very wise either. Take more lightweight spares than you think you will need, like gaskets, oil seals or bearings. Some can then be sold or exchanged for heavier parts if necessary.

What you include is somewhat dependent on the make, model and age of your vehicle, as well as the amount of space available in it. The actual list will also depend on the amount of preparation you have undertaken on the basic vehicle. Did you have a reconditioned injector pump or a new starter? Try to assess beforehand what might go wrong and what spares may be available locally *en route*.

You should get advice from a good mechanic who may know of typical problems regarding the make and model of your vehicle. Always remember to take all your workshop manuals with you. We have assumed you have a diesel engine.

We've also assumed that you will have the engine, gearboxes and clutch all reconditioned; that is, unless you are on a very tight budget and not too concerned about what happens to your vehicle afterwards. The front and rear axle differential units should be in good order.

It's best to have the following parts new or reconditioned: radiator, brake and clutch master cylinders, clutch slave cylinders, brake wheel cylinders, starter, alternator, water pump and brake hoses. Also suspension rubbers, engine mountings, brake pads and fuel lift pump. The injectors and injector pump must be reconditioned and the work done by recommended specialists. Injector pumps rarely go wrong if in good condition, but if they do it's a rather serious matter. Taking a spare would be a good idea if you can find an old version that works, but this is where the costs can rise quickly. In any case **all used parts should be kept as spares**.

After this, you need to take items that you will have to replace as part of a service: oil filters, fuel filters and air filters, unless your vehicle has an oil bath air system.

Old-fashioned oil baths are very good in dust and sand and there is no need to carry bulky filters, but most newer models don't have these. Take as many of these various filters as you can fit in: one for every 3,000–4,000 miles, as some local units may not be up to standard. You will have to change these more often than recommended by the makers. How often you change them partly depends on the terrain, dust, sand and temperature, and the quality of your oil. As a bare minimum, carry three of each type you require. Air filters can be cleaned out and reused at a pinch.

Don't forget all the little extras that save the day like radiator sealer, Araldite glue, plastic metal glue, bits of metal, string, duct tape, fuses and countless other items.

The following is a list of suggested spares, which should be tailored to your requirements. An asterisk denotes a part for a petrol engine.

Consumable spares
- 3 oil filters
- 4 fuel filters
- 2 or 3 air filters
- oil (enough for two changes)
- 5 litres of gear box/differential oil (check whether the same oil is used in each)
- grease
- 1 or 2 litres of brake and clutch fluid oil
- 1 litre of radiator coolant (you can use water)

General spares
- heater plugs/spark plugs★
- 1 spare diesel injector
- set of engine gaskets
- set of all oil seals (wheels, gearbox, engine, differential)
- set of wheel bearings
- set of engine mountings
- set of radiator hoses plus other hoses
- accelerator cable
- 2 fan belts
- set of brake pads
- brake master cylinder rubbers (if old units not serviceable)
- clutch master and slave cylinder rubbers (as above)
- wheel cylinder kit – rubbers (or kit for disc brakes)
- water pump
- lift pump
- suspension rubbers and bushes
- condenser★
- distributor cap★
- contact breaker points★
- spare fuel cap
- spare radiator cap
- U bolts/centre bolts for leaf springs
- main leaf springs (coil springs rarely break with careful driving)
- track rod ends
- clutch plate
- wheel nuts
- water temperature sensor unit

- sump/gearbox drain plugs (the silly things can fall into the sand – not guilty!)
- propshaft UJ
- flexible brake hose
- alternator (better a complete unit or at least the brushes)
- fuses
- light bulbs
- plastic fuel line and connectors

Other optional parts
- starter (for remoter areas, Sahara and Congo)
- fan (for seriously remote areas or constantly fording rivers)
- injector pipes
- injector pump (remoter areas, Sahara and Congo)
- injector pump solenoid if applicable (remoter areas, Sahara and Congo)

Useful bits and pieces
- funnel (make sure it fits the filler of your fuel tank and has a gauze filter)
- electrical tape
- electrical wires
- masking/duct tape
- assortment of wire
- assortment of nuts, bolts and washers
- 2m of fuel hose (long enough to be used as a siphon)
- flexible 'bathroom' sealant
- instant gasket paste
- plastic padding/instant fibreglass
- exhaust repair putty
- gasket paper
- WD40 or Q20
- radiator sealant
- towing eye/cable
- assorted small sheet metal, short drainpiping, square tubing, etc
- assorted bits of rubber, inner tube, old stockings – not for evening attire!
- old rags – lots and lots
- self-tapping screws
- cable ties in various sizes
- contact adhesive (spray-on contact is very quick and easy)
- Araldite and/or plastic metal epoxy glue
- superglue
- gasket cement
- radiator sealant
- plastic padding
- old bicycle/car inner tube
- wire or bicycle spokes
- thin gardening wire
- long piece of chain or steel cable
- small length of lighter chain
- plastic from oil tubs or similar containers
- pieces of sheet metal/aluminium sheet
- small pieces of plywood
- metal strips/old pipe/square tubing
- lots of assorted Jubilee clips/clamps
- various lengths of electrical wire

- assorted small springs (throttle, clutch, etc)
- various lengths of nylon rope/string/small rope
- ladies' nylon tights, for temporary filters or fan belt (you should be carrying a couple of spare fan belts anyway)
- assorted driver relaxants, tea, chair, hammock, etc, etc!

TOOLS Ensure you pack a good and comprehensive set of tools. Requirements vary from vehicle to vehicle and many jobs need 'special service tools'. However, there are general tools that will cover most jobs and, with a bit of lateral thinking, can be used in place of special service tools.

Suggested list of tools
- a good set of spanners (imperial or metric as required by your vehicle)
- a good set of sockets with a power bar and ratchet
- extra large sockets (check sizes needed)
- assortment of screwdrivers
- adjustable spanner
- mole wrench (large and small)
- pipe wrench (Stillson and adjustable-size versions)
- grease gun
- metal and rubber hammers
- torque wrench (essential for all engines)
- pliers (various)
- circlip removers
- multi-size puller
- jump leads for battery
- set of feeler gauges
- hacksaw and spare blades
- multi-meter electrical tester
- flat metal file
- coarse flat file
- small round file
- hand drill and bits (9V cordless drills can be connected directly to your battery)
- tyre levers
- tyre valve tool/valve extractor
- set of Allen keys
- centre punch/assorted punches and metal drifts
- wet and dry sandpaper
- length of pipe (to extend your power bar for those stubborn nuts)
- arc welding rods – a few
- G clamp/small vice to attach to bumper
- magnetic retrieving tool – for when you drop a nut that gets trapped
- plus the hydraulic jack

The lists are not exhaustive; but again space, weight and money determine which extras to take.

SUPPLIERS AND USEFUL CONTACTS

VEHICLE MANUALS A very good source of information specific to your chosen vehicle is the series of manuals/technical books produced by Haynes (*www.haynes.co.uk*). They cover most vehicles. They have a book that covers Land

3

Rovers from 1983 to 2007, which is excellent for all the technical data that the manufacturers will not easily divulge these days.

VEHICLE SELECTION *Autotrader* magazine can be found at major newsagents. It has information on used and new vehicles to sell or buy. Also look in local newspapers.

VEHICLE PREPARATION
UK

Black Diamond Warrington Transmission Centre Ltd Unit 2/7, Guardian St, Warrington, Cheshire WA5 1SJ; ℡ 01925 416619, technical hotline: 08457 125914; f 01925 230472; e sales@blackdiamond-ltd.co.uk; www.blackdiamond-ltd.co.uk. One of the largest independent re-manufacturers of gearboxes, differentials & axles. Nationwide delivery & they speak English, French & German.
Brownchurch Ltd Bickley Hse, 1A Bickley Rd, London E10 7AQ; ℡ 020 8556 0011; f 020 8556 0033; e sales@brownchurch.co.uk; www.brownchurch.co.uk. The largest suppliers of rooftop tents in the UK.
Essential Overland Preparation e info@allisport.com; www.allisport.com

Footloose 4X4 ℡ 01780 784781; www.footloose4X4.com
Formula 4X4 Ltd Stafford Rd, Stone, Staffs; ℡ 01785 811211; f 01785 817788; e info@formula4x4.com; www.formula4x4.com
Mantec Services Unit 4, Haunchwood Park Drive, Nuneaton, Warks; ℡ 0247 639 5368; f 0247 639 5369; e sales@mantec.co.uk
Superwinch www.superwinch.com. Worldwide suppliers of winches & recovery gear, based in Devon.
Westfield 4x4 Lancaster LA2 0HF; ℡ 01524 791698; f 01524 792653; e sales@west-4x4.demon.co.uk; www.west-4x4.demon.co.uk. Spare-part suppliers specific to Mercedes-Benz Type 411 & all makes of Unimogs worldwide.

For those of you in southern England, the following have been helpful to us:

Chichester 4x4 Lagness Rd, Runcton, Chichester, West Sussex PO20 1LJ; ℡ 01243 788805; Ask for Phil Haines, who is also a bike enthusiast, running trips in America.
H & J Potter The Old Railway Station, Singleton, Chichester; ℡ 01243 811277. For those tricky spare parts that have disappeared from dealers.

Harwoods When you really need genuine parts – ask Ian at Terminus Rd, Chichester, West Sussex PO19 8TX; ℡ 01243 781333; f 01243 836541; e harwoods@harwoods.uk.com; www.harwoods.uk.com. Also Keith in Pulborough.

And finally don't forget to see the *Land Rover* magazine for a full list of dealers and suppliers.

South Africa

Avnic Trading PO Box 532, Lanseria 1748, Johannesburg; ℡ 011 704 6147; f 011 704 6151; www.avnic.co.za. Suppliers of Garmin GPS 11 Plus.
Brakhah 4X4 Centurion, Pretoria; ℡ (012) 661 0583; f (012) 661 1481; e anton@brakhah.co.za or johan@brakhah.co.za; www.brakhah.co.za. Specialist vehicle equipment centre.
Outdoor Warehouse Randburg, Johannesburg; ℡ 011 792 8331/6818; *Pretoria* ℡ (012) 661 0505; *Durban* ℡ 031 579 1950/70; *Cape Town* ℡ 021 948 6221. Specialists in outdoor equipment.

Safari Centre Main Rd, Bryanston, Johannesburg; ℡ 011 465 3817; f 011 465 2639; e bryanston@safaricentre.co.za; www.safaricentre.co.za. Branches also at *Menlyn* e menlyn@safaricentre.co.za; *Windhoek* e windhoek@safaricentre.co.za; *Umhlanga* e gateway@safaricentre.co.za. The best-known & longest-established 4x4 outfitter.

OFF-ROAD DRIVING COURSES
UK

David Bowyer's Off-Road Centre East Foldhay, Zeal Monachorum, Crediton, Devon EX17 6DH; ℡ 01363 82666; f 01363 82782; e sales@davidbowyer.com; www.davidbowyer.com

Ian Wright Off-Road Driving Centre Ian Wright Organisation, Ashtree Farm, Teston Rd, West Malling, Kent ME19 5RL; ☎ 01732 529511; f 01732 529513; www.thewrightevent.co.uk

South Africa
Safari Centre offers off-road driving training & guided trails (see above).

OTHER
Expedition Advisory Centre (Royal Geographical Society) Kensington Gore, London SW7 2AR; ☎ 020 7581 2057

Africa Travel Centre 4 Medway Court, Leigh St, London WC1H 9QX; ☎ 020 7387 1211
Nomad 3–4 Turnpike Lane, London N8 0PX; ☎ 020 8889 7014; f 020 8889 9529

And see *Appendix 5*, page 332, for off-road websites.

MOTORBIKE SELECTION

David Lambeth (Rally & Overland ☎ 01205 871945; e bigbluecoach@hotmail.com; www.davidlambeth.co.uk) and Alex Marr

For those prepared to sacrifice comfort and space, travelling by motorbike offers a very exciting alternative. Although frequently physically demanding, most bikes also give the traveller an unparalleled freedom to explore off-the-beaten-track Africa. A bike can cope in a number of situations that a 4x4 vehicle cannot. Whether crossing rivers by canoe, negotiating narrow, rocky climbs or simply weaving a line along a badly pot-holed road, two wheels beats four nearly every time.

Another factor, often overlooked, is that bikes are not perceived by locals as great symbols of wealth (unlike cars) and they tend to be friendlier as a result. It helps at checkpoints and border crossings too – there is something about turning up at a remote road control tired and dirty that generates a sort of sympathetic admiration in all but the most hearted of officials. Someone getting out of a shiny new Land Cruiser is a lot more likely to be invited to participate in some underhand redistribution of wealth.

Of course, travelling by bike has its downside. It's hard to convince yourself it's a good way to travel if you get a puncture in a thunderstorm the day after you've had your tool kit stolen. Also note that bikes are not allowed into any national parks in Africa and must be left behind while you make alternative arrangements.

MAKES AND MODELS In virtually all of Africa a bike with some degree of off-road capability is essential. Two-stroke bikes are not suitable for long trips, as they are generally small, impractical and unreliable. These days there are myriad four-stroke bikes which are given an 'off-road' label by the manufacturers. The degree of 'off-roadability' varies enormously, ranging from superlight enduro bikes (designed for racing), which can tackle virtually any terrain, to large twin-cylinder bikes which are given trendy off-road styling but are really more designed for touring in comfort in easy conditions. The large middle ground is made up by versatile 'trailbikes' offering varying degrees of compromise between comfort, features, weight and off-roadability.

Just to confuse the issue, note that trailbikes are often called 'enduros' in Germany and are also sometimes referred to as 'dualsport bikes', particularly in America. What the British call enduro bikes – for competition use – tend to be called 'hard enduros' in Germany.

Listed below is a non-exhaustive selection of models that a fairly adventurous traveller who is not content with sticking to the main roads could consider. As with 4x4 vehicles, buying the latest models is not a good idea.

Yamaha (*www.yamaha-motor.co.uk*) The legendary reliability and unsophisticated engines of the XT500, and subsequently the XT600, meant Yamaha were the most popular overland bikes from the 1970s to the 1990s. The XT600 Ténéré models, with their 27-litre tank and bulletproof simplicity, were for a long time *the* bike to use in Africa. Discontinued in 1991, they are rarer, but there are still those who would never use anything else. Unfortunately, finding decent secondhand models can be a problem. One big advantage of their popularity is that a number of XTs are still found in Africa, having been sold by overlanders at the end of their trips, and scavenging spares is a reasonable possibility. If you do choose a 600 Ténéré, the best by far is the 1988–91 twin-headlamp electric-start-only 3AJ model. The earlier kick-only and kick-and-electric models suffer from some serious engine and gearbox problems.

The more recent electric-start XT600E is another good option, available new until early 2005 and can easily be 'Ténérised' with the addition of a large tank, a good screen and an 18-inch rear wheel. The best model is the 1997-onwards 4PT version with a rev counter and right-hand-side clutch actuator. The XTZ660 Ténéré, a water-cooled, 5-valve single, is a little over-complicated for overlanding, but worth a look if a good 600 can't be found. The XTZ750 Super Ténéré is Yamaha's twin-cylinder offering. It is a bit of a monster, but reliable and a good option for 2-up travel.

The TT600s are truer off-roaders than the XT, but are more limited in availability. They are a good choice but good ones can be hard to find as they are not imported officially into some countries and have often been used hard off road. The best are the TT600E and RE models. Both use the electric-start XT motor in a high-spec chassis and have a proper high-output generator.

Yamaha's four-stroke WR range, which in 1998 revolutionised the four-stroke competition scene, is a superlight bike, but as a high-revving out-and-out racer it is hardly designed with luggage-carrying in mind. It is an unlikely choice and definitely not suitable for those doing long distances on tarmac, but it may suit someone travelling light and regularly in very tough conditions. If you do choose a WR, go for the electric-start 450.

More recently the XT660R and XT660Z Ténéré have arrived on the scene and are sure to feature among the top overlanders' choices of the future once people become familiar with them – don't be frightened of electronic fuel injection and engine management systems – cars have had them for 20 years and they are reliable.

Honda (*www.honda.co.uk*) The Honda XR600, and since 1996 the XR400, are extremely robust off-roaders and utterly dependable. Offering the usual Honda high standard of quality, they are an excellent choice, with no frills – air-cooled and no electric start (electric start kits can be fitted), not even an ignition key. Comfortable they may not be, but they are built to last. Partly as a result of their use in desert rallies, a good range of accessories, such as large tanks, is available (see below).

The XR650L is a more street-legal version of the XR600 with the Dominator electric-start motor and a high-output generator (but over 20kg/44lb heavier) with a high seat that suits tall riders. The NX650 Dominator is slightly more road-orientated, but also a good candidate if fitted with an 18-inch rear wheel. Many high-mileage or overheated examples suffer from exhaust valve seats falling out – be careful! A good XL/XR/Dominator engine should make no rattling noises at all, hot or cold.

The Honda XR650R replaced the XR600 in 2000. With an aluminium frame and compact kick-start engine, this is an incredibly light bike for the power it produces, weighing in at under 130kg (285lb). It makes a good overlander and there is a whole host of good-quality overland kits available including various electric-start ones.

The Transalp, Africa Twin and Varadero are comfortable, larger, twin-cylinder bikes, but because of their weight, most people travelling on their own would consider them to be too cumbersome for a trans-Africa trip. Note that they also have expensive fairings, which would almost certainly not withstand the rigours of African travel.

Suzuki (*www.suzuki-gb.co.uk*) The long-established DR350 and DR650, simple air- and oil-cooled machines, have their fair share of fans, the smaller version having a reasonably low seat and being particularly popular with female riders. Unfortunately, the 650 has a 17-inch rear wheel. The DRZ400 (also badged as a Kawasaki KLX400R) was introduced in 2000, with a water-cooled motor which comes in both kick- and electric-start versions. It makes a great, lightweight, economical overlander for those of you who aren't after a monster. All the overland gear is available for the DRZ at affordable prices.

Kawasaki (*www.kawasaki.co.uk*) Not so frequently seen in Africa, the water-cooled KLX range (250, 300, 450 and 650cc) are very capable off-roaders, although, as with the Suzuki DR, the larger model takes a 17-inch rear. The KLR650 is heavier and more road-orientated. These models are popular in the US, so check out the internet for more information. We consider the KLR/KLX range a little over-complicated for overlanding, with its twin cams, water cooling and twin-balance shafts.

KTM (*www.ktm.co.uk*) The 640 'Adventure' is the closest you can get these days to a dedicated lightweight overlander's bike. With a 28-litre tank, twin tripmeters and options like side panniers, this bike is almost ready to go straight from the crate. However, they are expensive and there are question marks over engine vibrations and long-term reliability. One to consider for the more affluent 'must have' overlander could be a retired 660 Rallye. It's hugely expensive new (£15k), but built to endure the Dakar and more. It has 60-litre fuel capacity, and top-spec suspension, wheels and chassis, and comes with a full navigation equipment set-up. The 660 LC4 motor also seems now to have become reliable, while remaining simple to maintain and repair. You have four separate fuel tanks, so you could use one for water storage. The later models made after 2001 have better fuel consumption and a generally smoother response.

If you really think you need, and can handle a 200kg plus bike off-road, then the 950/990 Adventure is the one to go for. It's a proper trail/enduro bike with fine suspension and serious performance.

BMW (*www.bmw-motorrad.co.uk*) The F650GS/Dakar/G650X is BMW's single-cylinder trailbike, but at over 190kg (420lb) it is more at home on the road. Go for the Dakar or G650X as they have 21-inch front wheels.

The F800GS is the new parallel twin-cylinder trail/adventure bike and looks to have all the makings of a seriously refined overlander if a single cylinder just won't do.

The GS series of large boxer twin-cylinder bikes have been available throughout Africa for years. These creamy-smooth, shaft-driven machines are a pleasure to ride on the road, but for most people their sheer weight makes them a real handful in tough-going terrain. Even so, the latest R1200GS and HP2 are certainly marketed as real off-road machines and the GSs will probably never lose their faithful band of supporters, who will continue to manhandle them around the continent for years to come. Needless to say they are not cheap, and a massive range of equally expensive accessories is available from a number of German manufacturers.

WHICH TO CHOOSE? Your choice of bike depends upon a number of factors:

• Your mechanical knowledge. Don't choose a bike you can't fix, because you *will* have to fix it at some point. You must at least be able to carry out basic servicing. Go and do a short mechanics' course and take your bike to work on while learning.
• Your intended route. Generally speaking, the harder the terrain the more suitable a lighter bike will be. For example someone crossing central Africa in the rainy season would have a gruelling, if not impossible, time on an Africa Twin. At the other extreme, if you are going to be cruising around southern Africa, most of the time on tarmac roads, you may find a Honda XR400 slow and uncomfortable.
• Your size. Those short on leg length will not enjoy the comparatively high seat of an XR650L. Also very important for those travelling alone in remote areas, you need to be able to pick the bike up on your own – and you have to be pretty strong to right a fully loaded XTZ750 lying on its side in a pile of mud. Try it before you go – if you can't manage it, choose a smaller bike or get down to the gym!
• The availability of extra equipment, such as large tanks and luggage carriers. Yamaha XTs, Honda XRs and BMWs are the most popular overland bikes and so offer the best choice in this respect.
• How much the standard bike has to be modified – especially important for those people short on time or not mechanically inclined.
• Your budget.

MOTORCYCLE TOOLS AND SPARES LIST

• spare rear tyre
• heavy-duty inner tubes
• wheel and cush drive bearings and seals
• good-quality puncture repair kit with lots of feather-edge patches
• small mountain bike pump or compact electric pump
• a few spare spokes of each type – there can be two types per wheel
• connecting links for chain – clip and rivet (better) links
• short section of chain for repairs
• sprockets and lock washers
• clutch, brake and gear levers
• brake pads/shoes
• clutch cable
• throttle cable(s) – usually only pull cable
• air filters – fewer if cleanable type
• oil filters
• fuel filter
• spark plugs and HT cap and lead
• fuel hose and hose clips
• bulbs and fuses
• electrical wire and connectors
• regulator/rectifier
• stator/pickup/ignition pack/HT coil – if a very long trip
• assorted nuts, bolts, washers and Loctite

MOTORBIKE PREPARATION

David Lambeth (Rally & Overland ✆ *01205 871945;* **e** *bigbluecoach@hotmail.com;*
www.davidlambeth.co.uk) and Alex Marr

Thorough pre-trip preparation is the key to a successful time in Africa. Cutting corners at this stage will result in problems *en route* and you can almost guarantee that they will occur in the most remote and inconvenient places. As well as having a mechanically sound engine and chassis, considerable thought should be given to any peripheral items, such as mounting racks for luggage, fuel, water, tools and spares. These are the things that are going to break or cause problems.

Whatever bike you use, it goes without saying that it should be given a thorough mechanical overhaul before you leave. At the very least, you should start with new oil, filters (air, oil and fuel), spark plugs, chain, sprockets, clutch, tyres, inner tubes, brake pads and cables. Items which you know are going to get considerable wear, such as the non-engine bearings (wheel, swingarm, steering), should be thoroughly checked. It would be prudent to fit new ones before you leave. Whether or not you go for a complete engine strip-down depends on the age of the bike, how long you have owned it yourself and its general condition.

TOOLS It is a good idea at this stage to think about what tools you intend to take with you. With a view to keeping things as light as possible, select the smallest number of the best-quality tools you think you will need on the trip and prepare the bike confining yourself to using only these tools. It will soon become obvious what you do and don't need. Try to keep your tools in a dedicated, solidly mounted, waterproof, lockable toolbox.

- gasket set
- clutch friction & plain plates
- duct and electrical tape
- assorted cable/zip ties
- spare bungee rope/straps
- instant gasket
- multimeter electrical test meter
- epoxy glue
- liquid steel/JB weld two-part epoxy
- nitrile rubber gloves
- small tub of grease – 35mm film pot?
- one litre of engine oil
- air filter oil if using foam air filter
- small, high-quality toolkit (combination spanners, 3/8-inch drive ratchet and relevant sockets, screwdrivers, ball-end Allen keys, small mole grips, spoke spanner)
- Leatherman-type multi tool
- chain-splitting/riveting tool
- feeler gauges
- tyre pressure gauge (if not on pump)
- file
- spark-plug spanner
- tyre levers
- repair manual

BIKE MODIFICATIONS/ADDITIONS How you go about modifying the bike really depends on the length and intended route of your trip. When planning a trans-continental trip, for example, the following essential points need to be addressed.

Fuel and water tanks Generally speaking the ideal size for a fuel tank is around 25–30 litres. This is a good compromise between not being overly heavy or bulky and giving a decent range, around 500–600km (300–380 miles) for most bikes. This will be sufficient in all but a few circumstances. Realistically you are more likely to be constrained by what large tanks are available for your particular bike. Companies like Acerbis, IMS and Aqualine make large plastic tanks for a wide range of off-road bikes, though most of them tend to be slightly small, in the 18–24-litre range. The extra capacity can be achieved using side- or rear-mounted small auxiliary fuel tanks or cheap 10-litre jerrycans. Always fit transparent fuel filters to all your fuel lines. You can then see when you have contamination early enough to do something about it.

It's worth pointing out that in areas where you actually need more fuel than this, such as certain parts of the Sahara, for safety reasons you are more than likely going to be travelling with at least one other vehicle (a 4x4 or truck) which will be able to carry extra fuel in jerrycans or plastic containers for you.

For a long trip in the desert you will also need a considerable amount of water, say 20 litres, which just adds to the difficulty of carrying fuel on your bike. If there is no extra vehicle and if you don't have jerrycans to carry extra fuel, you can usually find cheap plastic containers which can be disposed of after transferring the fuel into your main tank. Another way is to use water 'bags', such as those made by Ortlieb, or flat foldable emergency fuel bags. They are very resilient and are fine for carrying fuel for short periods – and of course they take up very little space when not in use.

Hard luggage There are essentially two ways of carrying your gear, and the debate among experienced overlanders will continue forever about which is the better system! Hard luggage usually involves mounting hard aluminium side-boxes at the rear of the bike on to some sort of steel rack attached to the mainframe and subframe. This method is very popular in Germany and a number of companies manufacture the equipment.

Aluminium boxes have two big advantages over soft luggage: they are waterproof and they offer a much greater degree of security from theft. However, they are also heavy, unwieldy and annoyingly hard to mend if they break in a crash. You can find steel welders everywhere in Africa, but specialist aluminium welders are rare. Over time, friction on the aluminium creates a dark-grey dust, which means clothes and other sensitive items have to be kept covered. Tough fabric inner bags will prevent this problem and ease removal of contents. Tools and spares can be kept low in the boxes under a false bottom for protection.

Soft luggage Soft material side-panniers (Cordura, leather or similar) are also fitted at the rear side. Unless the contents are very light, they cannot just be thrown over; some sort of frame is needed to support the weight and resist constant abrasive movement and fatigue. Much cheaper and lighter, soft luggage is most people's choice on a short trip.

Actually, good-quality panniers are surprisingly hard-wearing and, provided they are well supported, should last a long trip. If damaged, they can easily be repaired with stitching. The obvious disadvantages are that they get wet in the rain and it is easier for people to pinch things from them. It is also harder to access the contents easily through a single zip on the top.

Whatever method you choose, it is very important to keep the weight as low down and as between the axles as possible. If the bike's centre of gravity is too high or too far back, it makes riding in difficult conditions, such as soft sand, even harder.

For my long trip on an XR400, I settled on a compromise of soft panniers at the sides and a small, lockable, 100% waterproof, aluminium topbox for camera, films, important documents, etc. This was designed so a spare rear tyre could fit perfectly around it. I had a waterproof Sealine drybag for camping gear sitting across the rear seat and panniers. I found this system worked very well. The key was fabricating a very strong steel framework which provided support and transferred a lot of the weight onto the mainframe. It also meant I could strap a 10-litre jerrycan under either pannier. The non-waterproof factor was not such a problem; I generally tried to avoid rainy seasons, but when it was wet I kept my clothes in dustbin liners. Maybe I was just lucky, but I never found security a big issue; in 23 African countries I never had anything stolen.

Within the luggage, it is important to protect all your belongings from the constant vibrations they will receive. Most things can be neatly stored in small Tupperware boxes and clothes within plastic bags. Apart from the main luggage, lightweight items can also be secured in front of the headlight.

Most riders also carry either a tankbag or a small rucksack for essential items which need to be accessed quickly. Kriega (*www.kriega.com*), based in the UK, produce some exceptionally well-designed and unusually comfortable overland-specific backpacks.

Tyres One important point to realise is that trailbikes which take anything other than a 21-inch front and an 18-inch rear tyre will have a restricted choice.

On a long trip, tyre choice requires careful thought, mainly because sourcing decent tyres in Africa (apart from some places in southern Africa) is a perennial headache. Tyres are always available in big cities, but they tend to be rather narrow and of light construction for small-capacity bikes. With a bit of persistence you can usually find something, but in west and central Africa, generally speaking, it is very difficult.

Ultra-knobbly motocross tyres offer the best grip in rough terrain, but they are not really practical because of their very limited life, particularly when ridden on tarmac, which is more often than you think. A better choice in tough conditions is a tyre like Michelin Desert, Pirelli MT21 or Metzeler Karoo. They have much harder-wearing knobbles, which are spaced closer together and consequently have a much longer life, although they still wear fast on the road.

More versatile 'trail tyres' – such as Metzeler Sahara, Avon Gripster and Dunlop Trailmax – with a broader, shallower tread pattern, are generally a good compromise, offering a longer life and an acceptable amount of grip in sandy or stony conditions; they are not so good in mud, however.

For those entering north Africa and crossing the Sahara, it is best to leave southern Europe with a pair of new Michelin Desert tyres and to carry a spare at the rear, space permitting.

For ultimate puncture and pinch resistance you can do no better than use Bridgestone, Conti or Michelin Ultra Heavy Duty inner tubes, lubricated with Michelin mousse gel and treated with a puncture-resisting 'slime'-type product.

Good tyres are of little use if your rims and spokes are about to part company. Make sure your wheels are true and that your spokes are tight and the nipples are free to be adjusted. Choose a good-quality rim tape to protect your tubes from spoke ends.

A rim lock on each wheel is a good idea and will stop the tyre creeping round and ripping out the air valve when running at low pressures in difficult conditions.

Miscellaneous Other essential modifications are:

- A bash plate, to protect the crankcase from flying stones.
- An O-ring (or X-ring) chain. Stronger than normal chains, the inside of the links is constantly lubricated, increasing longevity. Try to stick with DID as you will find it easier to find spare links. Always use a rivet link rather than a clip as clips can come free with time. Use genuine steel, not alloy, sprockets. They last a lot longer and are stronger.
- Good-quality, alloy-reinforced handguards, which protect your levers in a fall.

Desirable modifications include:

- Fitting an oil-temperature gauge, and for those bikes with a small oil-cooler (or none at all) replacing it with a larger unit.
- For those who intend using a GPS (global positioning system), a power lead and some sort of vibration isolating mounting bracket on the handlebars are necessary.
- Bland looks. The less new and shiny a bike looks, the better. Removing stickers from new bikes helps.

SPARE PARTS For those who have never travelled in Africa, one of the problems is not knowing in advance what spares you are likely to be able to pick up on the way. Generally speaking, very little is available for large bikes north of South Africa. In some large capitals you may find basic items, like oil filters for popular models, but not much more; there simply isn't the demand. In the more Westernised capitals like Harare, Windhoek, Nairobi and most of South Africa, you will find more choice, especially non-model-specific items such as tyres and chains.

What spares you take with you is a compromise between trying to cover all eventualities (the wrong approach), and taking as little as you can get away with (the right one). Only take what there is a good chance you will probably need. This may sound naively optimistic, but it is really a case of logical risk evaluation. If you have a fundamentally good bike, well prepared and properly looked after, it is pretty unlikely that anything serious mechanically will go wrong – and if it does, how can you possibly know what it is going to be and plan for it? If the worst does happen in the middle of nowhere, you will be able to get your bike to the nearest town eventually – although you may have to hire help and it will take a while – where you can try to repair it. You may need the right spares to be couriered out from your home country and you should be able to convince customs that, as you'll be exporting the spares again as part of your bike, you should not have to pay any duty. It is a good idea to have some arrangement set up in advance with your local dealer back home in case this is required.

Much more likely problems concern luggage carriers etc, so lots of bodge-it items such as glue, duct tape and plenty of cable ties are invaluable for temporary repairs.

CLOTHING Choice of riding gear is yet another compromise: protection versus practicality. While some degree of protection against a crash is essential, don't underestimate the amount of time you'll be off the bike, walking around villages or cities. A strong Cordura enduro jacket with built-in shoulder and elbow pads is a good choice. A simple spine protector with a waistband provides back support and protection without being too restrictive or uncomfortable.

Most riders use full-length motocross-style boots – an excellent safety measure – although some people find them too cumbersome when not actually riding and prefer the flexibility of normal strong walking boots which cover the ankle. This is something of a risk, given how vulnerable feet and legs are in the event of a crash, but again it boils down to personal preference.

As with the bike, the blander you look the better. Unfortunately nearly all off-road gear these days is distinctly unbland.

HELMET Off-road-style helmets with a peak and requiring goggles (which are easily lost) are best in dusty conditions, but normal road helmets are usually more comfortable and offer better all-round vision, though the visor can become scratched after a while.

CAMPING A lightweight tent, sleeping bag and mosquito net are essential. Some sort of mattress is highly desirable. Thermarest make one that can be packed to an incredibly small size.

A high-quality petrol stove (such as MSR) is the most practical way to cook.

WATER A camelback-style water system (a hose coming from a 'bladder' on your back) can be very useful when you need to drink often in hot and difficult conditions.

A filter bag (made of a material such as Millbank cloth) is the most space-economic method of filtering.

PERSONAL ITEMS Clothes, hygiene, books, etc are of course subjective things, but it is really a question of common sense based on the available space. Most people take far too much at the start of a long trip. A good general rule is to sort out what you would like to take with you and then halve it.

And see *Appendix 5*, page 332, for relevant books, magazines and websites.

BICYCLE SELECTION AND PREPARATION David Mozer of Bicycle Africa Tours

TYPES OF BICYCLE Most people cycling across Africa use mountain bikes. For some regional trips, touring and hybrid (or cross-bikes) are also practical.

I have a preference for mountain bikes (MTBs) over touring bikes for most excursions in Africa. The MTB is versatile, durable, stable and the disadvantages are few. I have found that once the bike is loaded with gear, a couple of extra kilograms in the frame are immaterial. The tyres and wheels are probably more of a factor, because that is where you'll find a lot of the extra weight. But for most excursions in Africa you won't want to give up the durability and stability of fat tyres.

Because the bike is going to be loaded with panniers, it is more important that it be able to accept sturdy racks than have a suspension system. Just the added weight of your belongings will help your bike to hug the road. An additional consideration about suspension systems is that they are an added element that might have mechanical problems.

In my opinion the hybrids, or cross-bikes, are crossed the wrong way. Instead of narrow tyres and straight bars, I would select fat tyres and drop bars as a better cross. The fat tyres increase stability and the drop bars increase control and the number of hand positions, as well as reduce wind resistance. This is especially useful if you know you will be doing some big mileage on paved roads, along with some challenging terrain on dirt roads. With narrow tyres you lose stability. The straight bar also tends to raise the centre of gravity, which further diminishes control. If you are looking for less rolling resistance and straight bars, put narrower tyres on an MTB.

As the airlines reduce their baggage allowances and increase their excess-baggage charges, folding-suitcase bikes become a serious consideration. I have ridden a Bike Friday 'World Tourist' in the sands of Mali, the rutted roads of Ethiopia and

3

the mud of Cameroon without failure. But the small wheel can drop further into holes and alter the inertia of the bike and a shorter wheelbase changes the centre of gravity to be much more over the front wheel. This is likely to catch up with you most going downhill on a rutted gravel road. Unless you are skilled at this, you will be better off with a full-size bike.

If you already have an MTB and want to increase your choice of grip positions, two options come to mind. Get some bar extenders (there is quite a wide variety available), or replace the whole handlebar assembly with the set-up you prefer. I have put drop-bars on an MTB with good results.

There are many good mountain bikes on the market and the choice comes down to personal preference. Though their names are different, many are made in the same factory, with the same inputs. Basically you get what you pay for. A rule of thumb is to pay enough to get what you feel you need.

SELECTING YOUR BICYCLE

Frames In addition to the geometry and size of the frame, there are other important factors: the size (diameter and thickness) of tubing; the quality of workmanship; the kind of metal; and the size of wheel that the frame uses. Many of these factors play more of a role in how comfortable the bicycle is to ride than how durable it is under normal use. Under normal conditions there is little or no performance difference between frames with high-top tubes (men's bikes) and slanted-top tubes (women's bikes).

Generally, new models have more efficient frame geometry than older bikes. Once you have the right style you probably won't have to worry too much about the specifics of the frame angles. In considering the kind, size and quality of the tubing, it is not necessary to get lured too far upmarket. Low-end bicycles, above the lower mass-market levels, simply don't fall apart very often.

Our advice is to not overlook the cost effectiveness and advantages of the solid US$300 bike with a frame of a weldable metal (chrome-moly steel). In the unlikely event that it should break, you usually don't have to go far to find someone who can fix it in some fashion. I have seen steel frames brazed over a blacksmith's bed of coals! On the other hand be wary of expensive frames made of materials or assembled with adhesive that might be weakened by vibration. I have seen expensive bikes shake apart even on 'paved' roads. Aluminium frames face the same problem of being difficult to repair if they break in a remote area.

An important variable dictated by the frame is wheel and tyre size. Not all frames use the same size of wheel and not all wheels have the same selection of tyres. For remote areas consider a frame with a wheel that takes a sturdy tyre.

Collectively, in terms of geometry, tubing, tyre availability and workmanship, this suggests a modest MTB as a starting point.

Size A bicycle that is too big or too small for the user can be a safety hazard and tiring to ride. Bicycles are sized, in inches or centimetres, by the measurement along the seat tube from the top tube to the bottom bracket (theoretically – it varies by brand). The final determination of a safe size comes when the bicyclist straddles the top tube, stands with both feet flat on the ground, and checks the clearance between the top tube and his/her crotch. The recommended clearance depends on the type of riding you will be doing – 3–5cm (1–2 inches) for road riding and double that for off-road riding. Your crotch and 7.5cm (3 inches) below it is a fixed distance above the ground, but because the bottom bracket isn't the same distance above the ground on all bicycles and 'sizing' varies by brand, the 'right size' may be different from bicycle to bicycle. Typically, people use MTBs 5–10cm (2–3 inches) smaller than they use touring bicycles.

PREPARING AND MAINTAINING YOUR BICYCLE

Speeds Once upon a time there were only single-speed bikes, then there were three speeds, and that expanded to five, ten, 12, 15, 18, 21, 24 and 27 speeds. Is there a difference? Sometimes. Is it important? Sometimes. Between one, three, five, ten and 15 speeds there are functional differences that can be important. In a flat area, with short trip distances and no loads, a one-speed might be sufficient and cost effective. In hilly terrain, on rough roads, over long distances and/or when hauling a load, 15 speeds are advantageous. Each additional chainring (front gear) you combine with a basic five-gear freewheel cluster (the rear gears) creates a substantial increase in the range of gear ratios. It's the 'range' that is important!

The same is not true for changing from a five-, six-, seven- or eight-gear freewheel. The incremental difference between speeds is smaller, but the range is usually unchanged. At the efficiency level that most people ride, the benefits from reducing increments between gears is not measurable. In fact, the fancy freewheels can cause new problems.

Freewheels, hubs and axles There are two systems for attaching the gears to the rear hub: traditional threaded freewheel units which screw onto the hub, and rear hubs with built-in freehub mechanisms that use cog cassettes. These are not interchangeable. To change from one system to the other you must change the hub, which requires rebuilding the entire wheel. In terms of remote-area maintenance, the main significance of this is on the rear axle. Mountain-bike rear hubs with screw-on freewheels generally use an axle similar to those on Chinese bicycles (and local knock-offs) found around the world. If you break this axle you can get a replacement axle almost anywhere. Good luck finding an axle for a freehub. If your freewheel should self-destruct you are more likely to be able to find a fill-in freewheel than cog cassettes.

Traditional hubs are available with solid nutted axles or hollow quick-release axles. Unless you need to take a wheel off frequently, solid axles are an economical and practical choice. Hollow axles can be replaced with solid axles and vice versa.

Hub bearings can be loose or sealed. Loose bearings may require adjusting (use standard-size bearings) and can be serviced and rebuilt easily with a set of cone wrenches. Sealed bearing hubs are difficult to service and require special parts and tools.

Protecting freewheels and hubs from dust, grit and rain Usually the manufacturer's instructions tell you to lubricate most of the ball bearings on a bicycle (the headset, bottom bracket and hubs) with grease, but to lubricate the freewheel with light machine oil. In some extreme climates and cycling conditions it also may be practical to protect the bearings in your freewheel by packing them with grease.

If you are cycling in conditions where dust or a lot of water is likely to get into the freewheel you should consider packing your freewheel with grease. This is done by screwing a fitting (freewheel grease injector, US$25) onto the back of the freewheel. It has an 'O' ring so it seals against the back. You then use a grease gun to pump grease into the injector. The injector directs the grease into the freewheel. When the chamber of the freewheel is full, grease will begin to come out of the front of the freewheel.

Problems can be created from doing this, so care is necessary. (This could be more of a problem when installing the grease in a cold climate. We have never had a problem during any of our activities in the tropics.) First a description of a freewheel: a traditional freewheel is essentially two frustums (cones with the top cut off by a plane parallel to the base), one nested in the other. There is a race and a ring of ball bearings at each end of the frustums to keep the two pieces evenly spaced and able to rotate independently. The outer frustum is grooved and threaded on the outside to support the gears and the inside is notched all the way around. The inside frustum screws onto the rear hub and has spring-loaded teeth sticking out of it. The springs are very small and not particularly strong. When a bicycle is coasting the teeth slip over the notches and this creates the familiar clicking sound. When the bike is pedalled the notches come up to the teeth and engage them, pulling the rear wheel along.

When you pack a freewheel the entire space between the frustums is filled with grease. As you ride the bike the bearings and the teeth carve out a path for themselves within the chamber of grease. Within their 'chambers' they are protected from dust and moisture. The potential problem lies in the strength of the small springs behind the teeth and the stiffness of the grease. If the grease is too stiff the teeth may not extend fully and may break off. You need to use a soft grease in the freewheel and start off coasting and riding easily after you pack the bearings. It will help if you do the process in warm weather.

On hubs (usually older) where the dust cap doesn't rotate with the axle, you can keep foreign material out of your bearings by wrapping the exposed part of the cone with a pipe cleaner and then twisting the two ends back on each other so that it fits snugly. This technique can also be used on the bottom bracket.

Chains It used to be that all chains more or less fitted all bicycles. No longer! The new seven-speed freewheels require narrower chains, and some of these chains require their own special tools, replacement rivets and service techniques for maintenance and repair. The high-tech chains are hard to repair if they fail on the road. Unless you have a certified mechanic working on your bike you may want to stay away from some of the advanced technology. You will maintain more options if you stay with five- or six-cog freewheels and the standard chains that fit these assemblies.

An ongoing concern for chains is lubrication. Africa is dusty. If you over-oil, your chain will get caked up. And once you get into the desert you will have to run dry as oil quickly attracts sand and this will destroy even the very best equipment.

Derailleurs Derailleurs are now built to close tolerances so that a specific movement of the shift lever moves the derailleur to a specific gear (indexing). To use this system the derailleur and shifter have to be matched. Generally, most models of derailleurs from one manufacturer are interchangeable. The main differences between the derailleurs within one manufacturer are weight, price and quality. As the weight goes down the price goes up.

But a higher price doesn't necessarily mean better quality. Grams are shaved by using more plastic or alloy metals, but this can also compromise strength. Generally at the level of performance at which MTBs are ridden a few ounces of weight is not as important as durability. Unless you are certain of their durability, derailleurs with plastic parts should be avoided. For remote locations, a high-quality, all-metal derailleur can be sufficient and is preferable. To continue to use an index system, any replacements should be the same brand as the original equipment. Whatever you use, if you go far enough on bad roads it will take a beating.

Gear shifters For years gear shifters were disks with a lever sticking out. The shift lever rotates through a continuous range of settings. To shift gears, the user moves the lever to the desired setting and the disk stays in place by friction. Any shifter would work with any derailleur. Engineers have now calculated the distance the disk needs to rotate for a specific derailleur to shift gears and have put stops (indexing) at these locations on the shifters. As long as the index systems continued to use over-the-bar shifters with both 'index' and 'friction' modes, even if the system came out of calibration from cable stretch or some other reason, you could switch to friction mode and things would work. Even if you needed to replace the derailleur with an incompatible model, you could move a lever, release the indexing, return to the friction system and continue on your way.

The world is no longer as interchangeable. The latest 'advance' is grip shifters which twist, and two-lever, under-bar ratchet systems (eg: 'rapid-fire' or 'express-shifting'). Just push a lever to ratchet up a gear, push another lever to release down a gear. Neither system offers a friction option. To work, the systems must be calibrated. If the derailleur breaks and you can't get a compatible replacement, the shifter is useless. Furthermore, the shifters are virtually impossible to repair. The best thing about a broken ratchet shifter is the opportunity to replace it with a dual-mode, over-the-bar shifter. 'Grip shifters' don't protrude out from the handlebars as far and have fewer moving parts to jam and break, so they are less prone to malfunction. But they are still single mode. If you are selecting a new bike, shifting systems with a friction mode alternative are highly recommended. Short of this, grip shifters are the choice.

Bottom brackets The bottom bracket is the mechanism inside the frame, between the two crank arms that hold the pedals. There are bottom brackets with sealed bearings and bottom brackets with free-bearings. The former are more expensive and harder to service. In contrast, the latter can be serviced worldwide and the bearings are available in many remote areas, assuming there are bicycles in the area.

Brakes It is said that a bicycle will always stop – brakes just let you determine where. If you want that choice, choose your brakes carefully. The heavier the loads and the more downhill travel, the stronger the brakes need to be. Among the strongest type of brakes are cantilever, v-brakes, u-brakes, roller-cam and disk brakes.

Disk brakes are expensive and usually found only on tandems and high-end MTBs. They are the best. V-brakes, u-brakes and roller-cam brakes have tended to be problematic and clog with mud very fast under those conditions. The most cost-effective brakes on the market today are cantilever brakes. The simplest designs use a standard brake cable from the brake lever to the cable hanger between the brakes. Standard brake cables are widely available. The more unique part of cantilever brakes is the way the two sides are connected. The simplest use a straddle-cable between the brakes, with a fixed anchor at one end and an adjustable cable-pinching plate on the other. These can be repaired with a short piece of standard brake cable.

Wheels and spokes There are alloy rims and steel rims. Alloy rims are more effective when wet, easier to keep true and easier to tap dents out of, but they dent more easily. Steel rims are strong, but they are dangerous in wet weather and when they start having problems they can be tough to re-true.

Spokes are available in different gauges. The standard ones are 15g spokes, but 14g spokes are stronger. Double-butted 14/15/14 spokes are strong and light. The preferred material for spokes is stainless steel.

Tyres One of the major features of MTBs is their durable wheels and tyres. The wheel is a small diameter and the rim is wider, so they are stronger, more trouble free and more stable than comparable touring bike wheels. The beefy tyres on MTBs are also relatively trouble free and if properly inflated they are very effective at protecting the rims from dents. The wider the tyre the higher the rolling resistance, so if you will be doing a lot of riding on smooth roads this is a drawback. If you will be cycling on both paved and unpaved surfaces, consider combination knobby tyres with a solid raised centre bead. The centre bead makes easier rolling on paved roads and the knobby tread will help you in the dirt.

Though the supply line for good tyres may be long, the longer life, less down time and additional versatility usually make them a good choice. MTB tyres are becoming more widely available in Africa's large cities. With a little planning ahead it is not hard to keep a sufficient number of spares on hand.

The price bears very little relation to suitability. Cheaper, gum-walled tyres can be better than skin walls at taking the weight on bad roads. On desert pistes deflate your tyres so they bulge, increasing the surface area in contact with the ground. Skin walls invariably split under this kind of treatment. Tyres with little tread proved to be the best at sitting on top of the sand – Chan Sheng and Michelin road tyres are particularly good.

Inner tubes Inner tubes can be made out of a variety of materials and there are at least three types of valves. Airless tubes are also available. The construction material of a pneumatic tube may affect its puncture resistance and will determine what type of glue and patches you need to repair a puncture. The most common inner-tube material is butyl rubber, which can be repaired with the glue and patches found in patch kits around the world.

'Thornproof' tubes are probably better labelled 'puncture resistant'. They are usually two to six times as expensive as regular tubes. Puncture-resistant tubes can be made of extra-thick butyl rubber, or of totally different materials, such as polyurethane plastic. When this punctures it requires its own special patch kit (twice as expensive as kits for butyl tubes). Combination latex/butyl tubes are an expensive hybrid (eight times the price of regular butyl) that can be patched with a standard patch kit.

Puncture-resistant tubes may be of the greatest advantage where there is a lot of glass or short, sharp objects on the road. If there are no sharp objects on the route all tubes are about equal. If you have long thorns to contend with, the best thing to do is avoid them!

Automobile tyres and tubes and most US bicycles use a 'Schraeder valve'. European cyclists often use a 'Presta valve'. The Chinese bikes use a third type of valve. One solution to the valve issue is to make sure that every bicycle has a pump that fits the valve of the tubes on that bicycle. A little more coverage can be gained by using one of the pumps that can be switched from Schraeder to Presta. If Schraeder valves are used, make sure that every pump for automobiles can also be used to inflate the bicycle's tyres.

Airless tubes solve some problems, but they offer a harsher ride, are six to ten times as expensive as regular tubes, at least twice as heavy, have twice the rolling resistance and don't carry heavy loads well. It is still probably most practical, for remote sites, to use butyl compound tubes that are repairable.

Tube protectors Some people praise tube protector strips. I know of several cases where the edge of the strips wore a line of holes in the tube, causing unrepairable punctures. The most plausible explanation is that the hot weather softens the tubes more than the plastic strip, making the tube vulnerable to abrasion from the edge. For off-road riding, there is no final decision on the effectiveness of protective strips. I have never used them in Africa and have only rarely had problems with a flat that I think a tube protector would have prevented. They would be most strongly advised for sections in severe thorn veld.

Pedals and toe-clips If you are likely to be dismounting in dirt (anything from dust to mud), it is best to stay away from any pedals that have hardware on the bottom of your shoes that can clog. This pretty much eliminates cleats and older clipless pedals. Some of the new designs of clip-in systems are not as susceptible to clogging. Conventional pedals give you the flexibility to use multi-purpose shoes, which cut down on the number of pairs of shoes you will have to pack.

You can gain some efficiency as you pedal by using traditional toe-clips. If you are trying them for the first time, or don't have a high level of confidence, don't tighten the straps initially nor when you are in urban traffic, sand, mud, rocks and other technical situations.

Saddles You are going to have an intimate relationship with your saddle; get one that is comfortable. Those that are too narrow or too wide may not support your pelvic bones properly or comfortably. Spring saddles will have you bouncing about all day. Gushy soft and rock hard can also leave you constantly searching for a comfortable way to sit. If you are not used to riding a bike, almost any saddle will leave you sore to begin with. Gel covers on saddles help to reduce saddle soreness, along with a comprehensive application of non-petroleum skin lubricant, bag balm, KY Jelly or something similar over the relevant parts of your body!

The angle of the seat and what you wear also play a role in saddle comfort. Thick seams and bunched clothing between you and your saddle quickly take their toll. Probably the most useful piece of specialised bicycle clothing is padded cycling shorts, which are designed to be worn without underwear.

Accessories The best advice on accessories is, be sure they are strong enough to take the beating they are sure to get. And, attach them securely. If accessories fail while in use it may not be fatal, but it can be very frustrating. Buy equipment that is properly designed and sufficiently durable for its intended use. One way to minimise lost screws is to apply Loctite (medium strength) or tyre patch cement to the threads before bolting on racks and cages.

Racks and packs There are two schools of thought on carrying anything on your back in a rucksack or backpack. Some people find that their back will ache very quickly and will overheat sooner. Even water packs can be a problem for some people and other people swear by them. If you plan to carry things on your back, test your system on a long ride in hot weather before your big journey. Waistpacks (bumbags) are more manageable, but can still be annoying. I like the versatility of a waistpack, but I rig it in front of the handlebars while I am riding.

To carry large loads you need a sturdy rack and saddlebags (panniers). Racks and packs can wear fast and screws loosen quickly when they vibrate for several hours on a daily basis. Choose racks and packs that are sturdy and stable enough to handle the conditions they will be subjected to. The weak points on racks tend to be the welds and eyelets. The weak points on panniers tend to be where the hooks screw into the backing.

Bicycles travel best if the weight of any load is distributed evenly and kept low. Four slim packs, two front and two rear, are better than two giant bulging ones. If you are travelling with only a moderate amount of baggage (say 10kg/22lb) you can get by with just a rear rack and medium-size panniers on each side. If the weight is too heavy in the rear the front wheel becomes hard to handle and you will expend extra energy trying to keep the bike under control. For heavy loads split the weight between front and rear.

Assuming you are looking at panniers made with strong materials and good workmanship, the trade-off tends to be between waterproofness and pockets to help you keep things organised. Regardless of which feature you favour, packing your items in plastic bags will help them stay more organised in a one-

3

compartment waterproof pannier, and will help them stay more waterproof in a multi-compartment pannier.

Strong lighter-weight racks divide into two groups: those made with aluminium rod or with steel alloy tubing. I have seen a lot of aluminium racks break and they tend to be hard to fix in the field. I have never seen a steel alloy tubing rack break, though if it did it would be easier to get it repaired.

The best mount is to screw the rack directly onto the frame. Look for a frame with rack braze-ons on the seat-stays and threaded eyelets on the axle drop-outs. If you expect to be riding on roads, trails or streambeds with high rocks or roots DO NOT USE low-rider racks. Low-riders will give your packs more of a beating than on racks that hold them higher. And if one of those rocks or roots gets hold of your pannier you may take a beating as well.

If you will be travelling on rough roads, it is preferable that the attaching system for the packs consists of strong hooks and non-stretch webbing straps with buckles or Velcro fasteners. Packs with suspension systems that rely solely on elastic cords and springs can bounce off when you hit bumps and pot-holes. Similar advice applies for attaching articles to the top of the rack: you will have more flexibility and fewer problems if you use non-elastic nylon webbing straps with buckles instead of elastic straps, shock cords or bungee cords. Webbing is also lighter.

Handlebar bags or waistpacks are not essential, but they are very convenient for cameras, snacks, sun lotion, notepads, etc. As they sit so high, you don't want to carry too much weight in a handlebar bag.

The advice on water-bottle cages is the same as for racks; they should be sturdy enough to handle the conditions they will be subjected to. It's best if they mount into braze-ons on the frame.

Fenders and kickstands Fenders and kickstands can be more of a disadvantage than an advantage: on trains, planes, buses and during the course of a normal day, fenders get knocked out of alignment. They are inconvenient to detach, reattach and keep adjusted. In dry weather they keep a little sand off the chain. In rain they will keep you happy and stop the chain from being washed, but if you ride off paved roads, they can quickly clog with mud and become a major aggravation.

If you have a rear rack, a less fragile (although less thorough) protection is available from snap-on commercial products which can be fitted to the top of the rack. Alternatively, you can improvise by cutting up a 1.5-litre water bottle and taping it onto the racks to provide a splash guard which keeps body, drive train and baggage drier.

The disadvantage of kickstands is that they are often not designed to support the weight of a loaded touring bike. If your bike is going to be fully loaded most of the time most kickstands are not worth the bother. You will have more success finding walls and other things to lean it against.

Mirrors Rear-view mirrors are not a substitute for good cycling technique, but they are useful. They tend to lead a rough life on tour. Whether they are attached to the handlebar, helmets or glasses, they tend to get a good bashing and have a short lifespan. I still love them.

Lights It is generally a good rule of thumb to make every effort to stay off the roads at night. A disproportionate number of accidents happen at night, and they are often fatal. If you have to be on the road after dark, lights and reflectors are essential. Plan ahead for your lighting system. If you don't expect to be riding at night much, you won't need a particularly elaborate one.

There is a choice of four kinds of power source. In ascending order of initial cost, they are: battery, generator, rechargeable battery, and combo generator/rechargeable battery. Prices can range from US$2 to US$100. Your budget, location and pattern of use will dictate which is the best system for you.

A versatile solution is to use a headlamp. These strap around your helmet or head and provide hands-free light on or off the bike. If you decide on battery power, choose a model that uses batteries that are easily replaced (D, C and AA are the most common worldwide). Remember that rechargeable batteries need a charger and electrical current or a solar cell to recharge.

Locks It seems that the further you are from the New York- and London-style cities of the world, the less sophisticated the bike thieves, the rarer the bolt cutters and the less need there is for heavy locks and chains. While on tour, my bike is usually loaded and conspicuous, securely stored at the hotel, or left for only a few minutes while I run an errand. In the latter cases I lock it. I use a rather ordinary lock and long cable. The long cable is attached to a fixed object to prevent snatch-and-ride. If you expect to be parking your bike unattended in cities, the more sophisticated your locking system needs to be.

Tools and spare parts To fully enjoy the self-sufficiency and independence that a bicycle can provide, you need to carry a few tools and spare parts – and know how to use them. They do not add much weight and could prevent you from having to push your bike on a long walk or having a long wait for a taxi. Select the tools and spare parts you need to do basic adjustments and maintenance on your bicycle and any special tools if your bicycle has esoteric components. Check with your local bike club to find out about classes on bike maintenance, if you need to bone up on this.

For a long solo trip, or any kind of group trip when supply lines could be long, bring enough tools and spare parts to be able to completely overhaul your bike and repair everything, short of a broken frame or rim. Essentially turn yourself into a mini-portable bike shop. If you are in a group of fewer than ten, usually only one complete set of these tools needs to be brought on a trip, though everyone should have their own tools for a patch and basic adjustments. The group leader or their designate is responsible for organising group tools.

If you should need a spare part or tool sent to you in an emergency, DHL and other worldwide package services are now available in most African capitals and many other major African cities. You will need a contact back home who can buy a replacement part and send it out via courier. Unfortunately, the shipping is not cheap.

WATER Dehydration can hit very quickly. Feeling thirsty is not a good indication; by then you could well be in serious trouble already. Basically there is no substitute for drinking plenty of water in a timely manner.

Water bottles It is essential to take a water bottle on every trip. In hot weather you will be drinking a litre of water or more every 15km (10 miles). For long trips you need a large water supply, such as water bags. Be sure you have sufficient water capacity for the kind of travel you plan. Safe drinking water is getting increasingly available in Africa, but it is still problematic in many places. It is also possible that some areas have no water during the dry seasons. Even when there is water you may find the pump that you expect to use is broken.

A tip is to use white-coloured water bottles, as the water inside doesn't heat up quite as much as in coloured or clear bottles.

Water purification A heavy, relatively expensive and high-tech option is to carry a filtering water pump. There are several brands of differing quality available, priced from US$30 to US$200. If you don't have a filter and are out of water, a few water purification tablets can save your life. Carry some on every trip. However, I don't like to rely on them because they can 'purify' your system in the same way that they purify the water – some of the organisms they kill are highly beneficial and protect you from pathogens. You don't want a purified intestinal tract.

FOOD AND COOKING UTENSILS Even if you start the day with a good breakfast and full of energy, as the day goes on you will burn it up. If you do not eat again, the calories will be consumed and you will reach a state of hypoglycaemia, or low blood sugar. It can hit you very quickly and leave you dead in your tracks. On any trip have extra food with you at all times. It needs to provide not just quick, but also sustainable, energy. Breads, local pastries, biscuits and bananas are widely available and are good choices. You should carry emergency packets of dried food for times of need. The dehydrated meals available from camping and outdoor shops are expensive and none too generous in size, so unless you are rich with a small appetite, you will have to look at alternatives. Good buys, particularly if weight is a problem, are packet soups, packets of instant Chinese noodles and other dried 'instant' food.

There's a wide range of lightweight billycan sets, though if you go for collapsible pots and pans pay particular attention to handles and how they clip or hook on. If some plastic slot-on handles chip you will never get them to stay put again.

PERSONAL EQUIPMENT

Helmets and gloves Many sports present a risk of head injury. Bicycling definitely has this hazard also, and it warrants precaution. Scrapes and broken bones heal, but scrambled brains may not. Helmets are not a substitute for good skills and judgement, and they won't prevent an accident, but they can reduce the severity of the consequence. Compared with the lifetime cost of a head injury or even death, the cost of wearing a helmet is small. I know of several crashes in remote locations of Africa where the cyclist's helmet took a hard hit and the cyclist rode on. None of these cases involved an automobile.

In direct sun, a helmet also serves to protect your head, which significantly reduces fatigue.

The value of gloves is similar to that of a helmet. Gloves don't prevent accidents but they can reduce injuries, such as the amount of gravel embedded in your palms. They are also invaluable in reducing road vibration.

Clothing On extended tours in remote areas all clothing – and bodies – get really filthy, as there can be a long time between washing opportunities. Perhaps the hardest aspect of travelling by bike is going for two weeks at a time without a decent wash, sweating every day in the same smelly clothes. Even if you are in an area where your body and day's clothing are being washed nightly, as the trip progresses, it is easy to get increasingly sloppy about things, for example cycling in flip-flops after shoes become too smelly and start falling apart. Leather gloves get forgotten for the same reasons. Don't lose sight of why these items were chosen in the first place and do have a plan for replacing them.

In choosing your clothes consider comfort, visibility and social standards. You can never make yourself too visible as a cyclist. Brightly coloured cotton T-shirts work well. Special cycling shorts have padding in the crotch, relatively long legs and no heavy inseams. Leather in cycling shorts is less durable than shorts with good synthetic material.

If you are going to be cycling at dawn, dusk or at night, an oversize, long-sleeved white shirt is an excellent item. It can be slipped on over anything and does not take up much space. A long-sleeved shirt also doubles during the day as protection from the sun. By covering your arms, you will reduce the amount of moisture you lose (for more information see *Health* in *Chapter 5*, page 117). Worn separately or together, a medium-weight sweater (or pile jacket) and nylon wind jacket will prepare you for a variety of changes in temperature and weather conditions. A pair of loose trousers or a wraparound skirt that can be slipped on over your cycling shorts will make you more presentable away from the bike in most cultures.

You can get shoes specially designed for cycling, but they tend to be uncomfortable to walk in. If you have a pair of shoes that you can cycle in without getting cramp in your feet and also walk in, then they are probably fine for general bicycle touring. As a rule cheaper athletic shoes have stiffer soles, so are better for cycling. If your feet get cramp using multi-purpose shoes to cycle in, then you will need to have two pairs of shoes.

Dust and exhaust are another problem. The irritation from exhaust can be the worst. When pollutants reach a choking level, a bandana over the mouth and nose helps considerably.

Sunglasses If you are used to sunglasses, you will want to wear them most days. They will not only protect your eyes from the sun but also keep dust out of your eyes and reduce eye fatigue from the drying wind. Do not wear sunglasses with opaque side blinders. They restrict peripheral vision, which is very important if you have to manoeuvre in traffic or swerve to avoid a hazard. In the afternoon, just when you are ready to take off your sunglasses, new irritants appear: gnats and small bugs. If you are going to be riding at dusk, it is worth buying a pair of glasses with clear lenses.

First-aid kit When people are in unfamiliar surroundings they can receive more injuries than usual. A lot of these are cuts and scrapes. Carry a first-aid kit and be able to give minor first aid. Prompt attention to even the smallest scratch is very important.

For an extended tour you should also prepare a medicine kit with prescription medicines and remedies for headaches, colds, upset stomachs, allergies and other common ailments. If possible get pills in 'blister packs' or individually packaged forms. Bulk-packed pills tend to vibrate into dust on long cycle tours. If you take a prescription drug, carry a duplicate prescription that gives the generic name.

Camping equipment You only need camping gear if you are going to camp. If you are taking a tent and/or stove, make sure you have all the pieces before you leave.

One of the problems with camping on a cycling tour is the security of your belongings – you're pretty much tied to your camp. A second problem is when it rains in Africa, it generally rains buckets, so no tent is going to be as nice as the simplest hotel room. When it is not the rainy season, what you really need, included in many hotel rooms, is a free-standing bug net.

The most practical of these is made by Long Road Travel Supplies (*111 Avenida Dr, Berkeley, CA 94708, USA;* ℡ *800 359 6040 (USA or Canada) or 510 540 4763 (USA only);* f *510 540 0652 (USA only);* e *sales@longroad.com; www.longroad.com*).

If you either take a tent or plan to sleep under the stars in your bug net, it is useful (if not essential) to have a dedicated ground cloth, ie: a piece of plastic, a woven mat, an old sheet, etc.

To self-cater you need not only a cooker, but also the pots, pans and utensils to use with it. You will also need space to carry some staples that you will need

3

EQUIPMENT

- bicycle
- helmet
- cycling gloves
- luggage rack(s)
- water-bottle cage
- panniers
- toe-clips
- mudguards
- rear-view mirrors
- lights
- cable and lock
- tool bag

SPARES AND TOOLS

- panniers, eg: Overlander by Carradice (www.carradice.co.uk)
- spare tyres (number depends on length of tour)
- inner tubes (number depends on length of tour)
- puncture-repair kit
- pump
- tyre levers
- gear and brake cables
- brake pads
- lubricants: grease and oil
- bearings
- wires and straps
- pliers
- a set of Allen keys
- cable cutter
- spoke tensioner
- set of spanners
- freewheel or cassette remover tool
- screwdrivers, blade and Phillips
- set of cone wrenches
- spokes
- box of nuts and bolts, etc
- chain link extractor
- gear brush or old toothbrush

MEDICAL

- rehydration mix and spoon
- gauzes, bandages and creams
- suture kit
- anti-malaria tablets
- antibiotics
- antacids
- antihistamine cream and/or tablets
- prescription medicine
- eye ointment
- non-petroleum skin lubricant
- Paracetamol or acetaminophen
- tooth repair kit

WATER

- filtering water pump
- Travelwell military water purifiers
- water bags or bottles sufficient for your tour

COOKING

- Coleman's multi-fuel cooker
- cooking pots
- spoons
- plastic bowls
- plastic cups
- penknife or pocket knife

CAMPING EQUIPMENT

- tent
- sleeping mats
- sleeping bags
- nylon string
- towel
- torch

MISCELLANEOUS

- maps
- whistles (as a warning and signal)
- binoculars
- compass
- camera

frequently but won't want to buy for every meal, like cooking oil, salt, pepper, sugar and spices.

The most versatile stoves are multi-fuel designs. Mountain Safety Research (MSR) and Coleman make ones that are highly regarded. You will need a safe container for carrying fuel. Sigg bottles work well for this. Make sure you have enough fuel storage capacity to last between fuelling points.

Other items for bicycle touring Depending on your plans there are a number of other special items worth taking:

- If staying in local houses or small guesthouses that don't necessarily provide linen, take sheets and a towel.
- If travelling in the cold season or at altitude, you might want to take a sleeping bag or blanket as well as the above.
- Rubber thongs or flip-flops are good for those slimy loos.
- Business cards are useful to impress officials and honour requests for your address.
- Extra passport photos are good for gifts and if bureaucracy invents an unexpected new form or you need to apply for an additional visa.
- Binoculars are good in game parks but otherwise they are just extra weight.
- Camera, film and batteries because some may be hard or expensive to obtain *en route*.

OTHER TIPS FOR CYCLISTS

Accommodation and food If you plan to stay overnight outside major cities and tourist destinations, which is the norm for bicycle tourists, it is usually difficult to plan your accommodation too specifically without the help of a travel consultant who has been there. In small towns and villages you may find you have no choice at all. You will get to stay in the best – and probably only – hotel in town. Where there is a choice it is often determined by price, so your selection will be dictated by your budget.

Many budget African hotels have only a few rooms and beds, so if you are travelling with a large group your choices may already be narrowed and the group may exceed the capacity of a village hotel. While camping is an option, we tend not to camp for a combination of reasons: you have to carry more gear (both shelter and cooking) or include a support vehicle (which negates much of any savings); setting up and taking down a camp uses time that is better spent on being more involved in seeing Africa; camping tends to be on the outskirts of towns and separated from the community.

I prefer to be more immersed in the village. The modest cost of most accommodation and meals does more to help the village economy and may be no more expensive than camping. Furthermore, many parts of Africa don't lend themselves to camping and there can be more security problems. Meal planning is similarly influenced by budget and by the availability of markets, cooking facilities and restaurants. In rural areas selection may be so limited as to constitute no choice. But if you are in an area where any Africans are travelling, cooked food is usually available.

Seeing wildlife One of the best experiences is seeing free-range animals from the freedom of a bicycle seat. If you know where to look it is possible to see a wide variety of wildlife and birdlife from a bicycle, but with the continuing encroachment on wildlife habitats by man, this is further and further away from inhabited areas.

3

If you choose to search for wildlife, be selective about your objectives. These are wild animals and, when threatened, they can be very dangerous. They have their own ideas on how to handle intrusions into their personal space. I have seen baboons and elephants from a bicycle in Burkina Faso, Togo and Zimbabwe, watched giraffes, zebras and gazelles in Kenya and Cameroon and enjoyed monkeys jumping overhead in Ghana and Liberia. I once heard the growl of a lion while on a bicycle and an elephant has chased me – not a relaxing experience.

Without an experienced guide, do not go in search of Cape buffalo, lions, elephants or rhinos by bicycle or on foot. Most countries help you with this by not allowing bicycles or foot travel in the major game parks. To see the big game you will have to store your bike and get into vans for a day or two. Unless you pre-arrange it, you will not find transport for game drives waiting at the park entrance. Usually game-watching safaris begin from major cities, so you need to plan accordingly.

4

Organised Tours

The concept of organised overland tours was pioneered in the mid 1960s by Encounter Overland. A number of 'fly by the seat of the pants' companies were formed, which soon began venturing across Asia and Africa with little back-up but a hammer and screwdriver. By the 1970s overland was booming and with its success came an equally rapid expansion in adventure travel. So successful were the destinations that the big travel companies finally followed suit, making 'adventure' a fashionable holiday. Sadly, overland and, to a degree, those off-beat original trips are now dwindling in popularity. Political events and, more often, bureaucracy at home and to some extent across the Third World, rear their ugly heads over the much cherished and fortunate freedoms of those who live in the West. It is to the credit of the few remaining overland and adventure companies that such travel is still an option.

If you have limited time, then an organised overland trip may be the best choice for you. Of course, you will need to sacrifice a degree of independence and be prepared to live and travel with a large group. However, there are quite a few compensations for this cheaper option.

How do these compensations add up today? There will be none of the planning, preparation and expense involved in getting your own vehicle ready. No *carnets*, no spare parts to worry about, no engines to overhaul and definitely no greasy hands to clean. There will be none of the hassles in dealing with border officials; you can just lie back while some other mug – usually the co-driver – deals with any cantankerous officials. You can enjoy the mesmerising lethargy induced by long hours in the truck and the camaraderie of like-minded travellers, while the countries roll by. You might even fall in love! Some of you may already be wondering why you would even think of taking your own vehicle!

There is little pre-planning to do. The company will brief you about things like visas, vaccinations, insurance and what to pack for the trip. All you need to do is be on time for departure. There are trips to suit all budgets. The company will be familiar with the routes, security, daily planning, good and bad places to camp and where to get water, fuel and food. The driver will have done most, if not all, of the trip at least once before.

Those who do choose an organised tour will probably never realise just how much they have been protected from African bureaucracy. Unless the group is very large, border crossings are likely to be quicker than for those learning the ropes as they go along. Most trucks operate some kind of rota system, giving those not on cooking duty time to explore at the end of the day. Tasks can be more efficiently divided and shared out. Travelling independently, you have to deal with all the daily tasks of guarding the vehicle, motor maintenance, shopping, pitching camp, making a fire, purifying water, cooking, cleaning and so on. Also, on a group overland trip, costs such as fuel, equipment, spares, *carnets* and insurance are spread across a much larger group.

Security is one of the most significant differences between the two options. The biggest headache for independent travellers is the need for constant vigilance over their vehicle and its contents. This can make it difficult to get away from the vehicle, perhaps reducing the possibilities for hiking and visiting more inaccessible spots. With an organised tour, there are more people to ensure a permanent security rota, allowing members to leave their gear behind and take off by foot, canoe, train or bus. Individuals can generally leave the tour at any time and travel independently (at their own expense) to a pre-arranged rendezvous point.

So what are the disadvantages of organised trips? You will have to put up with long hours in the back, covered in dust, sitting next to the obnoxious member of the group. Despite some pretence of democracy, you will definitely have less input when the driver dictates that safety, security and the well-being of the group take precedence. You will have to muck in with the daily chores, buying group food, cooking and, dare we say it, washing up 20 people's plates and mugs, as well as the black pots and pans. You will definitely have to push the truck out of sand and probably have to dig it out of thick sticky mud. You might fall out with your better half or significant other. Does this sound like fun?

There is also the lack of independence, which is why most of us consider doing a trip to Africa in the first place. The routes will be pre-designated and changing them can risk disagreement within the group. The leader will generally permit a measure of democracy, perhaps allowing the trip to deviate a little from the published route, but this isn't the same thing as finding a particularly nice beach and deciding to hang around for a week or so, deciding to miss some countries out altogether or to take a completely different route from the one originally planned. Only independent travel gives you absolute freedom.

Despite the common interest of crossing Africa, there is no guarantee that the members of the group will get along. On a six-month trip the group dynamics would be a university degree subject in its own right. Groups with a good cross-section of participants often work surprisingly well, but then again you could be on the trip that just never gels. You are very unlikely to be landed with an entire group that you can't stand. Although perhaps – no, we won't go there! It mostly requires some team effort, but you don't need to be caged in with the group all the time.

Mixing with the local people is all part of the routine, but perhaps making genuine friendships is more difficult. When a truck comes into town, the people will react very differently from the way they might react to a solitary Land Rover. Then again, coming into town in a solitary Land Rover might not be so relaxing either. So many decisions… Better let someone else make them and relax on an organised tour, or just go to the Maldives instead!

The boxed story opposite may perhaps be a good reason to join an organised tour if you are a little nervous!

THE ROUTES

There are many trips to choose from: two-week tours in Morocco to the original trans-African expeditions. Many of the routes are the same as those outlined earlier. For years the favourite routes were across the Sahara via Tamanrasset to Nigeria and then across the Central African Republic and what was formerly Zaire (DRC) to Nairobi before continuing south to Johannesburg.

Most companies who still operate trans-Africa will take the route from Morocco via Mauritania and through much of west Africa. However, with persistent problems in the Congo, some groups still fly to Nairobi, usually from Accra in Ghana, Douala in Cameroon or Libreville in Gabon. Another truck will then be waiting in Nairobi, where the trip will continue around east Africa before continuing south. The eastern

We'd been driving for hours, with nowhere to pull off the side of the new tarmac road, when we saw a small dirt track off to the left. That would have to do. A tin of Sainsbury's vegetable salad from our emergency reserves, and a cup of tea.

Halfway through our drinks, a plain white Toyota pulled up behind us. Five men got out, with large guns at the ready. That's it, we are going to be robbed, it's finally going to happen. We said our Salaams, and Good Mornings in case they weren't Muslims. Bob shook hands with them and Siân nodded her head respectfully from the interior of the vehicle. No-one spoke English, but it was intimated that we should drink up and get back on the road immediately. Wow, was this scary? They could have smiled a bit. Well, we hadn't been robbed yet. 'Police,' they claimed, but it was not in any way obvious. Local warlords, more likely.

With our adrenalin levels at an all-time high, we gulped down the remains of our tea and drove quickly back onto the main road, where we stopped at the next settlement, a small scruffy collection of permanent but temporary-looking shacks. At the pharmacy, the only proper shop in town, the man spoke English and translated. Were we international spies? Even spies have to stop for tea. It was all quite absurd, but no-one demanded any money and, after further consultations, the episode was closed. They decided we couldn't possibly really be spies – no, they drink alcohol, not tea. As for 'shaken not stirred', this experience had been a cocktail of both emotions!

Needless to say, we did not stop again on the side of the road until we reached a fuel station.

Nile route has opened up over the last couple of years and a few companies are now running trips each way between Cairo and southern Africa via Ethiopia. It is possible to link these with extensions into the Middle East and Asia. A limited number of shorter trips now operate in west Africa, but costs are higher. A few operators have recently run new trips in Libya and Tunisia.

Currently there is a boom in overland truck travel between Nairobi and Cape Town, either by routes through Malawi and Mozambique, or west through Zambia to Victoria Falls and Namibia. These shorter tours allow you to fly into a region for a few weeks and get a taste of it in a concentrated burst. Shorter expeditions also mean you can add them into your schedule once you arrive in a particular area, so giving you even greater freedom of movement. An organised tour could easily fit in with other parts of your journey by combining it with a hired car. Often, as one region closes off, others open up; that's the beauty and intrigue of Africa.

Throughout east and southern Africa there are now a number of good local operators. Smaller companies in South Africa (and previously in Zimbabwe) now offer a variety of expeditions, including South Africa, Mozambique, Namibia and Botswana. Local tours can respond to changing conditions much faster than the UK-based operators, perhaps providing a more interesting trip. The downside is that you have no way of assessing the quality of their operation until you arrive, and you probably have no 'comeback' options if you have a major complaint.

WHAT TO EXPECT

Of course, the way in which the tours are organised varies from company to company. They will generally organise briefing sessions to introduce themselves and explain how the trip will work, the everyday practicalities and precisely what you need to arrange in advance in the way of documents, vaccinations and so on.

They will usually also offer or suggest a comprehensive insurance policy, essential for any form of travel. Don't leave home without it.

Most tour operators aim to make the experience feel as close to independent travel as possible. As mentioned, there will be a fairly democratic approach to deciding on day-to-day details. Members of the group will normally set up a rota to cope with all the daily chores, especially cooking and security. Before leaving, most trucks will be partially stocked with food supplies, but fresh items will be bought locally and shopping will generally be the responsibility of those on cooking duty for the day.

Even where a company provides a cook as part of its team, you will be expected to help out with much of the actual work, with the cook acting more as an adviser. Participants will also be expected to volunteer for additional jobs such as stores, fire-lighting, water purification, security, first aid and rubbish collection. These vary from company to company and according to the number of people on the trip. Many drivers will also suggest the option of setting up a bar, which tends to be a popular job!

You will normally pay a deposit on booking. Most companies ask for a kitty at the beginning of the trip to cover food and other communal expenses, but others include this within the overall cost of the trip. Some companies only include transport; others will cover camping, game-park fees and other admission charges. It is important to be clear what is and what is not included in the basic price. A few companies add a 'Local Payment' in addition to the main charges. This may cover direct costs *en route* such as national park entrance fees etc. Remember to add in the cost of any airfares when you are budgeting for your trip. These will not be included in the tour operators' cost.

You will generally have to supply your own bedding, but tents are normally provided. Sleeping is generally in shared, two-person tents. Check the availability of camp beds and mosquito nets, as most do not supply these.

Most companies use Mercedes trucks, MAN or Scania, and the odd old Bedford, customised with their own seating configuration. They have very different layouts, but all of them can accommodate a group of around 18 to 24 people. South African companies often use Japanese trucks, (Izuzu or Hino); some are very well designed.

A very few trucks still pack luggage and tents into a separate trailer, making more space in the truck itself. It is worth checking out the seating design of trucks in which you are thinking of travelling. Has it been organised simply to fit in the greatest number of bodies, or does it look relatively comfortable with a decent view? Does it offer forward-facing or inward-facing seats? You will be spending a long time in that truck, so you ought to be quite sure you are happy with the layout.

Your drivers/leaders are the ones who can make your trip that bit better, but remember their job is an incredibly demanding one. They also have to be a motor mechanic, a diplomat, an actor, a social worker, an expert on everything and a friend to everyone. Most companies have extensive training programmes for their drivers, including both workshop experience and travelling with another leader/driver.

Some companies also provide couriers or cooks. On a short journey a good all-round leader/driver should be adequate. On a longer trip a second team member is invaluable in order to help with visas, bureaucracy and paperwork, as well as helping out with the driving and mechanics.

CHOOSING A TOUR

You can pay anything from £2,500 to £5,000 for a full trans-African trip, but the variations between them are not just a matter of cost. The range of choices offered can be quite bewildering. Make sure that you find out exactly what is included in the price and how the trip is organised.

As with most things, the general rule is that the more you pay the more you get. The cheaper end of the market can also tend to have less experienced leaders/drivers and use older and less dependable vehicles, though this is not always the case. Leaders/drivers with the larger operators keep in constant touch with full-time staff back at base, who can help out in the event of problems or emergencies.

One-off expeditions and budget trips are less secure when the going gets tough, but may offer a different style of trip. You might have to accept the possibility that the truck may break down more frequently, but this is not always the case. Anyone can break down in any place!

OTHER OPTIONS

For some parts of Africa it can be more beneficial to take shorter trips with local operators, some of whom will have representatives in Europe and elsewhere. Travelling with a European operator affords you the benefit of more financial security, of course. These shorter expedition options apply in particular to the Sahara, parts of west Africa and most of southern Africa. Two or three weeks in the Sahara, when safe, to places such as northern Mali, the Ténéré in Niger, Ennedi in Chad, Tassili N'Ajjer/Hoggar in Algeria are best done with specialist operators, who have experienced local guides and who travel with at least two 4x4 vehicles. Morocco, Libya, Egypt, Tunisia, Mauritania, Senegal, Gambia, Ghana and, to a degree, Gabon, in the west are other countries where local trips organised through European tour operators have a lot to offer. In east Africa there's no shortage of offers in Kenya, Tanzania, Uganda, Rwanda and Ethiopia. Of course there is a plethora of these shorter tours in South Africa, Namibia and Botswana in particular. Anyone planning a trip to unknown Guinea or Sierra Leone yet?

OVERLAND OPERATORS

UK

Acacia Adventure Holidays ☎ 020 7706 4700; e info@acacia-africa.com; www.acacia-africa.com. Operating since the 1980s, originally as an overland company. Now a more varied programme, including safaris, trekking, diving & short overland.
Africa in Focus ☎ 01803 770956; e info@africa-in-focus.com; www.africa-in-focus.com. Photographic specialist trips, mostly in southern Africa.
Africa Travel Centre ☎ 020 7387 1211 & 0845 450 1520; f 020 7383 7512; e sales@africatravel.co.uk; www.africatravel.co.uk. Offers a wide range of overland options including truck tours, self-drive in southern Africa, camping & coach tours, motorbike safaris, balloon safaris & game-lodge safaris.
African Trails ☎ 01580 761171; e sales@africantrails.co.uk; www.africantrails.co.uk. Have been running trips since 1980 with 1 driver & courier. No age limit quoted – most passengers 18–35. Also offers Kenya/Tanzania game-parks tour, & shorter trips in southern Africa. Nairobi to Cape Town.
Dragoman ☎ 0870 499 4484; e info@dragoman.co.uk; www.dragoman.com; & also

Encounter Overland (now part of Dragoman) www.encounter.co.uk. Has been running trips for over 20 years, using uniquely designed 16-ton Mercedes trucks with a crew of 2. Offers a very wide range of long & shorter tours in most of Africa. Also runs trips which feature visits to community projects helping local people to maintain their culture & benefit from tourism. Age guideline 18–45; most in their 20s & 30s.
Drive Botswana ☎ 0161 408 4316; f 0161 880 2414; e info@drivebotswana.com; www.drivebotswana.com
Exodus ☎ 0870 240 5550; e sales@exodus.co.uk; www.exodus.co.uk. Company with over 30 years' experience, using Mercedes trucks. Age range mainly 17–45 on trips from 2–12 weeks, mostly in east & southern Africa.
Expedition World ☎ 01243 789264; e sianpj@hotmail.com; www.expeditionworld.com. A small specialist company with a particular interest in trips to the Sahara (Algeria, Niger, Libya & Chad) plus Asia overland for older travellers.

4

Explore Worldwide ✎ 0870 333 4001; f 01252 760001; e res@exploreworldwide.com; www.explore.co.uk. Small group holidays using a mix of hotels, lodges & camping in north Africa, Kenya, Tanzania, Uganda, Malawi, Zimbabwe, Zambia, Botswana & Namibia.
Intrepid www.intrepidtravel.com. Has taken over **Guerba** (www.guerba.com), which had been running overland expeditions & shorter safaris for over 20 years. Off road & 4x4 tours with comfort-added camping & no camp chores.
Keystone Journeys ✎ 01722 620108; e malcolm@asapmz.co.uk; www.keystonejourneys.com. Offers overland & small group adventure in Africa from 7 days to 15 weeks.
Kumuka Expeditions ✎ 0800 068 8855; www.kumuka.com. Overland adventures for independent-minded travellers from 2–9 weeks.

Nomadic Expeditions ✎ 0870 220 1718; www.nomadic.co.uk
Oasis Overland ✎ 01963 363400; e info@oasisoverland.co.uk; www.oasisoverland.co.uk. Small company offering tours in Africa (also the Middle East & South America). Uses Scania & Leyland trucks with a driver/mechanic & courier. Passenger ages generally 18–40. Trips from 3 weeks to 7 months.
On the Go Tours ✎ 020 7371 1113; e info@onthegotours.com; www.onthegotours.com
Overland Club ✎ 0800 731 8841 (Freephone) or 01740 623633; e info@overlandclub.com; www.overlandclub.com. Budget camping expeditions throughout Africa from 2–26 weeks, for those who are free-spirited & have a passion to experience the real Africa.

Many of the UK-based companies above also have representatives in Nairobi, Harare and South Africa, as well as in Australia and the US. There are also other expedition companies worldwide. Here are some to look out for:

USA AND CANADA
The Adventure Center 1311 63rd St, Suite 200, Emeryville, CA 94608, USA; ✎ 800 227 8747; e tripinfo@adventurecenter.com; www.adventurecenter.com

Trek Holidays ✎ 888 456 3522 (toll free); *Calgary* ✎ 403 283 6115; *Vancouver* ✎ 604 734 1066; *Edmonton* Westcan Treks ✎ 780 439 0024; www.trekholidays.com

SOUTH AFRICA There are many companies offering specialist overland tours specific to southern Africa, with representation in South Africa only. You will need to shop around and your best bet is to visit a local travel agent for further information. Here are a few of these companies.

Affordable Adventures PO Box 1008, Sunninghill, 2157 Johannesburg; ✎ 011 465 9168; f 011 467 3913; m 083 325 7218; e info@affordableadventures.co.za; www.affordableadventures.co.za
Africa Tours Pretoria; ✎ (012) 333 7110; e info@destination.co.za; www.destination.co.za
Drifters Adventours PO Box 4712, Cresta, 2118 Johannesburg; ✎ 011 888 1160; f 011 888 1020; e drifters@drifters.co.za; www.drifters.co.za
Felix Unite ✎ 021 425 5181; e info@felixunite.com; www.felixunite.com

Harvey World Travel ✎ 0860 62 63 64; e adminoffice@harveyworld.co.za; www.harveyworld.co.za
Karibu Safari *Natal* ✎ 031 563 9774; *Johannesburg* ✎ 011 462 6414; e karibu@karibu.co.za; www.karibu.co.za
Umkulu Adventures ✎ 021 853 7952; f 021 853 0153; e umkulu@iafrica.com; www.umkulu.co.za. A budget operator.
Wildlife Africa ✎/f 011 782 3410; e info@wildlifeafrica.co.za; www.wildlifeafrica.co.za

EAST AFRICA
Africa Expedition Support Nairobi; www.africaexpeditionsupport.com. Dynamic company run by experienced overlanders & offering fully guided self-drive trips from Cairo to Cape Town or Cape

Town to Nairobi. A 4x4 vehicle leads these trips. Contact Debs or Thiemo.
Swala Safaris Arusha, Tanzania; ✎ +255 27 254 5144; www.swalasafaris.com

5

Practicalities

RED TAPE

PASSPORTS Make sure you have plenty of spare pages in your passport! Most visas will take up a whole page each, and sometimes the whole of the opposite page for entry and exit stamps when you reach the country. Some African countries are extremely 'stamp happy', and use up a lot of space. You may come across checkpoints where all your documents will be scrutinised and your passport stamped, sometimes over and over again. Some countries, like Egypt and Libya, put details of you and your vehicle in your passport as well as in the *carnet* (see below).

If you have dual nationality it may be worth taking both passports, as some visas may be cheaper for different nationalities. However, this can sometimes give you more problems at borders where you need to produce both passports. Some officials may act very suspiciously over a person holding two passports.

Remember you will not be allowed into certain countries if your passport has an Israeli stamp in it. Be aware too that a border stamp could imply a visit to Israel. This can happen at the Egyptian border south of Eilat, even where no Israeli stamps are shown in the passport.

Passport photos You will find when applying for visas that a lot of embassies demand two, and sometimes three, passport photos to attach to your visa application. We suggest you take around 30 passport photos with you; if you need more, it is relatively inexpensive to have your passport photograph taken in most capital cities of Africa.

CARNET DE PASSAGE (CARNET)

What is the *carnet*? The *carnet* is an essential and expensive document for everyone taking a vehicle (including a motorbike) across Africa. It is effectively the passport for the vehicle. *Carnets* are issued by national motoring organisations, eg: the RAC in the UK. This document allows you to import a vehicle into a country temporarily without paying customs duty, which in some cases can be many times its actual value.

Different countries have different regulations on the issue of *carnets*. Unfortunately, however, you cannot just shop around on the international markets, unless you go to the trouble of re-registering your vehicle. The *carnet* must be issued by an authority in the country where the vehicle is registered.

Although a *carnet* is likely to come in useful everywhere, it is not absolutely essential in north and west Africa. If you do not have a *carnet* here, a *laissez-passer* will be issued when you enter the country, for a 'small' fee. You should be able to cover much of western and southern Africa without a *carnet*. In central and east African countries, a *carnet* is essential.

The existence of *carnets* is the main factor that makes selling a vehicle at the end of your journey far more difficult than you might think. When you sell, you have

In 2008 it took us several hours to extricate ourselves from the border customs department in Guinea. The officials there claimed that we should not have been allowed into the country because our *carnet* did not state on the back that it was valid in Guinea. Luckily, after much talking in several languages, it took only a small gift (around £5) to smooth our way out, but following this up with the RAC in the UK was not entirely satisfactory.

Try to get the RAC or *carnet* issuer to list every country to which you will be travelling on the back cover of the carnet. Whatever they say in Europe, it is you who will be there in the jungle or bush trying to move on, not them!

to get your *carnet* discharged by the local customs office. This means the import duty will need to be paid before the deal can go through. Make sure that all the paperwork is correctly processed, or you could face a large bill later on. If you do sell without discharging your *carnet*, the motoring organisation or insurance company is still entitled to recoup the duty from you.

How do I get a *carnet* and how much does it cost? To obtain a *carnet* in the UK, you should contact RAC Carnets (*Great Park Rd, Bradley Stoke, Bristol BS32 4QN;* ☏ *01454 208304;* e *carnets@rac.co.uk; www.rac.co.uk*). For full details, look at http://www.rac.co.uk/web/know-how/going-on-a-journey/driving-abroad/carnet-de-passages.htm.

The cost of the *carnet* has now increased to £150, regardless of the number of pages you require, so you might as well ask for the maximum number. You should make absolutely sure your *carnet* has been validated for all the countries you have requested. Customs officers will check carefully to ensure their country is listed. You may as well play safe and request absolutely every country you may possibly wish to visit – the number of countries covered does not affect the cost.

You will need either to lodge a bank guarantee or deposit equivalent to several times the current value of the vehicle, or to take out a special insurance policy to cover this amount. The sum required is from one-and-a-half times the value of the vehicle for most countries, but up to eight times the value for Egypt. For this reason, you should value the vehicle as low as possible. The carnet-issuing authority reserves the right to adjust the declared value. Current valuations can be obtained from motoring magazines – go for the lowest option.

If you lodge a cash bond, you must send a cheque for the full amount to the RAC, who will hold the money until you return the *carnet* correctly processed to them at the end of your trip. The money will be returned to you without interest.

If you go for the insurance option, insurance is available from R L Davison (*31 Bury St, London EC3A 5AH*). 50% of the premium is refundable on return of the cleared *carnet* to the RAC. In Great Britain, *carnets* are only available from the RAC, and in general from the national motoring authority in the country where the vehicle is registered.

Note that previously *carnets* were issued by the Automobile Association (UK) (*Fanum Hse, Basingstoke, Hants RG21 4EA;* ☏ *0870 600 0371, international* ☏ *+44 191 223 7071;* e *customer.services@theAA.com; www.theAA.com*) and insurance was available from Campbell Irvine Ltd.

How is the *carnet* used *en route?* The *carnet* is a large booklet containing a number of pages that are identical (except for the page numbers). Each page has three sections with details of the vehicle such as chassis number etc. Details about the owner are also shown. When you enter a country the customs officer should stamp, remove and keep the third section. The first section should also be stamped in the entry part as a record. When you leave the country the second section should be stamped, removed and kept by the customs. The official should also stamp the exit part on the first section, which provides a record for you and the motoring association who issued the *carnet*.

The idea of this is that the main customs departments in the countries you visit will collect the two matching halves. If the two halves are not collected they will claim customs duty through the issuing authority. (One might ponder how long these pieces of paper take to find their way to the central customs of some countries.) It is therefore vital that you collect a complete set of entry and exit stamps. If you don't get an exit stamp for a country where you got an entry stamp, you could be in big trouble later on. It could also cost you a lot of money, because the *carnet* may not be cleared.

INTERNATIONAL CERTIFICATE FOR MOTOR VEHICLES Known as a *carte grise* (grey card) wherever French is spoken (even though it is white) it costs around £10, and is a vital investment. Available from motoring organisations, it provides an official-looking summary of the details and serial numbers of your vehicle. In fact we were always asked to produce the original registration document for our vehicle, but it is definitely advisable to have both close at hand at every border, police check-post or rain barrier you come across.

INSURANCE
Medical and personal belongings Medical insurance is essential. Shop around for a good deal, as prices and cover can vary substantially. Travel insurance policies generally include some cover for personal belongings, but this is unlikely to include theft from a vehicle.

Vehicle Comprehensive vehicle insurance is less important. You can try to get insurance through Campbell Irvine (*43 Earls Court Rd, London W8 6EJ;* ✆ *020 7937 6981;* 🖷 *020 7938 2250*). They are experienced in meeting the insurance needs of overlanders, though it is almost impossible nowadays to insure a vehicle for anywhere in Africa through a British insurance company. Currently a British comprehensive insurance policy should cover you for travel within most of Europe – check the back of your certificate.

Third-party vehicle insurance is not available in advance for most areas. It is both advisable and compulsory (policed to varying degrees) to buy third-party insurance locally. Once you reach Senegal, Niger or Mali it is possible to buy a single policy that will cover you for the whole of west Africa. Similarly, you can get another single policy covering central African countries (Cameroon, Chad, Central African Republic, Equatorial Guinea, Gabon and Congo). In Kenya, you can buy a policy to cover almost the whole of southern Africa, except Mozambique, though it may be marked as covered on the policy. Third-party insurance certificates are available at the border in some countries, including Zimbabwe and Zambia.

INTERNATIONAL DRIVING LICENCE These are available from national motoring organisations (such as the AA or RAC) on production of a current driving licence. You must get your international licence in the country where your domestic licence was issued. In the UK the cost is around £6 and requires a copy of your national driving licence and possibly passport details.

PERSONAL REFERENCES References can be useful if you are up against big bureaucratic problems. A reference from a bank or other financial representative can be used to prove that you will not be stranded through lack of funds. A character reference may also be helpful if you are in a tight corner. If at all possible, also get a character reference translated into French.

VISAS If there is any element of protracted red tape concerning a trip across Africa, it is that of obtaining visas. Getting many of the visas in your own country is sometimes more difficult than in neighbouring countries on the way, and it's getting harder and more expensive. Bear in mind, though, that for an African to get a visa to visit almost any country outside the continent is very difficult.

However, it will save you a lot of time *en route* if you can get visas for the first few countries you'll be visiting at the start of your trip, as well as any visas that are difficult to obtain in Africa. Visas for Libya, Sudan, Nigeria and Angola are notoriously difficult to get and it is well worth trying to get them before you leave. Angola may prove impossible beforehand, making planning difficult! Even if they run out before you arrive, at least you have something in your passport and that may just make the difference. For Libya, though, you need an Arabic translation of your passport and an invitation from a Libyan travel agency, who must send a guide to escort you throughout your stay in the country.

For other countries, depending on the route you take and the time you intend to spend in Africa, more often than not your visa will have expired by the time you have arrived in that country. Heading into west Africa, it's easier and cheaper to get them on the borders and within countries such as Burkina Faso, Benin, Togo and even Mali.

It is also not necessarily a good idea to get every visa before you leave, as the political situation in Africa is forever changing and by the time you intend to visit a specific country, it might not be safe or convenient. Clearly, if you are cycling, travelling will take a lot longer than in a vehicle, making visa validity and timing even more important.

On our last three expeditions we were able to get visas for all of the northern African countries in advance (down to and including Ethiopia, Gabon and Nigeria). Just be sure to make it clear when you intend to visit and they will

A VISA SAGA

Some things never change. It took six weeks to get a Sudan visa in 2004; but what happened on an overland trip to Africa in 1976? Some snippets from the diary…

BANGUI 3 JANUARY Crossed the Ubangui River, only to be turned back by the Zaïre Immigration. (The great Zaïre expedition falters before it's begun.)

Now trying for the Sudan visa, but the ambassador is a very bored fellow from Khartoum and has other ideas; he wants to wine and dine our girls before a visa is remotely possible. It's a good job the whole truck isn't loaded with females, or we'd never get out of here. Of course our CAR visa will expire before we get the Sudan one.

Managed a day trip down to the Congo border – that's another version of Zaïre run from Brazzaville not Kinshasa. That's if anyone is running Zaïre, with Mobutu Sese Seko Sese Banga Waza etc etc partying here in Bangui with Big Daddy Idi Amin and Emperor Bokassa.

9 JANUARY Looks like the Sudanese Ambassador is getting bored with our girls; not that anything underhand appears to be going on. Encounter Overland, another party, are here now for visas, so they have become more interesting for the fellow. We might be out of here tomorrow with visas.

We should have known better. Setting off into the darkest corners of Africa, one has inevitably to be fairly optimistic, thinking things will be all right. But setting off with barely enough time is not a good strategy for a successful overland. That though was what we did on our latest venture – London to Durban in 15 weeks, including Guinea, Sierra Leone, Liberia, Timbuktu and the two Congos. We tried to ignore the intermittent news about Angolan visa procurement.

Atakpame in Togo was the crunch point. The trip was going very well, seven weeks to here and on time for Durban by day 105. Then we received another email about the Angolan visa problem again and more web news of people ahead of us. It stopped us dead in our tracks; to go or not to go, that was the question! Of course, we had always known there was a chance that our African expedition might end prematurely this time; that was why we had explored Guinea, Sierra Leone and Liberia first.

This trip was like climbing Mount Everest – only getting to the top and safely back down again would be satisfactory. Now we were stuck on the equivalent of the South Col, not knowing whether to go on or back down. Retreating from here would be a big defeat, but going on could be considered foolhardy, like heading up with bad weather on the slopes above. This was perhaps the 'Hillary Step' of this trip; the decisive moment when we were almost bound to make the wrong choice.

We read that the group in front of us had been refused visas in every embassy that they had tried. Then we read that some motorcyclists who had got into Angola a few months earlier had had to ride through a rebel roadblock at high speed in Congo. They had managed to obtain their Angola visas in Kinshasa after much trouble, but having then arrived in Angola had found mines floating on the roads after the rainy season floods. Was this really what we wanted?

With other commitments in the summer ahead, waiting for weeks in Brazzaville was not a feasible proposition for us. Yet going back 'down' the mountain to the UK was 6,000 miles, even more than going on to South Africa. But 'what if' we got to Kinshasa and we really could not get a visa for Angola? A storm on the last summit ridge! Then the Land Rover would have to be shipped out of Pointe Noire, passing through dangerous rebel country, or we would have to drive back to Libreville, requiring another expensive Gabon visa, followed by uncertain shipping and flights. Frostbite for sure on the ridge. The sensible decision seemed to be to retreat – back to Bamako and Morocco – but it was a decision that was to haunt us for a long, long time.

What is the moral of this story? Try to have sufficient time to give yourself the best options to overcome the most awkward bureaucracy. And yes, be prepared for some regrets later back in Europe of course. Well that's overlanding in Africa these days. Perhaps if we were still 25 years old we would have 'climbed on up the South Summit Ridge' and found the clouds clearing ahead … but then again, perhaps not!

normally post-date the visa. But be careful – we arrived in Ethiopia one day before our visa had apparently been issued, which caused some consternation at the border. Most visas are issued as you go, from embassies in capital cities or consulates in larger towns. Consulates are often a better bet, as embassies can sometimes take several days to process an application, which can mean an enforced lengthy stay in an expensive city if you have several visas to get.

Generally speaking, you should be able to pick up a visa in the capital of a neighbouring country, but do not rely on it. For example, there is no Cameroon consulate in N'Djamena, Chad, despite its being only a few kilometres from the border. Major cities – Dakar, Abidjan, Nairobi, Dar es Salaam and Harare – have embassies for most other African states. Addis Ababa has the most representation when it comes to embassies and consulates, because of Ethiopia's early involvement with the OAU (Organisation of African Unity) and UNECA (United Nations Economic Commission of Africa) in 1958; most countries have some type of representation there. The moral is: if all else fails, go to Addis Ababa!

If there is no embassy in your country, contact the nearest embassy. Nowadays you can often get visa information from their website and download visa application forms. Getting any answers by email about visas, invitation letters, etc would be surprising, though.

Visa agencies It is often easier, and indeed cheaper if you live outside the capital, to get your visas via a specialist visa agency. They will send a courier with your passport to the various embassies, saving you time and effort, and of course money if you are still at work. They may ask you to download the visa application forms from their website, or from the websites of the countries concerned. You then simply complete the forms and send them, together with a cheque and the relevant photographs, and of course your passport, to the agency by registered post. Then you can sit back and get on with the vehicle construction and design. Two visa agencies we can personally recommend are:

Travcour Tempo Hse, 15 Falcon Rd, Battersea, London SW11 2PJ; ✆ 020 7223 5295; f 020 7738 2617; e amanda@travcour.com; www.travcour.com

Home Visas 111 Av Victor Hugo, 75784 Paris Cedex 16, France; ✆ 01 46 21 80 40; f 01 46 21 01 15; e contact@homevisas.com; www.homevisas.com

Visa requirements Specific visa requirements vary according to nationality. Most requirements for European travellers have now been harmonised, apart from special arrangements for UK travellers in most Commonwealth countries and similar arrangements for French nationals in former French colonies. Other travellers, such as those from Australia, New Zealand and the USA, will have to meet different requirements. If in doubt, contact your own embassy for further information.

There are many varying factors that need to be considered when applying for a visa. Firstly, costs can vary considerably from one country to the next, depending on your nationality and where you applied for your visa. On reaching a certain border, even though your embassy, and every guidebook, has told you that you are exempt from needing a visa, you may find that you will still have to pay to have your entry stamped in your passport. This is true when it comes to most Commonwealth nationals. It is a good idea to ask other travellers or locals about the latest status on visa applications for the next country you're visiting.

Remember that you may need a valid yellow fever vaccination certificate in order to obtain some visas.

E EMBASSIES AND CONSULATES

Below is a list of African embassies and consulates in the UK, South Africa, USA and Australia. A good website for further information is www.embassyworld.com, or www.yellowpages.co.za for South African embassies. Note that the details below can change without notice and we recommend you to check these websites for up-to-date information.

You can also check the British Foreign Office website (*www.fco.gov.uk*) travel advice section, which lists the relevant London embassy or consulate for each country. The French equivalent is www.diplomatie.fr/voyageurs and the German is www.auswaertiges-amt.de.

AFRICAN EMBASSIES AND CONSULATES IN THE UK

Algeria (embassy) 54 Holland Park, London W11 3RS; ✆ 020 7221 7800; (consulate) 6 Hyde Park Gate, London SW7 5EW; ✆ 020 7589 6885; algerianembassy@btconnect.com

Angola 22 Dorset St, London W1U 6QY; ✆ 020 7299 9850; f 020 7486 9397; embassyangola.org.uk

Benin Millennium Hse, Humber Rd, nr Staples Corner, London NW2 6DW; ✆ 020 8830 8612; f 020 7435 0665; e l.landau@btinternet.com

Botswana 6 Stratford Pl, London W1C 1AY; ✆ 020 7499 0031 & 020 7647 1000

Cameroon 84 Holland Park, London W11 3SB; ✆ 020 7727 0771–3; f 020 7792 9353

Congo The Arena, 24 Southwark Bridge Rd, London SE1 9HF; ✆ 020 7922 0695

Democratic Republic of the Congo (embassy) 281 Gray's Inn Rd, London WC1X 8QF; ✆ 020 7278 9825; f 020 7278 8497; (consulate) 2 Lowndes St, London SW1X 9ET; ✆ 020 7235 9719

Djibouti Request for visa may be handled by the French Embassy, 58 Knightsbridge, London SW1X 7TJ; ✆ 020 7073 1000; f 020 7073 1004; www.ambafrance-uk.org. Appointments can take 6 weeks.

Egypt 26 South St, London W1Y 6DD; ✆ 020 7499 2401; f 020 7491 1542

Eritrea 96 White Lion St, London N1 9PF; ✆ 020 7713 0096; f 020 7713 0161; e eriembas@erimbauk.com

Ethiopia 17 Prince's Gate, London SW7 1PZ; ✆ 020 7589 7212–5; e info@ethioembassy.org.uk

Gabon 27 Elvaston Pl, London SW7 5NL; ✆ 020 7823 9986; f 020 7584 0047

Gambia 57 Kensington Ct, London W8 5DG; ✆ 020 7937 6316–8; f 020 7937 9095; e gambia@gamhighcom.wanadoo.co.uk

Ghana 13 Belgrave Sq, London SW1X 8PN; ✆ 020 7235 4142; f 020 7245 9552; e ghmfa31@netscapeonline.com

Guinea 48 Onslow Gdns, London SW7 3PY; ✆ 020 7594 4819 or 020 7594 4811 (consular section); e ambaguineeuk@yahoo.co.uk

Ivory Coast 2 Upper Belgrave St, London SW1X 8BJ; ✆ 020 7201 9601

Kenya 45 Portland Pl, London W1N 4AS; ✆ 020 7636 2371–5; www.kenyahighcommission.net

Lesotho 7 Chesham Pl, London SW1 8HN; ✆ 020 7235 5686; f 020 7235 5023; e lhc@lesotholondon.org.uk

Liberia 23 Fitzroy Sq, London W1T 6EW; ✆ 020 7388 5489; f 020 7380 1593

Libya 61–62 Ennismore Gdns, London SW7 1NH; ✆ 020 7589 6120; f 020 7589 6087

Malawi 33 Grosvenor St, London W1K 4QT; ✆ 020 7491 4172–7

Mauritania Closed, so refer to their embassy in Brussels or Paris (see below). In theory the French Embassy (*58 Knightsbridge, London SW1x 7TJ;* ✆ *020 7073 1000; f 020 7073 1004; www.ambafrance-uk.org*) can do it but an appointment takes 6 weeks.

Morocco 49 Queen's Gate Gdns, London SW7 5NE; ✆ 020 7581 5001–4; f 020 7225 3862; e ambalondres@mace.gov.ma

Mozambique 21 Fitzroy Sq, London W1T 6EL; ✆ 020 7383 3800; f 020 7383 3801; www.mozambiquehc.org.uk

Namibia 5 Chandos St, London W1G 9DW; ✆ 020 7636 6244; f 020 7637 5694; e namibia.hccom@btconnect.com

Nigeria (embassy) Nigeria Hse, 9 Northumberland Av, London WC2N 5BX; ✆ 020 7839 1244; f 020 7839 8746; (consulate) 56–57 Fleet St, London EC4Y 1JU; ✆ 020 7353 3776; e information@nigeriahc.org.uk; www.nigeriahc.org.uk

Rwanda 120–122 Seymour St, London W1H 1NR; ✆ 020 7224 9832; f 020 7724 8642; www.ambrwanda.org.uk

Senegal 39 Marloes Rd, London W8 6LA; ✆ 020 7938 4048; f 020 7938 2546; www.senegalembassy.co.uk

Sierra Leone 41 Eagle St, Holborn, London WC1 4TL; ✆ 020 7404 0140; f 020 7430 9862; e info@slhc-uk.org.uk; www.slhc-uk.org.uk

South Africa South Africa Hse, Trafalgar Sq, London WC2N 5DP; ✆ 020 7451 7299; f 020 7451 7284; e general@foreign.gov.za; www.southafricahouse.com

UK EMBASSY ADDRESSES

Embassy addresses and telephone numbers in the UK are regularly updated and published by HMSO in the London Diplomatic List (ISBN 0 11 591746 2). The closest embassy in Europe is normally given for countries which have no embassy in the UK.

Sudan 3 Cleveland Row, London SW1A 1DD; ✆ 020 7839 8080; f 020 7839 7560; e admin@ sudanembassy.co.uk; www.sudanembassy.co.uk
Swaziland 20 Buckingham Gate, London SW1E 6LB; ✆ 020 7630 6611; f 020 7630 6564; e swaziland@swaziland.btinternet.com
Tanzania 3 Stratford Pl, London W1C 1AS; ✆ 020 756 91470; f 020 7491 8817; e tanzarep@ tanzarep.demon.co.uk; www.tanzania-online.gov.uk
Tunisia 29 Prince's Gate, London SW7 1QG; ✆ 020 7584 8117; f 020 7225 2884

Uganda Uganda Hse, 58–59 Trafalgar Sq, London WC2N 5DX; ✆ 020 7839 5783; f 020 7839 8925
Zambia 2 Palace Gate, London W8 5NG; ✆ 020 7589 6655; f 020 7581 1353; e immzhcl@ btconnect.com; www.zhcl.org.uk
Zimbabwe Zimbabwe Hse, 429 Strand, London WC2R 0JR; ✆ 020 7836 7755; f 020 7379 1167; e zimlondon@yahoo.co.uk; www.zimbabwe.embassyhomepage.com

AFRICAN EMBASSIES AND CONSULATES IN FRANCE AND BELGIUM

Angola 19 Av Foch, 75116 Paris; ✆ 1 45 01 58 20; f 1 45 00 33 71
Benin 87 Av Victor Hugo, 75016 Paris; ✆ 1 45 00 98 82
Burkina Faso 16 Pl Guy d'Arezzo, 1180 Brussels; ✆ 02 345 99 12
Burundi Sq Marie Louise 46, 1040 Brussels; ✆ 02 230 45 35
Cameroon Av Brugman 131-133 1060 Brussels; ✆ 02 345 1870
Central African Republic 30 Rue des Perchamps, 75016 Paris; ✆ 01 42 24 42 56
Chad Blvd Lambermont 52, 1030 Brussels; ✆ 02 215 19 75

Djibouti 26 Rue Emile Ménier, 75116 Paris; ✆ 01 47 27 49 22
Equatorial Guinea 29 Bd de Courcelles, 75800 Paris; ✆ 06 61 40 14 01; f 01 42 25 23 12
Guinea Bissau 94 Rue St Lazare, Paris; ✆ 01 45 26 18 51
Mali Av Molière 487, 1050 Brussels; ✆ 02 345 74 32; f 02 344 57 00
Niger 154 Rue de Longchamp, 75116 Paris; ✆ 01 45 04 80 60
Rwanda Av des Fleurs 1, 1150 Brussels; ✆ 02 763 07 38; f 02 763 07 53; also 12 Rue Jadin, 75017 Paris; ✆ 01 47 66 54 20; f 01 42 27 74 69
Togo 8 Rue Alfred-Roll, 75017 Paris; ✆ 1 45 80 12 13; f 1 45 80 06 05

AFRICAN EMBASSIES AND CONSULATES IN SOUTH AFRICA

Algeria 348 Hill St, Hatfield, Pretoria 0083; ✆ 012 342 5074
Angola 1030 Schoenman St, Hatfield, Pretoria; ✆ 012 342 0049; f 012 342 7039
Botswana 24 Amos St, Colbyn, Pretoria; ✆ 012 430 9640; f 012 342 1845
Burundi 1090 Arcadia St, Hatfield, Pretoria; ✆ 012 342 4881; f 012 342 4885
Cameroon 800 Duncan St, Brooklyn, Pretoria; ✆ 012 362 4731; f 012 362 4732; e hicoam@ cameroon.co.za
Congo 960 Arcadia St, Hatfield, Pretoria; ✆ 012 342 5508
Democratic Republic of the Congo 791 Schoemna St, Arcadia, Pretoria; ✆ 012 344 6475/6; f 012 344 4054
Egypt 270 Bourke St, Muckleneuk, Pretoria; ✆ 012 343 1590; e egyptemb@global.co.za
Eritrea 1281 Cobham Rd, Queenswood, Pretoria; ✆ 012 333 1302; f 012 333 2330
Ethiopia 47 Charles St, Mucklenuk, Pretoria; ✆ 012 346 3542; f 012 346 3867
Gabon 921 Schoeman St, Arcadia, Pretoria; ✆ 012 342 4376; f 012 342 4375

Ghana PO Box 12537, Hatfield, Pretoria; ✆ 012 342 5847
Guinea 346 Orient St, Arcadia, Pretoria; ✆ 012 342 4906; f 012 342 7348; e embaguinea@l.africa.com
Ivory Coast 795 Government Av, Arcadia, Pretoria; ✆ 012 342 6913/14; f 012 342 6713
Kenya 302 Brooks St, Menlo Park, Pretoria; ✆ 012 342 2249/50/51; f 012 362 2252
Lesotho Anderson St, Menlo Park, Pretoria; ✆ 012 460 7640; f 012 460 7649
Malawi 770 Government Av, Arcadia, Pretoria; ✆ 012 342 0146; f 012 342 0147
Mali 876 Pretorius St, Block B, Arcadia, Pretoria; ✆ 012 342 7464; f 012 342 0670
Morocco 799 Schoeman St, Arcadia, Pretoria; ✆ 012 343 0230; f 012 343 0613; e sifmapre@telkomsa.net
Mozambique 529 Edmund St, Arcadia, Pretoria; ✆ 012 401 0300; f 012 326 6388; consular section at 75 Hamilton St, Arcadia, Pretoria; ✆ 012 321 2288
Namibia 197 Blackwood St, Arcadia, Pretoria; ✆ 012 481 9100; f 012 343 7294/5998; e secretary@namibia.org.za

Nigeria 971 Schoeman St, Arcadia, Pretoria; ☎ 012 342 0805/06/63; f 012 342 1668; nhep@iafrica.com

Rwanda 983 Schoeman St, Arcadia, Pretoria; ☎ 012 342 6536; f 012 342 7106

Sudan 1203 Pretorius St, Hatfield, Pretoria; ☎ 012 342 4538/7903; f 012 342 4539

Swaziland 715 Government Av, Arcadia, Pretoria; ☎ 012 344 1910

Tanzania 822 George Av, Arcadia, Pretoria; ☎ 012 342 4371/93; f 012 430 4383; e tanzania@cis.co.za, the@tanzania.org.za; www.tanzania.org.za

Zambia Zambia Hse, 570 Ziervogel St, Arcadia, Pretoria; ☎ 012 326 1847; f 012 326 2140; e zahpta@mweb.co.za

Zimbabwe 798 Merton Av, Arcadia, Pretoria; ☎ 012 342 5125; f 012 342 5126

AFRICAN EMBASSIES AND CONSULATES IN THE USA

Algeria 2118 Kalorama Rd NW, Washington, DC 20008; ☎ 202 265 2800; f 202 667 2174

Angola 2100–2108 16th St NW, Washington, DC 20009; ☎ 202 785 1156; f 202 282 9049

Benin 2737 Cathedral Av NW (or consulate now at 2124 Kalorama Rd), Washington, DC 20008; ☎ 202 232 6656–8; f 202 265 1996

Botswana 3400 International Dr, Suite 7M NW, Washington, DC 20008; ☎ 202 244 4990/1; f 202 244 4164

Burkina Faso 2340 Massachusetts Av NW, Washington, DC 20008; ☎ 202 332 5577/6895; f 202 667 1882

Burundi Suite 212, 2233 Wisconsin Av NW, Washington, DC 20007; ☎ 202 342 2574; f 202 342 2578

Cameroon 2349 Massachusetts Av NW, Washington, DC 20008; ☎ 202 265 8790–4; f 202 387 3826

Central African Republic 1618 22nd St NW, Washington, DC 20008; ☎ 202 483 7800/1; f 202 332 9893

Chad 2002 R St NW, Washington, DC 20009; ☎ 202 462 4009; f 202 265 1937

Congo 1800 New Hampshire Av NW, Washington, DC 20009; ☎ 202 234 7690–1; f 202 237 0748

Democratic Republic of the Congo 4891 Colorado Av NW, Washington, DC 20011; ☎ 202 726 5500; f 202 726 1860

Djibouti Suite 515, 1156 15th St NW, Washington, DC 20005; ☎ 202 331 0270; f 202 331 0302

Egypt 3521 International Court NW, Washington, DC 20008; ☎ 202 895 5400; f 202 244 4319/5131; consular section ☎ 202 966 6342

Equatorial Guinea Suite 405, 2522 K St NW, Washington, DC 20005; ☎ 202 393 0525; f 202 393 0348

Eritrea 1708 New Hampshire Av NW, Washington, DC 20009; ☎ 202 319 1991; f 202 319 1304

Ethiopia 3506 International Dr NW, Washington, DC 20008; ☎ 202 364 1200; f 202 686 9551

Gabon Suite 200, 2034 20th St NW, Washington, DC 20009; ☎ 202 797 1000; f 202 332 0668

Gambia 1156 15th St NW, Suite 905, Washington, DC 20005; ☎ 202 785 1399; f 202 785 1430

Ghana 3512 International Dr NW, Washington, DC 20008; ☎ 202 686 4520; f 202 686 4527

Guinea 2112 Leroy Pl NW, Washington, DC 20008; ☎ 202 483 9420; f 202 483 8688

Guinea Bissau 1511 K St NW, Washington, DC 20005; ☎ 202 347 3950; f 202 347 3954

Ivory Coast 2424 Massachusetts Av NW, Washington, DC 20008; ☎ 202 797 0300; f 202 483 8482

Kenya 2249 R St NW, Washington, DC 20008; ☎ 202 387 6101; f 202 462 3829

Lesotho 2511 Massachusetts Av NW, Washington, DC 20008; ☎ 202 797 5533–6; f 202 234 6815

Liberia 5201 16th St NW, Washington, DC 20011; ☎ 202 723 0440

Malawi 1029 Vermont Av, NW, Washington DC 20005; ☎ 202 721 0270/74; f 202 721 0288; chancery at 2408 Massachusetts Av NW, Washington, DC 20008; ☎ 202 797 1007

Mali 2130 R St NW, Washington, DC 20008; ☎ 202 332 2249; f 202 332 6603

Mauritania 2129 Leroy Pl NW, Washington, DC 20008; ☎ 202 232 5700; f 202 232 5701

Morocco 1601 21st St NW, Washington, DC 20009; ☎ 202 462 7979–82; f 202 265 0161

Mozambique Suite 570, 1990 M St NW, Washington, DC 20036; ☎ 202 293 7146; f 202 835 0245

Namibia 1605 New Hampshire Av NW, Washington, DC 20009; ☎ 202 986 0540; f 202 986 0443

Niger 2204 R St NW, Washington, DC 20008; ☎ 202 483 4224–7; f 202 483 3169

Nigeria 3519 International Court NW, Washington, DC 20008; ☎ 202 822 1500

Rwanda 1714 New Hampshire Av NW, Washington, DC 20009; ☎ 202 232 2882; f 202 232 4544

Senegal 2112 Wyoming Av NW, Washington, DC 20008; ☎ 202 234 0540/1; f 202 293 4198

South Africa 3051 Massachusetts Av NW, Washington, DC 20008; ☎ 202 232 4400; f 202 265 1607

Sudan 2210 Massachusetts Av NW, Washington, DC 20008; ☎ 202 338 8565–70; f 202 667 2406

Swaziland 3400 International Dr, Suite 3M NW, Washington, DC 20008; ☎ 202 362 6683–5; f 202 244 8059

Tanzania 2139 R St NW, Washington, DC 20008; ☎ 202 939 6125; f 202 797 7408; *New York* e tzrepny@aol.com

Togo 2208 Massachusetts Av NW, Washington, DC 20008; ☎ 202 234 4212; f 202 232 3190

Tunisia 1515 Massachusetts Av NW, Washington, DC 20005; ☎ 202 862 1850

Uganda 5911 16th St NW, Washington, DC 20011; ☎ 202 726 7100–2 or 202 726 0416

Zambia 2419 Massachusetts Av NW, Washington, DC 20008; ☎ 202 265 9717–9; f 202 332 0826

Zimbabwe 1608 New Hampshire Av NW, Washington, DC 20009; ☎ 202 332 7100; f 202 483 9326

AFRICAN EMBASSIES AND CONSULATES IN AUSTRALIA

Botswana 52 Culgoa Circuit, O'Malley, ACT 2606; ☎ 026 290 7500

Cameroon PO Box 150, Wahroonga, NSW 2076; ☎ 029 989 8414

Egypt 1 Darwin Av, Yarralumla, ACT, 2600; ☎ 026 273 4437; f 026 273 4279

Eritrea 16 Bulwarra Cl, O'Malley, ACT 2606; ☎ 026 290 1991; f 026 286 8902

Ethiopia 38 Johnston St, Fitzroy, Victoria, 3065; ☎ 039 417 3419; e ethiopia@consul.com.au

Kenya 3rd Floor QBE Bldg, 33–35 Ainslie Av, Canberra, ACT 2601, ☎ 026 247 4788/6247; f 026 257 6613; e khc-canberra@kenya.asn.au

Lesotho 294 Old South Head Rd, Watsons Bay, NSW 2030; ☎ 029 398 3798; f 029 247 6384

Libya 50 Culgoa Circuit, O'Malley, ACT 2606; ☎ 026 290 7900

Morocco 17 Terrigal Cres, O'Malley, ACT 2606; ☎ 026 290 0755/6290; f 026 290 0744; e sifmacan@moroccoembassy.org.au; www.moroccoembassy.org.au

Mozambique 4/8 Lauderdale Av, Fairlight, NSW 2094; ☎ 029 907 8890

Nigeria 26 Guilfoyle St, Yarralumla, ACT 2600, ☎ 026 282 7411; f 026 282 8471; e chancery@nigeria-can.org.au

South Africa Cnr State Circle & Rhodes Pl, Yarralumla, ACT 2600; ☎ 026 272 7400; f 026 273 3543; e info@sahc.org.au; www.sahc.org.au

Zimbabwe 11 Culgoa Circuit, O'Malley, ACT 2606; ☎ 026 286 2281/6286; f 026 290 1680; e zimbabwel@iimetro.com.au

For other details look at www.info.dfat.gov.au/info.

$ MONEY

From a security point of view, you might expect it to make sense to take most of your money as travellers' cheques, but in fact in many places they are worse than useless. In northern Africa, if you can change them at all, you will almost certainly get a far worse rate than for cash. If you have travellers' cheques, make sure you carry your original purchase receipt, as many banks in Africa will not exchange them without it. You are not supposed to carry it with your travellers' cheques (for security), so, assuming you are travelling with someone else, you can carry theirs and they can carry yours. It's best to carry a photocopy and to keep the original securely elsewhere, hidden in the vehicle. Keep a list of the cheque numbers too.

Generally you should take as much hard currency in cash as you feel you can safely carry. At borders you will often want to change a small amount of money before you get to a bank or official moneychanger where you can check the current correct rates. You may also wish to take advantage of changing money on the street (a decision for each individual to make – be extremely careful if you do). Some banks will not change travellers' cheques. In some areas there may be no banks at all and you may have to rely on changing money with local traders. One bank in Cameroon actually sent us to the man 'behind the onion sellers', who they said would give us a much better rate! Some countries will demand payment for certain services in hard currency.

It is worth bringing both small and large denomination notes with you. Be aware though that there are a number of fake US$100 bills in circulation; most banks will not accept them because of this. But if you are using a moneychanger, he will usually prefer larger notes such as US$50 or €50. Small notes are useful when you have to pay low charges in hard currency, otherwise you end up getting your change in local money. Bring a mix of currencies to take advantage of swings in exchange rates. You will also find that only certain currencies will be acceptable in some countries. The two most important currencies to carry are euros and US dollars. The US dollar used to be the preferred international currency of exchange, but in some banks in west Africa, particularly in small towns, euros are now the only currency accepted.

Also make sure you have either euros or CFA francs with you when crossing the Sahara into Niger or Mali, as you must have these to pay various charges at the border. CFA (Communauté Fiscalière de l'Afrique de l'Ouest) is the common currency of the West African Monetary Unit. There are two CFAs—the West African CFA and the Central African CFA. They are not interchangeable, though they do have the same value. The western version is valid in Senegal, Guinea Bissau, Mali, Niger, Burkina, Togo, Benin and Ivory Coast. The latter is used in Cameroon, the Central African Republic (CAR), Chad, Congo, Equatorial Guinea and Gabon.

You do not necessarily need to take all the money you are likely to need. American Express cardholders can buy US$1,000 worth of travellers' cheques at any of their offices with a cheque guaranteed by an Amex card. It is sometimes even possible to buy hard currency with your credit and debit cards (shop around – different banks in the same town will have different rules). With the increasing number of ATMs around the world, you can also withdraw money in local currency in many places in many countries.

You can also have money wired to a bank in Africa, although it can take some time, sometimes up to 12 days. If you have someone to take care of your financial affairs back home, they should be able to help to transfer funds if necessary. For example, it can be done quickly (but quite expensively) by either Western Union or Moneygram, both of which are increasingly represented throughout Africa. For peace of mind it's best to arrange for all your regular outgoings to be paid by direct debit while you're away, with that same someone perhaps checking your bank statements to ensure all is in order.

We recommend you to find a relatively safe place in the vehicle to hide some money – a mixture of hard currency and local currency of the country you are travelling in – just in case you are unfortunate enough to be robbed. But do remember where you have hidden it.

✚ HEALTH with Dr Jane Wilson-Howarth and Dr Felicity Nicholson

Nomad Pharmacy (*3–4 Wellington Terr, Turnpike La, London N8 0PX;* ☏ *020 8889 7014*) supply all organised tours with their medical kits and are experts in what you will need when travelling in Africa. You can choose from a mini-kit or full truck kit. A full medical kit from Nomad Pharmacy costs about US$500.

We would also suggest that you go over your previous medical history with your local GP and take the appropriate medication with you. Hopefully you won't be needing it, but better be safe than sorry.

For women travellers it's important to carry all relevant medication regarding vaginal infections. See page 123 for more detailed information on health and women's issues.

The medical kit list in *Appendix 3*, page 326, includes everything we think you might need, but this does not necessarily mean that every item needs to be taken with you. The list should be discussed with either your local GP or a travel clinic, who can advise you on what you are more likely to need. Malaria, bilharzia, diarrhoea of varying kinds, constipation, skin infections, flu, and irritable eyes and ears from the dust are the problems you need to consider. Most of the travellers we spoke to while on the road had suffered from at least one of these.

It is also a good idea to attend a first-aid course for your own safety and security. In terms of intravenous (IV) treatment, it's best not to undertake this unless you are a qualified medic, doctor or nurse. Most travel kits include IV treatment packs as many medical institutions in Africa do not have these supplies. If you are seriously injured you should always take all of your own medical equipment with you. Medical staff in Africa do not find this offensive and in fact welcome good equipment.

Carry a medical self-help book with you. The one most travellers carry is *Where There Is No Doctor: Village Health Care Handbook for Africa* by David Werner, Carol Thuman, Jane Maxwell and Andrew Pearson. This book can be ordered through amazon.co.uk and is also available at Nomad Pharmacy. There are many other choices of self-help books, so you should shop around and take whichever one suits your needs. You may also find it useful to ask your local pharmacy for a copy of the BNF (*British National Formulary*). This book documents all the medicines available in Britain and their prescribed doses for the relevant diseases. It is updated every few months, so you should be able to get a recently expired copy.

BEFORE YOU GO

Vaccinations To ensure a healthy trip to Africa check on your immunisation status. It is wise to be up-to-date on tetanus, polio and diphtheria (now given as an all-in-one vaccine, Revaxis, that lasts for ten years), and hepatitis A. Immunisations against meningococcus and rabies may also be recommended. Proof of vaccination against yellow fever is needed for entry into many parts of Africa if you are coming from another yellow fever endemic area. The vaccine may also be recommended for those at risk of catching the disease. If the vaccine is not suitable for you then obtain an exemption certificate from your GP or a travel clinic. Hepatitis A vaccine (Havrix Monodose or Avaxim) comprises two injections given about a year apart. The course costs about £100, but may be available on the NHS; it protects for 25 years and can be administered even close to the time of departure. Hepatitis B vaccination should be considered for longer trips (two months or more) or for those working with children or in situations where contact with blood is likely. Three injections are needed for the best protection and can be given over a three-week period if time is short for those aged 16 or over. Longer schedules give more sustained protection and are therefore preferred if time allows. Hepatitis A vaccine can also be given as a combination with hepatitis B as 'Twinrix', for those aged 18 or over, though two doses are needed at least seven days apart to be effective for the hepatitis A component, and three doses are needed for the hepatitis B.

The newer, injectable typhoid vaccines (eg: Typhim Vi) last for three years and are about 85% effective. Oral capsules (Vivotif) are currently available in the US (and soon in the UK); if four capsules are taken over seven days it will last for five years. They should be encouraged unless the traveller is leaving within a few days for a trip of a week or less, when the vaccine would not be effective in time. Meningitis vaccine (ideally containing strains A, C, W and Y, but if this is not available then A+C vaccine is better than nothing) is recommended for all travellers, especially for trips of more than four weeks (see *Meningitis*, page 127). Vaccinations for rabies are ideally advised for everyone, but are especially important for travellers visiting more remote areas, and/or if you are more than 24 hours from medical help and definitely if you will be working with animals (see *Rabies*, page 127).

Oral cholera vaccine (Dukoral) is now available in the UK and is recommended for extended trips to west Africa or for shorter trips in areas of extremely poor hygiene. Older travellers or those with chronic health problems may also be recommended to take the vaccine. A primary course (adults and children over six years old) consists of two doses of vaccine taken between one and six weeks apart, the second dose being taken at least a week before entering the infected area. The vaccine gives good protection for up to two years.

Experts differ over whether a BCG vaccination against tuberculosis (TB) is useful in adults: discuss this with your travel clinic.

In addition to the various vaccinations recommended above, it is important that travellers should be properly protected against malaria. For detailed advice, see below.

Ideally you should visit your own doctor or a specialist travel clinic (see page 120) to discuss your requirements if possible at least eight weeks before you plan to travel.

Malaria prevention There is no vaccine against malaria, but using prophylactic drugs and preventing mosquito bites will considerably reduce the risk of contracting it. Seek professional advice for the best anti-malarial drugs to take. Mefloquine (Lariam) is the most effective prophylactic agent for most countries in sub-Saharan Africa. If this drug is suggested and you have never used it before then you should start two to three weeks before departure to check that it suits you. About 25% of people will experience some side effects but these are nearly always not serious. Stop immediately if it seems to cause depression or anxiety, visual or hearing disturbances, fits, severe headaches or changes in heart rhythm. Anyone who has been treated for depression or psychiatric problems, has diabetes controlled by oral therapy, is epileptic (or has suffered fits in the past) or has a close blood relative who is epileptic should not take mefloquine. Malarone is considered to be an effective alternative to Lariam. However, this drug is expensive and is therefore better for shorter trips. Malarone need only be started one to two days before arrival into a malarial area. It is taken daily and is continued for seven days after leaving the area. It is currently licensed in the UK for trips up to three months. It is also available in paediatric form for children under 40 kg. It is prescribed by weight so it is helpful to know how much your children weigh.

The antibiotic doxycycline (100mg daily) is considered to be a viable alternative when Lariam or Malarone cannot be used. (It also has the coincidental benefit of providing some protection against tummy bugs.) Like Malarone it need only be started one to two days before arrival; it is taken daily but needs to be continued for four weeks after leaving the malarial area. It may also be used by travellers with epilepsy, unlike Lariam, although the antiepileptic therapy may make it less effective. Users are warned that allergic skin reactions in sunlight can occur in about 1–3% of people. The drug should be stopped if this happens. Women using the oral contraceptive should use an additional method of protection for the first four weeks when using doxycycline. It is also unsuitable in pregnancy or for children under 12 years.

All prophylactic agents should be taken with or after the evening meal, washed down with plenty of fluid and continued for the recommended time after leaving Africa. Chloroquine (Nivaquine, Avloclor) and proguanil (Paludrine) are considered to be ineffective in sub-Saharan Africa and are only ever used now as a last resort.

There is no malaria above 3,000m; at intermediate altitudes (1,800–3,000m) there is a low but finite risk. Much of South Africa is free from the disease, although it is a risk in some parts; elsewhere the risk to travellers is great. It is unwise to travel to malarial areas of Africa when pregnant or with children: the risk of malaria is considerable and such travellers are likely to succumb rapidly to the disease.

Whether or not you are taking anti-malaria tablets, it is important to protect yourself from mosquito bites, so keep your repellent stick or roll-on to hand at all times. Some travellers carry a course of malaria treatment with them. Self-treatment is not without risks and diagnosing malaria is not necessarily easy, which is why consulting a doctor is the best option. If you are going somewhere remote in an area where malaria is a high risk, you probably have to assume that any high fever for more than a few hours is due to malaria. At present Malarone is considered the best treatment, but this will depend on whether you are taking prophylactic anti-malarial tablets and if so which ones. It is always wise to check for up-to-date advice before purchasing any malarial medication. Current experts differ on the costs and benefits of self-treatment, but agree that it may lead to people taking drugs they do not need. Discuss your trip with a specialist to determine your particular needs and risks.

Be aware that no prophylactic is 100% protective, but those on prophylactics who are unlucky enough to catch malaria are less likely to get rapidly into serious trouble.

Personal matters Remember to have a dental check before you leave home.

Read *Safe sex*, page 123; if you'll be using a coil, get it fitted at least six weeks before departure.

Take whatever tampons you may need initially; see page 123.

Finally, see the advice about multivitamins under *Weight loss and gain* (page 122).

TRAVEL CLINICS AND HEALTH INFORMATION A full list of current travel clinic websites worldwide is available from the International Society of Travel Medicine on www.istm.org. For other journey preparation information, consult www.tripprep.com. Information about various medications may be found on www.emedicine.com. For information on malaria prevention, see www.preventingmalaria.info.

UK

Berkeley Travel Clinic 32 Berkeley St, London W1J 8EL (near Green Park tube station); ℡ 020 7629 6233

Cambridge Travel Clinic 48a Mill Rd, Cambridge CB1 2AS; ℡ 01223 367362; e enquiries@ travelcliniccambridge.co.uk; www.travelcliniccambridge.co.uk; ⊕ 12.00–19.00 Tue–Fri, 10.00–16.00 Sat.

Edinburgh Travel Clinic Regional Infectious Diseases Unit, Ward 41 OPD, Western General Hospital, Crewe Rd South, Edinburgh EH4 2UX; ℡ 0131 537 2822; www.mvm.ed.ac.uk. Travel helpline (℡ 0906 589 0380) ⊕ 09.00–12.00 Mon–Fri. Provides inoculations & antimalarial prophylaxis, & advises on travel-related health risks.

Fleet Street Travel Clinic 29 Fleet St, London EC4Y 1AA; ℡ 020 7353 5678; www.fleetstreetclinic.com. Vaccinations, travel products & latest advice.

Hospital for Tropical Diseases Travel Clinic Mortimer Market Bldg, Capper St (off Tottenham Ct Rd), London WC1E 6AU; ℡ 020 7388 9600; www.thehtd.org. Offers consultations & advice, & is able to provide all necessary drugs & vaccines for travellers. Runs a healthline (℡ 0906 133 7733) for country-specific information & health hazards. Also stocks nets, water purification equipment & personal protection measures.

Interhealth Worldwide Partnership Hse, 157 Waterloo Rd, London SE1 8US; ℡ 020 7902 9000; www.interhealth.org.uk. Competitively priced, one-stop travel health service. All profits go to their affiliated company, InterHealth, which provides health care for overseas workers on Christian projects.

Liverpool School of Medicine Pembroke Pl, Liverpool L3 5QA; ℡ 0151 708 9393; f 0151 705 3370; www.liv.ac.uk/lstm

MASTA (Medical Advisory Service for Travellers Abroad) Moorfield Rd, Yeadon, Leeds, West Yorkshire, LS19 7BN; ℡ 0113 238 7500; www.masta-travel-health.com. Provides travel health advice, anti-malarials & vaccinations. There are over 25 MASTA pre-travel clinics in Britain; call or check online for the nearest. Clinics also sell mosquito nets, medical kits, insect protection & travel hygiene products.

NHS travel website www.fitfortravel.scot.nhs.uk. Provides country-by-country advice on immunisation & malaria, plus details of recent developments, & a list of relevant health organisations.

Nomad Travel Store/Clinic 3–4 Wellington Terr, Turnpike La, London N8 0PX; ☎ 020 8889 7014, travel-health line (office hours only) ☎ 0906 863 3414; e sales@nomadtravel.co.uk; www.nomadtravel.co.uk. Also at 40 Bernard St, London WCIN ILJ; ☎ 020 7833 4114; 52 Grosvenor Gdns,

London SW1W 0AG; ☎ 020 7823 5823; & 43 Queens Rd, Bristol BS8 1QH; ☎ 0117 922 6567. For health advice, equipment such as mosquito nets & other anti-bug devices, & an excellent range of adventure travel gear. Clinics also in Bristol & Southampton.

Trailfinders Travel Clinic 194 Kensington High St, London W8 7RG; ☎ 020 7938 3999; www.trailfinders.com/travelessentials/travelclinic.htm

Travelpharm The Travelpharm website, www.travelpharm.com, offers up-to-date guidance on travel-related health & has a range of medications available through their online mini-pharmacy.

Irish Republic

Tropical Medical Bureau Grafton Street Medical Centre, Grafton Bldgs, 34 Grafton St, Dublin 2; ☎ 1 671 9200; www.tmb.ie. A useful website specific

to tropical destinations. Also check website for other bureaux locations throughout Ireland.

USA

Centers for Disease Control 1600 Clifton Rd, Atlanta, GA 30333; ☎ 800 311 3435; travellers' health hotline f 888 232 3299; www.cdc.gov/travel. The central source of travel information in the USA. The invaluable *Health Information for International Travel*, published annually, is available from the Division of Quarantine at this address.

Connaught Laboratories Pasteur Merieux Connaught, Route 611, PO Box 187, Swiftwater, PA 18370; ☎ 800 822 2463. They will send a free list of

specialist tropical-medicine physicians in your state.

IAMAT (International Association for Medical Assistance to Travelers) 1623 Military Rd, 279, Niagara Falls, NY 14304-1745; ☎ 716 754 4883; e info@iamat.org; www.iamat.org. A non-profit organisation that provides lists of English-speaking doctors abroad.

International Medicine Center 915 Gessner Rd, Suite 525, Houston, TX 77024; ☎ 713 550 2000; www.traveldoc.com

Canada

IAMAT Suite 1, 1287 St Clair Av W, Toronto, Ontario M6E 1B8; ☎ 416 652 0137; www.iamat.org

TMVC Suite 314, 1030 W Georgia St, Vancouver BC V6E 2Y3; ☎ 1 888 288 8682; www.tmvc.com. Private clinic with several outlets in Canada.

Australia, New Zealand, Singapore

IAMAT PO Box 5049, Christchurch 5, New Zealand; www.iamat.org

TMVC ☎ 1300 65 88 44; www.tmvc.com.au. Clinics in Australia, New Zealand & Singapore, including: *Auckland* Canterbury Arcade, 170 Queen St, Auckland; ☎ 9 373 3531

Brisbane 75a, Astor Terr, Spring Hill, QLD 4000; ☎ 7 3815 6900
Melbourne 393 Little Bourke St, 2nd Floor, Melbourne, VIC 3000; ☎ 3 9602 5788
Sydney Dymocks Bldg, 7th Floor, 428 George St, Sydney, NSW 2000; ☎ 2 9221 7133

South Africa and Namibia

SAA-Netcare Travel Clinics Sanlam Bldg, 19, Fredman Dr, Sandton, P Bag X34, Benmore, JHB, Gauteng, 2010; www.travelclinic.co.za. Clinics throughout South Africa.

TMVC NHC Health Centre, Cnr Beyers Naude & Waugh Northcliff; PO Box 48499, Roosevelt Park, 2129; ☎ 011 888 7488; www.tmvc.com.au. Consult website for details of other clinics in South Africa & Namibia.

Switzerland

IAMAT 57 Chemin des Voirets, 1212 Grand Lancy, Geneva; www.iamat.org

IN AFRICA

Health, food and hygiene This is one area where it can be difficult to strike the right balance between justified concern and outright paranoia. A lot of common problems can be avoided by being sensible about hygiene. There will, of course, be times when you are more or less dependent on local standards of hygiene. Some health guides for travellers visiting out-of-the-way places will frighten you half to death. Basically you will find your own levels of hygiene and personal care but even then your standards will vary according to the different conditions you find yourself in. Most of the time all you need is common sense.

Do not hesitate to see a doctor or take advantage of medical insurance cover if you think there is something really wrong with you. Some countries have perfectly adequate hospitals and health clinics; some facilities are so basic they will make you cringe. Trust your judgement, but do not assume that health care will be bad just because it is African. After all, the doctors there are far more accustomed to tropical diseases than those at home.

Water sterilisation If you drink contaminated water, you will probably get sick, so try to drink from safe sources. Water should have been brought to the boil, passed through a good bacteriological filter or purified with iodine. Chlorine tablets (eg: Puritabs) are also adequate, although theoretically less effective and they taste nastier.

If you buy mineral water, make sure the bottle is properly sealed. Some mineral water has been found to be contaminated in many developing countries and may be no safer than tap water.

Hygiene One of the main problems you will face is trying to keep clean with only a limited amount of water after a hard day's driving with sweat, dust and sand clinging to every part of your body. Following the advice below will also help prevent dysentery:

- Carry a small, compact flannel with you and use a minimal amount of water, but still wipe the day's activities from your body.
- Disinfectant soap, like Dettol, can be found throughout Africa.
- Always wash your hands after visiting the local market and handling raw meat and vegetables, as well as before eating or drinking.
- When using a cutting board or any other surface to cut meat or vegetables, always use one side for meat and the other for vegetables.
- Wash any vegetables you want to eat raw in potassium permanganate or Milton, and always peel fruit before eating.
- When there is plenty of water available, give all your cutlery a good wash in hot water just to sterilise everything. This is a general rule in terms of clothing, too, but often not possible, unless you are intending to boil loads of water.

Day-to-day health issues

Weight loss and gain Travelling independently can cause weight loss and, while some lose weight, others gain it. Constipation is a common problem among women, particularly on organised tours. You are much less likely to lose weight on an organised truck tour. In fact, the high quality of the three square meals per day, as well as the lack of activity, sitting and driving all day, mean you are more likely to put on the pounds rather than lose them. Remember to bring some laxatives with you. If you find yourself losing weight, three square meals, if at all possible, should keep the weight loss under control and a multivitamin supplement will ensure your body gets any vitamins missing from your diet. Buy them before you leave home.

Dental care Toothpaste and toothbrushes are available in cities, but err on the side of caution and take everything you are likely to need. When you see some of the African versions of toothbrushes you'll be glad you did! Oil of cloves is good for numbing toothache, though of course it will not solve any real problems.

Safe sex Travel is a time when we may enjoy sexual adventures, especially when alcohol reduces inhibitions. Remember the risks of sexually transmitted infection are high, whether you have sexual intercourse with fellow travellers or with locals. About 40% of HIV infections in British heterosexuals are acquired abroad. Use condoms or femidoms. If you notice any genital ulcers or discharge get treatment promptly.

Condoms are usually extremely difficult to get hold of in Africa, though there is reputed to be a black-market stall in Abidjan that sells nothing else. And can they be trusted not to burst at that critical moment? Generally you would be advised to bring what you are likely to need – and more. In the more remote areas, thorough searches at border posts which concentrate on your washbags and medical box do so for a reason. Presumably the opportunity to relieve travellers of the odd three-pack of condoms is regarded as one of the perks of the job.

If you are only having sexual intercourse with your regular partner, condoms are not your only choice of contraception. If you are taking the pill, you should refer to the guidance set out on the packet for storage (normally in a cool, dry place) and follow it carefully. If you decide on a coil, it must be fitted at least six weeks before you leave, to check you are not at risk from infection or expulsion. Some women experience heavy and painful periods with a coil. You can also use a cap, which can be sterilised easily in a mug with an ordinary water-purifying tablet. But you should think about the number of times you will be using communal toilet facilities or washing in the open air before making a decision to rely only on your cap while you are away.

One other possibility is to have an injectable contraceptive (Depo-Provera), which will last for two or more months. Side effects can include irregular periods, or no periods at all, not necessarily a disadvantage on the road. Fertility can also be delayed for a year after the last injection. Another disadvantage could be needing another injection when you are miles away from anywhere.

If you are thinking of changing your normal method of contraception, talk this over in plenty of time with your doctor.

Tampons and sanitary towels You will be able to buy tampons and sanitary towels in most big towns in west Africa and more easily in east and southern Africa. Problem areas are north Africa, desert and other remote areas like the Congo and Central African Republic. Take enough supplies to get you through early problem areas and you will be able to stock up later on. If you have a definite brand preference and lots of spare space it's a good idea to bring extra supplies.

It might also be worth considering a reusable menstrual sponge, though if you have not used one before, make sure you practise before you leave so you know exactly what is involved.

Avoiding insect bites

Mosquitoes It is crucial to avoid mosquito bites between dusk and dawn. As the sun is going down, put on long clothes and apply repellent on any exposed flesh. This will protect you from malaria, elephantiasis and a range of nasty insect-borne viruses. Malaria mosquitoes are voracious and hunt at ankle level, so it is worth applying repellent under socks, too. Sleep under a permethrin-treated bednet or in an air-conditioned room. During the day it is wise to wear long, loose (preferably 100% cotton) clothes if you are going through scrubby country; this will keep ticks off and also tsetse and day-biting *Aedes* mosquitoes, which may spread dengue and yellow fever. Insect repellents should ideally contain around 50–55% DEET and can be safely used by children and pregnant women.

Tsetse fly Tsetse flies hurt when they bite, and they are attracted to the colour blue. Locals will advise on where they are a problem and where they transmit sleeping sickness.

Blackfly Minute pestilential biting blackflies spread river blindness in some parts of Africa between map co-ordinates 190°N and 170°S. The disease is caught close to fast-flowing rivers as flies breed there and the larvae live in rapids. The flies bite during the day but long trousers tucked into socks will help keep them off. Citronella-based natural repellents do not work against them.

Tumbu flies or putsi Tumbu flies or putsi are a problem in areas of east, west and southern Africa where the climate is hot and humid. The adult fly lays her eggs on the soil or on drying laundry and when the eggs come into contact with human flesh (when you put on clothes or lie on a bed) they hatch and bury themselves under the skin. Here they form a crop of 'boils', each of which hatches a grub after about eight days, when the inflammation will settle down. In putsi areas, either dry your clothes and sheets within a screened house, or dry them in direct sunshine until they are crisp, or iron them.

Jiggers or sandfleas Jiggers or sandfleas are another kind of flesh-feaster. They latch on if you walk barefoot in contaminated places, and set up home under the skin of the foot, usually at the side of a toenail where they cause a painful, boil-like swelling. These need picking out by a local expert; if the distended flea bursts during eviction the wound should be dowsed in spirit, alcohol or kerosene, otherwise more jiggers will infest you.

QUICK TICK REMOVAL

African ticks are not the rampant disease transmitters they are in the Americas, but they may spread tickbite fever and even Lyme disease. Tickbite fever is a flu-like illness that can easily be treated with doxycycline, but as there can be some serious complications it is important to visit a doctor.

Ticks should ideally be removed as soon as possible as leaving them on the body increases the chance of infection. They should be removed with special tick tweezers that can be bought in good travel shops. Failing that you can use your fingernails: grasp the tick as close to your body as possible and pull steadily and firmly away at right angles to your skin. The tick will then come away complete, as long as you do not jerk or twist. If possible douse the wound with alcohol (any spirit will do) or iodine. Irritants (eg: Olbas oil) or lit cigarettes are to be discouraged since they can cause the ticks to regurgitate and therefore increase the risk of disease. It is best to get a travelling companion to check you for ticks; if you are travelling with small children, remember to check their heads, and particularly behind the ears.

Spreading redness around the bite and/or fever and/or aching joints after a tick bite imply that you have an infection that requires antibiotic treatment, so seek advice.

Common medical problems

Travellers' diarrhoea At least half of those travelling to the tropics or the developing world will suffer from a bout of travellers' diarrhoea. The newer you are to exotic travel, the more likely you will be to suffer. By taking precautions against travellers' diarrhoea you will also avoid typhoid, cholera, hepatitis, dysentery, worms, etc.

Travellers' diarrhoea and the other faecal-oral diseases come from getting other people's faeces in your mouth. This most often happens from cooks not washing their hands after a trip to the toilet, but, even if the restaurant cook does not understand basic hygiene, you will be safe if your food has been properly cooked and arrives piping hot. The maxim to remind you what you can safely eat is:

PEEL IT, BOIL IT, COOK IT OR FORGET IT.

This means that fruit you have washed and peeled yourself and hot food should be safe, but raw food, cold cooked food, salad and fruit that have been prepared by others, ice cream and ice are all risky. Foods kept lukewarm in hotel buffets are usually time bombs waiting to explode! That said, plenty of travellers and expatriates enjoy fruit and vegetables, so do keep a sense of perspective: food served in a fairly decent hotel in a large town or a place regularly frequented by expatriates is likely to be safe. If you are struck, see box, *Treating travellers' diarrheoa* (page 126) for treatment.

Giardia Giardia is a type of diarrhoea or intestinal disorder caused by a parasite present in contaminated water. The symptoms are stomach cramps, nausea, bloated stomach, watery, foul-smelling diarrhoea and 'eggy' burps. Giardia can occur a few weeks after you have been exposed to the parasite and symptoms can disappear for a few days and then return – this can go on for a few weeks. Giardia is basically a form of amoebic dysentery and is best treated with tinidazole (2g in one dose repeated seven days later if symptoms persist).

Bilharzia or schistosomiasis
With thanks to Dr Vaughan Southgate of the Natural History Museum, London, and Dr Dick Stockley, The Surgery, Kampala
Bilharzia or schistosomiasis is a disease that commonly afflicts the rural poor of the tropics. Two types exist in sub-Saharan Africa – *Schistosoma mansoni* and *Schistosoma haematobium*. It is an unpleasant problem that is worth avoiding, though can be treated if you do get it. It is easier to understand how to diagnose it, treat it and prevent it if you know a little about the life cycle. Contaminated faeces are washed into the lake, the eggs hatch and the larva infects certain species of snail. The snails then produce about 10,000 cercariae a day for the rest of their lives. The parasites can digest their way through your skin when you wade or bathe in infested fresh water.

Winds disperse the snails and cercariae. The snails in particular can drift a long way, especially on windblown weed, so nowhere is really safe. However, deep water and running water are safer, while shallow water presents the greatest risk. The cercariae penetrate intact skin, and find their way to the liver. There male and female meet and spend the rest of their lives in permanent copulation. No wonder you feel tired! Most finish up in the wall of the lower bowel, but others can get lost and can cause damage to many different organs. *Schistosoma haematobium* goes mostly to the bladder.

Although the adults do not cause any harm in themselves, after about four to six weeks they start to lay eggs, which cause an intense but usually ineffective immune reaction, including fever, cough, abdominal pain, and a fleeting, itching rash called 'safari itch'. The absence of early symptoms does not necessarily mean there is no infection. Later symptoms can be more localised and more severe, but the general

TREATING TRAVELLERS' DIARRHOEA

Dr Jane Wilson-Howarth

It is dehydration which makes you feel awful during a bout of diarrhoea and the most important part of treatment is drinking lots of clear fluids. Sachets of oral rehydration salts give the perfect biochemical mix to replace all that is pouring out of your bottom, but unfortunately they don't taste nice. Any dilute mixture of sugar and salt in water will do you good, so if you like Coke or squash, drink that with a three-finger pinch of salt added to each glass. Otherwise make a solution of a four-finger scoop of sugar with a three-finger pinch of salt in a glass of water. Or add eight level teaspoons of sugar (18g) and one level teaspoon of salt (3g) to one litre (five cups) of safe water. A squeeze of lemon or orange juice improves the taste and adds potassium, which is also lost during diarrhoea.

Drink two large glasses after every bowel movement; more if you are thirsty. If you are not eating properly (or at all), you need to drink three litres of water a day plus whatever is departing from you. If you feel like eating, have a bland, high-carbohydrate diet. Heavy greasy foods will probably give you stomach cramps. If the diarrhoea is bad, or you are passing blood or slime, or if you have a fever, you will probably need antibiotics in addition to fluid replacement. Wherever possible seek medical advice before starting antibiotics. If this is not possible then a three-day course of ciprofloxacin (500mg twice a day) or norfloxacin is appropriate.

If the diarrhoea is greasy and bulky and is accompanied by eggy burps, the likely cause is giardia (see page 125).

symptoms settle down fairly quickly and eventually you are just tired. 'Tired all the time' is one of the most common symptoms among expats in Africa, and bilharzia, giardia, amoeba and intestinal yeast are the most common culprits.

Although bilharzia is difficult to diagnose, it can be tested at specialist travel clinics. Ideally tests need to be done at least six weeks after likely exposure and will determine whether you need treatment. Fortunately it is easy to treat at present.

Avoiding bilharzia

- If you are bathing, swimming, paddling or wading in fresh water that you think may carry a bilharzia risk, try to get out of the water within ten minutes.
- Avoid bathing or paddling on shores within 200m of villages or places where people use the water a great deal, especially reedy shores or where there is lots of water weed.
- Dry off thoroughly with a towel; rub vigorously.
- If your bathing water comes from a risky source try to ensure that the water is taken from the lake in the early morning and stored snail-free, otherwise it should be filtered or Dettol or Cresol added.
- Bathing early in the morning is safer than bathing in the last half of the day.
- Cover yourself with DEET insect repellent before swimming: it may offer some protection.

Skin infections Any mosquito bite or small nick in the skin gives an opportunity for bacteria to foil the body's usually excellent defences; it will surprise many travellers how quickly skin infections start in warm humid climates and it is essential to clean and cover even the slightest wound. Creams are not as effective as a good drying antiseptic such as dilute iodine, potassium permanganate (a few crystals in half a cup of water) or crystal (or gentian) violet. At least one of these should be available in most towns.

If the wound starts to throb or becomes red and the redness starts to spread, or the wound oozes, and especially if you develop a fever, antibiotics will probably be needed: flucloxacillin (250mg four times a day) or cloxacillin (500mg four times a day). For those allergic to penicillin, erythromycin (500mg twice a day) for five days should help. See a doctor if the symptoms do not start to improve in 48 hours.

Fungal infections also get a hold easily in hot, moist climates, so wear 100% cotton socks and underwear and shower frequently. An itchy rash in the groin or flaking between the toes is likely to be a fungal infection. This needs treatment with an antifungal cream such as Canesten (clotrimazole); if this is not available try Whitfield's ointment (compound benzoic acid ointment) or crystal violet (although this will turn you purple).

Prickly heat A fine pimply rash on the trunk is likely to be heat rash; cool showers, dabbing (not rubbing) dry, and talc will help; if it's bad you may need to check into an air-conditioned hotel room for a while. Slowing down to a relaxed schedule, wearing only loose, baggy 100% cotton clothes and sleeping naked under a fan will reduce the problem.

Damage from the sun The incidence of skin cancer is rocketing as Caucasians are travelling more and spending more time exposing themselves to the sun. Keep out of the sun during the middle of the day and, if you must expose yourself to it, build up gradually from 20 minutes per day. Be especially careful of sun reflecting off water, and wear a T-shirt and lots of waterproof SPF 15 or higher suncream when swimming; snorkelling often leads to scorched backs of the thighs, so wear Bermuda shorts. Sun exposure ages the skin and makes people prematurely wrinkly; cover up with long loose clothes and wear a hat whenever you can.

Foot damage If you wear old plimsolls or flip-flops on the beach you will avoid getting coral, urchin spines or venomous fish spines in your feet. If you do tread on a venomous fish, soak the foot in hot (but not scalding) water until sometime after the pain subsides; this may mean 20–30 minutes' immersion in all. Take the foot out of the water to top it up, to prevent scalding. If the pain returns, re-immerse the foot. Once the venom has been heat-inactivated, get a doctor to check and remove any bits of fish spines in the wound.

Meningitis This is a particularly nasty disease, as it can kill within hours of the first symptoms appearing. Usually it starts as a thumping headache and high fever; there may be a blotchy rash, too. The tetravalent vaccine (eg: Mengivax ACWY) protects against meningococcal A C W135 and Y strains of bacteria, which cause the serious forms of meningitis. It is recommended for most of sub-Saharan Africa, but specific advice should be sought. Other forms of meningitis exist (usually viral), but there are no vaccines available for these. Local papers normally report localised outbreaks. If you have a severe headache and fever, go to a doctor immediately.

Rabies Rabies may be carried by all four-legged mammals (beware the village dogs and small monkeys that are used to being fed in the parks) and is passed on to humans through a bite, a scratch or a lick of an open wound. You must always assume that any animal is rabid and medical help should be sought as soon as is practicably possible. In the interim, scrub the wound thoroughly with soap and bottled/boiled water for five minutes, then pour on a strong iodine or alcohol solution. This can help to prevent the rabies virus from entering the body and will guard against wound infections, including tetanus. The decision whether or not to

Snakes rarely attack unless provoked, and bites are unusual among travellers. You are less likely to get bitten if you wear strong shoes and long trousers when in the bush. Most snakes are harmless, and even venomous species will only dispense venom in about half of their bites. If bitten, therefore, you are unlikely to have received venom; keeping this fact in mind may help you to stay calm.

Many so-called 'first-aid' techniques do more harm than good. Cutting into the wound is harmful; tourniquets are dangerous; suction and electrical inactivation devices do not work. The only treatment is anti-venom.

If you think you have been bitten by a venomous snake, follow this advice:

- Try to keep calm – it is likely that no venom has been dispensed
- Prevent movement of the bitten limb by applying a splint
- Keep the bitten limb BELOW heart height to slow the spread of any venom
- If you have a crêpe bandage, wrap it around the whole limb (eg: all the way from the toes to the thigh), as tight as you would for a sprained ankle or a muscle pull
- Evacuate to a hospital that has anti-venom.

Here's what NOT to do:

- NEVER give aspirin; paracetamol is safe
- NEVER cut or suck the wound
- DO NOT apply ice packs
- DO NOT apply potassium permanganate

If the offending snake can be captured without risk of someone else being bitten, take it to show the doctor – but beware since even a decapitated head is able to dispense venom in a reflex bite.

have the highly effective rabies vaccine will depend on the nature of your trip. It is definitely advised if you intend to handle animals, or you are likely to be more than 24 hours away from medical help.

Ideally, three pre-exposure doses should be taken over a minimum 21-day period.

If you are bitten by any animal, treatment should be given as soon as possible. At least two post-bite rabies injections are needed, even by immunised people. Those who have not been immunised will need a full course of injections together with rabies immunoglobulin (RIG), but this product is expensive (around US$800) and may be hard to come by. This is another reason why pre-exposure vaccination should be encouraged in travellers who are planning to visit more remote areas. Treatment should be given as soon as possible, but it is never too late to seek help as the incubation period for rabies can be very long. Bites closer to the brain are always more serious. Remember if you contract rabies, mortality is 100% and death from rabies is probably one of the worst ways to go.

Treating local people You may be asked to provide medical help. Many local villagers believe that every white person is a doctor, perhaps because most travellers carry a significant amount of medicine with them.

Aspirin is particularly useful, as it is unlikely to harm anyone and is often seen as a cure for everything. Vitamin pills also enjoy a legendary status. NEVER hand out antibiotics carelessly, as you risk making someone seriously ill if you give them an inadequate dose or they fail to complete a course. Take care, too, when administering eye drops or bandaging sores, as infection is very easily passed on. If there is a local doctor nearby, it is better to send a person with these sorts of ailments to them. He or she will be there to continue treatment long after you have gone. If you do have some medical background, bear in mind that the local health post may be poorly equipped and may appreciate some of your surplus supplies.

ON YOUR RETURN

Health checks If you suspect you may have caught bilharzia, for example, you should certainly see a doctor when you return to your own country. This also obviously applies if you contracted malaria on your trip, or if you fall ill after you have come home. Remember to complete your course of malaria prophylaxis.

FURTHER READING Self-prescribing has its hazards, so if you are going anywhere very remote, consider taking a health guidebook. Here are some we recommend:

Bugs, Bites & Bowels by Jane Wilson-Howarth (Cadogan, 1999). For adult health matters.
Your Child Abroad: A Travel Health Guide by Jane Wilson-Howarth and Matthew Ellis (Bradt Travel Guides, 2005). For those travelling with children.
Where There Is No Doctor: Village Health Care Handbook for Africa by David Werner, Carol Thuman, Jane Maxwell and Andrew Pearson. (Macmillan Education, 1994).

SECURITY

> The black people possess some admirable qualities. They are seldom unjust and have a greater abhorrence of injustice than any other people. There is complete security in their country. Neither traveller nor inhabitant in it has anything to fear from robbers or men of violence. They do not confiscate the property of any white man who dies in that country, even if it be uncounted wealth. They are careful to observe the hours of prayer, and assiduous in attending them in congregations and in bringing up their children to them.
>
> *Ibn Battuta, Moroccan traveller, 1352; translated by H A R Gibb*

Of course things can go wrong anywhere and remote areas undoubtedly make things trickier. More often than not security issues are a matter of being as well informed as possible and making a sensible judgement. Avoid all current rebel areas and heed local advice. Remember that there are hundreds of thousands of visitors to Africa every year and only a small percentage may have a bad experience. Realistically, that person could well have had a similar experience at home or taken unnecessary risks.

PERSONAL With day-to-day security issues, you will need to make your own judgement on the situation and act accordingly, using common sense. Africa is generally a safe place to travel and, more often than not, you will be surprised by the kindness and hospitality of the African people; respect it. When walking around towns or cities, always look as though you know where you are going and stick to busy roads rather than isolated alleys. As always, dress respectfully and do not flash money, cameras and jewellery around. Moneybelts next to your body are the best way to carry cash and other valuables when away from your vehicle. If in any way you do feel threatened by a situation, drive away or find the nearest local police

5

station or security guard. When people in Africa have so little, looking rich will not help your security situation.

VEHICLE Lock everything up at night. Locking yourself in your vehicle at night is generally not necessary, but judge each situation for yourself. Do always lock and put everything away before leaving your vehicle. If you are on a motorbike or cycling, many campsites and backpackers' hostels have secure areas for you to lock up your valuables. We did not carry our passports or other important documents on us all the time, only when we left the vehicle unattended.

WILD ANIMALS Out in the bush, and particularly in areas where there are significant numbers of wildlife, there can be a danger from wild animals. Even when they are not a physical danger, monkeys can prove a great inconvenience, playing with your windscreen wipers, for example. In general the chances of encountering hostile animals is low. Nearly all instances of animal attacks occur when animals are surprised, protecting their young or where the animal perceives a danger to itself.

Avoiding these situations is nearly always a simple matter of exercising care and attention. Drivers already have protection in their vehicles, but frightening elephants and other large animals in game parks should be avoided. Be careful around waterholes, particularly at dusk when more animals come to drink. Most accidents occur where hippos are bathing near waterholes; watch out also for buffaloes. Crocodiles are another possible risk in some areas, but rangers will be aware of these problem places. Attacks on humans by the big cats are very rare. Hyenas may scurry about close to a camping area, but present no threat in the daytime. Monkeys can be a real pest in some campsites, and you should be wary of inquisitive warthogs. Since all visitors to the big parks with private vehicles have to camp in designated areas, the risks are minimised. That said, it is unwise to leave the confines of a tent or vehicle after dark. Plan ahead for that night-time loo stop.

Obviously those hiking or watching game on foot are more at risk. There are some minimal risks on the lower slopes of the big mountains, Mount Kenya, Kilimanjaro, the Ruwenzoris and other remote hilly regions. Never run from a wild beast; in the event of any danger try to get into the protection of trees. Hikers should be aware that there are dangerous snakes, and should be particularly careful in thick undergrowth and tall grasses. Fortunately most snakes, and indeed most animals, will be long gone before the approach of a human.

Also see vehicle *Security* in *Chapter 3*, page 57, and bicycle *Camping equipment* and *Accommodation and food*, *Chapter 3*, pages 97 and 99.

SAFETY FOR WOMEN TRAVELLERS

> Within this enclosed women's world, so to say, behind the walls and fortifications of it, I felt the presence of a great ideal, without which the garrison would not have carried on so gallantly; the ideal of a Millennium when women were to reign supreme in the world. The old mother at such times would take on a new shape, and sit enthroned as a massive dark symbol of that mighty female deity who had existed in old ages, before the time of the prophet's God. Of her they never lost sight, but they were, before all, practical people with an eye on the needs of the moment and with infinite readiness of resource.
>
> *Karen Blixen, Out of Africa*

We didn't often come across women or, for that matter, men travelling on their own. A lot of single women were either backpacking in loose groups or joining

The two men sat drinking beside the pool, as dusk settled over the country hotel just outside Bo in Sierra Leone. They looked like missionaries; who else would be driving around here apart from us? We had driven from Freetown along a road that we thought would be better by now – after all, the war had finished five years ago and the country has diamonds to pay for the improvements expected.

'Sit down; have a beer.' It was abruptly clear that the two guests were not missionaries. One had been living in the country for most of the last dozen years. The other had arrived from, among other places, Guinea. 'With the war over, where are all the developments promised?' we asked.

'Well, the war is technically over, but come into town [Bo, which was the rebel RUF headquarters during the struggles] and I'll show you where to buy an AK47 for a couple of hundred dollars.'

This was hardly encouraging news. In the streets of Bo there are many shops advertising diamonds for sale. A truce, then, for the sake of peace. So how was the road to Liberia, we asked. 'It's not good, but it's fine during the daytime; the villagers will help you and look after you if you have a problem. Just don't break down at night! … And don't stop to help anyone along the road – it might be a set-up,' they said. More encouragement.

We had already done that in Guinea, when a taxi-brousse full of desperate-looking locals had broken down and needed engine oil. For us, not to stop would have seemed harsh, but then just occasionally perhaps self-preservation should be the main consideration. It's a gut reaction thing; each traveller will have to make their own decision.

'So what is your mission in the country?' they asked.

'Just tourists,' we replied. We started to feel rather silly. 'Tourists in Sierra Leone!' one exclaimed. 'I thought that had stopped years ago! Even then it was only along the beachfronts of Aberdeen and Lumley, which the Chinese have bought up recently.'

Our hosts were clearly wise to many things that we could only imagine from media hype of the past and the recent film, *Blood Diamond*, which portrays the country in a grim light. So far we'd had a pleasant time in the country – the coastline near Freetown is spectacular, a paradise lost. Even frenetic, sweaty, overcrowded, dilapidated Freetown has a certain disintegrating charm. Our hosts were well liked around here – they must be doing some good for the people. The waitresses also showed attentive interest in us all.

For security reasons, we cannot divulge the names or occupations of our new friends, but we thank them for their entertainment and advice, even if it was rather scary!

PS The drive was exciting, but only because the route was another fun, off-road, dry muddy lane to the Liberian border. The village people were very friendly and we didn't break down. The first people to greet us at the Liberian border were Pakistani peacekeepers, but that's another story (see box, *'Salaam aleikum' in Liberia*, page 132).

organised tours. There may be hundreds of travellers who have done Africa on their own, but we have found that those who started out on their own hitched up with other travellers on a variety of transport. This is often the case where a country, certain borders or specific routes, has a dodgy reputation. The previous authors met a mother and daughter who were driving across the African continent and had successfully completed most of Africa without any hitches. It did help that the daughter was a professional auto mechanic!

Being greeted by a large white tank and soldiers with blue helmets was both welcoming and intimidating at the same time when we arrived at the Liberian border post of Bo Waterside. 'Salaam Aleikum.' The Pakistani soldiers nodded and seemed eager to talk. 'What is your country, madam memsahib? Pakistani cricket team, is it good, yes sahib?' This was the Pakistani Battalion, nicknamed PakBatt, motto 'Brave and Brisk'.

The main cart track 'road' from Sierra Leone had been a shock to the system, and escaping unscathed from the diamond smugglers of Bo was a relief, but getting this far was very exciting. We really hadn't thought it would be this easy to visit the country, nor had we guessed how safe it would feel. How many AK47-wielding rebels would we see? You really can't judge from any government travel website just how sensible it is to make these journeys. Yet on the whole trip we never once felt intimidated by anyone, even on this diversion to the recently war-torn former American colony. Optimistic, happy-looking people greeted us everywhere. We never saw any gun-toting soldiers of any persuasion, except the UN.

So what is Liberia like today? The capital Monrovia shows only a few signs of the wanton destruction of the war. The markets are stuffed with imported goods; huge generators hum all day. The restaurants are expensive, catering to the armies of UN advisers, and the hotel prices are set up to match their enhanced (fat) salaries. Huge numbers of American, British, European and Lebanese businesspeople are making the most of the new investment opportunities. However, the rainforest in the countryside that we saw is mostly devastated. The main roads are fair tarmac, but no-one has electric power other than from privately owned generators. The rubber trees are still dripping and the Firestone Tyre Company is said to be working again, as noticeboards advertised across the country.

Leaving Liberia upcountry for the backroads of southern Guinea, we were in the land of the BanBatt, the Bangladeshi Battalion. More smiling Asian faces and Salaam Aleikum to wish us goodbye.

Liberia is a great place. It has the first woman president of any African nation; perhaps that is reason enough for hope!

KNOWING YOUR VEHICLE An important difference for women travellers is in equipment weight on the vehicle. Rather than carrying 20-litre jerrycans, it is a good idea to carry 10-litre cans, which are easier to lift off the vehicle. Toolboxes should be smaller and sparingly distributed, once again making them easier to lift. Tyres could be kept inside the vehicle, rather than on top of the vehicle, so they are easier to access.

Otherwise, for women travellers everything else we have discussed regarding driving, biking or cycling through Africa is the same. One concern might be mechanical knowledge of your choice of transport, but then most men who drive on the African continent do not have much knowledge before departure either. After only a few weeks on the road, everyone will begin to learn very quickly the ins and outs of their vehicle, motorbike or bicycle. A helping hand is never far away in Africa and, although in more isolated areas you could run into problems, someone will always appear eventually (except perhaps if you get lost in the Sahara; be especially careful here; drive with at least one other vehicle).

It would be a good idea to do a 4x4 course and drive the vehicle or bike as often as possible. Even with a team of man and woman, it is best to learn, listen and get involved as much as you can. Your male counterpart might fall ill and be completely dependent on your skills to get you from A to B.

ATTITUDES TO WOMEN If you are a woman travelling on your own, your only other concern is going to be the mentality of the African people. Women are seen as having a specific role within the community, and in our eyes this may seem inferior. Remember that this has been part of their culture for centuries. Although not strictly true for every country you visit in Africa, many border posts, banks and embassies are usually run and staffed entirely by men. If you are travelling with a male, it is sometimes best to let the man do most of the talking. Obviously, if you are a woman travelling on your own, you have no choice but to communicate with whoever might be there. Be polite and respectful and you should have no problems.

When travelling through more isolated areas of Africa you will often see men lounging under the acacia trees, enjoying the shade, while the women are doing all the work – collecting water, reaping the fields, cooking, caring for the children and generally running around making sure home and family are looked after. Men are supposedly the financial providers within the community and often seem to do little else. But how do they provide the finances if they spend all their time lounging about under trees?

Most African women (or at least those who initially had the opportunity to attend school) never complete school. They start to help around the house as soon as they are able. It is also rare to see children playing. Girls in particular have to start helping around the house at a very young age. We were delighted whenever we came across children just playing with sticks and stones, or swimming and splashing around.

Through their indoctrination into helping the community at such a young age, women are usually very isolated and will speak only the local tongue, even when their male counterparts speak either French or English. Thus you will find that you will communicate mostly with men.

If you have been invited to somebody's home, the women will often provide the meal and then disappear, eating with the family in the kitchen. This is particularly so in Algeria and other Muslim countries. In that case women are perhaps privileged, because a male guest is only allowed into the guestroom, just next to the front door. If he were to venture into the rest of the house he might see the women of the house without their head coverings, and that would never do! As a woman, I was allowed everywhere in the house – the kitchen, living room, the television room, etc. Where we had a common language, I could communicate with the women and the men equally.

Women are also often shy in communicating with an outsider and are not used to being asked for an opinion, their lives revolving around their day-to-day responsibilities and survival. Their attitude may come across as, 'A European woman, what does she know? She is barren, no children, not married, driving this car, no home ...' This attitude is quite common and you should certainly not take offence. If time permits and you have the opportunity, it can make entertaining conversation between yourself and the local women. We can learn a lot from one another.

THE MOST DANGEROUS

Philip Briggs
The most dangerous animal in Africa, exponentially a greater threat than anything mentioned above, is the anopheles mosquito, which carries the malaria parasite. Humans, particularly when behind a steering wheel, run them a close second!
From *Tanzania: The Bradt Travel Guide*

Practicalities   SAFETY FOR WOMEN TRAVELLERS

5

Some of the greatest fun can be had at markets. In some Arab countries it is the men who trade, but often it is a woman's world. Sometimes, having walked for miles with their wares on their backs and heads, they transform a dust bowl into a riot of colour, smells and sounds. Children trace your every footstep, shouts offer you the local brew, food, cloth or even a sheep for sale ... you'll need plenty of patience and time to barter for whatever you want to buy.

Sometimes you'll experience African life as just a rest under the awning of a market stall, laughing and shouting with the women. You may never really learn much about African women, their joys and fears, laughter and tears. Just relax and enjoy the unspoken shared moments together. You'll have a lot in common.

HOW TO DRESS It is very important to dress in accordance with the social norms in the countries you are passing through, to avoid giving offence and indeed to feel more comfortable in the heat yourself. There are reasons for local people's choice of clothing beyond religious ones. In north Africa, it is best to cover up with loose tops that hang below your bottom, with loose trousers below. Long sleeves are advisable, again, not only for religious reasons, but because you will also be protected from the sun.

I have always worn a long Pakistani tunic-style dress when in north Africa, over Rohan or Regatta trousers, giving the advantage of lots of zipped pockets with the added security that no-one else can see them. Dressing down, as you might call it, also goes a long way to avoiding sexual harassment by African men, particularly in Muslim countries. Again, this is dependent on the area you are travelling in and can take many forms. You may be followed, laughed at, constantly touched, hissed or whistled at, usually innocently, but it can become uncomfortable and annoying.

When you're driving, you will probably be most comfortable in trousers, as a skirt can too easily get torn or caught on some protruding part of the vehicle; there's always something sticking out and waiting to catch you! I usually wore a loose long-sleeved shirt with the sleeves partly rolled up, and a scarf over my hair, tied Tuareg-style in a turban, to stop it blowing constantly in my eyes in the unavoidable wind. It also helps to keep some of the sand out of your hair, a special problem if it's long. I would sometimes wear a T-shirt when driving, but would always cover my arms when in towns or villages in Muslim countries.

Some European women in Africa prefer to wear a wraparound skirt, T-shirt and headband. Just be discreet.

Sometimes young women come off organised tours in their shorts and tight sleeveless or strapless tops, and you can see the reaction of the women – often tittering behind closed palms – and men, usually gawping in astonishment. This does not mean that you can never wear shorts, tank tops, bikinis or swimming costumes – just be very aware of your environment and what the other women are wearing.

Much of southern Africa is pretty relaxed when it comes to clothing, but again this is dependent on the area you are visiting. Most of the rest of Africa, however, is conservative and should be respected accordingly.

If you are a woman travelling on your own and you find that a particular town, city or even country is becoming a little overbearing regarding the attention of the opposite sex, you have three options. You could either find other travelling companions, use a guide (you'll have to shop around) who will often keep the masses at bay, or leave town. No travel is worth getting hurt. Egypt and Morocco can be particularly intensive regarding sexual harassment, though I did not ever feel threatened, just irritated by the constant hassle of touts wanting to sell their wares at inflated prices.

It was a lively and colourful ceremony when Wangari Maathai was awarded the Nobel Peace Prize in Oslo in December 2004, with vibrant singing and dancing bringing alive the black-suited observers.

She was the first African woman to win the prize since it began in 1901. The prize was awarded to her for setting up the Green Belt Movement in Kenya. As part of this project, over 30 million trees have been planted across Africa. An environmentalist, she links environmental issues with women's rights, democracy, development and peace. Each is dependent on the others. If we don't take care of our environment, how can we take care of each other?

She became an MP with the change of government in Kenya in 2002, but in the past was subjected to police brutality, and spent time in prison. She instigated the planting of trees in parks to demand the release of political prisoners, trees symbolising the struggle for democracy.

Her main theme is that the environment is a reflection of government: first we must heal the earth's environmental wounds, then in the process our own wounds will be healed. We must remember that we belong to a larger family of life. Humanity must shift to a new level of consciousness. We must shed fear and give hope – now!

With Wangari Maathai's shining example, there is indeed hope for Africa.

AVOIDING HARASSMENT Sexual harassment is not isolated to single women. Even if you're travelling with a male companion, he could be asked by an Arab man whether he can perform liberties with you. Or whether he will sell you for a certain number of camels! It is unfortunate that Arab men, particularly Muslims, tend to think that Western women are promiscuous and ready to jump into bed with any man at the drop of a hat. It is best just to try to ignore such a situation and state a firm 'No'.

There are certain things you can do to minimise sexual harassment:

- Dress is the most obvious. Do not flaunt yourself; dress conservatively. Your own personal experiences in Africa will be so much more fulfilling, with both men and women.
- A wedding ring is often helpful in Africa. If you are being hassled, refer to your husband as often as you can, even if you don't have one!
- Avoid eye contact and ignore all rude comments. If you are feeling threatened in any way, walk to the nearest public café and ask the owner for his or her help in getting a taxi home.
- Always know where you are and stick to busy roads rather than isolated alleyways.

SHEWEE What more can wee say? Speaks for itself really! A unique product specially designed for women only, for use in awkward places. See www.shewee.com for more information.

ACCOMMODATION

In Africa you will always be able to find a place to stay, whether it be with the local community, a hotel, bed and breakfast, pension, mission, youth hostel, backpackers' hostel, campsite, or just sleeping in the bush or desert.

One of the more enticing reasons for driving, cycling or biking through Africa is the fascination of meeting other cultures and tribes in the context of the

Practicalities ACCOMMODATION

5

continent's open spaces, beautiful scenery and often complete isolation from the outside world. Opportunities will arise for you to sleep out in the bush, something that you may come to love, giving you freedom to move as you please. The accepted rule that applies is *leave nothing behind but your footprints*.

If bush sleeping is not your cup of tea, or you cannot find a place where you feel comfortable and undisturbed, more conventional accommodation is available throughout the continent. In some parts of Africa, such as the east coast, there are plenty of lodgings along the coast, while in central Africa you will need to search to find accommodation for the night. Along the west coast, some countries accommodate campers, while others offer nothing but hotels.

Outside major cities in places like the Congo and Central African Republic, you are unlikely to find any type of accommodation unless you are lucky enough to come across a mission. Throughout southern Africa you will find a plethora of choices, except perhaps that idyllic wild bush camping spot for which you have been longing.

For more specific information about hotels, guesthouses, etc, see *Where to stay* in *Chapter 7* page 167, and *Chapter 9, A–Z Country Guide*.

✉ POST AND TELECOMMUNICATIONS

All over Africa, any reasonable-sized settlement will have a post office and a telephone. The question is whether the phone is working. Some systems are so old you wonder how they manage to get a line. And often they don't, or you may get cut off midstream. Now mobile phone networks are developing fast and have fairly good coverage in Africa, though not everywhere and certainly not in the jungles or parts of the Sahara. Internet access is available in the most unlikely places, as well as the larger towns and cities. Of course they may not always be online, sometimes they are very slow and sometimes they are expensive; but they are always a good means of communication.

POST In every capital city and larger town there is a post office with post, telephone, fax, poste restante and courier services.

Poste restante Poste restante is a postal service available at the main post office of almost every capital city. Although now generally superseded by email, it is still a general address to which family and friends can send post. Letters and parcels are kept for up to four weeks, and some form of identification will be needed for collection. You may also have to pay to collect it. All post is kept in alphabetical order. Make sure that your name is marked clearly in bold, black capital letters, underlining the first letter of either your surname or your first name. This will make it a lot easier to collect. For example: Joe **B**loggs, c/o Poste Restante, Central Post Office, Gonder (town as required), Ethiopia (country as required). Note that for all French-speaking countries you need to write 'PIT' instead of 'Poste Restante'.

The success rate of actually receiving a poste-restante letter or parcel depends on the individual country, and do remember that it can take at least two to three weeks for a letter to get to its final destination.

If you are collecting a parcel, it usually needs to go through an arduous customs check. It is advisable to indicate that the parcel contains old clothes and food, rather than new goods, otherwise you may have to pay duty.

If you are sending letters home, ask the cashier to frank all the stamps in front of you, as there are plenty of stories about stamps being removed from letters which then never reach their destination.

Morning comes and we cross the river to Gabon. Gabon too has its good bits of road and its strange aboriginal villages. The Pygmies are not far from here, but we don't see any. The road becomes a rutted dirt highway through the magnificent trees of the equatorial forest. Later, camping is a problem, with few places. Finally we stop to cook, but a local appears from nowhere and suggests that camping here is not a good idea; there are too many monkeys or elephants, but maybe it's too many inquisitive villagers. We don't really know; it's a bit forbidding.

We drive on and on into the dark night; the road brushes through thick bamboo forest. After hours some lights appear; it is 21.00, we are in Ndjolé, a town on the banks of the wide Ogooué River. We can't believe our eyes as we pull up outside the Auberge St Hubert. The building could be anywhere along the banks of the Loire in France, except it's hot, muggy and the cicadas are deafening. Inside we are greeted by 'Madame la Propriétaire' and some expatriate French guests. We have a beer and find ourselves discussing the state of the country with the expats. One is *en route* to Franceville on business; the other is out from the capital Libreville. Our room temporarily transports us to France, to a small hotel, a little tatty, a bit smoky and with rather tacky curtains. It could be in Amboise or Blois.

Alternative mail services A good and perhaps easier and safer alternative to post offices is that offered by American Express offices. Anyone carrying an Amex card or their travellers' cheques is entitled to use the company's offices worldwide as a mailing address. This service is free. A booklet is available from American Express (*Amex Hse, Edward St, Brighton BN2 1YL;* ✆ *01273 693555*) giving a complete list of its offices' addresses around the world.

TELECOMMUNICATIONS Fax, telephone and email facilities are widely available now, often even in the smallest towns. All capital cities and most larger towns will have public fax, telephone, skype and internet facilities, so there is no excuse not to keep in touch!

All these facilities obviously rely on the individual country's telecommunications network, the quality of which varies greatly. An overseas call is often clearer and easier to make than one to a neighbouring town, as overseas calls are routed via satellite.

Telephone calls and faxes to Europe (the international telephone code for the UK is +44, and for the US, +1) typically cost US$3–10 per minute, which can be much the same as an hour on the internet. It is well worth setting up an internet email account before you leave, so that you can check and send emails on any computer without incurring high phone charges.

The French cultural centres in francophone countries and the British Council often have email facilities open to the public, but they can be more expensive than the local internet cafés. Remember that computer viruses are much more of a problem when using public facilities, so do warn the recipients to virus-check all the mail you send them.

Practicalities POST AND TELECOMMUNICATIONS

5

Part Two

ON THE ROAD

DAVID LAMBETH
RALLY & OVERLAND

0044 (0) 1205 871945

www.davidlambeth.co.uk
N 53 02.751 E 00 09.041

bigbluecoach@hotmail.com

Lincs, UK.

Supply, construction and preparation of long distance Rally Raid and Overland Expedition motorcycles and 4x4s.

Experienced off road assistance team available for competition events, private expeditions and desert training.

Regular involvement in many international events including:

- **Dakar**
- **Tuareg Morocco**
- **Optic Tunisia**
- **Orpi Morocco**
- **Alto Turia Spain**
- **El Chott Tunisia**

Generously supported by
KRIEGA backpacks.

6

Your Vehicle

This chapter provides you with some useful information about driving in Africa, recovery techniques and an overview of daily maintenance, breakdown and repairs. It also deals with African bureaucracy and the challenges you will face along the way.

DRIVING TECHNIQUES

We aim to give you an insight into the different conditions you can expect to encounter and the best way to tackle them.

Become familiar with the 4x4 capability of your vehicle. Does it have permanent or selectable four-wheel drive? Does it have differential lock, and how can this be used to your advantage? Does it have freewheel hubs or not? All this information will be in the vehicle handbook and is essential knowledge, helping to prevent you getting stuck in difficult terrain.

Driving in Africa can be hot and exhausting. Conditions are harsh and days can be unavoidably long. It is preferable to share the driving and the experiences as much as possible. Do not drive at night unless it is completely unavoidable. With cattle and people straying onto the roads during the hours of darkness, there is constant danger. Many African vehicles have either pathetically poor or blindingly brilliant lights stuck on full beam. Some loads are wider than the vehicles and can be invisible at night.

Be very careful when you first reach the continent and watch out for the local drivers. Some car drivers drive phenomenally fast, including those share-taxis that have 11 people crammed inside and screech around corners with bald tyres! Buses are not always much slower, but are equally overloaded. The African travelling public have a lot to put up with.

You need to anticipate the driver's actions; many do not do the obvious. In fact expecting the unexpected should become second nature. Many vehicles don't have mirrors. Even when fitted, mirrors may not be used. You will soon learn how Africans drive!

Remember that a lot of African roads are quiet most of the time, and therefore people will not be alert for vehicles passing. This means you must drive **very slowly** through villages and towns; children run out unexpectedly, and women with heavy waterpots on their heads may not be looking out for traffic. If you should be so unfortunate as to knock someone down, it will always be your fault, whatever the circumstances. Animals are also a potential threat much of the time. Camels in particular, with their noses high in the air, seem oblivious to other road users.

Although some main roads are mostly good, there is always the possible threat at any time of large unmarked pot-holes; uncovered manholes aren't totally unknown and surfaces can be suddenly rough. With so many different road surfaces, gravel tracks, sandy pistes and muddy holes, driving in Africa can be great fun. But don't get carried away by the thrill of the moment; Africa will punish you severely. Always drive with great caution.

Keep to a moderate speed on the open road. We never drove anywhere over 80km/h (50mph); at this speed you can anticipate and react to obstacles and bad sections of road. A slower speed also helps to reduce wear and tear and is more economical on fuel. In sand and on bad roads and tracks it is preferable to coax the vehicle to go in the right direction rather than to fight the wheel and risk damage. Take it easy, be vigilant.

The benefits of walking through an obstacle before driving through should never be underestimated, particularly when faced with deep soft sand, water, mud holes and rocks. The chances of getting stuck or causing major damage because of an unseen object can be greatly reduced. Finally, keep your thumbs out of the steering wheel rim on rough roads, because hitting even small objects can make the steering wheel kick back, enough to bruise or even break them.

The three main conditions you will face are sand, mud and corrugations. Each requires a different technique and presents its own set of problems. Many main roads in Africa are not in such a bad condition (with the exception of much of central Africa, Ethiopia and northern Kenya). Going trans-Africa you will inevitably encounter one or all of the following situations depending on where and when you go.

SAND Driving on sand can initially be daunting, but within a short time you will be able to pick out the different types of conditions that sand presents. It can be hard packed, quite fast, smooth with some resistance, or seriously soft and deep. In between are countless variations. Sand can change abruptly from one condition to another; be very careful until you get a feel for it. Driving across sand dunes is potentially dangerous and needs extreme care. Vehicles can easily roll over in dune country. Never drive on a dune at any angle other than straight on and straight down. They have a habit of forming with hollow zones that cannot be seen. Consider a reconnaissance walk on any daunting sand dune sections. Most main desert routes avoid dunes of any significance. If you intend to follow sandy pistes for some days it will pay to let some air out of all your tyres. With flatter tyres a greater surface area exists, enabling the vehicle to float more above the sand. The effect this practice has on your mobility is immediately noticeable. Make sure your tyres are built for this, and have a gauge to check the pressure. Most dual-purpose tyres can be run around 1.5 bar (approximately 21psi) in sand. Keep a check on tyre temperatures frequently in sand if the pressures are low. Try to run them with the highest practical pressure for the conditions, unless there is no choice.

It's amazing how well a 4x4 vehicle copes in most sand. The key is momentum. Using high-range 4x4 is generally more appropriate for most desert crossings. We used low-range only when we could see a particularly soft patch ahead or were already stuck. It varies with the vehicle you have. Big throaty Toyotas have less likelihood of getting bogged. When you see a section that you feel needs low-range, give yourself plenty of room for the approach. Try to get into a suitable gear, probably low-range third, before you hit the soft sand. This will give you the momentum you need; try to change down smoothly to avoid losing it. Changing gear too suddenly in soft sand can bring you to a stop as quickly as braking. If you can change gear successfully, you can retain some momentum and avoid getting stuck. It takes some practice, though. After a while it becomes a bit of a challenge trying to avoid getting bogged, especially if you are in convoy with experienced Sahara drivers, including the locals. Avoid becoming over-confident, enjoy the adrenalin rushes and highs of desert driving, and act carefully; you'll have endless fun!

But we digress. Try not to use the brakes, as you will build up a wall of sand in front of your tyres, making it harder to get moving. If you have to stop, look for a harder area and just take your foot slowly off the accelerator. If you feel yourself getting stuck, try 'waggling' the steering wheel from side to side; this helps to reduce the build-up of sand. When you do come to a halt, drop the clutch immediately and check the situation. Sometime reversing out back to solid ground is possible and sufficient. Using excess power to get moving could seriously damage your vehicle, even snapping a drive shaft. In any case too much wheelspin will just make it worse, getting you bogged even more deeply.

Once bogged, you have more strenuous options. Often scooping away the sand from in front of and around the sides of all the wheels will be enough to get started. If not, and your vehicle has diff lock, then engage it, select your low ratio, first or second, and try to engage the clutch smoothly, edging forward until you gain momentum. Sand should also be removed from anywhere underneath if the vehicle is very deeply dug in.

If this fails, then it's out with the sand ladders or sandmats. Two will often be enough, but they must be well dug in and as level as possible. Placing them in front of the rear wheels is usually best. Watch out behind as ladders can be pushed forcibly backwards once motion is gained. Having your better half, whoever that may be, add some weight by pushing will also help, but they must be prepared to leap quickly out of harm's way as soon as you start to move. It can also happen that the sand ladders disappear below the surface of the sand, leaving no trace on top. If this is the case, it is obviously useful to have a person there to tell you where to dig for them! Sometimes it is possible to select reverse and sail out backwards. If you are unfortunate enough to be stuck in soft sand on an upward slope you may be in for a long slow session using your two ladders, or more if you have them. Once moving, don't stop until you are on a harder surface or on a downward slope. Don't forget to walk back and retrieve your sand ladders.

Driving on a good sandy piste is a rare experience these days, and one to be enjoyed.

MUD Mud can be worse than sand and, on a very bad section, hours can be spent extracting any vehicle except a bicycle, and your shoes too! Avoiding the main rainy seasons generally means avoiding the worst mud sections. However, be very careful driving on damp mud roads, particularly those in tropical rainforests that have exaggerated cambers. It is all too easy to start sliding sideways towards often deep ditch areas. Take these sections very, very gently, probably in your lowest gear.

A number of mud roads in Cameroon, CAR and DRC have quite steep hills, and going down these when sticky can also be a little hair-raising. Again use a low gear and crawl down. Always drive into a slide; turn the wheel into the wayward direction.

When you see a muddy section ahead, stop and engage 4x4. Select the appropriate gear before hitting the bad section. For vehicles with large engines, third-gear low-range or first-gear high-range is appropriate, and for smaller engines second-gear low-range. Don't head off thinking your speed will do the trick: this is just going to make things worse in most cases. Avoid wheelspin; it will just make you bog down deeper. When the wheels start to spin, ease off the accelerator until you pick up more traction, then accelerate gently, trying to avoid more wheelspin. Once you appear to be stuck, you'd better get out and assess the situation.

So now what? You could have a cup of tea if it's too bad. Then again, you could try reversing slightly. If you are not badly bogged, this might work. If not, then it's out with the shovel. Digging tropical mud can be rather tiring, so that tea may well be needed sometime soon. There are no quick ways out of this predicament. You need to clear away as much mud as possible. This can mean crawling about underneath to cut away compacted mud and even removing higher central mounds of the road itself. Using your sand ladder, jacks and wooden blocks may all be necessary, as well as utilising available resources like logs, rocks and bits of plank. You might have to fill in the road here and there, using whatever materials are to hand. Fortunately most muddy sections don't go on for miles, except in the Congo. Ho ho ho!

When you encounter a water-filled bog hole, or even long sections of flooded track, always stop. Walk through the hole first, and locate any logs or rocks that are often put in the hole by other drivers. These can do serious damage to the underside of your vehicle. Nine times out of ten it is better to drive through the middle of deep bog holes rather than to try to skirt round them. It is often muddier on the edges. You could end up sliding sideways into the hole, get stuck or, even worse, possibly overturn. Mud can be fun, but it can also be dangerous in certain situations.

CORRUGATIONS Corrugations are probably the most irritating and most common driving obstacle in Africa. Many roads are basically carved out of the existing terrain by grading machines. Some are excellent, but many more have not seen a grader since the day they were made or the last colonial left. Some are gravel, some hard-packed laterite (the red dusty ones); some are black murram, which is dreadful after rain. All these sorts of roads can develop corrugations: continuous ripples on the surface. They can occur after a soft section, where previous vehicles have taken the opportunity to speed up. Unfortunately they can often go on for hours at a stretch and can shake a vehicle to pieces. Invariably there is no ideal way to approach these frustrating sections. Sometimes there are other tracks beside the main route that are better.

With fairly regular corrugations, there seems to be an optimum speed at which to drive. This can often be disconcertingly fast and is potentially very dangerous. Beware! The vehicle tends to float over the bumps, doing immense damage to the suspension and also making the steering very light. It is very easy to lose control and clatter off the road. Also you may be going along at an apparently reasonable rate when the nature of the corrugations changes and the vehicle vibrates alarmingly, shuddering to a halt with tremendous shaking. In fact it's sometimes hard to slow down, as the vibration is so intense. Under these circumstances there is nothing to do but crawl along, hoping the torment will end soon. Going slowly will probably save time in the end, as speeding over corrugations invariably causes your vehicle to retaliate by breaking a spring or something else.

Once in the Cameroon jungle our engine stopped abruptly. No, it wasn't fuel problems, or any of the obvious problems, but a loose electrical connection on the injector pump solenoid, shaken apart.

VEHICLE RIVER CROSSINGS On most trips in Africa, having to drive through very deep water is not very common. That said, a flash flood in the Sahara or a raging torrent in the mountains can be encountered. The first thing to do is nothing. Park your vehicle well back and assess the hazards; crossing any torrent is potentially a very real risk. Invariably with seriously deep water the only action is to wait. Have a cup of tea.

Assuming it's safe and not too deep, walking through the water first is a must. Check for variable depth, large rocks and soft areas. If the depth of water is below the level of your radiator, fan and alternator you can fairly safely proceed slowly, trying to avoid creating any big waves as you go. Always keep a constant speed and do not change gear; correct gear selection is essential. Don't stall the engine. If you do, attempting to restart it could cause even more damage. Water and mud may have been sucked into the engine via the exhaust, which means you have a major job on your hands. So basically don't take the risk in the first place.

Recovering from this mess will probably involve other vehicles, unless you have the luxury of a winch. In deeper water you could take off the fan belt to prevent damage to the fan blades. At worst the fan can be smashed by small stones and churned-up gravel and the radiator might object as well. Another suggestion, which we have not tried, is to place a foot mat over the radiator. This is said to create a larger bow wave and larger draw down in the engine bay, hopefully keeping more of the engine out of the water.

Frankly the best options, if they exist, are to find another way or wait, unless you have any serious reasons for rushing on. We once waited three days for a river to subside, so have enough food and water on board in case. Don't even consider driving into deep water if you haven't prepared your vehicle properly (see *Chapter 3, Vehicle selection and preparation*). You will literally be landed in even deeper water.

RECOVERY TECHNIQUES

With luck and sensible driving, you may not need to use recovery techniques too often. Some of the recovery methods have already been touched on briefly in the driving section above. Below are some further points to consider. Getting stuck invariably happens when it's hot, windy or raining. Having the right equipment is the first step. Having extra equipment can make it easier. But taking every conceivable aid may in the end be the cause of your getting stuck in the first place, because of the weight factor.

How you go about extricating your vehicle from a tricky spot depends on what you are stuck in. What equipment you are carrying, what is available locally (manpower, other vehicles, logs, etc) and the availability of anchorage points all need to be considered. In almost every situation a certain amount of digging, common sense and hard work will be required. The following ideas about recovery techniques can be adapted as conditions dictate.

SAND LADDERS As we have mentioned above, and to summarise again, sand ladders (or sandmats) are most often used to get out of deep sand, but can also be used in mud, as a jacking plate for high-lift jacks and for repairing holes in damaged bridges. They can also be dangerous, especially in sand, where wheels throw them backwards. Removing the sand from around all the wheels, and from the chassis if the vehicle is grounded, is the first step. The mats should then be placed, the flatter the better, in front of the wheels with the least traction. Drive onto the mats and try to get as much speed up as possible. Do not stop until you are on a firm surface again. Sandmats can also be very useful when negotiating rotten log bridges in Congo, but again ensure they are secured in place before making any tentative advances.

HIGH-LIFT JACK Although we have not carried a high-lift jack, we would strongly recommend it to save time and energy. Always remember to put a jacking plate under it before jacking in soft ground conditions. This could be a sandmat, pieces of wood or a spare tyre. Two useful tips for recovering a vehicle with a high-lift jack are 'jack and pack' and 'jack and push'.

In 'jack and pack', the high-lift jack is used to lift the wheels clear of the ground so that material such as rocks, wood, sand ladders, etc can be packed under the wheels to increase traction. This method is useful when the vehicle is bogged up to its chassis in mud. The 'jack and push' method involves jacking the vehicle from the front or rear, so that both the wheels are off the ground. The vehicle is then pushed sideways off the jack. This method is useful when the vehicle is stuck in deep muddy ruts or grounded on a central ridge.

The high-lift jack can also be used as a winch, but it is limited to a pull the length of the jack before the whole assembly has to be reset. With all high-lift jack operations, it is important to remember always to leave the jack with the handle in the upright position when unattended.

If you do not have a high-lift jack you will probably have to spend more time getting 'de-bogged'. You can use your hydraulic jack, jacking plates, blocks of wood, spare wheels and any materials found around the site. Good luck!

WINCHING You will probably not be in a situation all that often where using a winch is the best solution. A winch could be useful if you are able to consider crossing the Congo, where there are trees and some roads have steep gradients and nasty, car-eating deep ditches. Winches are not much use in sand. When thinking about winching, you need to consider suitable anchoring points.

A natural anchor might be anything that is strong enough to take the strain, ie: trees, large boulders or rocks. Making your own anchors, from spare wheels or sand ladders stuck vertically in the ground, should only be considered when nothing else is available, as they can be potentially quite dangerous. These methods usually require a lot of effort. The spare wheel or sand ladder must be very well dug in, more so in sand. Be careful how you attach the anchor strap. Try using a bar behind the tyre or sand ladders. Cable eye clamps are another method. The direction of pull needs to be as straight and as low to the ground as possible; you will need to dig a trench for the strap to lie in.

A snatch block is another winching accessory. It is basically a heavy-duty, single-line pulley and can be used to double the pulling force by attaching it to an anchor point, then passing the winch cable through the snatch block and back to the vehicle. A snatch block can also be used to change the direction of pull when using another vehicle to winch you out.

Winches are potentially very dangerous. Whenever winching or towing, always ensure that the cable is securely fastened at both ends and all onlookers are well clear. This is very important in case the cable snaps or your anchor breaks. One person should co-ordinate the recovery and operate the winch and everyone else should stay well back while the cable is under tension. A heavy mat or blanket can also be placed over the cable to help stop it lashing if it snaps.

USING ANOTHER VEHICLE If you are travelling in convoy, many of the obstacles can be surmounted rather more easily. Using a cable between vehicles is the main method, but again be warned about snapping cables. Anchor points must be carefully considered, to limit any breakages. Also be very careful when using cables in mud, and especially if any local truck needs help.

MAINTENANCE, BREAKDOWNS AND REPAIRS

Above all, the key phrase to remember here is 'regular maintenance prevents breakdowns'. This cannot be stressed enough. Dusty conditions, extreme temperatures, contaminated fuel and bad roads all take their toll.

Consult the manufacturer's handbook for service intervals as a start, and then consider the conditions you are subjecting your vehicle to. More frequent checks will be necessary for sure. For example, desert driving means air and fuel filters will get clogged up more quickly. If you do a lot of wading, gearbox and differential oils will become contaminated and you can pick up a tank of dirty fuel just about anywhere in Africa.

The tables following are a guideline for maintenance and inspection intervals. Changing all filters more often will help prevent breakdowns. It may seem like overkill to suggest checking something like the wheel nuts every day, but the constant vibrations from corrugated roads mean that they can loosen themselves at a frightening rate. These things happen!

DAILY INSPECTION BEFORE STARTING ENGINE

Check for fluid leaks on the ground
Check for oil leaks around the engine
Engine oil level
Radiator water level
Brake- and clutch-fluid levels
Fan-belt tension
Spark plugs leads secure
Tightness of wheel nuts
Tyres visual check
Check for fluid/oil leaks around the wheels
Suspension – look for loose nuts and bolts
Shock absorbers visual check
Check for any other obvious loose nuts
General inspection of undercarriage and springs (daily when on rough roads)

After starting, check:

Water temperature
Oil pressure

EVERY THREE OR FOUR DAYS

These items should be looked at more frequently when on rough roads, and less on good roads:

Engine mountings
Exhaust system
Tyre pressures
Clean air filter – dust bowl or pre-filter if in dusty conditions
Drain plugs – check they're not loose
Spring U-bolt/nuts and spring centre bolt
Any movement between spring leaves
Cracks in coils or leaf springs
Rubbing of main leaf against the hangers
Check for any rubbing fuel lines, pipes and wires

WEEKLY

Battery acid level and corrosion of battery leads
Gearbox, transfer box and differential oil levels
Check steering-box oil
Check swivel housing oil/grease level
Steering damper
Air-cleaner oil bath – clean when in constant sand and dust
Brake cylinders and brake hoses

On old Land Rovers some of these may need to be looked at more often!

Your Vehicle MAINTENANCE, BREAKDOWNS AND REPAIRS

6

REGULAR MAINTENANCE You should get into the habit of checking certain things each day. Start by looking at oil and water levels, keeping both topped up without fail. Check the levels of hydraulic fluid for the brakes and clutch. Any noticeable drop will tell you that a problem may be developing. As you go around the vehicle, look at the wheel nuts, suspension fixtures, nuts, bolts and springs. As you go, watch for any telltale drops of oil and hydraulic fluid around the wheels. It pays to crawl underneath at least once a day and look for any changes: things coming loose, exhaust, wires, fractured mountings, fuel pipes touching and wearing. Water leaks often show up in the morning. Put a spanner on all the vital steering and suspension nuts regularly and fix any minor problems immediately.

If you have a mental imprint of how your vehicle should look, you will be able to spot any potential problems far more quickly and easily. Toilet stops or lunch breaks are a good time to have a quick walk-around and carry out the following checks:

- Check underneath for signs of leakage and loose nuts
- Visual check of hubs for signs of oil or brake fluid leakage
- Feel wheel hubs for abnormally high temperature – could indicate a worn bearing
- Feel the tyres for abnormally high temperature – could indicate low tyre pressure

COMMON PROBLEMS

Vibration damage It may seem obvious, but inattention to the small things leads to bigger difficulties. With continually rough roads, the effects of vibrations are the most common problem. Nuts and bolts need constant attention. Failure to do these checks will lead to potentially serious problems. Take time to look after the results of vibration.

Leaks Leaks too are invariably an effect of vibration; watch for weeping water hoses, brake pipes and fuel lines. Keep a screwdriver handy for those loose Jubilee clips. More seriously, watch for leaks from the radiator.

Suspension Suspension problems are an ever-present threat with the poor state of the roads. Careful driving and constant vigilance can reduce breakages. Fitting new springs on older vehicles before you set out is a good idea. Newer vehicles with coil springs are generally less trouble than those with leaf springs.

The chassis could crack if it was not in good condition before leaving. Older models are more prone to this. Most that are already in good condition will be fine if you take it steadily. It shouldn't be necessary to strengthen the chassis as a rule; this can distort things if not done professionally.

Many suspension problems can be prevented by careful maintenance. Check your suspension nuts are tight. Loose U-bolts can lead to the leaf springs slipping against the axle and eventually to a broken centre-bolt. When this happens the axle can then move fore or aft relative to the chassis and serious damage may follow. You will see a high number of trucks and buses 'going sideways' or 'crabbing' as a result of a skewed rear axle. Africans are not ones to worry over these potentially fatal matters.

Tyres Your tyres represent a considerable expense. Punctures are inevitable, but tyre damage is also a constant threat in Africa. Be vigilant when running your tyres at lower pressure, when they are more prone to damage from rocks and stones in sand. Stay away from sharp rocks, sticks and particularly the acacia thorns found under shady trees. Once back on a hard surface, be sure to pump them up or they'll rapidly overheat.

Keep a close watch for tyres going down slowly. Punctures are the main hazard. Be careful to ensure the vehicle is stable before removing wheels; use wooden

At the least the tyre problems meant interaction with the local people. It's quite easy to breeze by, cocooned in your own vehicle, passing villages, passing people whose lives are so different, clinically isolated from them by the very thing that gives you the freedom to see these places and people. Wherever we repaired our tyres, someone would speak English and ask us many things; sometimes we were offered cold drinks. The Sudanese have retained their great sense of self-respect; there was no blatant hassling, just a gentle friendliness and curiosity. In the meantime the media are making out the country is full of terrorists. What is the truth of the Darfur rebellion and humanitarian crisis? It is hard to know the true picture as a traveller.

blocks. It's an obvious point, but in the heat of the moment things happen. Some can be repaired locally, but keep a careful watch on the job; some are done well, others very badly. If in doubt, do it yourself. You need at least two levers for this. When deflating a partially soft tyre be careful to stop the valve flying into the sand or mud; they have minds of their own.

Breaking the bead between the tyre and the metal rim is the worst part. Soapy water can be used as a lubricant on stubborn tyres when levering. One way to break the bead is by jacking the tyre down away from the rim using the front bumper, if it's solid, or part of the chassis as the top jacking point. Be careful not to damage the tyre; use a wooden block if necessary. Africans often drive over the tyre to break the bead, but this can cause damage.

If repairing a tube, be sure to scratch and roughen the tube well, using a hacksaw blade. Once the repair has been done, take great care not to trap small stones, sand, grit or flakes of rust between the tube and tyre, otherwise another puncture could result very soon. A good dusting of talcum powder between tube and tyre can help lessen the friction between the two and reduce further troubles. It also pays to use graphite around the rim/tyre seal when installing new tyres before departure.

Be careful not to stand over a tyre when it is being blown up, in case it does not bed in properly. Carry a comprehensive selection of patches and repair material. It is also worth having tyre (rather than tube) patches to repair any large holes in the tyre itself. Tubeless tyres need special repair plugs. Old tubes can be cut for use as temporary liners if the tyre has sustained internal damage.

Fuel The poor quality of some fuel means your fuel filter is likely to get blocked more often than normal. It is a good idea to rinse the fuel tank before leaving, to get rid of any sludge that may be in the bottom, and flush the filter on the bottom of the pick-up (if fitted). This may not be necessary if your vehicle has been driven solely in countries with good fuel.

While on the road, clean out the sediment bowl regularly and change filters at the first sign of spluttering or loss of power from the engine. Filter your fuel through a fine gauze or cloth when filling the tank if you suspect it might be dirty.

If you have an apparent blockage in the fuel line, you can disconnect the pipe before the lift pump and blow through it. An obstruction can be located in this way; a short length of slightly larger pipe may be of use to avoid getting the fuel near your mouth. Keep an eye on the fuel lines; they can wear quite fast on bad roads. Also ensure that you can repair sections if necessary by taking spare pipe and joining links with ferals. In the event of a serious fuel feed problem in the lines or a leaking/damaged tank, a temporary fix can be made using your spare fuel lines fed from a jerrycan or small plastic container.

Electrical faults Electrical faults can be more puzzling than straightforward mechanical failures. You need to understand the basic principles first. All electrical systems involve a complete circuit for the flow of power. A logical analysis needs to be made before any drastic action is taken. The problem with wiring is that many wires are well hidden, in looms, and difficult to access. Vehicle electrical wiring is exposed to extremely unfavourable conditions: heat, vibration and chemical attack. Look for loose or corroded connections and broken or chafed wires, especially where the wires pass through holes in the bodywork or are subject to vibration. Fuses often blow as a result of such problems.

All vehicles have one pole of the battery 'earthed' and connected to the vehicle bodywork. Nearly all modern vehicles have a negative (-) earth terminal. Electrical current flows through the component and back to the battery via the metal bodywork. If a component mounting is loose or corroded, or if a good path back to the battery is not available, the circuit will be incomplete and malfunction will occur. The engine and/or gearbox are earthed by means of flexible metal straps to the body or subframe. If these straps are loose or missing, problems may result: the starter motor may not turn sufficiently, ignition may fail and the alternator may not recharge the batteries. Sometimes the straps do not make a good contact to the chassis and the contact points need cleaning with emery paper. Various other electrical components – wiper motors, bulb holders, etc – are also earthed directly by their mountings.

Assuming that the earth return is satisfactory, electrical faults will be due either to component malfunction or to defects in the supply wires. For example, if the starter is faulty or not activating, the cause could be the solenoid, the brushes inside or the wires linking it to the ignition, or even the battery leads. When wires are broken or cracked internally, this will result in an incomplete circuit. Sometimes wires become bare and the current is earthed on to bodywork, resulting in a short circuit. Most short circuits will blow a fuse. If not, the result could be burning of the wire insulation, more short-circuiting or, at worst, a fire. This is why it is inadvisable to bypass persistently blowing fuses with silver foil or wire. A good way to check out elusive problems is to bypass the suspect wire or component temporarily, using a length of wire with a crocodile clip or suitable connector at each end. A 12V test lamp can be used to verify the presence of supply voltage at various points along the wire and the break can be isolated.

TACKLING HIDDEN PROBLEMS With so many moving parts and extra strain, your vehicle will be very lucky to escape all mechanical difficulties. Some failures are obvious and can be located visually: oil leaks, water leaks, brake-pipe fractures, cracked exhaust, loose wheel nuts and so on. Others are not so simple. Some problems can be investigated by listening or smelling: hot rubber, piston rings or broken valve springs clicking, exhaust loose, etc. The worst problems are the hidden ones: hot engine, squeaking brakes, wheel noises, knocking suspension noises and other mysterious rumblings.

You can consult the manufacturer's manual first to see if the symptoms are indicated. Familiarity with your vehicle and personal experience are the best tools in checking out elusive problems. Try to think through exactly what is happening, and then try to isolate the problem with a few checks if possible. Clutch and gearbox noises are very hard to isolate, and often little can be done but soldier on.

Jumping up and down on the front bumper or a rear step and listening for any taps can sometimes locate suspension knocks. Squeaking brakes might be worn pads or, quite often, grit in the brake drum. It could be the wheel bearing too, but touching a hub for heat may help decide this. Some noises are worse on bad surfaces; others vibrate intermittently, suggesting less serious snags. With any new

Check the manuals for your particular model first.

ITEM	MAINTENANCE INTERVAL	
Diesel engine oil	6,000km (4,000 miles)	More frequently if doing a lot of low-range driving as mileage ceases to relate to engine hours
Petrol engine oil	9,000km (5,500 miles)	
Diesel oil filters	5,000km (3,500 miles)	
Petrol oil filters	9,000km (5,500 miles)	
Diesel fuel filters	5,000km (3,500 miles)	Loss of power can be due to clogged filters from bad fuel
Petrol fuel filters	9,000km (5,500 miles)	Loss of power can be due to clogged filters from bad fuel
Sediment bowl	10,000km (6,000 miles)	On diesels inspect regularly
Air filters	10,000km (6,000 miles)	Oil-bath and reusable types, clean with every oil change
Gearbox and transfer-box oil	15,000km (9,000 miles)	
Differential oil	15,000km (9,000 miles)	
Set tappets	10,000km (6,000 miles)	See manuals; it may be a longer distance
Set timing	10,000km (6,000 miles)	See manual
Change spark plugs	20,000km (12,000 miles)	
Greasing	Every two weeks or after every wade	
Injector pump	See manual, as some need small top-ups	
Windscreen	Washer reservoir – as needed	

noise that is constant you must diagnose the problem as soon as possible. Engine noises and overheating are of prime concern.

With an overheating engine there is an obvious symptom, but the cause may be due to a number of defects.

Here is an example. The water temperature light comes on; your engine is overheating not long after starting off. You need to understand what is happening so you can start eliminating possible causes:

- The engine is hot. Too much heat is retained or not enough lost, maybe both.
- Heat goes into the engine through burning fuel and friction from moving parts.
- Heat leaves the engine from the radiator via the cooling water, exhaust, oil and airflow over the engine.

The most likely cause is connected with the radiator and water system: a failure to lose heat. Water leaks are the first problem to look for and the easiest. The fan belt may have broken, although you can usually hear this happen. Is there an oil leak from the engine? Can you see oil weeping from gasket joints? If none of these seems to be the cause, it could be the heat sensor; even a wire problem is a remote possibility. Check out the following:

Your Vehicle **MAINTENANCE, BREAKDOWNS AND REPAIRS**

6

- Less airflow over the engine – a defective fan or a clogged radiator – or even the vehicle moving too slowly in the wrong gear.
- Reduced cooling from the radiator – water leaks, cracked rubber hoses, faulty thermostat, blocked radiator pipe, low coolant, faulty water pump.
- Check that it isn't simply a faulty radiator cap. Unimogs in particular have a complicated cap pressure system.
- Reduced cooling due to blown head gasket, or worse, cracked head.

Sometimes when a vehicle is ploughing through soft sand for long periods the engine will get hot because it's doing a lot more work at slow speed. Friction can be generated because of low oil. Low oil reduces the cooling ability of the oil. Oil more normally used in cold climates may be too 'thin'. Using heavier-duty oil in hot places may be preferred, but be sure to warm the engine up first thing before driving off.

GENERAL FAULT DIAGNOSIS Most common faults are caused by bad maintenance, defective parts, poorly installed parts, bad lubrication, blockages and sometimes just plain bad luck. In general, if a vehicle is prepared thoroughly beforehand, most troubles develop as a result of outside factors. Things shake loose, things touch moving parts, other items get too hot and so on. In general things do not suddenly fail. Many problems that develop take time to become obvious; eg: a wheel bearing overheated by a sticking brake shoe. Major mechanical failures in particular are usually preceded by characteristic symptoms over hundreds of kilometres; for example, the badly set up or worn thrust bearing in the gearbox that sounded slightly different. Components which do occasionally fail without warning are often small and easily carried in the vehicle, such as the thermostat or the ignition solenoid. Of course larger items – the starter, the lift pump or the alternator – do wear out; it's best to get new ones before you leave.

The first step is to decide where to begin the investigation. Often this is clear. Sometimes a fault can be apparently cured, only to recur. Often the key is observation, finding a problem before it becomes serious, and afterwards looking closely to make sure it has been fixed. Daily inspections can reveal potential hazards ahead. Sit down, have a cup of tea, smoke if you need to; a calm and logical approach is far more satisfactory in the long run. Take into account any warning signs or abnormalities that may have been noticeable in the period preceding the fault – power loss, high or low gauge readings, unusual noises or smells, etc – and remember that the failure of components such as fuses may point to some other underlying fault.

Whatever the fault, certain basic principles apply:

- Verify the fault. This is simply a matter of being sure that you know what the symptoms are before starting work. Don't rely on other people's assessments.
- Don't overlook the obvious. For example, in cases where the vehicle won't start, is there fuel in the tank? If an electrical fault is indicated, look for loose or broken wires before digging out the test gear.
- Cure the disease, not the symptom. Replacing a flat battery with a fully charged one will get you back on the road, but if the underlying cause is not attended to, the new battery will go flat too.

Take nothing for granted. A 'new' component may itself be defective (particularly if it's been rattling round in the back for months), and it's a mistake to leave components out of a fault diagnosis just because they were recently fitted. When you do finally diagnose a fault, you will probably realise it was there before the problem.

Whatever the problem, you will need to sit down and think through as many possible causes for the fault as you can. Below is a series of suggestions for fault-finding. Similar troubleshooting lists can be found in most manuals.

The following are some of the more likely problems:

Starting problems These include any problems when starting, and also a partial or complete failure to turn the engine:

- Flat battery: recharge, use jump leads or push start
- Flat battery caused by loose fan belt: re-tension
- Flat battery caused by loose or faulty alternator
- Battery terminals corroded or loose connection
- Battery earth to body defective: could be engine/starter strap
- Starter brushes, solenoid fault or loose or broken wiring
- Ignition/starter switch faults
- A corroded main earth lead: needs cleaning
- Insufficient power transmitting: engine fails to turn over
- Starter motor pinion sticking
- Flywheel gear teeth damaged or worn
- Starter motor mounting bolts loose

Fuel supply problems These include when the engine turns over but fails to start, fails to run cleanly or runs briefly before cutting out:

- No fuel in tank
- Lift pump failure
- Air in the line due to leaks and damage
- Blocked fuel filters
- Blocked outlet in the tank: blowing down the line might clear this
- Fractured fuel line joints
- Blocked air breather hole in fuel tank filler cap
- Injector pump failure: oh dear, seek specialist advice

Main engine problems These include when the engine turns normally but will not start, an engine that will not run properly and when it cuts out or overheats:

- No fuel in tank
- Other fuel system fault: air leak
- Fuel starvation: engine fires but will not run cleanly; blocked filters
- Injector pump fault/leaking pipes/broken injector nozzle
- Poor piston chamber compression
- Ignition warning light illuminated (no charge)
- Air leaks at inlet manifold
- Major mechanical failure, eg: camshaft drive, timing chain, head gasket
- Serious overheating; engine cuts out, as above, radiator, etc
- Overheating, slack or broken fan belt: adjust or renew

Other engine problems If there is a whistling or wheezing noise:

- Leaking manifold gasket
- Blown or leaking head gasket
- Leaking air pipes or air compressor
- Cracked exhaust pipe or leaking joints

If you hear any tapping, rattling or knocking sounds from the engine itself or close by:

- Incorrect valve clearance
- Valves and camshaft worn
- Worn or stretched timing chain
- Broken piston ring (usually a clicking or ticking noise)
- Inappropriate mechanical contact (eg: fan blades)
- Worn or loose fan belt
- Peripheral component fault, ie: generator, water pump, etc
- Big-end bearings worn (a regular heavy knocking, may be less under load)
- Main bearings worn (rumbling and/or knocking, may be worse under load)
- Piston slack in chamber (often more noticeable when cold)

Note: Do not add cold water to an overheated engine, as damage may result.

Ignition and warning lights If the oil gauge reads low, or the warning light is illuminated with the engine running, it may be one of the following problems. A low oil-pressure warning in a high-mileage engine on tick-over is not necessarily a cause for concern. However a sudden pressure loss at higher speed is far more significant. But it could be the gauge or warning light sender, and not in the engine.

- Low oil level
- Incorrect grade of oil
- Oil filter clogged or bypass valve defective
- Oil-pressure failure valve defective
- Oil light/bulb defective
- Oil pump loose
- Oil pick-up strainer clogged
- Oil pump worn
- Defective oil gauge or sender unit
- Wire to sender unit earthed
- Overheating engine
- Worn main or big-end bearings

Other warning lights are illuminated
- Low oil level
- Coolant loss due to leaking, internal or external, damaged hoses
- Low brake/clutch fluid
- Defective thermostat
- Binding brakes
- Clogged radiator, externally or internally
- Flat or non-charging battery/alternator fault

Other faults – clutch, brakes and axles, etc
- Clutch slipping: worn clutch plate or weak pressure-plate springs
- Clutch erratic or heavy: master cylinder or slave cylinder rubbers worn
- Clutch failure: fluid loss from master or slave cylinder, or pipes
- Wheel noise: worn or damaged bearings, brake drum grooved, loose wheel nuts
- Squealing brakes: brake pads worn or damaged
- Squealing or grating noise from wheel: grit or small stones trapped in disc brake

- Soft brake or clutch pedal: air in hydraulic fluid, hydraulic fluid leaking
- Deep grinding axle noises: low differential oil
- Knocking driveshaft: defective or worn UJ, or loose nuts
- Hot brakes: badly adjusted, worn pads or loose brake shoes
- Hot wheels: badly adjusted or worn bearings, leaking hub seals
- Poor braking: hydraulic fluid or hub bearing oil seeping on to brake pads
- Poor braking: badly adjusted brakes
- Steering knocks: loose or worn track rod ends, bent track rod
- Steering erratic: loose wheel nuts, worn ball joint bearings/kingpins
- Loud exhaust: loose nuts on exhaust joints, holed silencer, loose manifold
- Sagging springs: cracked leaf spring/s
- Loud knocking from suspension: worn or damaged shock absorber rubbers
- Other suspension noises: damaged shock absorbers, loose nuts
- Skewed motion: broken spring centre bolt
- Driver's aching back: driving too far or too fast, or old age!

Electrical faults
- Battery/ignition faults: as above under engine
- Lights fail: blown fuses, bulbs blown, loose wiring
- Indicator lights: bulbs, loose wire, fuses
- Engine cuts out: loose wiring on injector pump solenoid
- Any failure of electric units, wiper motor, horn, etc: fuses, loose wires
- Starter motor jams on: disconnect battery leads quickly and repair starter motor
- Petrol engines' electrical faults: condenser, points, distributor cap, and plugs
- Too much static electricity: driver's hair standing on end from African road users!

ROADSIDE REPAIRS Sooner or later African gremlins will decide it's your turn for a spot of bother. Something will fail or break on your vehicle and, of course, you may well be a long way from the nearest mechanical help, however basic. Now is the time for that quiet moment, in the hope of some enlightening inspiration.

Invariably some improvisations will not work or will work only partly, but patience and thinking around a problem will usually bring a viable solution, whether permanent or temporary. Keep ideas simple. This is the time for inspirational initiatives and inventive attitudes.

Assuming that you are carrying most or all of the items listed below as sundry accessories, you can often fix some quite daunting problems. It is often possible to make temporary improvised repairs. Sometimes it is better to bypass the main problem and work on a simpler solution, one that can be sorted out later where facilities exist.

A good example is where you have a brake problem. The wheel cylinder is leaking brake fluid and needs to be replaced or have new rubbers. It's late afternoon, you can't camp anywhere and this could be a long job. You might encounter difficulties removing a tight brake drum, or perhaps the nuts holding the wheel cylinder are corroded and not happy to come loose. Better then perhaps to disconnect the brake pipe leading to the mischievous wheel cylinder and block it off.

This could be done in quite a few ways, using Jubilee clips, spare fuel line joints, clamps on the rubber section, other miscellaneous plastic pipe, even a fuel line nut and some old tube rubber cut to act as a seal and then screwed onto a jointed part of the line. Once you reach somewhere to park up for a while, you can fix it properly yourself with parts, or try the local mechanic. African bush mechanics have some amazing tricks up their sleeves. But then of course most bush mechanics don't have sleeves!

This story is set in the east of the Central African Republic, on an overland trip on which Bob was a client. Most organised overland trips today are a little less fraught, but some of the happenings may not be so dissimilar. From the diary ...

BAHR AL GHAZAL, SOUTHERN SUDAN, 26 JANUARY Left Bangui then spent three days in Bangassou with brake trouble and officialdom delays. Drove on to Obo, road shocking; it's really an overgrown track and ferries not working. Delayed by a broke back spring. Next day a tooth came off the crown wheel on the back axle and made a neat hole in the diff cover. Also a tyre blew.

Just past Obo the second diff blew. With the rest of the party setting up camp in the bush for some time, the driver, Nick, Dave and I set off to look for parts in Wau, 300 miles on in the Sudan. No traffic at all, so we had to walk the 40 miles to the border, mostly in the cool of the night until some villagers warned us about large animals with big hungry mouths and fluffy, but not cuddly, manes. Ate stale bread and shared some tins of fish for two nights and a day. Spent the second night in a village, some locals invited us into their little thatched mud house. It was quite something – we were offered food and some straw matting; such hospitality, a pity about the bugs in the night, though.

We hitched from the border to Wau on the top of an old Bedford truck, overloaded with a boisterous host of passengers clinging to sacks of grain over every bump of the dirt road. It was hell under the burning sun, stomach cramps threatening at any moment. (A great story to relate from the comfort of leafy England later – you know, great white ashen-faced hunter explores the Sudan by exotic lorry.)

WAU, SUDAN, 27 JANUARY Dave took Nick, who was very ill, off to Khartoum by plane. I found a Bedford pinion but no crown-wheel. Later I found a complete axle in the customs house, but they weren't going to part with that. A few haggard-looking travellers arrived on the train from Khartoum, a five-day trip. Slept in the police station courtyard with other travellers. No beds, just sand and no spare parts.

Here are some useful tips and suggestions:

Starter failure

Pushing is the obvious choice, but there may not be any or enough pushers about. If there is an ignition/starter electrical problem, it's possible on some starters to shortcut the ignition/starter pre-solenoid by using a screwdriver across the terminal of the starter. Be careful though, as it can spark a lot if the connection is not right, and at worst the screwdriver might try to weld itself to a terminal. In case the earth is poor, you can also use jump leads from the battery to another earth point.

Some older vehicles still have starting-handle holes behind the number plates; it's worth a check before you leave. A starting handle might be a saver in a remote desert. Be very careful using these, as they can backfire and break your arm at worst. It is also said that you can jack up a rear wheel and, using a length of rope wrapped around the wheel, pull this to rotate the wheel. We have never tried it. It sounds rather hard and won't work on vehicles with permanent 4x4. Try it if you're bored of waiting for help to arrive. (A fuller description of this can be found in the Bradt *Zambia* guide (Chris McIntyre), edn 4, pp107–8.)

Damaged rubber suspension/shock absorber bushes

These could be replaced by using an old tyre tube cut into many small discs with a hole punched or cut out. Add as many discs as necessary. Africans sell strong bushes made of old tyres; they

TUESDAY, 3 FEBRUARY Back at the stricken truck the locals had been bringing food; water was found a mile away. The camp was set out with loos, a cold store on the evaporation principle, a summerhouse with mosquito nets all round, and a shaded area of poles and leaves. Early next day, Aussie Dave and Kiwi Mike set out to walk to Obo, where a mission was rumoured to exist. Next day they arrived back with a big Unimog from the mission. They proposed to tow the truck back to the mission.

THURSDAY, 5 FEBRUARY An amazing day – replaced the old Bedford axle with an abandoned Mercedes one. Had to replace one bearing; luckily the truck's one was exactly the same. The mission blokes welded the truck propshaft onto the new axle with the only electricity and welding gear between Bangui and Juba. The brakes didn't really work and we had to put four discarded bald Land Rover tyres on the wheels. The girls kept us all plied with great fruit salads, pineapples, papaya, bananas and lemon juice.

***EN ROUTE*, 10 FEBRUARY** Departed from the mission, full of trepidation. Nearly came off the road where some terrible rock steps in the track barred the route. Had to camp and use rocks next morning to build the road up under the truck. It took six hours to get 50 yards. Had a puncture afterwards, but got the tyre off using a screwdriver, hammer and jack handle. Used one of the two patches left and later got stuck in a mud hole for hours. Met some tourists going west; our notoriety has spread along the bush telegraph – 'So you're the lot who've been stuck in the bush for four weeks.'

Crossed into Sudan, all the officials were most helpful; they could hardly believe their eyes with the truck a good two feet lower at the back than the front. Had another puncture; we seem to be on three rear wheels longer than four.

NAIROBI, KENYA, 24 FEBRUARY Finally pulled into the big city. Ate almost continuously for three days; mostly bacon, eggs and cake at the Thorn Tree Café.

last much longer than the genuine spares. They won't pass an English MOT test, though. Temporary fixes can be done using string wrapped around damaged bushes to get a tight wad.

Leaking water hoses These can be temporarily fixed with wire/duck tape reinforced with old tube rubber and large Jubilee clips. But you ought to be carrying spare hoses anyway.

Broken throttle cable or pedal Tie a piece of cord or electrical wire around the injector pump or carburettor arm and pass it through the window. We once did this on an Indian motor-rickshaw on the way to Delhi Airport and managed to co-ordinate the gear changes with the large Sikh driver. After we'd barely made it to the airport in time, the flight was then cancelled anyway!

Loose exhaust, broken mounts or holes Wire can be used to secure a loose exhaust pipe and make temporary mountings onto a suitable anchor point on the chassis. A hole in the exhaust can be patched from old food cans and wire or Jubilee clips. Dum-dum exhaust paste is a good standby; it hardens fast.

Broken radiator cowling Wire can be used to secure a loose or broken cowling mount, but take care the fan is not touching.

Radiator holed or damaged Soap, softened with a little water, will temporarily fix the leak. Other methods are to put an egg into the radiator water, but it's better to use proper Radseal, available from any motor factor trader. Araldite can also be used to seal a badly leaking radiator with limited damage. Otherwise, in cases of severe damage, it is possible to block off any leaking channels or part of the radiator that is damaged.

Cracked or leaking fuel tank Fuel tank leaks can be reduced or cured by using plastic padding or Araldite. The tank needs to be drained first to ensure the surfaces are dry and free from oily diesel. Fuel lines are best repaired properly by carrying the necessary pieces and joints.

Broken main leaf or coil spring Insert one or more wooden blocks between the axle and chassis. They need to be securely held in place with rope etc. Any largish lump of rubber might do the trick – always assuming that you can find a largish lump of rubber in the first place. A spare tyre, in certain situations, might work, but it would need to be well secured and away from brake lines, propshafts and other moving parts. Where some leaf springs have broken, you can insert small wooden blocks, bits of flat metal or any other suitable filler, and then bind the springs up as tightly as possible with thin nylon rope.

Damaged propshaft or UJ Best to have a spare UJ. Otherwise remove the broken shaft and continue in 4x4. Take care though, as all the torque from the engine is now being transferred through one shaft that is not designed for this. It's fine on part-time 4x4 vehicles only. On permanent 4x4 vehicles it may not work where there is a transfer box differential. Using the diff lock will overcome this problem, but don't drive fast or for too long without releasing the wind-up by jacking the vehicle up periodically.

Clutch not functioning Start the engine in the lowest gear and change gear by matching the engine and road speeds. Otherwise crawl on using whatever gears you can get moving in.

Differential or pinion broken On some vehicles the front and rear differentials and pinions are interchangeable. Check your workshop manual to see if it's the case with your specific vehicle. If they are interchangeable and your rear is damaged, swap the front units to the back to maintain rear-wheel drive. This is advised only as a last resort. You need to reset the crown-wheel and pinion backlash and interface gaps. Normally this is done using a special gauge, but it's possible to get a reasonable match using instant gasket squeezed on to the pinion interface gear. Rotate the pinion; it will leave marks on the crown-wheel. Some manuals have a sample diagram showing the pattern required.

Sticking thermostat Remove the thermostat, but then let the engine warm up for longer.

Leaking heater hoses You can use another piece of hose and Jubilee clips to isolate and bypass the troubling leak.

Sump or differential holes Use plastic padding, Araldite or epoxy metal glue and, if necessary, a small sheet of metal for repair. Again all surfaces need to be free from oil before starting the repairs.

Track rod sheared Sounds unlikely, but it happened on a Bedford truck in Amboseli National Park in Kenya. Bind the rod up using any clamps, Jubilee clips, nylon rope and a length of piping or a strong metal bar and hope the nearest welder is close by. Bent rods should be hammered back as well as possible.

Damaged bolt or nut threads All stripped bolts are best replaced if accessible. Try Araldite where possible as a temporary fix. Nut threads on such things as clutch slave cylinders are prone to damage and can be awkward to fix. Threads on exhaust manifold nuts and studs often strip easily because the nuts are softer. Try metal epoxy glues, or use wire as a quick fix.

Piston ring breaks/damage God forbid, but a known suggestion that has worked in remote areas on an ancient 6-cylinder Bedford Truck is to remove the damaged piston and seal the piston chamber with a very tightly fitting, fashioned piece of wood. This blocks oil from the sump. The injector pipe to the affected chamber needs to be disconnected, as you don't want diesel in the oil system. This can be re-routed using a plastic pipe into a reservoir, or diesel will spray everywhere. We haven't actually tried this and it can only be a desperate last resort!

We did once have a Bedford truck aluminium piston welded and turned down with new ring grooves in Turkey. The welder was amazingly skilled.

Tyres damaged When the last spare has blown and you are desperate, it is said to be possible to fill a tyre with sand for a limited distance. Otherwise you can use old tubes to line damaged tyres. Africans even stitch up old tyres or bolt them together and use them again. There are no vehicle safety regulations; if it works it's OK!

OTHER REPAIRS, ETC

Extreme heat It is possible to do a limited number of repairs using heat and your battery. Apparently, in a worst-case scenario, you can use your battery and arc-welding rods to effect simple repairs. We haven't tried it. Repairing metal brake pipes or loosening press-fitted parts can be done using an air pump or compressor to super-heat charcoals. Pump air down a metal pipe into the fire to generate the higher temperature a repair might require. However, none of these techniques should necessarily be your first course of action. Keep it simple. Normally it's better to effect a temporary cure and get along to a decent workshop if you can.

Degreasing A 50/50 mixture of diesel and washing-up liquid makes an excellent degreaser for pre-cleaning very dirty areas – rinse off with water after several minutes.

Old oil It is prudent to keep old oil both for extra insurance against sudden loss through damage and for ecological reasons. In the worst case, it can be filtered and re-used until a new source is found.

Suggested bush spares See *Chapter 3*, page 74 for a list of suggestions.

MOTORBIKE DRIVING TECHNIQUES AND REPAIRS

David Lambeth and Alex Marr

Once on the road, the two most important things are undoubtedly keeping your air filter clean (in very dusty conditions this can be necessary every day) and performing regular oil changes (around every 3,000km/2,000 miles). Foam air

And so to Khartoum; the name conjures up visions of the exotic. We camped at the Blue Nile Sailing Club, basically a large car park next to the river. The shower worked, and after three days in the desert that was truly essential. There was also a pleasant green lawn with shady trees, where we met some fellow travellers – Ina and Alex, who were planning to cycle across Africa over a period of two to three years. But they had already been on the road for over a year, and were about to fly back to Germany for a couple of weeks so that Alex could sort out his tax returns. They must be a little crazy. Even crazier than us, we thought!

Then another white man arrived with just a tiny bag of personal possessions. He was Reinhardt, in the process of shipping his vehicle from Aqaba to Port Sudan to avoid getting a *carnet* for Egypt. He planned to drive his almost-new Land Rover into the desert and make a film following the progress of a particular tribe of Sudanese nomads throughout the year. On the vehicle, at least when it left Aqaba, was all his expensive camera equipment, not to mention sleeping bags and other essentials for life in the desert. How much would remain when it arrived in Port Sudan? His girlfriend was due to fly out to Khartoum at the weekend, then they would take the weekly public bus to Port Sudan and wait for the ship to arrive. To get back to Europe, he was planning to ship the vehicle to Jeddah in Saudi Arabia, but, not being married to his girlfriend, she could not get a visa to travel through Saudi with him, so would have to fly to Aqaba and wait for him there. The whole thing sounded far too much hassle…

Mirror, mirror on the wall,
Who is the craziest of them all?
Cyclists, motorcyclists or car drivers?

filters can be washed in petrol/diesel (wear your nitrile rubber gloves), dried, soaked in air filter (or engine) oil and the excess squeezed out.

Other frequent checks should include chain tension, spoke tension and tightness of nuts and bolts (Nylock nuts help, as does Loctite thread-locking fluid).

There is a long-running debate as to whether you should lubricate your chain in very dusty and sandy conditions. From direct experience gained from thousands of miles of desert racing events, I believe that a chain will always last longer if lubricated. The rubber O or X rings in a modern chain need to be kept moist to be able to seal the internal lubricant. When run dry, a chain can get very hot, and the rings can dry out and split. Sand can also be very salty and lubricant can help to protect the chain and sprockets from corrosion.

RIDING IN DIFFICULT CONDITIONS

Sand Reducing tyre pressures considerably – as low as 8psi – increases the surface area of the tyre in contact with the sand and makes riding a lot easier. However, if the sand is in stretches alternating with rocky terrain, do not reduce tyre pressure too much, as you risk a puncture on the rocks. In really deep sand which has been rutted by other vehicles, it can be easier to just move through at walking pace, paddling along with your feet until you feel in control enough to ride properly. If you feel the rear wheel getting bogged down, it is best to dismount immediately and push, simultaneously applying gentle engine power. If you do get completely bogged down, slowly start moving the bike from side to side until it is free enough to be lifted out of the hole. This may require removing the luggage and, if it happens often, a sense of humour is very helpful!

Mud A real nightmare with a heavy bike, deep mud can mean you lose almost all grip and control. Stop before really bad sections and choose the best route; sometimes there is an easier way round the edges or side. Check the depth of water-filled sections before riding through.

River crossings The golden rule is to walk through first, checking the depth and the state of the bottom. Riding on large, rounded mossy rocks in deep water is going to have only one result.

In high-risk situations it is better to push the bike through, taking the luggage off first if necessary. If the bike is going to fall over in the water, make sure you switch the engine off first.

Punctures Everyone should know how to mend punctures. It is not difficult, but does require technique and practice – make sure you do the practising at home before you leave. Using heavy-duty inner tubes significantly reduces the chance of punctures. Check regularly for thorns, nails and sharp stones in the tyre carcass even if you don't have a puncture. Get them out as soon as possible so that there is less chance of them slowly working through to the inner tube.

BICYCLE TROUBLESHOOTING

Generally it is very clear when you have a major malfunction on a bike, but minor and subtle problems can sometimes be more difficult to decipher.

- Numb hands – should this happen, check the angle of the tilt on your seat or the direction of the bend of your handlebars and adjust as necessary.
  Faced with unexpected noises, try the following:
- Click (only when pedalling) – make sure crank arms and pedals are screwed on tight. Make sure crank arms are not hitting the front derailleur cage, the wire on your front derailleur, or kick stand. Check if the derailleurs, chain and gears are all aligned.
- Click or rubbing sound (even when you don't pedal) – check that everything attached to the rack is free from the wheel; check for deformed rim hitting brake pad or mudguard; check for broken spoke or broken axle.
- Rattle – check for loose screws all the way around on racks, water bottle cages or other screw-on accessories.

7

Day-to-Day Issues

BUREAUCRACY

Bureaucracy proliferates around the world and our own country is no exception. In fact, given that it was the British who perfected the art of bureaucracy that now persists in its ex-colonies, who are we to blame the Africans? However, in Africa bureaucracy can sometimes be encountered at its most intense, so we give some guidelines as to how to deal with it below.

There are a few golden rules to remember: be patient, stay calm and keep smiling. There will be times when this is easier said than done, but remember that you have time on your side. Make a cup of tea for yourself, and offer one to the officials, too. This will help you to relax, and make them realise that you're not going to be rushed into something you don't want to do. It can be a useful way of getting through a tricky border or check-post, so make sure you have a spare cup or two available for such an eventuality.

African red tape is something that may drive you crazy in the short term, but after the event you will probably be amused at the memory. It is sure to enliven your dinner-party conversations for years to come. If you are travelling with a vehicle or motorbike, you are almost certainly going to have to deal with officialdom and talk your way through Africa. Always be friendly and polite, even when you feel you are getting nowhere. African bureaucrats are no different from any others, in that they will not want to lose face. Be patient and kind and you will eventually get there. Be rude and you may spend the night there.

DJIBOUTI – A BORDER CROSSING

Just before the border with Djibouti, the road suddenly cascaded down a fantastic volcanic wall, the remains of a long-extinct caldera with dark brooding lava cliffs and a brilliant white-and-pink dried-out lake bed. This salt lake stretched into the dark, almost blue, mountains beyond. It was lunchtime at the border, even though it was now well past two o'clock. The Ethiopian immigration officers were very helpful, but customs were not to be found. Eventually a soldier sheepishly took us to one of many rusting cabins, old cargo containers and railway carriages. Here in air-conditioned comfort sat the elusive customs crew, cross-legged and chewing away to take their minds off the sweltering heat outside.

Qat is a plant which resembles the privet hedge from an English country garden. That's how every guidebook describes it, and we cannot better the description. As the sun hits its strongest period, that is the time for the whole of the Horn of Africa and neighbouring Yemen to start the daily ritual of munching and chewing qat. Nothing can disturb this ritual; well, almost nothing. Exceptions are apparently made when a foreign tourist appears on the scene, such a rare occurrence is this.

'However hard life is, approach it with humour and courage'

An apt description of this unbelievable place!

BORDERS AND POLICE CHECKS

Borders and police checks vary from country to country. Some border crossings will take hours, with a tedious amount of paperwork, while others have an easy and convenient system that doesn't take long at all. Never underestimate the systems of African border posts and always allow enough time to cross from one country into another. However, bear in mind that things sometimes move faster when they are about to close, and you can often park safely at the customs post for the night, so that you're ready for a quick getaway in the morning.

It is worth seeking advice from other travellers who have recently crossed a specific border. Most border crossings will involve first immigration and then customs, where your vehicle or bike will be cleared; your *carnet* will be stamped in or out, your international vehicle certificate and driver's licence will be checked. Vehicle insurance usually needs to be purchased, and there may be a police or military check on the vehicle. In Libya and Egypt you have to have local number plates attached, and of course you have to pay for these. In fact in Egypt they even crawled around under the vehicle looking for the chassis number, which is engraved into the chassis next to the front wheel. We didn't know where it was until they showed us. Luckily it was the same as on the *carnet*, otherwise who knows what might have happened. There may also be an import tax or fuel tax to pay. But with a *carnet* you do not have to pay import duty, so don't let anyone talk you into doing so. Keeping on top of all this can become a major occupation, but remember – be patient, stay calm and keep smiling!

Police or military checks are apparent not only at every border crossing, but often also on the outskirts of towns and sometimes in the middle of nowhere. The officials may just want to relieve the boredom and say 'hello', or they may insist on seeing everything you have, but the latter is rare nowadays. We personally had no serious problems at any border posts on our last three trips in 2003, 2004 and 2008, but the previous authors reported that some bikers in southern Ethiopia ended up at a border post for three days while every one of their items was meticulously searched, regardless of gifts offered. However, you may be lucky. In Nigeria, which has a terrible reputation for police corruption, we were stopped at nearly every roadside check-post, but they simply said 'Good morning, how are you? Have a safe journey.' See also box, *Warning re countries listed on the back page of the* carnet!, *Chapter 5*, page 108.

Receipts for administration fees are not uncommon; in this case the request is probably genuine. In fact when we left Arlit in Niger we had to pay a road toll for the first tarmac road we had been on for several days. After our experiences at the Assamaka border and then the police station in town, we said we were not going to pay any more money, but the policeman looked at us very apologetically and said 'It's not for me, sir, it's for the road,' as he gave us a genuine receipt. We felt very embarrassed at not having trusted him.

The best advice we can give is to play it by ear. It is up to you how to handle it if you are asked for money. Sometimes a cigarette (buy some to give away even if you don't smoke) or a pen and a smile is enough – sometimes a smile alone will suffice. Unfortunately, some travellers and tourists in the past have given in too easily to requests for money or gifts. Some officials now expect that you will pay

South of Tamanrasset and the broken rocky remnants of the Hoggar Mountains, the road becomes open desert, with many pistes. The tracks cross plains dotted with isolated craggy outcrops of boulders, destroyed by heat and cold, smashed by gripping winds and sandstorms, slowly decomposing to sand.

We camped close to the border with Niger. On the roof of the vehicle, we slept intermittently. A cool breeze rustled the plastic bag behind our pillows. The stars were amazing. A large eerie shadow was cast by a 150ft tower of rock erupting vertically upwards from the warm sands. Sentinels of similar rock towers marched across the desert in the black of the night. Suddenly the headlights of the leading car brushed the Land Rover, and a convoy of two vehicles came to a halt some short distance away. Too stunned to be afraid, we peered out from below the bedding, not daring to breathe. A group of men in turbans got out of the vehicles. Leaping around and shouting, they seemed to be arguing. Then another car came past us. This was it; bandits, kidnappers, smugglers, whoever they were, we were sitting ducks and might as well pretend to be asleep.

After what seemed like an eternity, they drove off into the darkness of the night, leaving us waiting for our hearts to slow down again. Perhaps our crummy old Land Rover wasn't worth the bother.

At In Guezzam, the Tabaski festival was under way, the diesel station was closed and everyone was dressed in their finest robes and colourful *cheches* (turban-style colourful headscarves). Sheep were nervously corralled in pens awaiting their fate. 'We cannot find the fuel pump man; he is with one of his wives!' While waiting, we were invited to partake in the celebrations at the police station. After much delay, large plates appeared loaded with freshly grilled lamb and salad. All we could offer in return was a McVitie's chocolate cake, which went down very well with the local officers. 'What about the men we saw last night?' we asked.

'Oh, they're just smugglers; cigarettes, you know. We don't have any bandits here, you are quite safe.'

or give a gift. If you can get away with it, it's best not to hand anything over, except for a smile and a handshake.

Do remember that often the police and military, especially in more remote areas, are not paid regularly by the government. Some of them also perform important services, for example restricting access to dangerous or remote areas. They may be totally dependent on donations from tourists as well as the local community, so don't always just refuse to pay; consider their situation and be fair. Assamaka (Niger) is a particular case in point.

VISAS

Whenever you arrive in a large African town, particularly a capital city, you will probably have a long list of things that need doing: fixing the vehicle, buying spares, changing money, getting visas, making phone calls, sending and receiving emails, collecting post, replacing food supplies, etc. These will probably take longer than you think!

Visa applications can be a waiting game, taking from 24 hours up to three days (the exception is a Sudan visa – it took us six weeks in London, the previous authors three months! But we heard you could get it in a week or less in Cairo).

See *Visas* in *Chapter 5* (page 110) for information about which visas to get before leaving home.

Once in Africa you are dependent on the capital cities and the embassies represented there. Not every country has an embassy in every African country, but with some careful planning, depending on where you want to go next, you'll be able to get your visa within a day or two. Some visas can take weeks, but that is very unusual. Try to get your visas where it is the least hassle, perhaps when you are staying a few days somewhere in any case. It is best to apply for a visa as soon as you arrive in town, as it may take longer than expected for it to be issued.

Filling out the application forms can be time-consuming and involve lots of paperwork. Most embassies have specific opening times for visa applications, so check beforehand. Some embassies demand a letter from your embassy, called a 'Letter of Introduction'. This is literally a form of introduction from one embassy to another, a really unnecessary form of bureaucracy, since your passport proves your nationality. These letters usually take 24 hours to process and vary in price, costing anything between US$20 and US$100, depending on the embassy. Sometimes your own letter typed on official-looking letterhead notepaper may suffice.

Photographs – one, two or three depending on the country – need to be attached to the visa application. Passport photos are useful not only for visa applications, but

THE PANTOMIME SEASON IN ASWAN

To get to Sudan is not easy: first the visa then the ferry across Lake Nasser. Sunday morning in Aswan. Oh yes we can, oh no we can't. The ferry does go on Monday, but will there be enough cargo to attach the barge? Wait till Monday.

Monday morning bright and early we arrived at the high dam. Four hours later we were still at the high dam and nervous with anticipation. We were dealing with Mohammed; they are all called Mohammed. Yes, there is enough cargo; no, there isn't enough cargo. There aren't any other foreign devils with cars, so it's not looking too optimistic. We sit, and sit. How much are we willing to pay for this once-a-week mayhem? Can we consider coming back next week? What about driving back to Cairo? No more convoys, please! It's going to be pay up, Wadi Halfa or bust. The game is played out all day.

The Sudanese cargo manager, Mahmoud, seems to be the one who pulls the strings, although he claims he is consulting with a higher authority in the building conveniently out of sight. The first Mohammed seems to be on the sidelines, but his cut must surely be in the pie somewhere. More cargo arrives and it looks promising. It's all an illusion, but it's conducted with a great air of honourable pretence on both sides. They say they really are sorry that there isn't enough cargo and we'll have to pay more. Of course we are totally over a barrel, and pretend that it's really too much, we'll have to drive all the way back to London. What a shame.

Two pm and a deal is done. It's outrageous but it's better than going back to Cairo in a convoy. Four pm and we are still waiting to be loaded. There is so much cargo there is barely room for the Land Rover. A barge crammed with potatoes, tomatoes, cans of cooking oil and much else is lashed to the side of the main ferry. Finally we drive the Land Rover up two wobbly planks on to the deck of this narrow barge, without driving straight off the other side. The brakes mercifully stop us ploughing into the lake. They take us proudly to our cabin.... What a heap of ... and this is the new ferry. The communal toilets have already overflowed and are awash with eight inches of water, or whatever. In order to use them, you must stay above floor level on raised bulkheads and stand in the dark, hoping that your aim is straight and accurate. Judging by the state of the paintwork around the hole, the men are not very skilled.

also for other documentation that you may need for a specific country, such as photo permits.

When you apply for a visa it is useful to know the name of a hotel in the country you are proposing to visit. It may help if you can say you're staying at the Sheraton or another respectable hotel, rather than a backpackers' hostel or campsite. Visa costs can vary from US$10 to US$100 depending on your nationality and the country you are visiting.

Visa requirements for different countries and different nationalities alter regularly, and it's unlikely that they'll all remain unchanged throughout the life of this book. Always check beforehand. Some east African countries will issue visas at the border, but in the rest of Africa you almost certainly need to obtain one before you arrive. If in doubt, get it in advance. Your embassy or other travellers can give current advice.

The same applies to most francophone countries (ie: ex-French colonies). Visas for these can sometimes be obtained from a French embassy. Check with your nearest French embassy or consulate for the current list of countries for which they issue visas, as it seems to change frequently. The following countries are relevant: Benin, Burkina Faso, Cameroon, Central African Republic (CAR), Chad, Congo, Ivory Coast, Equatorial Guinea, Gabon, Mali, Niger, Senegal and Togo. Several of these have embassies or consulates in the UK; for others you will have to send your passport to Paris or get the visa *en route*.

Some border guards will ask to see a receipt for the visa. You cannot be certain whether this is a genuine requirement, or simply an excuse to ask for money. Try to get a receipt from the embassy or ask them to write the amount paid for the visa in your passport with an official stamp next to it.

$ MONEY

Finance is the art of passing currency from hand to hand until it finally disappears.
Robert W Sarnoff

Visiting a bank can take a whole day, if not longer. Trying to find somewhere to change travellers' cheques is a nightmare in most countries (impossible in Sudan); in others, particularly in southern Africa, it is easier and you'll get a better rate than for cash. If you have five things you want to get done on a particular day, you may be lucky to get through two. But you never know. Just relax and slow down into the pace of Africa.

CURRENCY DECLARATION FORMS Fortunately these are rare these days, but some countries require you to fill in a declaration on entering, saying exactly how much foreign exchange you are bringing in and whether it is in cash or travellers' cheques. If so, all your money might be counted out in front of you and listed on the form. You cannot change any money at a bank without this form. On leaving the country your leftover money, change receipts and declaration form should all tie up – don't get caught out.

Make sure you have hidden some money in a safe place, not only so you can perhaps get a better rate, but also so you can change money even if there is no bank around or open. This can often happen.

CASHING MONEY ON THE ROAD The best option is to take a mixture of euros, pounds sterling and US dollars, in small and large denominations. For more information on suggested amounts and types of currency to take, see *Money* in *Chapter 5* (page 116).

Still in a convoy, we visited the magnificent temples and ruins of Idfu and Kom Ombo on the way. Idfu was magnificent, stunning, despite the hordes of daytrippers and silly prices at the tea stand. As soon as we hit Aswan the armed escort melted away into the chaos. The perennial problem: where will we stay here? No campsite, no hotel with safe parking. No lonely oasis, no shady delightful palmeries to hide in, just concrete and walled compounds. We had harboured a notion of camping in the lush gardens of the Old Cataract Hotel; well, it had been possible 20 years ago according to an ancient guidebook. Now, we could not even get into the hotel grounds without paying an entrance fee. Death on the Nile. Choking by mass tourism and choking by security concerns – the death knells of the independent traveller.

Finding somebody to change hard currency is hardly ever a problem, but travellers' cheques (and in some places moneychanging banks) are another matter. Most travellers carry them for security, but they can be almost impossible to change. If you're lucky, you might find a bank or bureau de change that will accept them. Some campsites and backpackers' hostels, mostly in the south, will change travellers' cheques for you and sometimes even accept travellers' cheques as payment. But generally speaking cash is best.

Changing money, like visa applications, can be time-consuming and filled with paperwork. Some banks are computerised and changing money is a simple process, while others need to go through all sorts of hassles before you see the cash. Always check opening and closing times of banks and leave plenty of time to change money, particularly in Arab countries where the opening hours vary between 08.30 and 09.00 – like in the Sudan – or 09.00 and 10.00. Though guidebooks may state that banks are open from 09.00 to 11.00, it is better to go earlier rather than later, even if you do have to wait for the attendant to have tea and say good morning to everyone. Remember that Friday is usually a holiday in Arab countries.

Most banks in Africa will charge a commission for changing travellers' cheques. Rates and commissions vary widely (from 1% to 10%) from bank to bank, so it is worth shopping around to ensure you get the best rate. It is also advisable to check where your next bank will be and change enough money accordingly.

In Sudan it is not possible to change travellers' cheques, although it is possible to change US dollars cash. Banks almost never change money in Nigeria.

Credit and debit cards can be convenient in southern Africa and parts of east Africa. ATMs are now fairly widely available in larger towns and you can get your cash on the spot, but some countries have no facilities for plastic cards at all.

WHERE TO STAY

Also see general information under *Accommodation* in *Chapter 5*.

HOTELS Hotels are plentiful in most parts of Africa, though many of them do not come close to what we would call a hotel. But then nor do the prices. In some places they are run by the local community with no star structure at all, while in southern Africa, the east coast, parts of the west coast and parts of north Africa, there is one- to five-star accommodation.

In many African countries, and particularly in the capitals, you will find a Hilton or Sheraton, a temporary escape from the Third World to the First and the so-called civilisation that you are trying to evade and forget for a while. Such hotels can be a great place to relax and recover your energies when you have been on the road for sometime. They usually offer all sorts of amenities, normally at roughly European rates. However, we were exceptionally lucky in Djibouti, when the manager of the Sheraton offered us a room for a very reasonable rate at 17.00; we had been looking for hours for somewhere safe to camp. We used every minute of our air-conditioned comfort before check-out the next day.

'Hotels' in African terms can often be just the bare minimum, so always ask to see the room and negotiate the rate before booking yourself in. If you have your own vehicle, make sure that the hotel has a secure parking area; some hotels will allow guests to keep motorbikes in their rooms.

In many of the French-speaking countries along the west coast, you will struggle to find campsites or hostels, particularly in the larger towns, and you may have to depend on the kindness of a hotel manager to let you stay in his parking lot and use the hotel facilities. In fact we found that many of the hotels in Africa would allow us to sleep in the car park and use a room for shower and toilet facilities. It may not work every time in the Hilton or Sheraton, but it's worth asking and explaining that you're driving across Africa. Often the novelty value of such a trip may inspire sympathy as well as incredulity and wonder.

BED AND BREAKFAST Bed and breakfasts are found mostly in southern Africa and along the east coast. Often quaint and family run, they offer a wonderful opportunity to relax and get information on what to do, or not to do, in that specific town or country. Most bed and breakfasts belong to the National Hotel Association and/or are accredited by the tourist board, Automobile Association or various guidebooks. They are usually reasonably priced, around US$15–25 for a double room. Tourist information offices should be able to supply you with a list of bed and breakfasts in the area and relevant prices.

PENSIONS AND AUBERGES Perhaps if you're driving across wildest and deepest, darkest Africa, you won't be in need of a pension! But let's be serious. Pensions are similar to bed and breakfasts, but are specific to the French-speaking countries such as Chad, Ivory Coast, Mali and Niger. They are often family run and are abundant in Morocco. Most of the pensions we experienced were economical, clean and well run. They are often also a wonderful introduction to the local community, usually offering an abundance of information about the town and surrounding areas. Most pensions cost between US$20 and US$40 for a double room.

MONKEY BUSINESS

South of Addis a good road drops down from the highlands into the Great Rift Valley of east Africa. We passed a lone Japanese cyclist on this road – we will never know his story. The lakes of the Rift are famous for their birdlife and pleasant scenes. We were surprised how dry the area just out of Addis was, with dusty plains of acacia and bush. On each side of the valley the land rose to distant heights. Awasa is one of the more developed towns, with a superb hotel on the lakeside. Massive shady trees offered a cool retreat in the gardens, while flocks of colourful birds skimmed low over the lake. Vivid blue-bottomed monkeys looked inquisitively at the discarded icing off our last remaining piece of Christmas cake; the icing had become discoloured with aluminium dust, which seems to get everywhere in the back lockers, but the cake itself was still delicious! And the monkeys seemed to enjoy the icing too, once they dared to taste it. So much so that we had to keep the windows of our room firmly shut.

MISSIONS Throughout Africa, missions, hospitals and aid organisations will often let you camp in their grounds or even offer you a room. Some will expect a small fee, others a large one – either way, a donation based on current camping rates is always welcome.

Missions can be found in nearly every country in Africa. Unfortunately some travellers have abused their hospitality, so those that follow after them are not always welcome. You won't find yourself being turned away by every mission, but it is more and more difficult to depend on them. Most missions adhere to strict rules and regulations in terms of curfews, shower time, kitchen and leisure time. If you don't want to keep to such rules, find alternative accommodation. Others coming after you may like to use the opportunity, even if you don't.

YOUTH HOSTELS Youth hostels are located in most capitals and other large cities. They are often the most convenient and cheapest places for a lone traveller, but two people travelling together can usually get a double room for the same price and greater privacy elsewhere. Some are spartan, with night-time curfews, daytime closing and no cooking facilities, often lacking in privacy and overrun by school groups. Others, however, are conveniently located and hassle-free, offering a wonderful opportunity to meet other travellers.

BACKPACKERS' HOSTELS Backpackers' hostels are found mostly in southern Africa and along the east coast, with an occasional one dotted along the west coast and in north Africa. They are economical, ranging from US$12 to US$20 for a single room, and often you can camp in the courtyard or garden. They offer a huge variety of information on what to do around town, and are a good place to meet up with other travellers.

CAMPSITES You will often find that your day revolves around finding a good spot to stay for the evening, if not for a day or two. Along the more frequented Africa overland routes, there are campsites at fairly regular intervals. Major towns and out-of-the-way places will often have a site, but, if you're intending to do a loop around west Africa, you may struggle to find any at all. Campsites are not common in Libya, Sudan, Ethiopia, most of west Africa, Nigeria, Cameroon, Gabon, the two Congos and Angola. Sites vary from one- to five-star ratings, and prices will usually vary from US$5 to US$12.

Most campsites are visited on the recommendation of other travellers. They also give you the opportunity to meet other travellers, do some maintenance and repairs to your vehicle and catch up on all the other odd jobs that you might have been neglecting. Campsites are often a great source of information regarding vehicle repairs; where to go and who to see. Sometimes they even have their own individual mechanic, a sort of Mr Fix-it and perhaps an ex-driver for one of the tour companies. Information on some of the main campsites is included under individual countries in *Chapter 9*.

BUSH SLEEPING Don't miss it! It is an indescribably wonderful experience to sleep out in the bush, listening to the cicadas whispering, or rather chattering at high volume, in the stillness of the night. Or to sleep out in the Sahara, where nothing at all disturbs the silence. Looking up, watching the stars and pondering the immensity of the universe, you can hear your own heartbeat.

For your own security, the less visible you are from the road, the better; unfortunately, not everyone in this world is friendly and you don't want the wrong kind of person to find you alone in an isolated spot. But trying to steer away from prying eyes can often prove difficult. Find a spot earlier rather than later, as problems tend to multiply once it gets dark; then you can't see where you're going, whereas anyone else who might be around can see your headlights for miles. Having spotted an area, try to make sure that no other drivers or villagers are watching when you turn off. This is easier said than done, as villages tend to develop alongside a country's road network.

Make sure that you respect the bush and be aware of the environment around you. If the surrounding area is particularly dry and there is a gale, don't light a fire. It would in any case make you extremely visible for miles around. Leave only your footprints in the sand – bury only biodegradable products. Do not bury any goods in national parks. Animals will usually dig them up and could cause major damage to themselves, if not the environment. It's best to carry all your rubbish with you until you find an appropriate place to discard it.

In Congo, Gabon or any other tropical rainforest area, bush sleeping can be very difficult, with solid vegetation right up to the sides of the road and wild animals on the prowl at night. One option, often the only one, is to find one of the 'gravel pits' that have been dug out for material to build the road. Such pits are few and far between and may often contain large pools of water, making mosquito nets absolutely essential. You are also almost guaranteed to have visitors, as these pits are frequently sited close to a village. It can also be hard to find a spot for bush camping in South Africa, Botswana, Namibia or Zimbabwe, as almost all land is fenced off. In north Africa you can occasionally camp in palmeries (palm groves), but as these are privately owned you should ask permission if possible.

The other option is to find a village and ask if you may camp there. It is all too easy to forget that we are guests in the communities through which we are driving. Where there are a few roads or tracks the population is likely to be concentrated along them. In this case, try to find the head of the village and ask permission to camp. A small gift of appreciation such as a bottle of Coke, pens or cigarettes is often welcomed. Even empty plastic water bottles are useful. Villagers are by nature curious, as we are of them, and you may feel a little intimidated by ogling adults and children. Mostly they are just friendly, though, and would like to communicate with you. A sense of humour, or being able to play a musical instrument, drawing or just communicating in some way or another usually helps to ease the situation, and is one of the better ways of getting to know a particular tribe, culture or village.

Remember that the vast majority of people in the world are friendly; if you didn't believe that, you would have stayed at home. By taking reasonable precautions, you can have a fantastic experience out in the bush.

✖ EATING AND DRINKING

LET'S GO LOCAL Going local is inexpensive and can be great fun. All of Africa's countries have their own unique meals and local brews. Some can be an acquired taste, others will be something you want to eat over and over again, and a few you will hope never to taste again. For the local flavour of the day go to the markets, street vendors, restaurants or local cafés. But do be cautious about the standard of hygiene. Avoid fresh uncooked salads and fruit you haven't prepared yourself. You can't always choose where to stop the car in an emergency!

Each African country has its own beer, often brewed and bottled locally. In addition to this are fermented rice water, honey beer, millet beer and all sorts of other local delicacies brewed up 24 hours a day. In some Muslim countries, alcohol is prohibited, so be careful about this.

In most African cultures, people eat with their hands. If you are invited into somebody's home, they will often offer you their one spoon or any other cutlery

No matter how much food you take or what you can find to eat, there's always some item that you crave. Chocolate melts, bacon is taboo in Muslim countries and bread with bananas can get tedious every day. If you can have yoghurt on cereals every day or with curries, your day is sure to go well! But unless you have a big fridge you can't store a yoghurt for every day – and it just isn't found in many shops. A solution is, however, at hand.

It took a rather eccentric former American missionary (no names yet) to teach us a thing or two about Africa. His recipe below for making your own yoghurt on the road was a winner for us and may be for you too.

UTENSILS

1 small measuring cup, espresso size or similar
2 empty jam jars, thoroughly cleaned with boiling water
Saucepan for stirring in (optional)

INGREDIENTS

2 cups of water at room temperature
2 cups of milk powder
1 cup of live yoghurt
2 cups of boiling water from the kettle

METHOD Put the two cups of 'cold' water in the saucepan and mix with two cups of milk powder. Stir well to dissolve the powder as much as possible.

Add one cup of ready-made live yoghurt, which you can probably buy from the hotel or campsite you are staying in, or try a supermarket. Or if this is your second or more attempt, you already have it! Stir again gently.

Now add two cups of almost-boiling water and stir again gently. Don't worry if it is slightly lumpy.

Pour into the two heated and cleaned jam jars.

Wait and watch. If the ambient temperature is right, the yoghurt will start to set in less than one hour.

Leave it overnight with a damp cloth over it, so in the morning it will be fresh and cool.

Et voila! Next morning you have a delightful breakfast feast.

Don't forget to save a little to make more for the next day, then it will go on and on. Ours lasted six weeks and only died when we returned to the frozen wastes of northern Europe.

Sadly this method does not work very well in cold places, so added heat may be necessary in northern or southern Africa. If the outside temperature is too cold, you can try leaving the yoghurt in the cab or near the engine, so long as it's not an oil-covered Land Rover block! But that's where the difficulties arise, as it sometimes ends up as 'lassi' – a yoghurt drink found in India – or it may separate into semi-solid cottage cheese and whey. At least it always seems edible, in whatever form.

Bon appetit! Enjoy your experiments.

PS: Does anyone know the former missionary (from Mali – a hint) we are talking about?

Charlie Shackell and Illya Bracht

EGYPT
Stella Local beer.
Alwa turki Turkish-style coffee and a great energy booster, particularly with large amounts of sugar.
Molokhiyya A soup made by stewing leafy vegetables with rice, garlic and chicken or beef broth. Do not be put off by its appearance.
Grilled samak (fish) Served by the kilogram and chosen by you. Usually includes salad, bread and dips like tahini (sesame spread with olive oil, garlic and lemon) and *baba ghanoug* (a mix of aubergine and tahini).
Gibna beyda White cheese like feta.
Gibna rumi Hard, sharp yellow-white cheese.

ETHIOPIA
Tej A very potent honey beer that you will either hate or love.
Coffee ceremony A must; be ready to experience a caffeine overdrive.
Shiro wot Vegetable stew, great for vegetarians, and eaten by Ethiopians during religious fasting.
Doro wot Hot chicken stew served on the famous *injera* bread.
Injera Flatbread, generally made to cover a table. Food is placed on top for communal meals. Not to everyone's taste; can be quite sour.
Kitfo Raw meat with yellow pepper (*mitmita*).
Coffee shops Serve fresh coffee, fruit juice and cakes.

GHANA
Apateche Traditional firewater found everywhere. Try it.
Star Local beer.
Shitor din Traditional dark chilli *sambal*.
Palava sauce *Palava* means 'trouble'; this is a variation of vegetable and meat stew.

IVORY COAST
Attiéké Grated *manioc* (cassava) served with fish and pepper sauce.
Maquis Chicken with onion and tomatoes.
Rice and offal balls A great delicacy.

KENYA
Tusker Local beer.
Irio Corn mash and maize which most Kenyans think is dull, but it's worth a try.
N'dizi Swahili for bananas, wrapped in groundnut. Crunchy *n'dizi* is self-explanatory.

MOROCCO
Green tea Very sweet, served with fresh peppermint leaves.
Tagine With chicken and prunes: a stew cooked in the traditional tagine bowl and said to be one of the oldest recipes in Africa.

that might be available. If this does not happen, there is just one golden rule you need to remember; always eat with your right hand. The left hand is used for all other, dirty business.

NIGER
Green tea Traditionally brewed up by Tuaregs over an open fire in very small teapots.
Fresh camels' milk Like a warm milkshake and not to everyone's taste.
Goat's cheese A Tuareg delicacy and delicious if you're a lover of cheese; should be accompanied by dried prunes.
Tuareg bread Baked in the sand.

NIGERIA
Lager Star Local beer.
Gari foto Based on the root vegetable of the African diet.
Gari Like rice, the base for many dishes.
Okra soup Looks like slime but never say no to a new experience!
Kyimkying West African kebabs and great street food, but not recommended by the local expat community.

SOUTHERN AFRICA
Castle Local beer.
Red wines From Cape Town.
Amarula A liquor made up from the amarula tree, which bears a fruit that elephants particularly like to eat.
Biltong Dried game, not to everyone's taste.
Bobotie A Malay dish served in southern Africa.
Boerewors A type of sausage, delicious grilled over an open fire.

SUDAN
Guava juice A must if you like guavas, freshly squeezed, served out of enormous cooler boxes.
Fuul Fava beans with oil, lemon, salt, meat, eggs and onions.
Ta'amiyya Deep-fried ground chick peas – very 'moreish'!

TANZANIA
Amstel Local beer.
Chapati ya n'dizi tamu Banana fritters, common throughout Africa.
Chilled banana cream Good, depending on its freshness.
Mboga ya maboga Pumpkin leaves and flowers in cream.
Plantain or banana chips

TUNISIA
Brik A thin, crisp, pastry envelope filled with egg, cheese or meat. If you choose egg, bite carefully – the yolk may spurt out.

ZIMBABWE
Black Label Local beer.
Nhopi dovi Like pumpkin.
Sadza Like the west African *banku*, the east African *ugali*, Zambian *ntsima* or South African *mealie-meal*, *sadza* is a stiff, steamed dumpling made from white maize flour. It is regarded as Zimbabwe's national dish.

If you are unsure about how to react to a specific situation, watch what others do. In some cultures, they will only begin eating once you have started. Ask to wash your hands before a meal, then help yourself. Often your insecurity and any mishap in eating with your hands can break the ice; it's your turn to be the entertainment.

In much of Africa you'll have no problem finding local produce at markets or from street vendors. Onions, garlic and tomatoes are nearly always available. Goat, mutton and chicken are also readily available, and fish is plentiful near rivers and on the coast. Many other fruits and vegetables can be found according to the country's economy and the season. But food is not always so easy to find, so make sure you always have some emergency supplies of tinned food with you. For example, in some parts of Ethiopia we found only garlic for sale along the roadside; in one town there was no food for sale in the shops, but the hotel we camped at had a wonderful orchard where our carrots were picked fresh from the ground while we waited. See box, *Ethiopia in Nutshell*, below.

It can be great fun haggling and bartering your way through smiling vendors, each protesting that their produce is the freshest, nicest and cheapest. Visit a few stalls and ask around, so you can get a feel for prices and always keep in mind the average local income. Sometimes you will be ripped off, but if you are happy to pay the price asked, then pay it. Most supermarkets have local produce, but at an increased cost, as many of the products are imported from neighbouring countries, or even from Europe.

SUPERMARKETS Most capital cities in Africa have a supermarket or two, from well stocked to nearly empty. West African capitals all have expensive supermarkets with French products. Local shops, often only a hole in the wall or a table set up on the pavement, have basic goods like toothpaste, toilet paper, margarine and other odds and ends. One hole-in-the-wall shop in Omdurman, Khartoum, had an amazing array of goods, which we browsed through while our punctured tyre was being fixed next door. Orange juice, Egyptian fava beans, clean loose sugar…

For more luxurious items such as fresh cheese and chocolate, you will need to shop in large supermarket chains, like the Nakomat or Uchumi in Nairobi, which are found in most east African countries. Morocco now also has several chains of European-style supermarkets, including Marjane. If you have a favourite brand, take enough to last your entire trip, although this is only possible if you have your own vehicle.

INTERNATIONAL RESTAURANTS There will come a time when you are tired of eating locally or cooking for yourself. Perhaps there is a special occasion on the horizon. Cuisine from all over the world can be found throughout Africa, particularly in the capitals, from Chinese to Italian, Indian to Lebanese, pizzas to hamburgers. The restaurants cater to every need and every pocket. Some are based on European prices, while others are more affordable. Ask other travellers or wherever you are staying for advice on restaurants in the area. Most campsites and backpackers' hostels also offer basic international meals.

WATER There is a saying in Agadez, Niger, that once you have tasted the water you will always want to return. In Agadez, the artesian wells are thousands of years old and the water is pure, coming deep out of the ground. It is checked regularly, too. But this is not always the case everywhere, and it's better to be safe than sorry; better to spend time purifying the water than be sick for days in your vehicle, or worse, on your bicycle.

You must respect local water sources. Water, especially clean water, is one of the most important commodities in Africa. Never do anything to a well that might contaminate it, such as throwing anything into it, or washing yourself or your clothes close by. This is particularly important in Arab countries, where water is also used for prayer.

Obtaining water and the amount you need to carry depends on the time of year you are travelling, where you are and how dedicated you are to washing both yourself and your clothes. Drinking is more important than washing when water is scarce or unavailable. Remember also that your radiator may be thirsty or, in the worst case, spring a leak. Never waste water, especially when you're on the road.

In the desert at the hottest time of year you should allow six to eight litres a day intake per person, and even in January or February you will easily get through two or three. It is absolutely vital to drink as much as you need, as you could run into serious problems if you do not. If your urine becomes concentrated in colour, you could be heading for trouble. A good guide is that you should urinate often and it should be clear.

Cyclists will face the greatest difficulties in terms of how much they can carry, and motorcyclists will also be restricted by weight. It is best to stick to the more major desert routes, where water is more likely to be available from other travellers. Cyclists will need a good filter, because they are less able to carry supplies of good water and will be more likely to rely on poorer sources. If water is not clear in any way, filter before purifying it. We drank either bottled mineral water, or boiled water that locals would drink straight from the tap. Very rarely, and only in parts of the Sahara, we drank water straight from the source without purification. Other travellers have recommended Chloromyn T.

In general, wherever there is a village you will find a source of water. Open bodies of water, streams, lakes, etc are probably going to be contaminated and should be treated with caution. If you take water from an open source, always purify it, preferably by boiling. Water from the tap can vary in quality; the best advice is to ask the locals if they drink it straight. Then purify it anyway just in case. When faced with a village well, use some common sense. If people are washing nearby or the toilets are close, then don't trust it. Even if you are at a remote desert well which is well maintained and covered, you should still purify the water before drinking it; there may well be a dead goat or camel down there.

For more information see *Water and water purification methods* in *Chapter 3* (page 69) and *Health* in *Chapter 5* (page 117).

SOFT DRINKS, BEER AND SPIRITS A cold refreshing beer under a fading African sky is bliss after a hot day on the road. Except in north Africa, beer and local spirits are generally easy to find. Local beers at local prices are nearly always pleasant and of varying levels of alcohol content. Imported spirits can be found in most capital cities at European prices. In Arab countries, where alcohol is often banned, don't try to smuggle any in. You could end up in prison, or worse. Soft drinks can be found almost everywhere and Coke or Pepsi is always available.

SHOPPING

Wherever you travel in Africa, the following are some of the local products and crafts available: weaving and cloth; sculpture; masks; silver crosses from Agadez, Niger; other jewellery; wood carvings; papyrus paintings from Egypt… enough to inspire the most reluctant consumer or, conversely, to keep the most ardent shopaholic occupied, while contributing directly to the local economy. See also *Cultural interaction and respect* in *Chapter 8*, page 186.

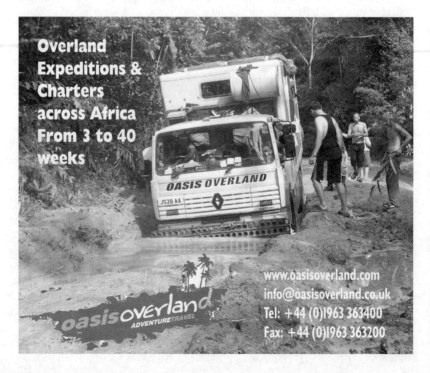

Part Three

THE GUIDE

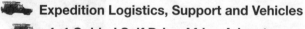

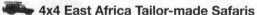

8

Background

GEOGRAPHY, VEGETATION AND CLIMATE

In this section is a brief outline of the main physical features of Africa. All of the north, from the Mediterranean to the 25° latitude, is **desert**. It is amazingly varied and has the mountainous areas of the Hoggar, Tassili, Tibesti and Ennedi. South of the desert is the transitional zone known as the **Sahel**. This is a region of hardy fine grasses, sandy sparse scrub, acacia trees and limited low tree cover. Moving south, these scrub areas become steadily thicker bush, with very striking baobab trees. This whole transitional area is known as **savanna**, a wooded zone with tall grasses that becomes steadily denser. Finally, around the Equator are luxuriant thick **rainforests** with tall trees and dark undergrowth. Heading into the southern hemisphere, the vegetation has similar patterns in reverse, but the desert is confined to the western region of Namibia. South Africa is generally classified as a Mediterranean climatic zone, but with variations depending on altitude. East Africa and Ethiopia present the other main variations, where altitude is the dominant influence on the landscape and vegetation.

Africa's climate has gone through many changes. It is thought that most of Africa and indeed Europe had a wet and warm period between 13000BC and 9000BC. After this the climate became drier, but there is strong evidence from rock art that most of the Sahara area was fertile, with herders and some sedentary groups. Some of the rock art of the Tassili Plateau in Algeria/Libya, the Tibesti and Ennedi mountains in Chad is thought to be as much as 7,000 years old. The desertification of the north to form the Sahara steadily expanded from around 3000BC. Climatic changes are still in progress in Africa today, as the Sahara steadily moves southwards. The droughts of the 1980s bear witness to this.

NATURAL HISTORY AND CONSERVATION

Detailed examination of this vast topic is beyond the remit of this guide. Suffice to say that any extended trip across the continent will encompass all the major natural features it has to offer. Apart from the well-known safari parks in east and southern Africa, there are many new and amazingly diverse additions to the conservation list. Almost every country in Africa, whether desert, savanna, rainforest or mountain region, has set aside areas of significant natural habitat, many with attendant wildlife. Increasingly Africa is embracing the new forms of tourism: ecotourism, wildlife preservation and conservation, cultural tourism and village development through small tourist initiatives. Botswana, Namibia, Tanzania, Kenya, Uganda and Gabon in particular have made great efforts towards conservation. It is no longer enough to chase around game parks or climb high mountains without giving something back. Endangered species are now at the forefront of conservation. That said, there are still serious problems. The most intractable are along the DRC/Uganda/Rwanda border, where political instability and saving the

In the morning, bleary-eyed and tetchy from the long drive, we head for Lake Assal nearby. The scenery is again stunning. The road snakes over broken lava fields and past currently dormant volcanic cones. Most are not large, but the sheer number of old cones is breathtaking and somewhat sinister. Lake Assal, although only ten miles from the sea, is below sea level and separated from the sea only by the lava fields. The heat is already stifling by 08.00. The brilliant blue lake is surrounded by the walls of an ancient cauldron, multi-coloured but mostly dark and jagged. Around the lake is an almost fluorescent white collar of super-brilliant crystalline deposits. The road descends into this vast cauldron of colour and seemingly dead wasteland.

Yet life is found here too. Small antelopes hop agilely across the rough landscape, tentatively watching the intruders. Distant flamingos gather around the shore. Down by the lake's edge are amazingly shaped crystals and rare volcanic rocks, halite being the strangest, with its hollowed-out rugby-ball shapes and brown crystals locking into each other. Brilliant yellow sulphur crystals grow from the water's edge. This is not a place to walk around carelessly without a guide. Here is the birthplace of a new ocean, where Africa is being ripped apart along its famous Rift Valley. Here Somalia and most of Kenya will be cut adrift by the forces from below the earth of Djibouti.

Suddenly a thunderous deafening, screeching roar breaks the silence of the desert. We jump out of our skins in fright. The French are playing soldiers across the desert, and their air force is terrifying everyone with its low-flying supersonic fighter jets. Djibouti, it seems, is the playground of the French military. The noise is enough to awaken the demons of the dormant cones and send their boiling bellies of molten lava into crescendos of explosive rage.

The road east to Tadjoura holds more surprises: massive dried-out whirlpools of solidified lava, where hardy scrub acacias are trying to stay alive. The Land Rover can barely cope with the gradients and the gearbox sounds noisy. The views south of the narrow Bay of Ghoubbet are stupendous. The waters are almost cut off from the Red Sea. The mountains to the north are stark and rugged. Towards Tadjoura the greenery increases, and soon we can make out the Forêt du Day, a small zone of intensely forested hills: a freak of nature, born from the sea mists and very infrequent rains.

mountain gorillas conflict. In years to come, the need to preserve the continent's natural attractions will always be tempered by the need to eradicate poverty and increase economic development. Protecting nature will hopefully be seen in future as a means of protecting the planet and aiding human development.

HISTORY

It is generally agreed that human development began in Africa. Recently the oldest remains were found in Chad, 300km north of N'djamena. Until the discovery in Chad, the oldest hominid had been found in Ethiopia's Danakil region. The name given to this find was Lucy. Dated at just over three million years old, these remains confirm the existence of transitional humanoids that were neither apes nor fully developed humans.

There is evidence to suggest that five main ethnic groups existed in Africa. There were the Nilotic peoples, generally tallest in stature. In the north were people from whom the Berbers have descended. In the west were stocky black people. In central areas were the diminutive Pygmies and in the east and south were the San, who are now known as the Bushmen of Botswana. A date for the emergence of these groups is around 100,000 years ago. The Egyptians seem to have developed later, before or around 6000BC and separately from these groups. The Egyptian civilisation was at its zenith after 3000BC. It finally died out after being engulfed by the Nubians around 300BC. Then the Nubians too were overrun, by the Assyrians and Persians. Meanwhile, from central and east Africa, the Bantu people spread south between 100BC and AD200–300.

The next great civilisations to impose their will on north Africa were the Greeks and the Romans. The great cities of Carthage, El Djem, Sbeitla, Leptis Magna, Sabrata, and Apollonia arose. Further south another great kingdom, possibly with a Jewish connection, arose in the 4th century: that of Aksum in Ethiopia. Christianity spread into the empire, but in the face of the new religion, Islam, it was driven up into the highlands where it continued to flourish. Perhaps the greatest change in Africa occurred with the rise of Islam, from its beginnings in Arabia in the mid 7th century. Arab traders and slavers moved down the coast of east Africa, where the Swahili language developed. Arab zealots moved swiftly across north Africa, the Sahara and deep into west Africa.

Way to the south, the only significant civilisation to develop in the rest of the continent was centred on Zimbabwe. Its famous ruins date from the 11th century. In west Africa three great civilisations or empires arose, mainly with the development of cross-Sahara trade routes using camels. The earliest was the Ghana Empire. It existed from AD700 to approximately AD1000. This was not centred on the area known as Ghana today, but located in southeastern present-day Mauritania. Later the Mali Empire arose, around AD1200, lasting until AD1500. This was a great period of wealth and trade, with the cities of Djenné, Mopti and Timbuktu at their zenith. Finally the Songhai Empire gradually developed, taking over from the Mali Empire, with its centre around Gao.

Slavery, which had already existed since the Arabs arrived, was further developed with the coming of the seafaring Europeans. The Portuguese began the process in 1450. Officially it was abolished in 1870, but did not completely die out. In fact tendencies towards slavery have not long been discontinued in Mauritania. The great wave of European expansion and subsequent colonisation began around the 1850s. By 1884 the great colonial powers were in such conflict over the territories that a meeting was called in Berlin to delineate the boundaries of the various countries. The British and the French took most of the continent, with Germany, Belgium and Portugal occupying most of the rest. Spain got Western 'Spanish' Sahara and Rio Muni/Fernando Po, modern Equatorial Guinea. Ethiopia remained virtually independent, but the Italians had some of its territory, as well as Libya.

After World War I, Germany lost Tanganyika and parts of Togo and Cameroon, but remained influential in Namibia. Independence finally arrived, from the early 1950s onwards. Libya was one of the first to become independent, in 1951, followed by Ghana in 1952, after agitation by Nkrumah. Many countries gained independence in the 1960s, including most of east Africa, Nigeria and the French and Belgian colonies or protectorates. The last were the Portuguese colonies, Guinea Bissau, Mozambique and Angola, finally succeeding in the years of 1974–75. In southern Africa different problems existed. Zimbabwe gained freedom in 1980, after a protracted period under the Smith government and various interim arrangements. Namibia was the last country here to gain independence. It had been under South African administration, which had long been separated from the British yoke, but retained its unique racial separation with apartheid. South Africa finally became a multi-racial democracy in 1994.

AFRICAN EXPLORERS Today we can pore over glossy maps and calculate travel times and distances in Africa with ease. However, the early exploration of Africa

Just south of Iringa is Kisolanza Farm. This haven of peace sits at some 7,000ft and is much cooler. As we drove in, two young white women came across and said in perfect Sussex accents, 'Do come and have a cup of tea when you're ready.' The campground was very well organised and the food was tremendous. For less than a pound we gorged on best fillet steak, so tender it could be cut with a butter knife. A party of four South African vehicles and their ageing occupants shared the camp.

The evening was spent exchanging stories. Where did you break down? How is your vehicle going? What sort of engine do you have? (Note that we all had Land Rovers.) Jasper and Emma, Justin and Becki had met in Nairobi after completely separate journeys from England, but lived only five miles apart in Kent and did not then know each other.

The farmhouse stands on a hill not far from the camp; the roof is thatched, the walls of local stone. Such a magnificent house could easily fit into a Dorset village. The farm had run down during the excessive socialist years of Nyerere, when landed gentry were considered undesirable in a left-leaning Utopian regime. New but admirably set bungalows have now been added to encourage ecotourism, the new byword in development in modern-day Tanzania.

was a haphazard affair. Some adventurers had official backing, others explored clandestinely; some were fanatical missionaries and others travelled with a deep faith in their hoped-for discoveries. Most set forth in the footsteps of Arab traders and slavers. An overland journey today follows these illustrious adventurers, but does not need to be so haphazardly planned.

One of the first African explorers was James Bruce, who set out for Ethiopia in 1769, ostensibly to find the source of the Nile. His journey took him into the highlands of the country, from the port of Massawa on the Red Sea. Climbing onto the high plateau, he first visited Axum then headed south across the Simien Mountains to the capital, Gonder. Bruce was briefly appointed court physician to Ras Michael in Gonder after an epidemic of smallpox. He was also bewitched by one of his wives. After much drinking of honey wine at a wedding, he took his leave and travelled to Lake Tana and the Tissisat Falls on the Blue Nile. Avoiding the various intrigues of power in Gonder, he eventually made his way home via the Sudan and Nile. On his return in 1773 his exploits were doubted, although his books prospered. He received no acclaim until after his death in 1794.

The Scotsman Mungo Park was another adventurer to be sent out to find answers to African geographical mysteries. Heading inland from the Gambia, he passed Segou but got no further than Silla in his quest for the route of the Niger River. This was in 1795. After recovering in England, he returned to Africa in 1805. This time his progress was better and he followed the river through Mali, Niger and Nigeria. He was killed at Bussa in Nigeria before completing his mission.

Three strong-minded but incompatible adventurers, Oudney, Clapperton and Denham, crossed the Sahara in 1822 via Murzuk to Bilma and Agadez. They eventually reached Lake Chad, seeking routes to the Niger River. Oudney died in Nigeria and only Clapperton succeeded in making any significant journeys, reaching Kano and Sokoto. In 1825 he again set out with Landers to find the route of the Niger. It was left to the Landers brothers to solve the mystery of the Niger and its mouth in 1830.

Stories of great wealth and gold lured others to Timbuktu. Alexander Gordon Laing was one such explorer. He travelled across the desert via Ghadames and the Fezzan. Having once been left for dead after a Tuareg raid, he reached the fabled

above   *Injera* – the national dish of Ethiopia (AZ)

left   Swazi girl preparing porridge, Matsamo village, Swaziland (AZ)

below   Banana fritters, Tanzania (AZ)

bottom   Djerba market, Tunisia (SPJ & BG)

above   **Paintings inside Debre Birhan Selassie Church, Gonder, Ethiopia** (AZ)

left   **Luxor Temple, Egypt** (SPJ & BG)

below   **Country house, Guinea** (SPJ & BG)

bottom   **Cape Town, South Africa** (SPJ & BG)

above   **Ksar Ouled Soltane, Tunisia**
(SPJ & BG)

right   **Ennedi rock art, Chad**
(SPJ & BG)

below   **Amphitheatre, Leptis Magna, Libya** (SPJ & BG)

above	**Black-backed jackal** (AZ)
above left	**Mountain gorilla** (AZ)
left	**African elephant** (AZ)
below left	**Springbok** (AZ)
below	**Forest buffalo** (AZ)
bottom	**Lions** (AZ)

above	**Senegal parrot** (AZ)
above right	**Lesser flamingoes** (AZ)
right	**Black rhino and warthogs** (AZ)
below right	**African penguins** (AZ)
below	**Hippo and calf** (AZ)
bottom	**Nile crocodile** (AZ)

above   **Road to Djanet, Algeria** (SPJ & BG)

below   **Zebras at Mlilwane Wildlife Sanctuary, Swaziland** (SPJ & BG)

city and lived there in a house that can still be seen today. He never returned alive though, being killed by Tuaregs in 1826. The Frenchman René Caillié reached Djenne and Kabara by canoe, and arrived in Timbuktu in April 1828. He returned to France alive, crossing the Sahara to Morocco.

In 1850 Heinrich Barth and James Richardson left Tripoli southbound across the Sahara. Despite hostile Tuaregs, Barth succeeded in being the first 'infidel' Christian to reach Agadez. Richardson later died, but Barth continued to explore the area of Nigeria, Cameroon and west to Timbuktu before returning alive to Germany in 1855. The Swiss explorer Johann Ludwig Burckhardt learnt Arabic and made a daring visit to Mecca, having travelled across Egypt and the Sudan. Another adventurous German, Gustav Nachtigal, explored the Sahara and in particular the unknown Tibesti Mountains. He was lucky to escape from the fiercely independent and unfriendly Tubu tribes of those mountains. The Tubu still resist outsiders today.

In 1854 Richard Burton, having studied Somali customs, made a daring visit to Harar in Ethiopia, a city of devout Muslims where no infidel was likely to survive. But survive he did, being welcomed by the Amir. On a further expedition to Somaliland, Burton travelled with John Hanning Speke. In 1856 Burton and Speke were sent by the Royal Geographical Society to discover the source of the Nile. Having caught yellow fever, both were holed up in Zanzibar until June 1857. Travelling inland, they made it to Tabora and on to Lake Tanganyika. Here they split up, with Burton continuing to look for the source of the Nile in the area, while Speke headed north to a large lake, Lake Victoria, from which he came back convinced it was the source of the Nile.

TIMBUKTU OR BUST IN 2008

Timbuktu – city of explorers, mysterious blue men of the desert, of mesmerising mud mosques and stories of untold wealth in days gone by. Here is the tangible melancholy of a former glory, its quiet decay arrested by modern infections. Timbuktu today is an enigma, where the incessant wind blows a plastic bag across a sand-laden street, where grubby children follow the tailcoats of a stranger and where modernity still struggles to impose its antiseptic character. Timbuktu does not disappoint.

Alexander Gordon Laing, Heinrich Barth and Rene Caillie all reached the city of Islamic learning, mostly in disguise, at great personal cost and a great deal of physical discomfort. Laing was the first in, but he was killed on his journey home. Caillie made it back; Barth stayed for years and just survived his journey. The houses of these great adventurers, where they hid or lived, still exist within the sandy old city. Why would anyone, particular an 'infidel', want to come to Timbuktu?

Having first reached the city in 1978, Bob was apprehensive about our impending return. Familiar sights remained, though – the impressive Dinguerey Mosque now given a new paved access path, the Sankore Mosque extended in tasteful style and the house of explorer Laing still signposted but with at least 3ft of sand removed from the street. The former metal-structured supermarket, the only modern blot on the place before, was now painted a greener yellow, but ceased to function.

Where the early explorers awaited uncertain fates on their return journeys, those reaching the fabled city of the Mali Empire now have a good chance of getting back home afterwards. The internet of course has arrived in Timbuktu, but the overland access is still rough, wild, lonely, rugged and, yes, achieved with a significant degree of physical discomfort.

Long may it last!

Background HISTORY

8

Back in England, the debate between Burton and Speke continued acrimoniously. In 1862 Speke returned to Lake Victoria with James Grant. They explored the western shore, found a river and waterfall at Jinja, headed to Lake Albert and then continued up the Nile to Khartoum. However, they did not actually follow the river from Jinja for its entire course. Burton and others, with some justification, still doubted the assumption that this was the true source of the Nile. Around this time, an adventurer, Baker, and his former slave girlfriend met Speke and Grant in Gondokoro. Baker and his girlfriend continued south, exploring Lake Albert and locating the waterfall later called Murchison Falls. But still the absolute facts were not settled.

After Burton returned from another journey to west Africa and Gabon in 1865, a debate was organised between Speke and Burton. This ended with the notorious self-shooting of Speke just before the meeting. The death of Speke, however, did not once and for all solve the mystery of the source of the Nile.

David Livingstone, part explorer and part missionary, arrived in southern Africa in 1835. After a series of expeditions into the Kalahari and the interior, he discovered Victoria Falls in 1855. Livingstone's exploits and exploration in Africa brought him acclaim in England, but the death of his wife affected him deeply. Then, in 1865, the Royal Geographical Society asked him to seek out the source of the Nile for final clarification. Livingstone was of the opinion that the river rose well to the south of Lake Victoria, possibly in Lake Bangweulu. After a series of fruitless journeys characterised by ill health and hostile tribes, he finally arrived at Ujiji on Lake Tanganyika. This was in 1869. Joining Arab traders, he sought out the Lualaba River for the next two years. The famous meeting with Stanley occurred in Ujiji in 1871. Revived somewhat, Livingstone travelled north with Stanley up Lake Tanganyika, but the source of the Nile eluded him. He died in 1872 heading south again.

Henry Morton Stanley, though born in north Wales in 1841, was an American citizen and quite a different character from the stiff-upper-lipped British explorers. Yet he had as much grim determination as any of his predecessors. In 1874 he set out to explore Lake Victoria fully. He then attempted to check out Lake Albert, but warring tribes prevented this. He set out for Lake Tanganyika and then, having ascertained that it had no outlets, he headed west to the Luabala, which he followed. Continuing west, he discovered a larger river and the falls, which became known as the Stanley Falls, near modern-day Kisangani. Without knowing where his journey would take him, he finally arrived at the sea. But it was the Atlantic Ocean he found; he had followed the mighty Congo River to Boma. The mystery of the Nile had been solved, and it was Speke's original theory that was proved correct.

Stanley continued to explore Africa with the celebrated Tippu Tip and a massive retinue for protection, finally mapping out the remaining geographical conundrums of the great central African lakes. After his death in 1905, the colonial scramble for Africa began.

PEOPLE

Africa has a very diverse cross-section of people. In the far north are the Arabs, who migrated and brought Islam from Saudi Arabia. They mixed with the indigenous Berbers of the Maghreb. Further south are the famous nomads of the desert – the Tuareg and Tubu people of Algeria, Libya, Mali, Niger and Chad, who probably developed from the Berbers. The Moors of Morocco spread along the Atlantic coast to Mauritania. Much further to the east are the Nubia and Dinka of Sudan and the Amharic-speaking groups of Ethiopia. West Africa is well known for its diverse peoples, and it is they who add such colour and interest to trips in the region. The Fulani or Peul are the famous cattle herders. Other major west African groups are the Wolof, Bambara, Malinke, Songhai, Mossi, Bobo, Djerma, Bozo, Dogon, Hausa, Ibo and Yoruba.

In central Africa, Pygmies are still found in Cameroon, the two Congos and Gabon, where the Fang are also found. Some of the Bantu-related groups in east Africa are the Buganda, Kikuyu, Masai, Rendille and Samburu. In Rwanda and Burundi the two main ethnic groups, who have been bitter enemies, are the Hutu and the Tutsi; the pygmoid Twa are only a small minority. Across southern Africa

DOWNTOWN DJIBOUTI – A MELTING-POT OF TRIBAL PEOPLE

The old colonial quarter of town has some picturesque buildings, many with arched façades that give much-needed shade to the vendors and pedestrians. There are street cafés and ancient tamarisk trees. Well-dressed businessmen mingle with entrepreneurial ladies dressed in amazingly colourful attire, laughing and gossiping over strong coffee. The African quarter and market area is totally absorbing. Shopkeepers and street vendors promote their wares, groups of men sit beside the old whitewashed mosques smoking hookah pipes and cigarettes. The women in the clothes market are deep in animated conversation. We, of course, are probably the source of most of their laughter and humorous gossip, but no-one is threatening. We drink tea; it's the milky Indian-style tea, which is a big surprise, as there aren't many Indians about. There are lots of Somalis, Ethiopian truckers, Eritrean refugees, Afar and Danakil tribals, Yemenis and Arab traders, but hardly any white faces in the markets. Djibouti city is a fascinating place and should not be missed.

Check-out time in our own 'Paradise' Hotel is 13.00 but 14.00 is fine. We savour the cool luxury, watching the television. Our world is one of make-believe, cocooned in this small place where we can travel in time and space. We are transported back to little England. The budget is being discussed – we don't know if it's over or due next week; the weather forecast is of course for rain and the cars are just as expensive as ever on *Top Gear*. Down in the car park the Land Rover is cooking, the steering wheel is too hot to touch and the guards are half-asleep in the great fog of humidity.

the following make up most of the people: Shona, Ndebele, Himba, Herero, Ovambo, Makua, Chewa, Basotho, Zulu and Xhosa.

Finally, set apart from these Bantu peoples, are the San, who are the original Bushmen, the people who inhabited Botswana and parts of South Africa before retreating.

CULTURAL INTERACTION AND RESPECT

Africa has such a rich cultural heritage that you will probably only be able to scratch the surface. As you travel through Africa, you will begin to discover the diversity of this huge continent. Wherever you go, an understanding of local culture and history will go a long way towards enriching your experience.

Before you leave home, get as much information as you can about Africa, its culture and people. The more you know and respect the places you plan to visit, the less likely you are to disrupt local culture when you get there, and the more you will get out of your trip. Travelling carries responsibilities as well as bringing pleasure – dress in a manner to suit the different cultures; respect people's dignity and wishes, particularly when taking photographs; respect religious sites and artefacts; keep the environment clean by burning your rubbish wherever possible; and do not encourage dependence by casually handing out gifts, unless some small service has been rendered.

Africa is home to possibly the most diverse peoples on the planet, yet it also has common themes across its vast expanse. Each area has a great mix of distinct tribal groupings, defied by the illogical borders that the modern world ascribes to the continent. It is impossible to learn the spoken word of all these differing groups, but any usage of even the most basic words will open doors and enable greater interaction. Most guidebooks will give a few common greetings and phrases in the local language.

Despite the cultural divide, most Africans are welcoming, interested and lively. Many African societies have very elaborate greeting rituals from person to person that seem to go on and on. Some rituals amongst the nomadic peoples involve lengthy tea ceremonies and not much actual tea drinking. A simple handshake will, however, suffice for the rest of us.

One of the subjects most guaranteed to cause inadvertent offence or misunderstanding is that of traditional Islam in Africa. The nature of Islam in black Africa is generally more laid back and tolerant than that in the Arab regions. This does not mean, however, that one should act in a more liberal way, particularly regarding dress. Clothing, together with general appearance, is the one thing that defines your approach and can have negative as well as positive impacts.

RELIGION

ISLAM Apart from the well-known countries along the north African coast that adhere to Islam, a surprising number of sub-Saharan countries also have substantial numbers, if not all of their population, observing the religion. Islam spread south across the Sahara with the caravan routes from Egypt, Libya, Tunisia, Algeria, and Morocco after its founding in the middle of the 7th century in Saudi Arabia. Places on the southern fringes of the desert became rich and powerful, places like Agadez, Gao, Djenne and Timbuktu, the most famous and mysterious of all. Vast wealth was accumulated by the empires of Ghana (not the current state), Mali and Songhai. With the coming of ships, much of the cross-Saharan trade declined and the cities were eclipsed. By now the Islamic faith had become well and truly embedded in the populations of much of west Africa. Countries like

Guinea have surprisingly large numbers of devout Muslims, as do east African coastal districts. Swahili is a modified form of Arabic; the word Swahili is derived from the word for 'coast' in Arabic.

There are five main pillars of Islam. These are:

- Witness (*shahadah*): submission to God (Allah) and acceptance that Muhammad is his prophet.
- Prayer (*salat*): five times a day, at sunrise, midday, afternoon, sunset and evening. Before praying, Muslims must wash head, hands and feet. They can pray in any place that is clean and not polluted, and they must face Mecca. On Fridays at midday, it is more beneficial to pray collectively at a mosque. Otherwise they may pray alone, wherever they may be. Men and women pray separately.
- Alms giving (*zakat*): according to the Koran, faith in God should be expressed by doing good to others. A devout Muslim should, once a year, give 2.5% of his money to others in need.
- Fasting (*sawm*): the month of Ramadan is a holy month, when all Muslims must fast from dawn till dusk. If they are ill or travelling, or if they are pregnant women, they are permitted to postpone the fast until they are well. Elderly people and young children are excused from the fast. The purpose of the fast is to teach discipline to the soul. Eid al-Fitr is when the fast ends and all Muslims celebrate with a great feast – sheep and goats are not lucky, as hundreds of them are ritually slaughtered on this special day.
- Pilgrimage (*hajj*): At least once during his lifetime, it is a sacred duty for every Muslim to go to the Ka'aba, the sacred mosque in Mecca. This should be done ideally between the seventh and tenth days of the month of Zuul-Hijja, the twelfth month of the Muslim year. This is usually between March and July, depending on the moon. The hajj includes, among other things, the *tawaf*, seven anticlockwise circuits of the Ka'aba, prostrations at the site of Abraham, and the sacrifice of either a sheep or a camel, depending on one's wealth. This meat is given to the poor. The pilgrimage ends with another feast, the Eid al-Adha, after which the pilgrim must visit the tomb of the prophet in the holy city of Medina.

Some more basic tenets of Islam are: the Koran is the word of God; Muhammad is his prophet; the Sunna is the right way of life, which represents everything that the prophet Muhammad did or said. The books of Hadith record the Sunna, the way to live. Note that the Sunna is the guidance given by Muhammad; it is not the same as the Koran, which is the direct word of God. The Koran and the Sunna together are known as the al-Asl, the foundation of Islam. A madrasa is an Islamic school.

Muhammad's daughter was Fatima. Ali was his cousin. Muhammad favoured Ali as his successor, and married Fatima to Ali. Those who follow Ali are known as Shi'a Muslims.

CHRISTIANITY Christians probably just outnumber Muslims in Africa as a whole. The colonial expansion across Africa that began in the mid 19th century brought with it the missionaries, explorers and traders who sought to exploit Africa for its natural physical wealth as well as its people. Slavery, long endemic in the continent, had already expanded to provide cheap labour for the Arabs and later the American colonists.

Christianity found favour with the peoples of the sub-Sahara, often where slavery had its prime locations. The west African coastal people suffered the greatest impact of slavery. These areas are now some of the main heartlands of the religion. The

It was a fairly typical scene: a long line of vehicles stuck at the side of the road awaiting who know's what. I got out and walked up the line of cars to investigate. Various police or army personnel stood officiously controlling the traffic, ie: blocking the road for no good reason other than that the president's house was nearby and he might come out at any moment … or not.

We waited. In front of us was a flashy car full of men in smart suits. After a while, one of the men got out and crossed the verge into the long grass, where he started to gather it up. What could a man in a snazzy suit be doing with his arms full of grass, I wondered. He opened the boot.

Inside was the answer … a goat sat behind the spare wheel, resting his tired head on the tyre. His spirits lifted as well as his head when the delicious grass was placed in front of him.

religious divide in the countries of the Sahel, particularly Nigeria, Chad and Sudan, has been the source of communal tensions and periodic violence that continues to this day. The Coptic Christian movement found homes both in Egypt and in the highlands of Ethiopia. Further south, Christianity is the dominant faith. As with most things African, the energy and vibrancy of the people manifest in its faiths, with lively and robust forms of preaching and worship. Isolated on the highlands of Ethiopia, Christianity is the main religion and churches are a focal point for the very devout.

TRADITIONAL RELIGION Although less common, the practices of Africa's original animistic beliefs are still to be found almost anywhere except the north. Along the coast of Togo, voodoo has survived and retained its traditions. Its followers worship the cult of ancestors and fetishes. Most African animistic ideas incorporate such ideas. The Dogon people of Mali have retained their ancient beliefs. Their traditions are linked to the stars, sun and moon through their god.

FESTIVALS

West Africa has a number of colourful and vivid festivals. In Mali there is the annual Cattle Crossing at Diafarabe, which takes place in December. This festival is when the Fulani herders reunite with their families. The famous Dogon of the Bandiagara escarpment in Mali have a number of masked dances and ceremonies, usually from March onwards after the harvest. In recent years a desert music festival has been taking place north of Timbuktu in Mali, subject to security factors. In Niger is the famous Cure Salée around In Gall. It takes place in September and basically involves young men dressed and made up to impress and woo partners. The Bianou festival in March is another spectacle in Niger, with Tuaregs riding camels into Agadez.

Across all of north Africa and amongst all the Muslim communities are the normal Islamic holidays and fastings. Tabaski, the most important festival, involves the eating of sheep and goats in large quantities and is a time when people dress in their finest clothes, particularly in places like Mali and Niger (the dates for this festival are not fixed; see below). Eid al-Fitr is the day that celebrates the end of the month-long fast of Ramadan. Eid al-Moulid is celebrated as the Prophet's birthday (dates not fixed; see below).

Timkat is probably Ethiopia's most colourful festival. It is the celebration of Christ's baptism. Across all of Christian Africa, Palm Sunday is a particularly colourful time for processions and gaiety. Versions of the carnival or Mardi Gras are celebrated, mainly in the ex-Portuguese colonies. There is a biannual film festival in Burkina Faso, and the Fêtes des Masques in Ivory Coast in November.

Not so much a festival has been the annual blast of technology, the dusty raid in the Sahara of the Paris–Dakar Motor Rally. Unfortunately, after the murder of four French tourists in Mauritania in late 2007 and the implied terror threats, the 2008 rally, which would have been the 30th Paris–Dakar Rally, was cancelled completely. In future the 'Paris–Dakar' rally will be held in South America (Buenos Aires–Chile–Buenos Aires).

DATES FOR 2009–10

Eid al-Kebir (Tabaski)	28 Nov 2009/17 Nov 2010
Ramadan	22 Aug 2009/11 Aug 2010
Eid al-Fitr	20 Sep 2009/9 Sep 2010
Eid al-Moulid	9 Mar 2009/27 Feb 2010

ARTS AND ENTERTAINMENT

It is a good idea to build up a knowledge and enjoyment of all things African such as its religions, music, literature and history before you leave home. The visual arts are closely tied to the craft traditions of carving and weaving. These will be appreciated best as you travel.

ARTS AND CRAFTS

Sculpture This is one of Africa's greatest art forms. Wherever you travel, you are sure to come across wonderful sculptures of one kind or another, each of them distinctive to their own particular region. Of course, the main tourist areas are swamped with souvenir reproductions of little merit, but take the trouble to visit the many national museums in Africa and you will discover a treasure trove of astounding proportions.

If you would like to get a flavour for African sculpture before you go, there is much on display in European museums. A comprehensive guide to African sculpture that can be seen in England and Scotland has been published as *African Assortment* by Michael Pennie (Artworth, 1991). It discusses and illustrates works on display in 34 separate museums.

Nigeria/Benin The famous Benin bronzes are some of the finest artworks that west Africa has produced. They date from the 10th or 11th century; the region where they were found is in today's southern Nigeria.

Tanzania The famous Makonde carvings are to be found along the coast in Kenya and Tanzania; they are often remarkable works of art.

Zimbabwe Zimbabwe has gained a particular reputation in the world of sculpture, with some experts claiming that the country has no fewer than six of the world's top ten stone sculptors. A visit to the Chapungu Sculpture Park in Harare is an absolute must.

Masks These are another art form, many designs and styles having their origins in the ancient animistic beliefs. Mali, Burkina Faso and Ivory Coast are well known for their masks and Togo for its fetishes.

Weaving and cloth The astonishing array of colourful materials in almost any market is overwhelming. Although increasingly made locally, a lot is still imported, much of it from Holland. Ghana has a thriving textile industry, mostly village-based around Kumasi. Kente cloth is its most famous product. Elsewhere most of the material is produced on a small scale. Indigo cloth is produced mostly in north and west Africa, and is widely used by the Moors and Tuareg people, as well as other nomadic tribes.

Miscellaneous Egypt is famous for its papyrus paper and delicately painted images. Agadez has its silver crosses. And so on. The list is endless …

MUSIC One of the easiest and most enjoyable ways to start learning about Africa is through its music. Africans love to talk about their favourite artist. The growing interest over recent years in modern African music is a refreshing development and means a vast catalogue of material is now available. Most good music shops stock a reasonable selection of African CDs. The variety and volume of African music means that any guide to the highlights will necessarily be a partial and personal selection. Below is a suggested list of musicians to look out for.

Benin One famed artist, Angélique Kidjo (*www.angeliquekidjo.com*), who has successfully hit the European market, is worth a listen. Her albums include *Ayé* and *Fifa*, released in the late 1990s. For further information look at her website.

Democratic Republic of the Congo (DRC) This is the heart of African music; you will hear the sounds of *soukous* wherever you go in Africa, with its infectious jangling guitar lines and sweet vocals.

The king of *soukous*, Franco, sadly died in 1990. For a taste of him at his best, listen to the 1985 release *Mario* and the compilation of his 1950s classics *Originalité*. Franco's band, OK Jazz, was for many years effectively a training school for all of the greats of DRC music. Thankfully, they continued after their leader's death, immediately recording the impeccable *Champions Du Zaïre* (they were rejoined for this album by former member Ndombe Opetum, whose solo albums are a delight). One former member of OK Jazz who warrants special mention is Papa Noel, if only because he rarely receives the praise he so richly deserves. Two albums, *Nono* and *Ya Nono*, are among the most prized records in our collection. Pass them by at your peril.

Franco's great rival over many years was Tabu Ley, who has a similarly large catalogue of releases. Check also on his protégés Sam Mangwana and top female vocalist Mbilia Bel.

The 1980s saw a shift in the music of the Democratic Republic of the Congo (then known as Zaire), with the rise of a new generation of younger stars preferring to leap straight into the faster dance sections of the *soukous* style and dropping the traditional ballad sections. Top of this group of musicians is Kanda Bongo Man, possibly the most commonly played throughout Africa. Many of his albums are available; look out for *Non Stop Non Stop*. Other bands at the forefront of this new wave are Pepe Kalle's Empire Bakuba, Zaiko Langa Langa and Papa Wemba.

Gabon An honourable mention should go to the Gabonese *soukous* band Les Diablotins. Their best-known albums are a whole series recorded in Paris in 1983 – the best is *Les Diablotins à Paris Volume 7*.

Ghana The greatest musical contribution from Ghana is 'highlife' – the danceband music that has developed throughout the 20th century with its synthesis of African and Western styles. The acknowledged king of highlife is E

T Mensah. Look out for the excellent compilation of his 1950s hits, released under the title *All For You*. Also look out for Daddy Lumba, Highlife 2000, entitled *Aben Woaha*.

A superb compilation of 1950s and early 1960s highlife hits is *Akomko*. It features tracks from such greats as the Black Beats, Stargazers Dance Band and Red Spot. For a taste of more recent music from Ghana, the *Guitar And The Gun* compilations are also worth a listen.

Guinea Guinea shares the *griot* traditions of Mali (see below) and many musicians have moved between the two countries. Guinean *griot* Mory Kanté, for example, replaced Salif Keita in the Super Rail Band (and see *Mali* below). He subsequently left and has since released a number of excellent solo albums. Mory Kanté is now the best-known musician from Guinea. His breakthrough album was *Akwaba Beach*, but he also appears with Kanté Manfila and Balla Kalla on the rootsy *Kankan Blues* – a much more raw sound recorded at the Rubis Nightclub in Kankan, Guinea.

For many years, the national band of Guinea was the Beyla group Bembeya Jazz, who used modern electric instruments to interpret traditional themes. Although they have now disbanded, many of their recordings are available. Guinea's most popular performer of semi-acoustic Manding music is now former Bembeya Jazz singer Sekouba Bambina Diabaté. The all-woman equivalent band was Les Amazones. Two of its members, Sona Diabate and M'Mah Sylla, released an excellent album in 1988, called *Sahel*, featuring acoustic instruments.

Kenya and Tanzania East African music is dominated by three main styles – a local version of the *soukous* of the Democratic Republic of the Congo, the unique sound of Swahili Taarab music and the big-band sound of Tanzania. For *soukous* try Orchestra Virunga or Orchestra Maquis Original. For the Swahili sound, try Black Lady and Lucky Star Musical Clubs' *Nyota: Classic Taarab from Tanga*. Of the Tanzanian big band stars, the all-time great was Mbaraka Mwinshehe. By the time of his death in 1979, he had recorded dozens of albums. Look out particularly for the *Ukumbusho* series.

Mali The traditional music of Mali is dominated by the *griots* – singers who have been charged through history with maintaining the oral literature of the area. Their pure voices typically combine with two beautiful instruments – the 21-stringed *kora* and the *balafon* (xylophone). Since gaining independence, Mali has also produced a number of tremendous and quite distinctive large bands. Its contemporary music typically integrates traditional patterns and styles with modern instruments. Several former *griots* have made the transition.

One of the country's most successful musical exports has been Salif Keita, a singer with a voice of pure gold. If you are happy for the music to be filtered through modern Western pop, then solo albums like *Soro* and *Ko-Yan* are worth a listen. But if you want to hear Salif Keita at his best, look for the albums made between 1974 and 1984 with Les Ambassadeurs (the easiest to find is probably the 1984 release *Les Ambassadeurs Internationaux*).

One classic album from Mali that is reasonably easy to find is by Salif Keita's former group, the Super Rail Band. He left in 1973, but it was not until 1985 and the band's first UK release, *New Dimensions in Rail Culture*, that it achieved international success. This album features the voices of Sekou Kanté and Lanfia Diabate. The Super Rail Band is based in Bamako, but the second-largest town in Mali, Segou, is home to the excellent Super Biton Band. Their best album is simply called *Super Biton de Segou*.

Make sure you don't bypass the work of the magnificent Ali Farka Touré. His work is some of the most accessible to Western tastes, even though his music is based on traditional forms of Malian music. He reached an even wider audience with the 1994 release of *Talking Timbuktu*, recorded with American guitarist Ry Cooder.

More recently female artists have become popular, like Nahawa Doumbia's *Didadi* and Oumou Sangare with *Bi Furu*.

Niger Worth looking out for is the Guez Band from Arlit. This is the new style of the Sahel.

Nigeria As well as having the largest population in Africa, Nigeria also has the most developed music industry. Its best-known musical style is *juju* – typically guitar-based bands, weaving melodies around a core of talking drums. Its best-known exponents are Ebenezer Obey, King Sunny Ade and Segun Adewale. A good introduction is Segun Adewale's *Ojo Je*.

No account of Nigerian music would be complete without reference to Fela Kuti, whose politically charged 'Afro-beat' music has ensured continual conflict with the authorities – he was even jailed from 1984 to 1986. A live concert is a real experience, with as many as 40 musicians on stage putting together complex patterns of cross-rhythms.

Senegal Another famed artist to hit the European market is Youssour N'Dour from Senegal. His albums feature a few solo hits and some with his band, the Super Etoile.

South Africa Paul Simon may have popularised the music of southern Africa with his *Graceland* album, but, if you enjoyed the singing featured by Ladysmith Black Mambazo, far better to check out the records from their own large output. The music of South Africa is incredibly varied, with everything from traditional music to township jive via some of the best jazz in the world. There are a number of very good compilation albums of various artists, in particular *Zulu Jive* and *The Indestructible Beat of Soweto*. Also listen out for Johnny Clegg, who has recorded various albums. More traditional and with a Mozambique influence is Steve Newman and Tananas. The ex-exiled Miriam Makeba and Dollar Band (Abdullah Ibrahim) are traditionally South African and are also worth a listen.

Zimbabwe The modern music of Zimbabwe has been popularised in the West by the Bhundu Boys and the Four Brothers. Albums by both are readily available. Also try to listen to Oliver Mtukutzi and Thomas Mapfumo, Zimbabwe's number-one singers and band leaders. A classic collection of Mapfumo's earlier work is *The Chimurenga Singles*. For Mtukutzi try *Shoko*. A great introduction to the dance music of Zimbabwe is provided in the compilation of various artists on *Viva Zimbabwe*.

The live music scene in Harare used to be one of the best in the world. All the top names played most nights of the week in the various hotels, beer gardens and clubs. If the situation improves, make sure you build in enough time for the music when you reach there.

Record stores and websites Any of the above-mentioned music can be found and bought locally in Africa. Always check the tapes if you can; some will be of dubious quality, but that's part of the fun of it. Better-quality recordings can be found outside Africa. If you would like to get a feel for African music beforehand, try the Africa Centre in London or www.africana.com.

LITERATURE The best of modern African literature has brought together the oral traditions of the past with alien Western traditions of the novel and theatre. A good starting point for anyone interested in the whole range of contemporary African writing is the anthology *Voices From Twentieth-Century Africa – Griots And Towncriers* (Faber and Faber, 1988). Edited by African poet Chinweizu it is a collection that will lead you towards the strongest writers of the continent. *The Traveller's Literary Companion to Africa* by Oona Strathern (In Print Publishing, 1998) takes readers on a country-by-country literary tour.

The following is a guide to a handful of the most important writers to look out for.

Chinua Achebe Nigeria's great man of letters. The two novels that are most highly recommended were written some 30 years apart and reflect themes of very different periods in the country's history. The effect on African society of the arrival of Europeans is the subject of his first novel, *Things Fall Apart* (Heinemann, 1958). His subject matter moves on to the problems of corruption and governing modern Africa in his 1987 novel *Anthills of the Savannah*.

Ayi Kwei Armah Ghanaian novelist, much influenced by black American writers. Novels include *The Beautyful Ones Are Not Yet Born*, *Why Are We So Blest?* and *Two Thousand Seasons*.

Sembene Ousmane The Senegalese writer and film director is best known for his masterpiece novel *God's Bits of Wood* (Heinemann), which vividly tells the story of the great strike on the Bamako-to-Dakar railway. It is particularly recommended if you plan to take that route.

Stanlake Samkane Zimbabwe's best-known novelist and historian. His classic novel *On Trial for my Country* puts both Cecil Rhodes and the Matabele King Lobengula on trial to discover the truth behind the 1890 invasion of what became Rhodesia.

Wole Soyinka This prolific Nigerian playwright and poet was awarded the Nobel Prize in Literature in 1986. *The Man Died* (Arrow) is a vivid account of the two-and-a-half years he spent in prison at the time of the Nigerian civil war in the late 1960s. *A Dance in the Forests* is one of his most ambitious and powerful plays, steeped in the beliefs and background of a Yoruba heritage.

Ngugi Wa Thiong'o Kenya's greatest writer has been highly critical of his homeland and has had many conflicts with the authorities as a result, including time in jail and in exile. Earlier books concentrated on the struggle against colonialism but he then moved on to criticise post-colonial Kenya as well, most forcefully in the classic *Devil on the Cross* (Heinemann).

Literary criticism The South African critic, novelist and short-story writer Es'kia Mphahlele is reckoned to be the father of serious study of African literature. His *The African Image* was the first comprehensive work of African literary criticism.

One other particularly interesting work we can recommend is *Land, Freedom and Fiction* by David Maughn-Brown (Zed). This successfully weaves together the history, literature and politics of Kenya by discussing the distortions and reworking of history by writers about the Mau Mau struggle that led to independence.

We arose early to see the famous Abu Simbel monuments. Later, as the ferry crossed into Sudanese waters, a speedboat shot up to us. Was this the police or the customs? We could only stare in disbelief as the cables tying the barge to the ferry were disconcertingly unleashed, and our Land Rover sailed off into the distance. We'd paid too much and now they were stealing the vehicle!

We disembarked at Wadi Halfa and then the barge appeared a few moments later with the Land Rover still intact. We followed everyone to the immigration area; at least the building was new and the hot sugary black tea in surprisingly clean glasses was more than welcome.

A largish man who could be anyone's jolly old grandfather came over. 'Where is your car? Please get it now.' Kamal Hassan Osman was the customs man, and he wasted no time. We quickly rushed back to the ferry barge and somehow drove down two wobbly planks to get the Land Rover on to the narrow jetty. The brakes still worked. The paperwork was quickly sorted out and then we waited. Some other work had to be done. We waited and waited. We were in Sudan but we couldn't go anywhere. It was getting dark, too. We sat and brewed up more and more tea.

And then without explanation we were off. Oh yes, could we give our friendly customs man a lift to town? Did we have a choice? Off we went; we headed not into town but over some low dunes to the next bay around the lake. Here was a small settlement set in a sandy valley with some irrigation near the lake. We stopped outside a walled mud house. It wasn't much to look at from the outside, but inside it was a treasure. The elegant wooden dresser displayed exquisite bone china tea sets, cut glass and family photos. This was the house of Kamal Hassan Osman's sister. We took tea and biscuits, hardly daring to breathe in case we dropped a china cup. He spoke English well and we had a decent conversation. They showed us some photos of the old town, before the Egyptians decided to build the dam and flood the Nile valley upstream forever. Wadi Halfa has never recovered from its flooding, and there is obvious distress about the loss of their old homes and the beautiful oasis now below the waters.

After tea, we took Kamal to his own house, doing the rounds of shops, to buy fresh bread and cheese, and visit more friends en route. We were starving by now, but he invited us for dinner. His house was inside a large walled enclosure, with many rooms carpeted by sand. A big fridge took pride of place, with basic furniture and some decorations, posters and old photographs. Various nieces and nephews seemed to call by all evening and eventually we had a superb meal of beans, rice, cheese, omelette, spaghetti and goat, washed down with copious amounts of tea. His nephew invited us to a wedding party, but unfortunately it was rather late and, after our sleepless night on the ferry, we were somewhat low on energy.

Non-fiction

Nelson Mandela *The Long Road to Freedom* is the autobiography of the great man himself and should be part of any reading on South Africa.

Not by Africans, but about Africa, is a book by Peter and Beverly Pickford. Their *Forever Africa* is a visual feast of sepia and colour photographs, depicting the people, landscapes and wildlife seen on their journey from Cape Town to Tangier.

Further information There are several websites with more information. Try www.heinemann.co.uk or www.africanwriters.com.

No matter where you travel in Africa, you are bound to see poverty, urban squalor and occasionally genuine hunger. Life for the poor in both cities and rural areas may prove harsher than you'd imagined. Your reaction may well be a mixture of sadness, perhaps shock and often a feeling of guilt. The imbalance seems unjust, and the scale of the problem daunting. Why do some have so much when others do not? The reasons are complex, rooted partly in culture, partly in ignorance and poor education, partly no doubt in foreign exploitation – and these are only the more obvious causes.

African tradition has cast women in the role of workers, fetching water, looking after the children, cooking and washing. Men were traditionally the hunters. In rural Africa it is very common to see men sitting under trees, apparently deep in thought or conversation but otherwise inactive. As the continent becomes more urbanised, so they have needed to become more industrious and many have enormous reservoirs of energy and initiative. Still tradition dies hard, and 'development' often requires painful compromises. As choices increase, so do pressures. Adapting to the pace and the advanced technologies of the 21st century isn't necessarily easy.

So, where can we fit in? Isn't it enough that we've shopped in local markets, paid local mechanics, stopped at some local campsites and used local ferries? Aren't the big charities and governments dealing with 'development' as such? Have we as individuals got anything to offer (apart, obviously, from our hard-earned cash, which we don't want to throw away into such a bottomless gulf of need) that can really make a difference to this vast, teeming, vibrant, contradictory, maddening and stunningly beautiful continent? Maybe we all have different answers. Below are just a few suggestions in case you need a starting point.

LOCAL CHOICES Of course shopping locally and using the services of local people are ways to contribute. Buy souvenirs from the craftspeople who seem to have made them rather than via middlemen who will siphon off profits, and patronise small street vendors rather than big supermarkets. Don't bargain to a price below what is reasonable; the difference may be the price of a drink to you but the price of a whole family meal to the vendor. Stay in small local hotels rather than foreign chains. Use the services of a local guide or a child who wants to help, and pay a fair rate. Bring with you only those supplies that you know you won't be able to find in Africa, and buy the rest in local stores and markets.

EDUCATION Education is the future of Africa. In many places you will see children dressed in smart, brightly coloured uniforms, bouncing along to school with great exuberance and energy. In others they may be ragged, crammed together on rickety wooden benches or grouped in the shade of trees, eyes fixed earnestly on the teacher and learning by rote because they have no books. Whatever the conditions, there is an insatiable wish to learn. If you have spent time in a village and made some contact with its inhabitants, why not consider donating some pens, crayons and notebooks to the local school? (See also *Gifts* in *Chapter 3*, page 73.) School equipment is easy to buy in local markets. Ask to be introduced to the schoolteacher, so that he/she can receive and officially distribute the gift. Offer to spend some time in the school, being questioned by the children about your home country. If an adult language or literacy course is running locally, offer to drop in on that, too. After all, knowledge is about stretching horizons and learning new things, which is just what you're doing by travelling, so why not make it a two-way process? Anyway, it's fun!

In 2002, having spent some time in Guinea's bustling capital city Conakry, we were keen to explore the offshore islands. We took the ferry – alone – past rusting wrecks in the harbour, and across a clear blue sea, with tropical islands dotted in the distance. Gradually our destination came closer, and soon we stepped off onto a remote beach. 'Just follow that path through the forest, and you'll reach the other side of the island in three or four minutes,' our boatman said. As we arrived, a gorgeous golden retriever appeared, with two young foreign travellers. 'He'll follow you everywhere,' they said. 'We're going back to the mainland on the boat you just came on.' So we were alone again, but for the dog.

Our room was a beautiful straw chalet overlooking a deserted beach. Later we walked along the smooth sand and lay down in the sun. The dog ran up to greet us, our own personal bodyguard. 'What's his name?' I asked the man at the restaurant, where we stopped for a drink.

'Espérance,' he replied. That means hope. In such a poor country it seemed a fitting name.

'Where are you from?' we asked. 'You speak very good English.'

'I'm a refugee from Sierra Leone,' he replied. 'I speak English, so I persuaded Madame to give me a job here for board and lodging only. She said she can't pay me anything because business is bad, but I'm happy because I have food and a roof over my head, and, above all, I am safe here. But I hope I will be able to go home soon.'

Having visited Sierra Leone ourselves in 2008, we are also full of hope that he has gone home to a new Sierra Leone full of the promise of better things to come.

As we left for the ferry the next day, Espérance sprang along the path to see us off. As they say, 'Hope springs eternal' in Africa.

If you have contact with schools back in your home country, consider whether it might be possible to set up a link. If the schoolteacher wants to stay in touch and you feel able to take on a correspondence, agree to this, but do warn him/her that mail can be very slow and envelopes sometimes get lost. Maybe someone nearby has an email address. When you get home, if you feel able to undertake the sponsorship of an individual child or older student in Africa, the big international organisations offering this are easy to find via the internet. And education is a gift for life.

Note: Travellers often collect up pens/biros at home beforehand and bring them over, but, in this case, *please* check that they work and have plenty of ink before donating them. To an impoverished rural child, a new pen is a huge and thrilling gift. He/she is so proud and happy and then so bitterly disappointed when it stops working after only a few hours. It would have been better never to have had it. (Also see *Begging*, page 198.)

IN THE VILLAGE As you pass through – or stay in – small towns and villages, you'll come across missionaries, expatriates, aid workers and various development projects. If the work that they're doing interests you, make a note of their contact details. Once back home, you may be able to organise fundraising or other support. This is development 'on a human scale' – a well, a school, an orphanage, a village hall, a water pump, a plot of farmland – so the local organisers will appreciate your individual interest as much as you enjoy being personally involved.

While you're driving, you may also spot wooden signs beside the road advertising small development projects – housing schemes, irrigation, cooperatives, agriculture – and giving a contact address or phone number. Jot them down: you never know what may be useful later.

If you felt drawn to a village or a community but didn't manage to get details of any current activity there, it's worth trying an internet search for its name when you get home – try various spellings, just in case – as this sometimes produces unexpected contacts.

VOLUNTEERING If you want to return to work as a volunteer in Africa and have some relevant skills ('relevant' covers a wide range), start by checking out Voluntary Service Overseas (*www.vso.org.uk*) or Earthwatch (*www.earthwatch.org*). VSO also welcomes donations, from small amounts up to the cost of maintaining a volunteer in a developing country. An internet search for organisations using volunteers will provide many more possibilities, including ones specialising in shorter projects, which may involve anything from teaching English to manual labour. If teaching English appeals, why not take a short course in TEFL (Teaching English as a Foreign Language; *www.tefl.com*)? An internet search will reveal various colleges; one where you can learn at a distance by post or email is Global English (*www.global-english.com*). UK-based, it has students from as far apart as Thailand and the USA.

A way to volunteer without leaving home is via the Online Volunteering Service (*www.onlinevolunteering.org*); it's managed by the United Nations Volunteers Programme (UNV), which is the volunteer arm of the United Nations. Volunteers need reliable access to a computer and the internet, and some relevant skill or experience. Via the OVS they undertake a variety of computer-based assignments for organisations in developing countries: for example translation, research, web design, data analysis, database construction, proposal writing, editing articles, online mentoring, publication, design, etc. Also check out Netaid (*www.netaid.org*) and see Peter Lynch's *Wildlife & Conservation Volunteering: The Complete Guide* (Bradt Travel Guides, 2009).

BIG INTERNATIONAL CHARITIES The big international charities are colossal, and it's sometimes hard to remember that their work does reach down to benefit the poorest at grass-roots level. It's particularly hard to believe, although it's true, that they need our small donations. Most of them don't deserve their poor reputation for spending too much on administration, and they respond magnificently to

---

STUFF YOUR RUCKSACK – AND MAKE A DIFFERENCE

www.stuffyourrucksack.com is a website set up by TV's Kate Humble which enables travellers to give direct help to small charities, schools or other organisations in the country they are visiting. Maybe a local school needs books, a map or pencils, or an orphanage needs children's clothes or toys – all things that can easily be 'stuffed in a rucksack' before departure. The charities get exactly what they need and travellers have the chance to meet local people and see how and where their gifts will be used.

The website describes organisations that need your help and lists the items they most need. Check what's needed in the countries you are visiting, contact the organisation to say you're coming and bring not only the much-needed goods but an extra dimension to your travels and the knowledge that in a small way you have made a difference.

www.stuffyourrucksack.com
Responsible tourism in action

disasters such as the 2004 tsunami in Asia and the 2008 earthquake in China. If you want to make a general donation 'for work in Africa', you could do far worse. They advertise extensively, so check their ads and their websites to see which comes closest to your interests. If it's wildlife that appeals to you, then you'll already know about the Worldwide Fund for Nature (WWF) (*www.panda.org*) which works just about everywhere and has had some remarkable conservation successes.

SMALLER CHARITIES Nowadays the smaller international charities are amazing in their range and variety; whatever you want to support, you'll find it somewhere. The handful of lesser-known ones listed below are small enough to have a personal approach but large enough to make a useful impact. This is only a tiny sample of the many available, so you'll certainly come across others in the same or different fields.

Firelight Foundation www.firelightfoundation.org. This US-based organisation works through local people & groups, & currently supports projects in Cameroon, Ethiopia, Kenya, Lesotho, Malawi, Rwanda, South Africa, Tanzania, Uganda, Zambia & Zimbabwe. Its remit, which is interpreted very broadly, is 'to support & advocate for the needs & rights of children who are orphaned or affected by HIV/AIDS in sub-Saharan Africa ... & to increase the resources available to grassroots organisations that are strengthening the capacity of families & communities to care for children made vulnerable by HIV/AIDS'.

Good Gifts Catalogue www.goodgifts.org. This novel idea enables you to support development schemes while remembering friends & family at anniversaries, Christmas, etc. For example you can buy a 'Goat for Peace' for your aunt's birthday; it'll be delivered to one of the goat schemes in Africa, & you get a card for your aunt explaining the gift. As the brochure says: 'This is no ordinary goat: this is a revolving goat. Where communities are slowly rebuilding themselves, a revolving goat (with the aid of a revolving ram) starts families. Kids go to restock families without goats & so on. A goat is a milk & fertiliser factory & goes a long way to improving the local diet; a 4-legged step towards self-sufficiency.' The goat is only one of a huge range of gifts — check the online catalogue at the website above.

Intermediate Technology Development Group www.itdg.org. Founded in 1966 by the radical economist Dr E F Schumacher, the ITDG works to show that the right technologies can help people to find lasting, appropriate solutions to poverty, & that a small-scale approach can bring results that benefit whole communities long into the future. ITDG enables poor communities to discover how new technologies, adapted in the right way, can improve their lives. Current activities are in east Africa, southern Africa & Sudan, with other countries due to be added soon.

Send a Cow (*www.sendacow.org.uk*) Based in the UK, this small charity (chosen as one of its Christmas charities by *The Independent* newspaper in 2004) provides not only cows but also goats & chickens on a self-help basis to impoverished families & individuals (widows, orphans, etc) so that they have a means of livelihood & hope for the future. It gives training in livestock rearing & organic farming, & access to low-cost veterinary & advice services. Projects are in Ethiopia, Kenya, Lesotho, Rwanda, Tanzania, Uganda & Zambia.

War Child www.warchild.org. War Child works with children suffering the effects of conflict. Current African projects are in Angola, Burundi, DRC, Ethiopia, Eritrea, Rwanda, Sierra Leone & Sudan.

Water Aid www.wateraid.org.uk. Dedicated exclusively to the provision of safe domestic water, sanitation & hygiene education to the world's poorest people. In Africa, it works in Burkina Faso, Ethiopia, Ghana, Malawi, Mali, Mozambique, Nigeria, Tanzania, Uganda & Zambia.

BEGGING There's no way you can escape beggars in Africa, and how you handle the problem is a very personal matter. Remember that the 'visible' misery of those thrusting their hands out to you as you pass is not necessarily any worse than the 'invisible' misery of those suffering silently at home; a donation to a relevant charity (for the homeless, or the orphaned, or the disabled, or the abandoned…) is likely to mean that your money is used more effectively. But sometimes it's hard to walk on by.

If you decide to give cash on the spot, then do look the person in the eyes, smile and say an appropriate 'Good morning'; being given a coin is probably far less of a

For those of you heading into northern Togo or Benin, be sure to detour to the Tamberma settlements (in Togo) or the Somba (in Benin) for an amazing experience.

The houses are not set in villages, but are found isolated across the savanna. The two- or occasionally three-storied, mud-walled circular buildings are like mini-fortresses. Each is a family unit and each is 'guarded' by fetishes. Superstition is still rampant here, so it's definitely necessary to go with a local guide or you risk offending. A small fee is requested for the guide, who in turn interacts with the villagers and donates appropriately. Interesting fetish-style figurines are for sale here as well as other small local crafts, but it is all very low-key with few visitors.

The lower part of the structure acts as a defensive entrance, with hidden chambers for poisoned arrow-armed residents. Fetishes are prominent again. Climbing up round rough steps to the next intermediate level you reach the kitchen or cooking area. Yet further on, you normally come round on to the roof terrace. Various different small, rounded chambers here provide living areas and sleeping places. Most are extremely low, better suited to Pygmies. In particular, there is a low-roofed room where a woman must live when giving birth. She is not allowed to go downstairs until sometime afterwards; she must wash on the roof and the water runs off through a channel. The men's room up here is significantly higher.

It is extraordinary to see people living like their ancestors, with few items of the modern era, but no-one could say that these people were down at heel or in real poverty. Their vibrancy was a testimony to the human spirit of self-sufficiency and proud independence.

---

novelty to him or her than being treated like a human being. (And prepare for the onslaught as others nearby spot that you're a soft touch and suddenly materialise.)

Just occasionally you can turn begging into an encounter that's pleasurable for you both. Many children do it from habit and would much rather be playing, so if you turn it into a game, they'll remember the fun of it far longer than the handing over of a coin. Also try learning 'What is your name?' in a few appropriate languages – perhaps French, Arabic and Swahili. The effect is astonishing, on someone, whether child or adult, who's used to being ignored or pushed aside. Even if you learn only their name, tell them yours and then say goodbye; you've lifted them several rungs up the scale of humanity and that's what they'll remember. Or if you're refusing to give, then use their name politely as you say 'No'. In fact this is a great way to connect with children at any time; by using their name, you give them dignity and they respond.

Again, do bear in mind the damage you can do by giving little gifts (sweets, pens, biscuits or whatever) to a child or youngster who comes up and begs, however cutely. If the begging bears fruit (and if the gift isn't immediately grabbed by a bigger child), he/she will start to pester all visitors, some of whom may react aggressively or unpleasantly. However it's fine as a 'payment' for genuine helpfulness.

WHEN YOU LEAVE Here's a final chance to be useful to Africa. Don't take home that T-shirt you probably won't wear again, that almost-full bottle of baby lotion, that soap, that pen, that pad of paper, that length of rope, that torch, those batteries, those duplicate tools… collect them up and give them to a local charity. Organisations looking after the homeless or running children's homes can turn pretty much anything to a good use. As an added bonus, you'll have more space in your vehicle for all those bulky souvenirs that you couldn't resist.

Background **GIVING SOMETHING BACK TO AFRICA**

8

TOURISM IN GENERAL It goes without saying that responsible tourism is vital to the future of interethnic relations and cultural interaction. The actions of the visitor today are the seeds of the reaction to the visitor tomorrow. Tourism can offer Africa another source of employment, a tool for development and a direction for understanding. Ecotourism is a new word and concept in Africa, but one that will develop with greater education. It is incumbent on us to keep Africa as we found it in most aspects, and maybe somehow in other aspects to leave it a better place.

However we travel in Africa, we are always going to be seen as the rich people, but it is still a source of surprise how little this can matter sometimes. Interaction between peoples is the only way of developing greater understanding, and at least in that, if in nothing else, we may be seen to be doing some good.

9

A–Z Country Guide

Your road is everything that a road ought to be ... and yet you will not stay in it half a
mile, for the reason that little, seductive, mysterious roads are always branching out
from it on either hand, and as these curve sharply also and hide what is beyond,
[you] cannot resist the temptation to desert your own chosen road and explore them.
Mark Twain (1835–1910)

This section, of necessity, gives just a brief introduction to each country. It includes
a guide to visa requirements, some of the red tape you may encounter, an
indication of accommodation and fuel costs and a general overview of some of each
country's highlights. Please note that fuel prices are given as a relative indication
only, since the cost of a barrel of oil has fluctuated dramatically of late and oil prices
are quoted in US dollars with very variable exchange rates. We also advise you to
check the latest visa requirements, as these change frequently. For more detail you
should buy the relevant Bradt travel guide for the specific countries you intend to
visit – see pages 332–3 and www.bradtguides.com.

RED TAPE

You might think that driving across Africa would be a huge bureaucratic
nightmare, with money disappearing from your back pocket all along the way. But
in fact, it's not as bad as it might at first seem. In Nigeria, for example, there is an
anti-corruption drive in the police force and immigration department. We were
stopped at most roadside check-posts just so they could ask after our health and
wish us a safe journey.

Gabon was the only country where we were really hassled by any of the
authorities, and Equatorial Guinea, when we crossed the border for half an hour
without a visa. In Cameroon we were 'fined' for travelling on the unmarked
private road of the president (but only one pound sterling), and in one part of
Nigeria some local bureaucrats tried to force us to pay a local road tax, which
was not necessary. To stop us moving on, they threw a long plank studded with
nails between our wheels. Only by standing in the middle of the road and
stopping the traffic did we manage to get out of this mess, but that was an
isolated incident, and we found the Nigerians perfectly civil and helpful on
nearly every other occasion.

Of course we haven't visited every country in Africa on our last four trips, and
no doubt things have changed and will continue to change. So all you can do is be
flexible, keep up to date with websites – there are internet cafés everywhere – and
keep smiling. Most people are kind-hearted and want to help you. There are
bureaucrats everywhere and some of the worst are back home in our own
countries. Remember that.

See page 107 for more information on red tape.

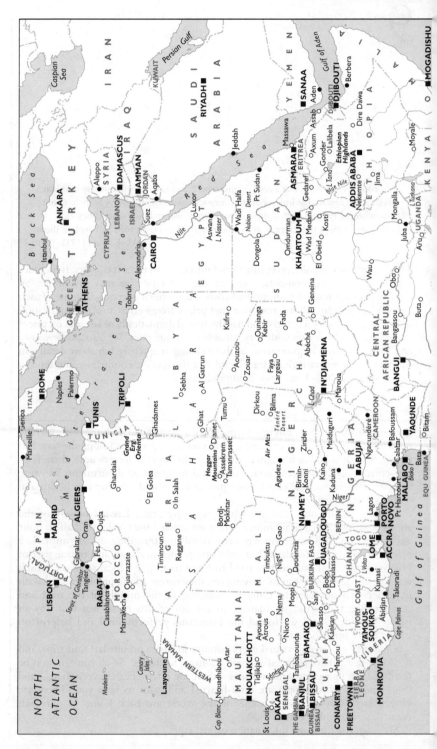

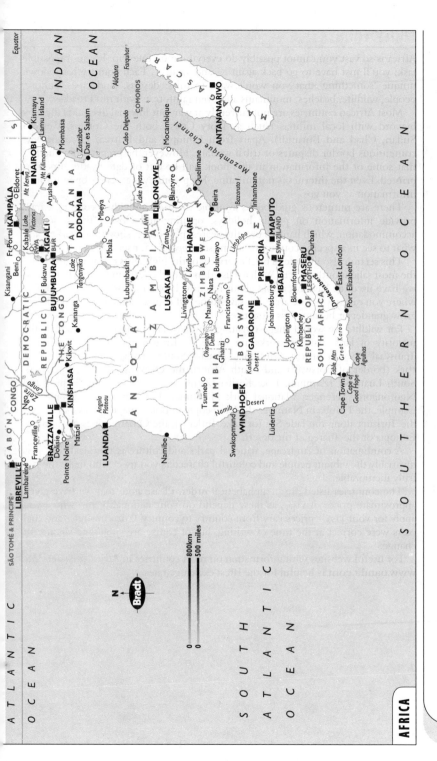

AFRICA

Africa is so vast you cannot possibly do everything on one trip. It's an impossible task; you'll just have to go back again ... and again ... Each country has its own unique 'something' that you won't want to miss: deserts, landscapes, culture, people, wildlife, beaches, mountains and even rainforests with mud roads.

Most African countries are not currently at war, but internal dissent is the new byword with local militias (such as Ivory Coast, both the Congos, Western Sudan, Chad and Burundi). Apart from Ethiopia and Eritrea, there are few contentious border disputes or tribal warfare. However, be prepared for the fact that some of the information in this book will be out of date by the time it is printed. Even the internet is not immune. Keep your eyes and ears open for new information as you go.

There are numerous guidebooks available for each individual country, which provide information on public holidays, opening and closing times, specific accommodation, which bank to use, the nearest post office, shopping, markets and what to see in a specific country or town (see *Appendix 5*, page 332).

This section also includes a brief overview of the highlights of each country and the most salient outline facts. We have listed most of the camping places/hotels that we have used, or have been told about recently. It often helps to have an idea of where you can stay before arrival; it saves time. Of course, some places shut down, grow grander or become less attractive.

For wildlife we would suggest visiting southern and eastern Africa, where the majority of large national parks are located – Kruger National Park (Eastern Transvaal – South Africa), Umfolozi (Natal – South Africa), Kalahari Gemsbok Park (border of Botswana and South Africa), the Okavango Delta (Botswana), South Luangwa (Zambia), Lake Kariba (Zimbabwe), Masai Mara (Kenya) and Ngorongoro, Serengeti National Park (Tanzania). For culture and people, for example, the Himba in Namibia, the San people in Botswana, the Masai in Kenya, the Turkana along the Jade Sea (or Lake Turkana), the Omatic tribes of southern Ethiopia or the Tuareg of the desert.

A combination of landscape, national parks and culture is the ideal. But it is invariably the vibrant people and colourful characters you meet who make the trip truly memorable.

The countries listed are in alphabetical order. Please note that we have given approximate prices of visas, as these depend on your nationality and where you apply for your visa – prices vary from country to country. Currency rates and fuel costs were correct at the time of writing, but of course are subject to significant change.

For useful websites with information on most countries in Africa, see page 336. **www.oanda.com** is helpful for the latest exchange rates.

☞ *WARNING!* Having been off-limits for several years, overland travel in Algeria was again possible in the early 2000s, but is currently not very safe because of the kidnapping of 32 foreign tourists in early 2003. Groups linked to al-Qaeda are believed to be operating in the area. However, the scenery and people are outstanding and it is undoubtedly worth a visit if the situation improves. Seek sound travel advice if you do intend to visit.

CAPITAL Algiers

LANGUAGE AND TELEPHONE Arabic is the official language. International telephone code +213.

CURRENCY AND RATE Algerian dinar (DZD); US$1 = DZD65.49

RED TAPE The *carnet* is not accepted and a *laissez passer* will be issued at the border. A currency declaration form might still have to be completed on entry and surrendered on departure. You may or may not have to prove what you have spent when you leave. Be prepared for this.

Visas Visas are required for all except nationals of other Arabic countries. Estimated visa costs can vary between US$55 (UK citizens) and US$100, depending on the country of application. You will also need three photographs, an invitation from the agent who is hosting you in Algeria, and an introduction from your embassy if you are not getting the visa in your home country. Double-entry visas are available. Visas are not issued at the border.

African embassies

🇪 **Benin** 16 Lotissement du Stade, Birkhadem, Les Sources Birmandreis, Algiers; ☎ 21 56 5271
🇪 **Burkina Faso** 20 Rue des Cèdres, El Mouradia, Algiers; ☎ 21 59 4436
🇪 **Cameroon** PO Box 343, Algiers; ☎ 21 78 2864
🇪 **Ghana** 62 Rue Parmentier-Hydra, Algiers; ☎ 21 60 6444
🇪 **Libya** 15 Chemin Cheikh Bachir; ☎ 21 92 1502
🇪 **Mali** BP 05, Bir Mourad Rais, Algiers; ☎ 21 54 7214

🇪 **Morocco** 8 Rue des Cèdres, El Mouradia, Algiers; ☎ 21 69 1408
🇪 **Niger** 54 Rue de Vercors; ☎ 21 78 8921
🇪 **Nigeria** 77 Cites des PTT, Djenane El Malik, Hydra, Algiers; ☎ 21 60 6050
🇪 **Sudan** 8 Shara Baski Brond, El Yanabia, Beir Murad Reis, Algiers; ☎ 21 56 6623
🇪 **Tunisia** 11 Rue du Bois de Boulogne, El Mouradia, Algiers; ☎ 21 69 138

DRIVING AND ROADS Drive on the right. Good surfaced roads throughout the north and most of the way down the central route to Tamanrasset and also the eastern route to Djanet. Construction of tarmac northwards from In Guezzam continues. Many desert pistes of varying quality.

Fuel costs Diesel: US$0.30; petrol: US$0.40 per litre.

CLIMATE The best time to visit the desert is December to March. October, November, April and May are hotter but just about bearable. Desert temperatures are hottest in July and August.

HIGHLIGHTS The main highlight is without doubt the Sahara; also Tamanrasset, the volcanic Hoggar Mountains, the hermitage of Père Foucauld, Djanet and the

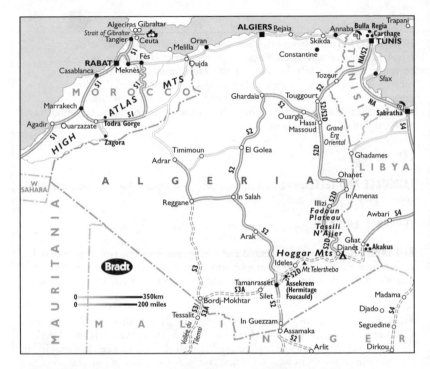

Tassili N'Ajjer Plateau with its prehistoric art and fantastically shaped rock towers, and the remote Tassili du Hoggar in the far south. The kasbah in Algiers is also a highlight, but it has been too dangerous to visit recently. Along the eastern coast it is said to be worth visiting Constantine, Djemila and the Kabylia Mountains. On the way south it is worth stopping in Timimoun and Ghardaia. The black Tademait Plateau south of El Golea, and the Arak Gorge, are stunningly stark, and there are some beautiful sand dunes in various places along the route.

🏠 **WHERE TO STAY** Bush sleeping is a currently a dodgy option, though it is wonderful to sleep out in the open desert if you can find the right spot. If you do so, make absolutely sure you are well out of sight of the road or piste. Basic accommodation costs between US$5 and US$25, depending on what you are after. With or without a lack of tourism in the country, the Algerians are extremely friendly and will go out of their way to help you, sometimes even offering accommodation. You can also ask to camp in the back yard of some hotels.

Ouargla The Hotel Tassili has allowed parking/camping behind the hotel. It is north of the main road.

Ghardaia Try either the central Hotel El Djenoub with secure parking nearby or the Hotel Rym, which has parking below. Campsite closed at the time of writing.

El Golea There was a nice but sandy campsite in the palmeries on the way south out of town; look for the camping sign on the gates. The central Hotel Boustane also has parking.

In Salah The Hotel Tidikelt allows camping outside in the garden area.

Tamanrasset The Hotel Tinhinane in the old main street has economical rooms with safe parking. There were two campsites east of town. Try the Hotel Tahat for a splurge with safe parking.

Djanet In the centre of the town is the famous and still pleasant Camping/Hotel Zeriba.

OTHER Currency declaration forms may need to be filled out on arrival and will be asked for on departure, though they may not be checked. If you are unlucky enough to be checked, it may be thorough. All other money found could be confiscated. Ensure that you get valid receipts when changing money at a bank, although the black market is thriving, particularly in euros. Remember that your declaration form needs to tally with bank receipts. But it may be that you cannot find a bank when you need to, and have to change money on the black market. Put some aside (hidden) for this eventuality. Also be aware that it is almost impossible to change travellers' cheques anywhere in the country. Take enough cash with you. Insurance must be purchased at the border or, if coming north from Niger, at Tamanrasset.

FURTHER INFORMATION
Sahara Overland, Chris Scott (see *Appendix 5*, page 333)
Algeria: The Bradt Travel Guide, Jonathan Oakes

ANGOLA

☞ *WARNING!* Although the civil war in Angola finished a while ago, there are still vast numbers of unexploded mines littering the countryside. **Do not** leave any road to camp; **stay on the road** overnight if necessary.

CAPITAL Luanda

LANGUAGE AND TELEPHONE Portuguese is the official language. International telephone code +244.

CURRENCY AND RATE Angolan new kwanza (AON); US$1 = AON75.158

RED TAPE There are reported to be lots of checkpoints along the roads. You may have to register with the police in any main settlement. The few travellers who have managed to get into the country from the DRC have said that the Angolan border officials there have often been most helpful.

Visas Visas are required for all. Obtaining an Angolan visa is currently extremely difficult. Applications can be attempted directly to: Ministerio de Hostelaria e Turismo Angola office, Largo 4 de Fevereiro Palcio de Vidro, 2 Andar Luanda; ☏ 244 2 338 625; f 244 2 338 770 or 244 2 331 322. Good luck!

Visas cost US$80 and are valid for 15 or 30 days. Visas are not issued at the border. *En route* try in Lomé, Abuja, Yaoundé, Libreville, Brazzaville, Kinshasa or the consulate at Matadi in the DRC. The consulate here has sometimes given five-day transit visas.

Note: If heading to Angola from Pointe Noire, try to get a multiple-entry visa to go through Angola and its enclave of Cabinda. Note that the consulate at Pointe

Noire had reportedly stopped issuing visas for overland travel into Angola at the time of publication, though they were still issuing visas for people to fly into the country. A transit visa for Cabinda for five days previously took three days here and cost 20,000CFA. Necessary paperwork included two photocopies of the passport outside cover, the inside pages of the cover and the information page, as well as vaccination certificate.

African embassies

Congo Brazzaville Rua Fernando Pessoa, Vila Alice, Luanda; ☎ 231 0293

DRC Rua Fernando Pessoa, Vila Alice, Luanda; ☎ 231 0293

Ghana Rua Vereador Castelo, Branco 5.10, Caixa Luanda; ☎ 233 8239

Gabon Rue Eng Armindo Adrade 149, Luanda; ☎ 244 9289

Ivory Coast 41–43 Rua Karl Marx, CP 432 Luanda; ☎ 239 0150/233 3992

Mozambique 55 Salvador Allende, Luanda; ☎ 334 871/331 158; f 322 250

Namibia Rua dos Coqueiro 37, Luanda; ☎ 239 5483; f 233 9234

Nigeria Rua Houari Boumedienne, 120 Miramar, Luanda; ☎ 234 0098; f 234 0089

South Africa Rua Kwamime Nkrumah 31, Luanda; ☎ 39 8726

Zambia Rua Rei Katyavala 1618, Luanda; ☎ 244 7496; f 233 1241

Zimbabwe Edevicio Secil, 42 Av 4 de Fevereiro, Luanda; ☎ 233 2337/8/9; f 233 2339

DRIVING AND ROADS Main roads were once good, but many along the coast are in a dreadful state of repair. Current information would imply that many roads had deteriorated badly, but are now being repaired and rebuilt by Chinese teams. Some routes that used to take days can now reportedly be done in a few hours. Look at the internet for the latest travellers' reports.

Fuel costs Diesel: US$0.40; petrol: US$0.55 per litre.

CLIMATE Angola has a varied climate with rains inland from October to May. The dry season is from June to August. The south coast is drier.

HIGHLIGHTS South of N'zeto are some turbulent rivers, savanna, jungle and some beautiful rock formations, all close to the sea. The Ponta des Palmerinas south of the capital offers a viewpoint where some unusal rock formations are seen. In the southwest there is an extensive mountainous region inland from Namibe. The area close to Lubango is said to have some volcanic features, including a deep fissure in the plateau. Lubango is likely to become *the* tourist destination of southern Angola, as more people discover its long-unexplored delights. Known highlights of the far south are the Quedas do Ruacana waterfalls, when flowing, on the border with Namibia.

WHERE TO STAY Finding places to stay in Angola is problematic, but things should improve if more people come this way. As a last resort, after churches, missions, police stations, half-open national parks and the bush, you can ask at the limited hotels with secure parking. Hotel prices in Angola are not inexpensive, ranging from US$80–100 for tiny rooms to over US$360 for international standard hotels in Luanda.

Luanda Security issues here are paramount but you might be able to park near the Hotel Panorama around the bay or at the Clube Nautico (yacht club) in Luanda on the Ilha (basic conditions).

WARNING! Crime levels in Luanda are high, so beware.

Parque Nacional da Quicama South of the capital, this may have camping options.

Cabinda Some overlanders have stayed at the Catholic mission by the church near the immigration, where registration might have to be done again.

M'banza Congo Again try at the church where a French priest has been helpful to travellers.

N'zeto Ask at the police station, or camp along the coast 15km south of N'zeto.

Caxito Stay near the police station.

Quedas De Agua Da Binga A bit off the 'main highway' with bush camping almost at the falls, with a toilet.

Benguela It's back to the police station probably, or the bush quarries.

Lubango There might still be a campsite in Lubango near the botanical gardens. There is also a quarry about 30km south of Lubango on the route to Namibia that may be suitable for bush camping.

Namibe Town There is a campsite just before the Diversi Lodge hotel on the promenade.

Namibe province Look for the Flamingo Lodge (*www.aasafaris.com*). Camping is US$20 per person per night.

Ruacana You can camp at Osheja Guest House or camp on the Namibian side.

FURTHER INFORMATION
Angola: The Bradt Travel Guide, Mike Stead and Sean Rorison (due November 2009)
www.angola.org

BENIN

CAPITAL Porto Novo

LANGUAGE AND TELEPHONE French is the official language. International telephone code +229.

CURRENCY AND RATE West African franc (CFA); US$1 = CFA415

RED TAPE Of little significance in Benin, except visas.

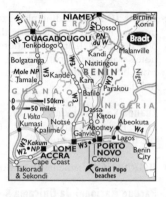

Visas Visas are required for all except nationals of the Economic Community of West African States (ECOWAS). Entry visas cost US$85 for a month, in the UK. They are normally available at the borders of Benin for 48 hours' transit only, costing US$50 (20,000CFA). You will need two passport photos. Yellow fever vaccination certificates are also officially required, but are not often checked.

Non-African embassy
🄴 France Av du Pape Jean-Paul II/Rue 232, Cotonou; ✎ 30 0225. British citizens with a problem should come here.

African embassies
🄴 Ghana Av du Pape John Paul II, Haie Vive, Cotonou; ✎ 30 0746 ; ⏰ mornings. Visa takes a day; a one-month tourist visa needs four photos.
🄴 Niger Rue 651A, Cotonou; ✎ 31 5665. A one-month tourist visa needs two photos & takes one day.

🄴 Nigeria Bd de France, Cotonou; ✎ 30 1142. Tourist visas issued only to residents of Benin. Transit visas available & can be extended in Lagos.

DRIVING AND ROADS Drive on the right. Most roads in Benin are paved and even those that aren't are in good condition, with only a few pot-holes.

Fuel costs Diesel: US$1.30; petrol: US$1.20 per litre.

CLIMATE Humid everywhere, with steady temperatures of 27°C. The dry seasons are from December to April. Northern Benin, being part of the Sahel, is less humid but very hot during March and April. Its dry season lasts from November to May.

HIGHLIGHTS The capital city of Porto Novo, which is a sleepy town, has some interesting buildings and markets. Ganvié, a village built on stilts in the middle of a lagoon and accessible only by dugout canoe, is near Cotonou. The voodoo museums of Ouidah, Grand Popo and the coastline are worth a visit. Inland are the historic palaces of Abomey. The three-storey houses of the Somba/Betamaribe people around Natitingou are worth seeing and, in the north, the Parc National du W. The railway, one that still works, is a fine way to travel.

 WHERE TO STAY
Cotonou Finding secure parking is a big problem. It might be much pleasanter and safer to avoid Cotonou and stay in Ouidah to the west, where a couple of cheap beach resorts exist. If you have to stay in Cotonou try the Hotel de la Plage near the beach; it had parking but the area was not wonderful or that safe. Better first try asking to park/camp at the Hotel Aledjo east of the city on the beach. Further out is Auberge au Large which may allow parking/camping along Route des Peches.

Porto Novo The choice is bleak; suggested is the Hotel Beaurivage, where rooms are expensive but the view is pleasant.

Ouidah Try the Hotel Jardin Bresilien in the beach area. Rooms from US$12.

Grand Popo L'Auberge de Grand Popo has camping at around US$4 per person. It is a hotel, restaurant and campsite with a view of the ocean in an extremely beautiful setting. A meal at the restaurant is a must. Also look for camping at Awale Plage for a similar price.

Abomey A little way from the centre of town, Chez Monique has a shady tropical garden and straw roof restaurant. You can camp at the back of the hotel in the courtyard for around US$6 per person. The staff are extremely helpful and will go out of their way to show you parts of Abomey – even a voodoo festival if one is in progress.

Dassa The Dassa Motel (Auberge de Dassa Zoume) is on the west side of town, past the dramatic rocks near the ring road. Parking is available here, with good value rooms.

Parakou The very rundown but atmospheric Hotel de la Gare had large rooms and good parking. It may be called Buffet Hotel now. Nearby, just 4km away on the road to Natitingou, on the barrage by the Voie de Djougou, a new fish farm may offer accommodation overlooking a series of beautiful lakes.

Natitingou It might be possible to park in the grounds of the Hotel Tata Somba. Another hotel option might be the Auberge le Vieux Cavalier east of town, where trips to the villages can be organised. Rooms from US$12.

Kandi Look for the Motel de Kandi north of town. In town is the pleasant Auberge la Rencontre with a roof terrace.

Parc National de la Pendjari You can stay at the Campement de la Pendjari where camping costs about US$7 per person. Bookings possible through Hotel Tata Somba in Natitingou.

OTHER Taking of photographs is permitted, but please be respectful, especially when visiting fetish temples and shrines. Crime in Cotonou has increased significantly.

FURTHER INFORMATION
Benin: The Bradt Travel Guide, Stuart Butler
www.hotels-benin.com is a good website for finding accommodation.

BOTSWANA

CAPITAL Gaborone

LANGUAGE AND TELEPHONE English and Satswana are the official languages. International telephone code +267.

CURRENCY AND RATE Pula (BWP); US$1 = BWP6.58

RED TAPE Although we had no problems, the Botswana Defence Force (BDF) sometimes take their duties extremely seriously and can be aggressive.

Visas Visas are not required for nationals of the USA, UK and most other Commonwealth countries, or from most of western Europe, as long as the stay does not exceed 90 days. Entry permits for 30 days are issued at the border. Botswana embassies worldwide are found at www.gov.bw.

African embassies
Θ Angola 2715 Phala Cres & Nelson Mandela Rd, Gaborone; ☎ 390 0204; f 397 5089

Θ Mozambique 758 Robinson Rd, Gaborone; ☎ 319 1250/1; f 319 1261

Θ Namibia Debswana Hse, Lobatse Rd, Gaborone; ☎ 390 2181; f 390 2248; e nhc.gabs@info.bw

Θ Nigeria High Commission, The Mall, Gaborone; ☎ 391 3561; f 391 3738

Θ South Africa Queens Rd, Gaborone; ☎ 390 4800/1/2/3; f 390 5502

Θ Zambia Zambia Hse, The Mall, Gaborone; ☎ 395 1951; f 395 3952

Θ Zimbabwe Orapa Cl, Gaborone; ☎ 391 4495; f 390 5863

DRIVING AND ROADS Drive on the left. There are good surfaced main roads and the rest are tracks and pistes.

Fuel costs Diesel: US$1.50; petrol: US$1.60 per litre.

CLIMATE It is hot throughout the year, with the main rainy season from December to April.

HIGHLIGHTS The Okavango Delta, Moremi Wildlife Reserve and Chobe National Park are obvious highlights. All have an array of wildlife in various environments. Maun has various campsites and organisations that arrange tours into each of these national parks. The Kalahari Desert, with its vast open spaces and Central Kalahari Game Reserve, is worth a visit, as are the Makgadikgadi and Nxai Pans and Tsodilo Hills with ancient San paintings. The Makgadikgadi and Nxai Pans can be crossed only with 4x4 and in the dry season, April to December. Only use well-marked tracks on the pans, or your vehicle will sink. It is advisable to go with another vehicle.

WHERE TO STAY
Gaborone With only a few cheap hotels in town, try camping in the Mokolodi Nature Reserve US$25 for two.

Francistown There are quite a number of places to camp. Look for Tati River Lodge, Marang Motel camp and the Kharma Rhino Sanctuary.

Makgadikgadi and Nxai Pans Camps in these parks are expensive options. Nata is the nearest town with places to stay. Look for Nata Lodge. In the Nata Sanctuary camping is allowed at basically serviced designated places (US$5 each). In Nxai Pan there are north and south campsites.

Kanye The Hotel Motse is delightful and you can camp in the orchard behind. It's rather hard to find, but is on the north side of town; ask at the fuel stations. Cost US$15 (car plus two).

Kang Just about the only place on the trans-Kalahari road between Kanye and Ghanzi with a motel, shop and fuel. Secure parking.

Central Kalahari region It has a few basic camping areas within the vast area.

Ghanzi Try the Kalahari Arms Hotel and the Thakadu Camp.

Maun A good choice is available: Alfa, Audi Camp, Back to the Bridge Backpackers, Crocodile Camp, Island Safari Lodge, Maun Rest Camp, Drifters Safaris, Okavango River Lodge and Sitatunga Camp all offer basic camping facilities from US$6. Each is a great stopover for excursions into the delta, and a safe spot for your vehicle. Most 'camps' in the delta area are luxury style.

Okavango Delta No visit to the Okavango Delta (or any other national park in Botswana) will be cheap, but the delta is a unique attraction. The Sepupa Swamp Stop, located on the northwest side of the delta, not far from the Tsodilo Hills, offers camping for around US$5 per person. Others are Mbiroba Camp, Guma Island Lodge and Makwena Lodge. They can usually set up cheaper trips into the delta.

Moremi Reserve There are several options here: try the north gate Khwai Camp, Xakanaxa Campsite, Third Bridge Campsite or South Gate Maqwee Campsite. These are inside the park, so the costs will be higher. Allow about US$30–40 per person per night, including entry, camping and vehicle.

Kasane/Chobe National Park The main area is along the Chobe River east of Kazungula around Kasane. The Ngina Safari camping is basic. Kabu Lodge has camping options as does Toro Safari Lodge. About 5km out is the Thebe River camping for US$17 per couple; further away from the river you find Luyi Campsite. Also look for Ihaha Campsite and Linyati Camping Site. There is also a campsite at Savuti further south.

Tsodilo Hills Getting to the Tsodilo Hills, a World Heritage Site, is now easier with road improvements, and is worth the effort. It is possible to camp here: try Makoba Woods Camp, Squirrel Valley Camp or Malatso Campsite. It should be possible to bush camp *en route*.

Panhandle region Well-developed places are found here. Drotsky Cabins and Camp, Shakawa and Sepupa Swamp Stop, Guma Lagoon Camp. Prices from US$10 camping per person.

Bookings for the national parks are recommended and can be done at their offices in Gaborone or Maun.

OTHER The importing of meat is prohibited, with some checks.

FURTHER INFORMATION
Botswana – Okavango Delta, Chobe, Northern Kalahari: The Bradt Travel Guide, Chris McIntyre
www.botswananet.org

9

CAPITAL Ouagadougou

LANGUAGE AND TELEPHONE French is the official language. International telephone code +226.

CURRENCY AND RATE West African franc (CFA); US$1 = CFA415

RED TAPE Police checks were once numerous, but now things are less frenetic all round.

Visas Visas are required for all except nationals of ECOWAS countries. They cost US$50 to US$100, depending on the country of application. Visas are normally and more cheaply issued at the main borders, but check first. The *Visa Touristique Entente* intended to cover Benin, Burkina Faso, Ivory Coast, Niger and Togo seems to be unavailable these days. In countries where there is no representation, the French Consulate usually handles Burkina visas. Vaccination certificates for yellow fever may be checked.

Non-African consulate
⊖ French Consulate (issues visas for Central African Republic, Mauritania & Togo) Av de l'Independence, Ouagadougou; ☎ 5030 6774

African embassies
⊖ Ghana Av d'Oubritenga, Ouagadougou; ☎ 5030 7635/5030 1701
⊖ Ivory Coast Av Raoul Follereau/Bd du Faso, Ouagadougou; ☎ 5031 8228/5030 6637
⊖ Mali 2569 Av Bassawarga, Ouagadougou; ☎ 5038 1922; f 5038 1923
⊖ Nigeria BP 132, Av d'Oubritenga, Ouagadougou; ☎ 5030 6667
⊖ Senegal Av Yennenga (southern end), Ouagadougou; ☎ 5031 2811

DRIVING AND ROADS Drive on the right. Main routes have mostly good surfaced roads. Secondary roads are quite reasonable, with some maintenance.

Fuel costs Diesel: US$1.30; petrol: US$1.50 per litre.

CLIMATE The cool dry season is from November to mid April and the rainy season from June to September. The north has less rain and is hotter.

HIGHLIGHTS Although the 'Grand Marché' in Ouagadougou remains closed after a huge fire, the area is still a shopping zone. Ouagadougou is a food connoisseur's delight, known for its variety of restaurants ranging from African and European to American. Visit Banfora, which is excellent for cycling, and the surrounding area. Bobo Dioulasso, with its mud mosque, has long been a favourite. The Sultan's Palace (Na Yiri) at Kokolongho, 45km

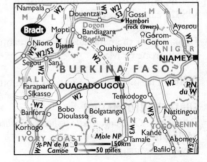

west of Ouagadougou, is a worthwhile stop *en route*. Built in 1942, it is the home of Naaba Kaongo and has an interesting story, which guides will relate. The small town of Bani, near Dori, has some amazing mosques. In the north, on the desert fringes, a melting pot of people gathers in the market of Gorom Gorom every Thursday starting at 11.00. The Parc National du W is another attraction in the southeast.

WHERE TO STAY

Ouagadougou The best and most secure place is at the Mission Catholique, within the compound near the cathedral. Try the sisters (Les Soeurs Lauriers) or the brothers (La Fraternité). You are not allowed to sleep in your car; rooms are compulsory, but very cheap. Otherwise try at Hotel Les Palmiers with parking. Also look out for Le Pavillion Vert (e *pavillionvert@liptinfor.bf*). If you prefer to stay well out of town, look for Campement Phargon, 12km east on the main highway to Niger. There is also a campement at Rapadama, 53km east of Ouaga.

Bobo Dioulasso As well as the main mud mosque, the biggest attractions are the Bobo (local tribe) houses, distinguished by their tall, conical roofs, in the surrounding countryside. Casa Africa is still by far the best option, with shade, camping, cheap rooms and a restaurant. It's southwest of town across the railway. Also near here is Campement le Pacha (e *lepachabobo@yahoo.fr*), another option with a shady garden, at US$6 for two, but they seem to be discouraging campers. Near the Grande Mosque is Hotel Les Cocotiers with hot but cheap rooms and some parking without shade. It's popular with backpackers. For a big splurge try the Hotel Les 2 Palmiers not far from Le Pacha. It's a good place for a drink in any case.

Boromo About halfway between Bobo and Ouaga, centrally in town on the south side of the road, is the Campement Relais Touristique where rooms are 11000/18000CFA with fan/air conditioner. It's a great stop for a drink and/or snack.

Banfora The best place for campers is the Campement Baobab 4km from town near the Domes of Fabedougou, with great atmosphere, thatched huts and camping options. Allow US$3–4 per person. If you want a hotel, try the atmospheric Hôtel le Comoé, on the southern edge of town; they may allow you to camp in their courtyard for a minimal fee. Equally charming but more expensive is the Hotel la Canne à Sucre (e *hotelcannasucre@fasonet.bf*).

Close to Banfora are the unusually shaped hills of the Pics du Sindou. You can stay at the Sindou village at Campement Djatiguiya.

Oronawa West of Bobo Dioulasso in this small town is the delightful Hotel Le Prestige. Internet café here.

Ranch de Nazinga (e *phillippe_trepagny@yahoo.fr; www.ranchdenazinga.com*).

Dori/Bani The Camping de Djomaga about 7km out of Dori is a good option, US$4 each for camping. Hebergement Le Nomad can set up dune trips from Bani.

Gorom Gorom Le Campement Rissa is a decent option, where camping costs US$8 for two. Also here is Campement Hotel Gorom Gorom, a quiet place with a rocky outcrop. Oursi, with a lake and dunes nearby is a gem; stay at Campement Aounaf.

Tenkodogo On the way to Togo is the great Hotel Laafi with good parking inside, garden and restaurant. You can camp or have a room with air conditioning for 13000CFA. It's on the west side of the road.

Fada N'Gourma The Belle Etoile is a cultural experience as well as a place to stay.

OTHER Photographic permits used to be a requirement, but this is no longer the case. Just be aware of what you are photographing and remember that photos of government institutions are completely forbidden. Video permits are required and these are issued by the Ministère de l'Environnement et du Tourisme. For repairs and parts check Burkina Motors in the centre of Ouagadougou.

FURTHER INFORMATION
Burkina Faso: The Bradt Travel Guide, Katrina Manson and James Knight

BURUNDI

☞ **WARNING!** Due to the ongoing political unrest in Burundi we strongly advise you to seek sound travel advice if you intend to visit. Basic information has been listed. The 'latest' new peace deal was signed in May 2008, but will it hold?

CAPITAL Bujumbura

LANGUAGE AND TELEPHONE French and Kirundi are the official languages. International telephone code +257.

CURRENCY AND RATE Burundi franc (BIF); US$1 = BIF1187

RED TAPE You can expect some roadblocks, as security is still not assured.

Visas Visas are required for all visitors. A one-month tourist visa costs US$60 plus, depending on the place of issue. You will need two passport photos. Again, depending on the place of issue, visas can be issued within 24 hours. Visas are issued at the airport and possibly at the main Rwanda/Burundi land border, but check beforehand.

African embassies
ⓔ DRC Av de Zaire/Republic du Congo
ⓔ Rwanda 24 Av de Republic du Congo, Bujumbura; ☏ 226865/228755; f 223254

ⓔ Tanzania Av Patrice Lumumba, Bujumbura; ☏ 228636

DRIVING AND ROADS Not much information available. The main road between Bujumbura and Kigali is reasonable.

Fuel costs Diesel: US$1.50; petrol: US$1.60 per litre.

CLIMATE The climate is varied. The general rainy season is from November to May. A dry period lasts from June until October, but seasons are not clearly defined.

HIGHLIGHTS Bujumbura has an attractive setting and some old colonial buildings. Other sights are the Parc National de la Kibira with its rainforest, the Parc National de la Rurubu, and the waterfall, Chutes de la Kagera, near Gitega.

WHERE TO STAY

Bujumbura Look for the Hotel le Doyen (US$30–40), an old colonial place with parking and garden. Out of town and with parking is another former colonial place called Safari Gate (US$40 plus) on the lakeside. Saga Beach Resort is another possibility nearby.

FURTHER INFORMATION
Africa on a Shoestring, Hugh Finlay et al (Lonely Planet)

CAMEROON

☞ *MILD WARNING!* There were riots and civil disorder in March 2008 over food and fuel price rises, but such things are normally very limited in scope.

CAPITAL Yaoundé

LANGUAGE AND TELEPHONE French and English are the official languages. International telephone code +237.

CURRENCY AND RATE Central African franc (CFA); US$1 = CFA415

RED TAPE You will be stopped sometimes for passport and vehicle checks. Beware of accidentally driving on the president's road in Yaoundé.

Visas Visas are required for virtually everyone. The cost is US$115 in London and requires proof of funds, as well as a hotel booking with a local police stamp from Yaoundé or Douala, making obtaining a visa impractical in Europe. Visas are not issued at the border. *En route* you could try in Dakar, Lagos or Calabar, Nigeria. One has to wonder if they really want any tourists.

Non-African consulate
❸ French Consulate (issues visas for Burkina Faso & Togo) Rue Joseph Atemengué, Yaoundé; ☏ 223 4013/6399 or 222 1776

African embassies
❸ Central African Republic Rue 1863, Bastos, Yaoundé; ☏ 220 5155
❸ Chad Rue Mballa Eloumden, Bastos, Yaoundé; ☏ 221 0624
❸ Congo Rue 1816, Bastos, Yaoundé; ☏ 221 2455/223 2458
❸ Democratic Republic of the Congo Bd de l'URSS, Bastos, Yaoundé; ☏ 222 5103

❸ Equatorial Guinea Rue 1805, Bastos, Yaoundé; ☏ 221 0804
❸ Gabon Rue 1816, Bastos, Yaoundé; ☏ 220 2966
❸ Ivory Coast Bastos, PO Box 11357, Yaoundé; ☏ 221 7459
❸ Liberia Bd de l'URSS, Bastos; ☏ 221 1296/5457
❸ Niger ☏ 221 3260
❸ Nigeria off Av Monseigneur Vogt, Centre Ville, Yaoundé; ☏ 222 3455

DRIVING AND ROADS Drive on the right. Road surfaces range from exceptionally good tarmac to diabolically corrugated dirt, with all variations in between. North of Ngaoundéré or south and west of Yaoundé are some fairly good, tarred roads. Otherwise there are some reasonable dirt roads that shut if it rains. Then there are a few awful stretches of corrugated dirt, best not dwelt on – east of the capital and on the road to Mamfé. There are also some new road projects, so the situation is improving all the time. A better road from Bertoua to Yaoundé is via Abong-Mbang. Good road to Gabon.

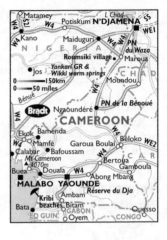

Fuel costs Diesel: US$1.30; petrol: US$1.50 per litre.

CLIMATE Coastal Cameroon is very wet almost all year. The north is hot and dry, with a long rainy season from May to October. The south is hot and humid, with a short 'dryish' season from December to February and rains from March until October, with a less wet period in July and August away from the coast.

HIGHLIGHTS Climb Mount Cameroon, which is west Africa's highest mountain at 4,070m; visit the Waza and Benoué national parks. The beaches at Kribi are excellent. In the north, explore the villages and markets around Maroua, and hike in the Mandara Mountains, including Roumsiki. Southern Cameroon has some spectacular hill regions with the last of the Pygmy tribes left in the area, but they are extremely difficult to reach; take an organised expedition with a volunteer organisation in Yaoundé.

WHERE TO STAY

Yaoundé Finding a reasonably priced hotel with parking in the capital is hard. Hotel Meumi is a good choice. Double rooms cost US$22. The Foyer International de l'Eglise Presbyterienne near the water tower near Carrefour Nlongkak is OK for US$5.

Douala Best avoided, but if you have to stay, try the German Seamen's Mission in Akwa district. Despite its name, it's popular (US$30+).

Mamfé In 2004 we stayed at the Heritage Inn. By chance, or perhaps because it's a good retreat, so did Charlie and Illya much earlier. We were told, 'Sorry, we have only the most expensive room left. It's $12.' This was a suite with air conditioning, sofas and a huge bathroom. We didn't mind at all. This small town is close to the border with Nigeria. Fuel comes from Nigeria and is only available from large barrels; there is no fuel station.

Buea The town is on the lowest slope of Mount Cameroon and is also the base camp. You must have a permit and guide; both are available in the main street in town. Climbing Mount Cameroon can take between three and four days. A good place to stay in Buea is the Presbyterian church with parking and camping. In town is the Hotel Mermoz, where a double room costs from US$16.

Kumba The Azi Motel is one parking/camping possibility, especially if you have dinner in the restaurant.

Limbé In town try at the Park Hotel Miramar behind the botanical gardens. Also it may be OK to camp at the 6 or 8 Mile Beach area. The First International Inn has bungalows.

Kribi Stay at Tara Plage with a good restaurant, from US$7 per person for camping.

Ebolowa Try a hotel with tennis courts on the edge of town.

Bamenda There is the Baptist Mission Resthouse.

Foumban The town is rich in historical sights. Try staying at the Catholic Mission, which has a nice garden.

Maroua Try at Hotel le Sare or Hotel Sahel. There is a campement called Boussou, which is cheaper.

Waza National Park Camping is possible at the Centre d'Accueil de Waza for US$6.

Roumsiki This is a hill retreat with good trekking and outer villages where it is possible to stay. In 'town' you could stay at Kirdi Bar, a cheap option for camping, or at Auberge Le Kapsiki.

Garoua Try the plush hotel, Relais St Hubert. It has air-conditioned rooms and secure parking. A double room costs US$40. Camping might be allowed.

Benoué National Park About 30km from the main road at Banda. There is camping at the Campement du Buffle Noir.

Ngaoundéré On the south side of town try Hotel Transcam, which has secure parking. Southeast of town, about 35km away, Ranch de N'Gaoundaba has been mentioned as a good option in the hills and near a volcanic crater lake.

OTHER Photographic permits are not required, but many officials will tell you that they are. If hassles continue, go to the Ministry of Information and Tourism and let them, for a small fee, write a letter stating as much. Crime is on the increase, particularly in Yaoundé and Douala. Again, don't drive on the president's unmarked private road, a large roundabout area in central Yaoundé; it could be a costly error.

FURTHER INFORMATION
Cameroon: The Bradt Travel Guide, Ben West

CENTRAL AFRICAN REPUBLIC (CAR)

☞ ***WARNING!*** Due to the ongoing civil disturbances in the Central African Republic the information listed may be out of date. We strongly advise no overland travel into the country. Seek sound travel advice if you do intend to visit.

CAPITAL Bangui

LANGUAGE AND TELEPHONE French is the official language. International telephone code +236.

CURRENCY Central African franc (CFA); US$1 = CFA415

RED TAPE Avoid all military personnel and try not to stay longer than one day in one area.

Visas Visas are required for all and may cost US$70–100. Two photos, two application forms, a yellow fever certificate, a letter from your company stating that the applicant will resume work on returning and a return ticket are all required. Nationals of Australia, New Zealand, France and the Republic of Ireland need permission from Bangui before a visa application is accepted. Visas are not issued at the border. Visas may only be given for short stays, requiring extensions in Bangui.

Non-African consulate
❺ French Consulate (issues visas for Burkina Faso, Gabon, Ivory Coast, Mauritania, Senegal & Togo) Bd Général de Gaulle, Bangui; ✆ 61 3000

African embassies

❺ Cameroon Rue de Languedoc, Bangui; ✆ 61 1687
❺ Chad Av Valéry Giscard d'Estaing, Bangui; ✆ 61 4677
❺ Congo Av Boganda, Bangui; ✆ 61 1877
❺ Democratic Republic of the Congo Rue Gamal Abdel Nasser, Bangui; ✆ 61 8240

❺ Nigeria BP 1010, Km3, Av Boganda, Bangui; ✆ 61 0744/3910/3911
❺ Sudan Av de la France, Av de l'Indépendénce, Bangui; ✆ 61 3821/5011

DRIVING AND ROADS Drive on the right. There are sealed roads to the northeast and northwest of Bangui for a limited distance, but closer to the borders of Cameroon, Chad and Sudan roads are in very poor condition, particularly during the rainy season.

Fuel costs Diesel: US$1.50; petrol: US$1.50 per litre.

CLIMATE It's hot and humid in the south, drier in the north. The rainy season is from March to October, starting later and finishing earlier the further north you go.

HIGHLIGHTS The rolling savanna forest across the border from Cameroon gives a feeling of vastness. The Chutes de Boali north of Bangui are spectacular, particularly during the rainy season. Also worthwhile are the Kembe Falls east of Sibut, and the remote forests beyond. In

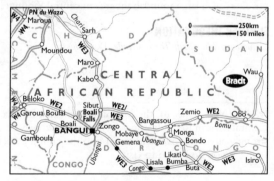

220

Bangassou you can take dugout canoe rides along the river in search of hippos. The Dzanga-Sangha Nature Reserve is opening up to tourism and has some great wildlife, including lowland gorillas. The Worldwide Fund for Nature is involved (*www.panda.org*).

WHERE TO STAY

Bangui Overlanders used to go to the Centre d'Accueil Touristique Dalango (✆ 61 1772) which charged US$5 for camping. It was located in the African Quarter, on Avenue Boganda, 1.5km to the west on Km5. We do not know if it is still open.

Bayanga Doli Lodge is a remote and rustic eco-lodge built by the Worldwide Fund for Nature (WWF) with aid from Germany. It is used by tour operators and researchers as a base for trips into the Dzanga-Sangha Nature Reserve.

Obo The Obo Mission allowed camping and had a very well-equipped workshop some years ago (see pages 156–7).

OTHER We would suggest that your camera stays in its case in Bangui. Ask people in the countryside for their permission, as some in the Central African Republic are extremely sensitive about photography.

FURTHER INFORMATION The WWF (*www.panda.org*) currently have conservation, health and education projects in the CAR, so their website has some relevant information.

CHAD

WARNING! Yet another rebellion took place in early 2008, this time both in the east and around N'djamena. Although quiet at present, the situation is clearly unstable.

CAPITAL N'djamena

LANGUAGE AND TELEPHONE French and Arabic are the official languages. International telephone code +235.

CURRENCY AND RATE Central African franc (CFA); US$1 = CFA415

RED TAPE The eastern border with Sudan is currently closed, so we leave this information from the previous authors for reference should it reopen: 'On entry from Sudan at the Adré border in Chad, we found the military and police to be extremely aggressive and drunk. It also took up to four hours to clear all paperwork, which was not due to inefficiency, but to having to find the right person for the job who was having a game of cards with friends on the other side of town. Throughout Chad we found the military to be particularly aggressive – they are best avoided.'

When we travelled there ourselves in the desert (Ennedi Plateau) in a local agent's cars, our drivers always tried to avoid police check-posts wherever possible, suggesting that the situation is not much different elsewhere in the country.

In theory a *carnet* is not required but some adjacent countries will need them anyway. For those without a *carnet*, a 'Laissez-Passer pour Vehicules' will normally be issued at all custom border posts for a fee, (from CFA5,000).

9

VISAS Visas are required for all Westerners. Three application forms and three photos are needed. Officially you also should have a return air ticket. Visas are valid for three months. The estimated cost of a visa is US$50–100, depending on country of issue. Yellow fever vaccination certificates will be checked on entry. Visas are not issued at the border. It was possible to get an invitation by fax from a local tour operator and have a visa issued at the airport on arrival by air.

Non-African consulate

❸ French Consulate (may issue visas for Burkina Faso, Gabon, Ivory Coast, Mauritania, Senegal & Togo) Rue de Lieutenant-Franjoux, off Av Félix Eboué,

N'djamena; ☎ 52 2575/6; f 52 2855; www.ambafrance-td.org

African embassies

❸ Cameroon Rue des Poids Lourds, N'djamena; ☎ 52 3473
❸ Central African Republic was at Rue 1036, N'djamena; ☎ 52 3206
❸ Democratic Republic of the Congo Av 26 de Août, N'djamena; ☎ 52 5935

❸ Nigeria Av Charles de Gaulle, BP 752, N'djamena; ☎ 52 2498
❸ Sudan Off Rue de la Gendarmerie, N'djamena; ☎ 52 5010/51 3497

DRIVING AND ROADS Drive on the right. There are short sections of tarred road on either side of N'djamena; the rest are either sandy desert tracks in the north or very bad mud roads in the south.

Fuel costs Diesel: US$1.45; petrol: US$1.55 per litre.

CLIMATE The desert climate in the north is very hot and dry all year round. The heavy rains are from June to September in the south.

HIGHLIGHTS The bustling central market and Grand Marché in N'djamena are colourful. Also worth seeing are the village of Gaoui, which is just outside N'djamena, Lake Chad and Abéché, on the edge of the Sahel. The Tibesti Mountains in the north would be a highlight if they were safe and accessible. The Ennedi Plateau, including Guelta d'Archei, is usually more accessible with a local guide and offers stunning desert scenery with natural arches, freshwater crocodiles and prehistoric rock art. Ounianga Kebir and the northern lakes are amazing.

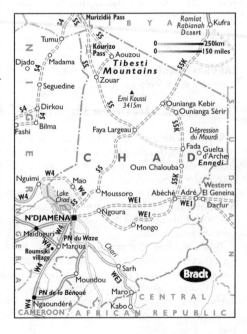

WHERE TO STAY
N'djamena There are a few hotels in N'djamena and you may be able to park in their

yards. We stayed at the centrally located Hotel Sahel. It has a nice airy courtyard and parking. Or ask at the Novotel – formerly Hotel Tchadienne – if you can camp in their grounds. If you're lucky, you may be allowed to use the staff showers and the hotel's pool. Email facilities are available in town. La Caravelle is rumoured to be a new camping place near Rondpoint du Pont.

Abéché In Abéché Charlie and Illya were lucky enough to meet the sultan's brother, who put them up for the night. We would otherwise suggest bush camping. Abéché is not a very large town and the surrounding area is typical Sahel.

Ennedi The Ennedi Plateau is a beautiful desert area, similar to the Tassili du Hoggar in Algeria. But it is equally wild and we do not suggest going there alone. Travel with a local agent to avoid the risk of landmines remaining from the civil war. Mostly you will camp out wild, but there is a vague resemblance to a hotel in Faya, Hotel Restaurant Emi Koussi, where we camped in the yard. In Faya we camped at our driver's cousin's house – the toilet was just outside.

Tibesti Mountains Bush sleeping is the only option and a travel permit for the area is required. There has been a long-standing border dispute between Chad and Libya, as well as fields of uncharted landmines; a tour of the Tibesti is definitely not for the faint-hearted. In fact we do not recommend you to go there at all at the moment. If and when it becomes safe, you will need enough fuel, water and food supplies for approximately 1,000km (600 miles). Obtaining permission to travel in the area will be difficult and you will probably be rejected. If it ever becomes safe, it will still probably be best to avoid officialdom when wise and safe to do so.

OTHER A photographic permit is said to be required, but can take up to a week to issue, so most travellers don't bother. The answer is not to take any pictures, or be extremely discreet when you do. Out in the desert this is not a problem, though you should always ask if photographing people. The Tubu people are particularly averse to having their photos taken.

At the time of writing, the border between Chad and Sudan (Adré) is closed due to the situation in Darfur. How this will develop, we have no way of knowing. In any case it is a very remote and lonely area. Be careful and make sure you have sufficient supplies of fuel and food.

FURTHER INFORMATION
www.expeditionworld.com

DEMOCRATIC REPUBLIC OF THE CONGO (DRC)

☞ **WARNING!** Due to the recently concluded civil war in the Democratic Republic of the Congo, the situation is variable but mostly stable. Seek sound travel advice if you do intend to visit and, depending on the state of the country, travel in convoy if possible. The western areas have improved, but in the northeast there is still sporadic fighting.

CAPITAL Kinshasa

LANGUAGE AND TELEPHONE French is the official language. International telephone code +243.

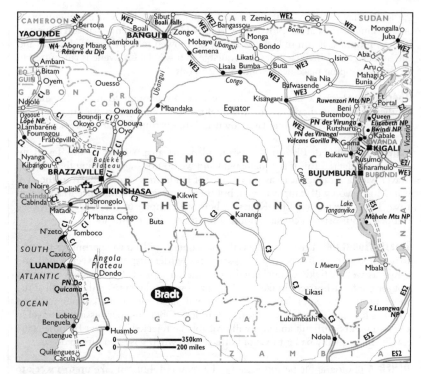

CURRENCY AND RATE Congolese franc (CDF); US$1= CDF437

RED TAPE Officials of the DRC are notoriously bad and known for their corruption and drunkenness (from palm wines). Avoid them at all times. Never stay in one place longer than a day and never walk or drive at night. You will probably have to register each night with local police. Keep a copy of passport details – in fact, dozens.

Visas Visas are required for all and costs vary depending on where you get the visa. Prices range from US$85 for a one-month visa to US$100 or more for multiple entry. You will also need three to four photographs and an introduction letter from your embassy. Vaccination certificates are obligatory. Visas are not issued at the border.

African embassies

E Angola 44/13 Bd du 30 Juin, Gombe, Kinshasa;
↘ 12 32 415; f 12 27 890. Consulate in Matadi may give visas to overlanders, but check if this is still possible.

E Benin 3990 Av des Cliniques, Kinshasa; ↘ 12 28 822

E Burundi 4687 Av de la Gombe, Kinshasa; ↘ 12 33 353/21 327

E Cameroon 171 Bd du 30 Juin, Kinshasa; ↘ 12 34 787; m 099 16822

E Central African Republic 11 Av Mont des Arts, Gombe, Kinshasa; ↘ 12 33 571

E Congo 176 Bd du 30 Juin, Gombe, Kinshasa;
↘ 12 34 028

E Gabon Bd du 30 Juin, Kinshasa; ↘ 12 50 206

E Ivory Coast 68 Av de la Justice, Kinshasa; ↘ 12 21 028; f 12 21 214

E Kenya 4002 Av de l'Ouganda, Kinshasa; ↘ 12 33 205; m 099 31936

E Nigeria 141 Bd du 30 Juin, Kinshasa; ↘ 12 33 343/43 274; m 081 700 5143

E Rwanda Was at 50 Av de la Justice, Kinshasa;
↘ 12 33 080

E Sudan 83 Av des Treis, PO Box 7347, Kinshasa

DRIVING AND ROADS Drive on the right. There are not many stretches of road in the DRC that are good; they become a sea of mud during the rainy season.

Fuel costs Diesel: US$1.50; petrol: US$1.50 per litre.

CLIMATE It is impossible to summarise the climate for the whole of the DRC, as it is such a huge country. Along the northern route (the one formerly taken by most travellers) the only time of year it is likely to be fairly dry is from December to February. If travelling from Gabon to Angola through the two Congos, after May can sometimes be better, but since rain is possible at any time, avoiding wet conditions cannot be guaranteed.

HIGHLIGHTS Crossing the Congo River from Brazzaville. In the east is the Parc National des Virunga, known for its gorilla trekking and volcanoes (although access has been affected by the civil war). Climbing the Nyiragongo active volcano is spectacular. See the lakes of Tanganyika, Kivu, Edward and Albert, plus the Epulu Reservation for Pygmies, and the Okapi reserve. Mount Hoyo and the eastern mountain ridge are good for a cool respite and a taste of the villages. Don't forget the music of the DRC. And if it ever becomes safe, there are even worse roads to test your driving skills, your vehicle and your staying power.

WHERE TO STAY Because of dense forest it is hard to get off the 'road', so sleeping/parking/camping in disused road quarries will be the best option. Travellers used to stay at the various missions dotted around the country; this is one of the few reasons why certain roads are still driveable. The current state of the missions is uncertain, even if the state of the roads and bridges is predictable.

Kinshasa The city is a vast sprawl. It's worth checking the missions in town, because there's little else on offer without blowing a hole in the budget.

Muanda It might be worth checking at the convent school near the hospital.

Boma About 20km before town is a cattle ranch that might allow bush camping.

Matadi There was a convent beside a truck park, which offered some security for a fee. (There may still be a mechanic and electrician called Dodo here as well.)

Goma There are now two campsites. One is close to the Rwandan border; the second is behind the Chez Kamanza supermarket – US$7 each. Another option is the Colibri Hotel, where camping is allowed for US$5 each.

Parc National des Virunga The park was closed from 1997 until 2004 but is now functioning again. There is an office in Goma now for information. Entry permits are paid for here at the headquarters in hard currency – gorilla-tracking permits from US$300–400. Climbing Nyiragongo is also organised from here. In the park there are basic camping facilities at Bukima and a small lodge at Djomba. Camping is also just about again possible at the Rwindi Lodge for US$5 each.

Bukavu Not a very safe place yet, but the nearby Gorilla reserve of Kahuzi-Biega will hopefully rise again. Hotel Tourist is said to have parking.

OTHER Photographic permits are required, but are only valid in the region of issue. Try in Kinshasa, Kisangani and Lubumbashi or, easier perhaps, don't get caught taking pictures. The cost is dependent on the official. There were also special requirements for travel in central DRC in the mining regions. These permits were only issued in Kinshasa and could take up to two weeks to get. Most travellers bribed their way through these areas.

FURTHER INFORMATION
Congo and Democratic Republic of Congo: The Bradt Travel Guide, Sean Rorison
For wildlife and nature information, the Institut Congolais pour la Conservation de la Nature (ICCN) (*www.iccnrdc.cd*). Access to this site is very unreliable.

PEOPLE'S REPUBLIC OF THE CONGO

☞ **WARNING!** Due to the on–off rebellion in the People's Republic of the Congo we advise all overland travellers to check the latest security situation. Since 2004 a few overlanders have taken the route, so it may get better. In 2008 the main problems are in the regions west of Brazzaville along the road to Dolisie. The road north of Brazzaville is currently safe.

CAPITAL Brazzaville

LANGUAGE AND TELEPHONE French is the official language. International telephone code +242.

CURRENCY AND RATE Central African franc (CFA); US$1 = CFA415

RED TAPE As with most war-torn countries in Africa, try to avoid all military personnel. It is also advised that all travel at night be avoided here.

Visas Visas are required for all except nationals of France. Visas will cost US$140 or so, depending on country of application. Visas are not issued at the border. There are embassies in Cameroon and Gabon.

Non-African embassy
❸ France (issues visas for Burkina Faso, Ivory Coast & Togo) Av Alfassa, Brazzaville; ☏ 81 5541

African embassies
❸ Angola CP 388, Brazzaville; ☏ 83 6565. Consulate in Pointe Noire; ☏ 94 1912
❸ Cameroon Rue Général Bayardelle, Brazzaville; ☏ 81 1008
❸ Central African Republic Rue Fourneau, Brazzaville; ☏ 81 4721
❸ Chad 22 Rue des Ecoles, Brazzaville; ☏ 83 2222

❸ Democratic Republic of the Congo 130 Av de l'Indépendance, Brazzaville; ☏ 81 3052
❸ Gabon Av Monseigneur Augouard, Brazzaville; ☏ 81 5620
❸ Nigeria 11 Bd du Maréchal Lyautey, Brazzaville; ☏ 81 1022

DRIVING AND ROADS Drive on the right. Roads are extremely poor.

Fuel costs Diesel: US$1.50; petrol: US$1.50 per litre.

CLIMATE The climate is mostly hot and humid. The main drier season is from May or June to September.

HIGHLIGHTS For a start there are the clean beaches along the coastline around Pointe Noire and the nearby Jane Goodall Chimp Sanctuary. In the east, isolated in dense rainforest, is Parc National de Odzala, known for its gorilla trekking. Brazzaville is a lively place. The Congolese music and food are well-known bonuses of a visit here. The bad roads are another highlight if you like that sort of thing.

WHERE TO STAY

Brazzaville Like most west and central African countries' capitals, Brazzaville is expensive and it is difficult to find camping accommodation here. You could try either of the Catholic missions in town – Eglise Sacré Coeur (*Av Maréchal Foch, behind the Méridien Hotel*) or Eglise Kimbanguiste (*Plateau de 15 Ans, near the Hotel Majoca*). Also recommended, with glowing reviews, is the 8th Novembre Hotel near the Hippodrome; ask for Olivier. There is a Chinese restaurant here.

Pointe Noire Most accommodation is along the Cité. Campers can try at La Requiem on the beach and use the shower and toilet at the back.

Jane Goodall Chimp Sanctuary Bush-style camping is available at the sanctuary; ask for Victor.

OTHER
Parc National de Odzala Extremely difficult to get to, but very rewarding for those who do make it; the amount of wildlife here is astounding. For further information contact WCS in Brazzaville (*www.wcs.org*).

A photographic permit is not required, but be extremely cautious when taking photos and stay clear of all government institutions.

FURTHER INFORMATION
Congo and Democratic Republic of Congo: The Bradt Travel Guide, Sean Rorison

DJIBOUTI

CAPITAL Djibouti City

LANGUAGE AND TELEPHONE French and Arabic are the official languages. Afars is spoken elsewhere. International telephone code +253.

CURRENCY AND RATE Djibouti franc (DJF); US$1 = 178.71DJF

RED TAPE None of any significance, except visas.

Visas Visas are required for all. They are valid for one month and cost around US$75. Visas are not issued at the border. There are not many embassies; in Europe there is one in Paris.

Non-African consulate
€ French Consulate (issues visas for most French-speaking African countries) Av Maréchal Lyautey, Djibouti City; ☎ 35 2503; f 35 0007

African embassies
€ Egypt Ilot du Heron, Djibouti City; ☎ 35 1231
€ Eritrea PO Box 1944, Rue de Kampala, Djibouti City; ☎ 35 4951/35 0381/35 4961

€ Ethiopia PO Box 230, Rue Clochette, Djibouti City; ☎ 35 0718
€ Sudan PO Box 4259, Iron Hse, IE12, Djibouti City; ☎ 35 6404; f 35 6662

DRIVING AND ROADS Drive on the right. The main roads to Ethiopia and Tadjoura are generally good; desert tracks and piste outside the main routes. Be very careful if going to Lac Abbé; take a guide to avoid quicksands and getting seriously lost.

Fuel costs Diesel: US$1.30; petrol: US$1.61 per litre.

CLIMATE The climate is generally very hot and humid on the coast, with a cooler season from November to mid April and occasional rain during that period.

HIGHLIGHTS Djibouti City has some colourful markets, old colonial buildings, tea shops and old mosques. You could take a boat trip across the Gulf of Tadjoura, but driving there is very spectacular, with black lava flows and volcanic cones. Lac Assal lies below sea level with amazing brilliant-white salt, sulphur and halite crystals. The Forêt du Day, a small zone of luxuriant growth, is accessed by a shocking rocky track. Randa is a nearly defunct retreat, but a pleasant drive. Lac Abbé is known for its birdlife. Enjoy the flamingos and natural chimneys formed by the escape vents of underground steam dotted along the foreshore.

WHERE TO STAY
Djibouti City Try the Sheraton; it has secure parking. In town try the Auberge Sable Blanc on Boulevard de la République; it may still have parking/camping. In the African quarter there is some budget accommodation available, but no obvious secure parking.

Tadjoura With superb coral reefs 10m from the shore, this is a great place for a stopover. Bush sleeping well outside the town is one option. Try Hotel Le Golfe or the hotel opposite nearby, which have parking.

Randa Look for Campement le Goda just before town.

Forêt du Day Try Campement de Dittilou, but getting there is shockingly rough.

Dikhil Try the Hotel le Palmerie on the main road. Camping is not encouraged.

Lac Assal Bush sleeping is not recommended; stay close by at Le Plage du Goubbet, with camping and small thatched huts.

Lac Abbé Lac Abbé can be reached only by 4x4 and requires at least two days, including a guide. Bush camping is possible, but beware of quicksands, or better, try the new Campement Asbole.

Border: Galafi We camped/parked here close to the customs on our way back into Ethiopia.

OTHER Photographic permits are not officially needed, but officials particularly may act petulantly and in any case people in Djibouti are not happy to be photographed, so beware! Djibouti is an expensive country.

FURTHER INFORMATION
Africa on a Shoestring, Hugh Finlay (Lonely Planet)

EGYPT

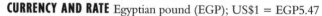

CAPITAL Cairo

LANGUAGE AND TELEPHONE Arabic is the official language. International telephone code +20.

CURRENCY AND RATE Egyptian pound (EGP); US$1 = EGP5.47

RED TAPE The roads south of Aswan and Ras Banas have been closed to all by the military since the tourist attacks and we suggest that you get advice on routes if you are intending to drive that way. Convoys are also compulsory between the Red Sea resorts, Luxor and Aswan.

Visas Visas are required for all except nationals of Malta and Arabic countries. Visas can now be obtained at airports and at some borders. For those entering by road, it is better to get it in advance. One-month single-entry visas cost US$30–40.

African embassies

ⓔ **Algeria** 14 Sharia Brazil, Zamalek, Cairo; ✎ 341 8257/341 1520

ⓔ **Burkina Faso** 9 Fawakeh St, Mohamdessine, Cairo; ✎ 360 8480/341 6077

ⓔ **Cameroon** 15 El Esraa St, Mohamdessine, Cairo; ✎ 344 1101

ⓔ **Chad** 12 Midan al-Rifai, Doqqi, Cairo; ✎ 349 4461

ⓔ **Democratic Republic of the Congo** 5 Sharia Al-Mansour, Mohammed Zamalek, Cairo; ✎ 341 1069341 7954

ⓔ **Djibouti** 11 Sharia al-Gezira, Agouza, Cairo; ✎ 345 6546

ⓔ **Eritrea** 87 Shahab St, Mohamdessine, Cairo; ✎ 303 0517 or 344 4409

ⓔ **Ethiopia** 3 Ibrahim Osman St, Mohamdessine, Cairo; ✎ 347 9002; e ethio@ethioembassy.org.eg

ⓔ **Ivory Coast** 39 Rue El Kods El Cherif, Madinet, Mohamdessine, Cairo; ✎ 346 0109/4952; f 346 0109

ⓔ **Jordan** 6 Goheiny St, Doqqi, Cairo; ✎ 348 6169

ⓔ **Kenya** Hboulos Hanna St, Doqqi, Cairo; ✎ 345 3907; e embacia@hotmail.com

ⓔ **Libya** 7 Sharia As-Saleh Ayoub, Zamalek, Cairo; ✎ 735 1864

ⓔ **Morocco** A10 Rue Salah ad-Din, Zamalek, Cairo; ✎ 340 9849/ 9677

ⓔ **Niger** 101 El Ahram St, Haram, Cairo; ✎ 337 4038

ⓔ **Nigeria** 13 Gabalaya St, Zamalek, Cairo; ✎ 340 3907

Ⓔ Somalia 27 Sharia Somal, Doqqi, Cairo; ☏ 337 4038

Ⓔ South Africa 21–23 Sharia al-Giza, Giza, Cairo; ☏ 571 7234

Ⓔ Sudan 3/4 Ibrahim St, Garden City, Cairo; ☏ 354 5658/ 794 5043; f 794 2693

Ⓔ Tanzania 9 Sharia Abdel Hamid Lotfi, Doqqi, Cairo; ☏ 37 4286; tanrepcairo@infinity.com.eg

Ⓔ Tunisia 26 Sharia al-Gezira, Zamalek, Cairo; ☏ 341 8962

Ⓔ Uganda 9 Midan al-Missaha, Doqqi, Cairo; ☏ 348 6070/248 5975

Ⓔ Zambia 25 Abdel Monein Riad St, Mohamdessine, PO Box 253, Doqqi, Cairo 12311; ☏ 361 0281–3; f 361 0833

Ⓔ Zimbabwe 36 Wadi El Nil St, Obandessin, Cairo; ☏ 351 4427

DRIVING AND ROADS Drive on the right. All the main routes are well surfaced. Outside the major routes you will find road signs in Arabic only. Convoys operate on the Hurghada to Luxor and Aswan routes and south to Abu Simbel.

Fuel costs Diesel: US$0.11; petrol: US$0.26 per litre.

CLIMATE Egypt is hot and dry for most of the year, except for the winter months of December, January and February.

HIGHLIGHTS One of the Seven Wonders of the World – the Pyramids of Giza. Also in Cairo are the Tutankhamun treasures and, close by, the Pyramids of Sakkara including the newly discovered 4,300-year-old tomb. The Coptic monasteries of St Paul and St Anthony are further south, close to the Red Sea coast. Along the Nile are the temples of Karnak and Luxor, plus the Valleys of the Kings and Queens in Luxor. Kom Ombo and Idfu are worth stopping at on the way to Aswan. Aswan has the Philae Temple and a pleasant riverside environment. Abu Simbel is spectacular if you have the time and money to go that far. The Sinai has its own highlights of St Catherine's Monastery, climbing Mount Sinai and the fantastic snorkelling and diving along the coast. Plus the Red Sea has the popular resorts of Hurghada and Safaga, while the western desert has the oases of Kharga and Siwa etc.

 WHERE TO STAY

Cairo The Motel Salma is near the Wissa Wassef Art Centre just south of Giza on the Sakkara road. Camping will cost around US$5 and there's lots of space but little shade.

St Anthony's and St Paul's monasteries These monasteries do not allow camping. Do not go there expecting to be allowed in to stay the night.

Luxor The Rezeiky Camp is fairly basic, but pleasant with some shade; US$10 for camping (vehicle plus two people).

Hurghada Try Hotel Snafer; parking will be sorted out with the police for security reasons. US$15–20 double room.

Safaga Camping at Sun Beach is the only option, as far as we know. It's pleasant with a beachside tent bar. US$10 (car plus two people).

Aswan We stayed a mile or two south of the very swish Old Cataract Hotel at the pleasant **Hotel Sara**, with safe parking and good rooms, all negotiable. There was nowhere at all to camp.

Between Libya and Alexandria We did not find anywhere, and the military do not allow desert camping. There are plenty of expensive hotels near El Alamein.

Between Alexandria and Cairo

Try the Fisherman's Village, a local mini-resort in a quiet spot west of the main highway.

Sinai Try the Pigeon House in Na'ama Bay, Sharm el Sheikh, which had comfortable huts with fans, and serves breakfast. Accommodation costs around US$20. Nuweiba has a camping area.

OTHER *Baksheesh* (tipping) is widely expected, whether for somebody carrying your bags or opening a door or for another service. Haggling is an art form in Egypt and, whether it be for accommodation or curios, be aware of local prices and never quote a price you are not prepared to pay. This includes the ferry from Aswan to Wadi Halfa.

FURTHER INFORMATION
www.tourism.egnet.net
www.touregypt.net
www.cairo.com

EQUATORIAL GUINEA

CAPITAL Malabo

LANGUAGE AND TELEPHONE Spanish is the official language. International telephone code +240.

CURRENCY AND RATE Central African franc (CFA); US$1 = CFA415

RED TAPE The police are said to be a little pushy, but if all your paperwork is in order there shouldn't be a problem. You might be allowed to cross the border for a brief visit from Cameroon, for a small fee.

Visas Visas are required for all and one-month visas cost US$65–80. You will also need two photographs. Visas are not issued at the border, but you could ask at Ebebiyin on the northern border with Cameroon.

Non-African embassy
❸ **France** (issues visas for Burkina Faso, Central African Republic, Chad, Ivory Coast & Togo) Carretera del Aeropuerto, Malabo; ✆ 092 005

African embassies
❸ **Cameroon** 19 Calle de Rey Boncoro, Malabo; ✆ 092 263
❸ **Gabon** Calle de Argelia, Malabo; ✆ 093 180

❸ **Nigeria** 4 Paeso de los Cocoteros, Malabo; ✆ 092 487

DRIVING AND ROADS Drive on the right. Roads are mostly very poor, but new oil wealth should change this one day.

Fuel costs Diesel: US$1.40; petrol: US$1.60 per litre.

CLIMATE Equatorial Guinea has a wet tropical climate, with a drier spell from June to September on the mainland. December and January are driest on Bioko Island.

HIGHLIGHTS Malabo, with its old Spanish architecture, and Luba's nightlife on Bioko Island with beautiful beaches. There's a Bioko Biodiversity Protection Programme under way (*www.bioko.org*). The rainforests of the mainland.

WHERE TO STAY

Ebebiyin If you visit Equatorial Guinea at all by road, it will be through the border here. Try at the hotels, eg: Hotel Mbengono.

Bata Finding any secure parking would be difficult in Bata. Hotel Yessica might have parking.

OTHER Photographic permits are essential and you will be asked for your permit on a regular basis. These can be obtained from the Ministry of Culture, Tourism and Francophone Relations. You will need to type up a request, preferably in Spanish on official stationery. The permit will cost you US$60 and will be issued within 24 hours. Do not take pictures of any government organisations.

FURTHER INFORMATION
www.bioko.org

ERITREA

☞ **WARNING!** The border disputes between Eritrea and Ethiopia have still been only partially resolved. It is currently impossible to drive into Eritrea from Ethiopia. It may be possible to drive in from Kassala in Sudan, but security may be an issue. Crossing into Djibouti is said to be possible, according to one local, but check first as you might be stuck in the country. Tourists need permits to move around the country. Within the country, security has improved and visiting should be a pleasant experience. However, seek current advice before entering.

CAPITAL Asmara

LANGUAGE AND TELEPHONE Arabic and Tigrinya are the official languages. International telephone code +291.

CURRENCY AND RATE Nakfa; US$1 = 15.0Nakfa

RED TAPE It is currently necessary to obtain travel permits for destinations out of Asmara. Check security issues before heading into the Danakil areas.

Visas Visas are required for all and should be applied for in your home country. Of course this is not always possible and proof of visas from other countries, a letter of introduction from your embassy and two photographs should suffice. A one-month visa will cost US$50+ and is valid from the date of entry. Visas are not issued at the border. Make sure you have a valid yellow fever vaccination certificate.

African embassies

€ Djibouti Andinnet St, Asmara; ☎ 125990
€ Egypt Marsa Fatuma St, Asmara; ☎ 124835;
f 123294

€ Ethiopia Was at Franklin D Roosevelt St, Asmara;
☎ 116365; may not be open now.
€ Sudan Hazemo St, Asmara; ☎ 124176/189544;
f 129287

DRIVING AND ROADS Drive on the right. Roads are in good condition on most major routes, deteriorating as you get off the beaten track. The road south from Massawa to Assab is substantially improved now and possible with a well-equipped vehicle. Security issues are still of concern. It is said to be rather risky to go south of Assab into Djibouti, but this may change. Hard information about this route is difficult to find.

Fuel costs Diesel: US$0.60; petrol: US$0.80 per litre.

CLIMATE Eritrea has a varied topography, so the climate is different in each of its three main zones. In the highlands, the hottest month is usually May, with highs of around 30°C. Winter is from December to February, with lows at night that can be near freezing. Asmara's climate is pleasant all year round. Short rainy seasons are in March and April; the main rains are from late June to early September. On the coast, travel is not recommended between June and September, when daily temperatures range from 40° to 50°C (and considerably hotter in the Danakil Desert). In winter months the temperature ranges from 21° to 35°C. Rain is rare, and occurs only in winter. In the western lowlands the rainy seasons are the same as the highlands; the temperature pattern is the same as that of the coast.

HIGHLIGHTS Asmara is known for its pleasant ambience, Italian buildings and cool climate. The dusty alleys of Massawa are being restored, across the first causeway on Taulud Island. Keren is a predominantly Muslim town and has a colourful daily market, renowned for its silversmiths' street, and the livestock market every Monday. Churches and monasteries close to the Ethiopian border are interesting and Qohaito has Axumite remains. The Danakil Desert is an incredibly remote area, sparsely populated by the Afar nomads. It will be increasingly possible to drive through this area and possibly on to Djibouti as roads improve. However, with temperatures generally around 40°C, and with no facilities or main roads, it is really only for the seriously adventurous. A guide is recommended and seeking local advice is **essential.**

WHERE TO STAY There are said to be a few campsites, but good-value accommodation is available and rooms are usually clean and well kept. You will need to shop around for parking if you managed to get your vehicle into the country in the first place.

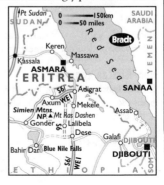

Asmara There are quite a few *albergos* (inns) to be found along Liberation Avenue. For camping, try the Africa Pension, which is an old converted villa. The Hotel Sunshine and Hotel Khartoum, which has car hire, may be possible places to park.

Massawa Massawa does not have any campsites, but does have accommodation on the mainland and on Taulud Island. Ask at the Gurgussum Beach hotel if parking is possible; it's north of the old city area.

Keren Try the noisy Eritrea Hotel or the nicer Sicilia, with shady courtyards.

Agordat Try at the Alwaha Oasis hotel a bit out of town.

Barentu On the way to Sudan is this small town. Hotel Selam is a quieter suggestion.

OTHER There are uncharted mines throughout Eritrea, so stay on main roads rather than off the beaten track, particularly after dark, and always ask the locals for route advice. The *faranji* (white man) hysteria can get a bit much, but you'll become used to it and it's generally harmless.

FURTHER INFORMATION
Eritrea: The Bradt Travel Guide, Edward Denison
www.eritrea.org is still for sale
www.asmera.nl

ETHIOPIA
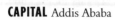

> Ethiopians are completely bonkers. I knew, too, that I had to visit their country.
> *Philip Briggs,* Ethiopia: The Bradt Travel Guide

CAPITAL Addis Ababa

LANGUAGE AND TELEPHONE Amharic is the official language. International telephone code +251.

CURRENCY AND RATE Ethiopian birr (Birr); US$1 = 9.70birr

RED TAPE None of any significance, except visas. Ethiopians are generally pleasant people, if more than a little inquisitive!

Visas Visas are required for all except nationals of Kenya. Visas are single-entry only and cost US$50–65. You may also need to prove you have sufficient funds. Yellow fever vaccination certificates are mandatory. Visas are not issued at the border.

Non-African consulate
✪ **French Consulate** (issues visas for most French-speaking African countries) Omedia St, Addis Ababa;
✆ 155 0066; f 551 1180

African embassies Just about every African country is represented in Addis Ababa and the tourist board office (*near Maskal Sq*) issues a useful booklet listing all the embassies. Here are just a few. For others see www.mfa.gov.et/consular.

Cameroon Bole Road, Addis Ababa; ☎550 4487;
e ambcamaa@ethionet.et
Congo PO Box 5571, Addis Ababa; ☎ 661 0012
Djibouti Off Bole Rd, Addis Ababa; ☎ 661 3200;
f 661 2504
Egypt Entonto Av, Addis Ababa; ☎ 155 3077;
f 155 2722
Ivory Coast Bole Kifle Ketama/Jimma Rd, Addis
Ababa; **e** coteivoire_aa@yahoo.fr
Kenya Maryam Aba Techan St, Addis Ababa; ☎ 661
0033; **f** 661 1433; **e** kenya.embassy@telecom.net

Nigeria Gulele Kifle Ketama, Addis Ababa; ☎ 120
644; **e** dmoffice@ethionet.et
Somaliland ☎ 663 5921
Sudan Ras Lulseged St, Addis Ababa; ☎ 551 6477;
f 551 8141; **e** sudan.embassy@ethionet.et or
sudan.embassy@telecom.net.et
Tanzania Bole Rd, Addis Ababa; ☎ 663 4353;
e tz@ethionet.et
Zimbabwe House 007, Higher Kebele 19, Addis
Ababa; **e** zimbabwe.embassy@ethionet.et

DRIVING AND ROADS Drive on the right. Roads are mostly poor with some tarred sections along the major routes. The road from Addis Ababa to Moyale is nearly all tarred, as is the new road to Djibouti, the main port now for landlocked Ethiopia. Roads in the highlands are very rough gravel and extremely slow going. The eastern highland road from Adigrat to Addis is not all tarred, as indicated by the Michelin map.

Fuel costs Diesel: US$0.70; petrol: US$0.90 per litre.

CLIMATE The main rainy season is from June to September, with lighter rains from February to April. In the lowlands it can get extremely hot from April to June, while the colder season in the highlands can be very cold.

HIGHLIGHTS The northern historical route includes Gonder, for its castle compound, and Bahar (Bahir) Dar beside Lake Tana, source of the Blue Nile, and close to the Blue Nile Falls. The route also includes the Simien Mountains and Axum, plus the famous rock-cut churches of both Lalibela and Tigre. South of Addis are the lakes of the Rift Valley and the Omo region, with its traditional village life and culture. Ethiopian cuisine (memorable to say the least), and the elaborate coffee ceremony are a must, as well as the traditional music and dance.

WHERE TO STAY

Addis Ababa There are a few options apart from hotels. We stayed at the Hotel Amba, a small but friendly compound on Maryam Aba Techan Street, east of town. We also camped at the Swedish Mission, just beyond the American embassy north towards Entoto. Cost US$6.

Gonder The Terera Hotel has a view of the royal enclosure – it is located just to the north. Camping costs US$3–4 per person. Gonder often has a shortage of water and getting a shower can be a little frenetic.

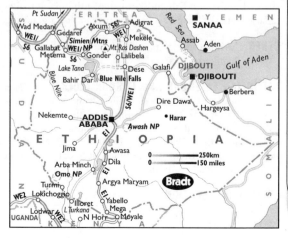

Bahar Dar We camped in the exotic lakeside garden of the Ghion Hotel. Camping cost US$6, rooms are US$12–15. It's hard to beat for a restful interlude. Nearby is the new hotel Bahir Dar Pension.

Axum At the time of writing, not many travellers in vehicles had visited Axum, partly because of the terrible road and the long distance. But don't let this deter you; fill up with fuel in case of shortages. Some tour groups were flying into Axum. Try the Axum Touring Hotel. Also suggested as being a pleasant watering hole is Africa Hotel.

Lalibela We camped in the driveway of the Seven Olives Hotel; it's not very busy. There's a nice view and enough room to spread out. Cost US$5 per person for camping. The food is traditional; try injera wat in the restaurant. The Roha to the west of town also offers camping at US$6.

Woldiya The Lal Hotel allows camping in its backyard; it has a bar, comfortable lounge and good rooms. It is a super place with an amazing vegetable and fruit garden; a rare example of local personal initiative in the highlands, where fresh food other than garlic is often scarce. They will sell you some of the produce. A bread shop is also on the site. Camping US$5 for two. See box *Ethiopia in a Nutshell* in *Chapter 7*, page 174.

Kombolcha The Hotel Tekle is very good value, with pleasant rooms, restaurant and parking on a hill. Double room US$10.

Nazret Along the main road on the south side is the Hotel Adama Ras with a quiet garden and good parking. Rooms are good value, costing just over US$10 for a double.

Awasa On the lakeside try Hotel Woye Shebele; it's shady and the gardens host lots of birdlife. Camping cost US$6 for two and a room will be around US$12. Watch out for the monkeys.

Yabello The Yabello Motel is the only decent place, with parking and a nice garden. There is a basic garage next door if you need it. Double room costs around US$12.

The Omo region The best bet here is to bush camp. If you decide to stay a night in Arba Minch, stay at Roza's Place, where camping is allowed in the courtyard and she makes the best fish cutlets in all of Ethiopia. It makes a great break from *injera* (a large pancake-shaped substance made of *tef*, a grain that is unique to Ethiopia).

OTHER Currency declaration forms are not now needed on arrival, but keep all bank exchange receipts.

THE JULIAN CALENDAR AND 12-HOUR CLOCK Ethiopians use the Julian calendar, which means that their year falls seven or eight years behind the European calendar, and there are 13 months in the calendar of the Orthodox Church. Ethiopian time is also measured in 12-hour cycles starting at 06.00 and 18.00. In other words, their 19.00 is our 13.00 and vice versa. Be very aware of this when booking a bus or flight, and double-check departure times. Most banks and other such institutions have both Western and Ethiopian calendars and times.

FURTHER INFORMATION

Ethiopia: The Bradt Travel Guide, Philip Briggs
www.ethiopia.org

GABON

CAPITAL Libreville

LANGUAGE AND TELEPHONE French is the official language. International telephone code +241.

CURRENCY AND RATE Central African franc (CFA); US$1 = CFA415

RED TAPE Police are suspicious of all foreigners, so approach with care. Some officials at road checkpoints are a little unfriendly, but not all.

Visas Visas are required for all and can take as long as a week to be issued, as all applications are theoretically telexed through to Libreville for approval. You may need a letter of introduction from your embassy, two photographs and US$100. Visas are not issued at the border. A yellow fever vaccination certificate may be needed.

African embassies

Ⓔ Angola Quartier Louis, Lot 34 du Plan, Cadestral, Libreville

Ⓔ Benin Bd Léon Mba, Quartier Derrière Prison, Libreville; ☎ 73 7692

Ⓔ Cameroon Bd Léon Mba, Quartier Derrière Prison, Libreville; ☎ 73 2800

Ⓔ Central African Republic North of Voie Express, Libreville; ☎ 73 7761

Ⓔ Congo Gué-Gué, off Bd Ouaban, Libreville; ☎ 67 7078/73 2906

Ⓔ Democratic Republic of the Congo Gué-Gué, off Bd Ouaban, Libreville; ☎ 73 8141

Ⓔ Equatorial Guinea Route d'Ambowe, Gué-Gué, Libreville; ☎ 73 2523/ 75 1026

Ⓔ Ivory Coast Immeuble Diamant, Bd de l'Indépendance, Libreville; ☎ 72 0596/73 7412; f 73 8287

Ⓔ Nigeria Av du Président Léon Mba, Quartier de l'Université, Libreville; ☎ 73 2111/73 1017

Ⓔ São Tomé BP 489 Bd de la Mer, Libreville; ☎ 72 0994

Ⓔ Senegal Quartier Sobraga, Libreville; ☎ 73 6675

DRIVING AND ROADS Drive on the right. Roads are a mixture of good new tarmac interspersed with generally poor corrugated dirt. Between Oyem and Ndjolé there are both good and bad sections, which are slowly being worked on. Libreville to Lambaréné is good but quite hilly. To Réserve de la Lopé, the road was narrow, remote and very hilly. We gave up. There is a train!

Fuel costs Diesel: US$1.50; petrol: US$1.00 per litre.

CLIMATE The climate is hot and humid, with the dry season from May to September and another short drier spell in mid December.

HIGHLIGHTS Gabon has extensive virgin forest covering very hilly country, which can be seen by visiting the various reserves. The most famous is the Réserve de la Lopé, where one can go in search of lowland gorillas. In Libreville are extensive local markets, and a few resorts along the ocean to the beach at Cap Estérias. Lambaréné is set on the beautiful banks of the Ogooué River, with the Albert Schweitzer Hospital and Museum.

WHERE TO STAY

Libreville We stayed at the Michèle Marine, which is one of the cheaper places but still expensive. A double room costs US$75. Camping may be possible in the parking area, but rather unpleasant with high humidity. The Hotel Tropicana resort, near the airport, is a more pleasant and cheaper option used by expatriates. US$40 a double. It has a beachside café-restaurant, but check that the overnight parking is secure. The Maison Libermann on Boulevard Bessieux has been suggested and is said to be clean, quiet and offering hot showers. Camping also said to be possible in Sablière beach, a suburb just out of the centre near the airport, but with dubious security.

Cap Estérias Cap Estérias is just north of Libreville and very pleasant. Camping is possible at the L'Auberge du Cap. It also has rondavel huts and a restaurant. Also suggested is La Marina.

Lambaréné We parked for free in the grounds of the Ogooué Palace Hotel, which is on the river to the north of town near the church and mission. The mission (*Soeurs de la Conception*), the red brick complex on the nearby hill, is not that cheap and does not allow camping. They have rooms for US$18. Another suggestion was Le Petit Auberge, two blocks southeast of Bar Dancing Le Capitol, but camping facilities would need to be negotiated. It could be noisy.

Réserve de la Lopé If you take the train, this is the easiest national park to get to and has abundant wildlife. In your own vehicle, be prepared for a remote drive. Camping is not allowed inside the reserve. The Hotel Lopé is very expensive. It might be possible to stay in cheaper lodgings (*casa de passage*) in the village, but come well prepared. A motel owned by Jules could be another option.

Bitam Try the Hotel Escale, which has parking and a nice restaurant.

Oyem South of town on the west is the Oyem Motel with parking and cheap rooms at US$12.

Ndjolé The amazing Auberge St Hubert on the west of town along the river looks like a hotel set on the banks of the Loire in France. The inside is not much less comfortable; a welcome retreat in a sea of jungle and pot-holed roads. Double room costs US$40. See *Est-ce que c'est la Loire* box in *Chapter 5*, page 137.

Lastoursville Try a hotel or head south to find a place in the jungle.

Franceville Check if you can camp at the Hotel Masuka. Camping is possible in the Lekoni canyons, but check security in Franceville first.

OTHER Be wary of what you photograph, as the Gabonese are quite touchy about photography and your camera could be confiscated.

FURTHER INFORMATION
Gabon, São Tomé & Príncipe: The Bradt Travel Guide, Sophie Warne
www.wcs.org for information on national parks in Gabon

CAPITAL Banjul

LANGUAGE AND TELEPHONE English is the official language. International telephone code +220.

CURRENCY AND RATE Dalasi (GMD); US$1 = GMD20.48

RED TAPE Roadblocks can be tiresome, with officials surly at the best of times.

Visas Visas are required for all except nationals from the Commonwealth and most EU countries. There are different visa requirements for nationals of the United States, Australia, New Zealand and South Africa, so it's best to check. British nationals do not currently need visas. Ensure that your passport is valid for six months or more. Yellow fever certificates are obligatory.

African embassies

🇪 **Ghana** 18 Mosque Rd, Latrikunda
🇪 **Guinea** 78A Daniel Goddard St, Banjul; ☎ 422 6862
🇪 **Guinea Bissau** Atlantic Rd, Bakau; ☎ 449 4854
🇪 **Mali consulate** VM Company Ltd, Cotton St, Banjul; ☎ 422 6942

🇪 **Mauritania** Off Kairaba Av, Fajara; ☎ 449 6518
🇪 **Nigeria** 61 Buckle St, Banjul; ☎ 456 1717 also Garba Jahumpa Rd, Bakau.
🇪 **Senegal** Off Kairaba Av, Fajara; ☎ 437 3752
🇪 **Sierra Leone** 67 Daniel Goddard St, Banjul; ☎ 422 8206

DRIVING AND ROADS Drive on the right. Roads along the coastal strip and the airport road are good, but inland expect some deteriorating surfaces.

Fuel costs Diesel: US$1.10; petrol: US$1.30 per litre.

CLIMATE Cool dry season from December to April, followed by a warmer dry season and rains between June and October.

HIGHLIGHTS Visit the mysterious Wassu Stone Circles. Take a trip in a local boat up the Gambia River and admire the birdlife. Relax on the Atlantic beaches and visit the market at Basse Santa Su. Banjul should be seen for its run-down ambience.

WHERE TO STAY

Banjul Banjul town is not a place suitable for camping.

Serekunda/Bakau Look out for Sukuta Camping (*www.campingsukuta.de*), which costs about US$7 for a car plus two. It's advertised on various rock outcrops all the way from Laayoune to Nouakchott just so you don't miss it. Also, there are cheap rooms at New Atlantic City Guest Inn for US$10 along Atlantic Road.

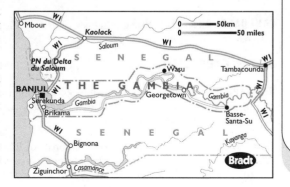

Fajara You will have to shop around for camping, but try at Fajara Guesthouse south of Kairaba Avenue or Dutch Compound, which you will have to ask for. US$7.

Sanyang Down the coast is Sanyang, where two places offer basic African cultural experiences – Sanyang Nature Camp and Rheakunda Camp with dancing and drumming school.

Gunjur There are some pleasant restful locally run spots, like Gunjur Guesthouse (good parking), Rasta Kunda Beach Camp and the Balaba Nature Camp. Prices around US$10 each.

Kartong South of Banjul near the Senegal border, try the Boboi Beach Lodge (*www.gambiaadventure.com*), where camping is US$10 per tent. Also here is Country Edge Lodge with camping; Tamba Kruba, a cheaper option at US$4 each; and a new place, Kartong Tesito Ecotourism Camp.

Tendaba Camp One of the most popular nature areas. Bungalows from US$10 per person.

Assau Stone Circle Camping at Village Camp for US$5 each.

Janjangbureh (formerly Georgetown) There are various camps set up here, primarily for birdwatching. Look for Baobolong, Janjangbureh Camp, Dreambird Camp, Alaka-bung (*alakabung@qanet.gm*) and Bird Safari Camp (*www.bsc.gm*). Prices are reasonable, from US$5 per person upwards.

OTHER Crime is on the increase in Banjul, so do not walk on your own at night along the beaches of Bakau and Fajara. There have also been many complaints about beach boys, known as 'bumsters' or 'bumsan', who offer you everything and anything. Ignore them unless you would like to use one or other of their services. Motorists may be fined for strange infringements!

FURTHER INFORMATION
The Gambia: The Bradt Travel Guide, Linda Barnett and Craig Emms
www.gambia.com

GHANA

CAPITAL Accra

LANGUAGE AND TELEPHONE English is the official language. International telephone code +233.

CURRENCY AND RATE New Cedi (GHS); US$1 = GHS1.01

RED TAPE There are occasional roadblocks with minimal hassle; just ensure all your paperwork is in order. At the border between Ghana and Togo, the touts can be a nightmare. Politely ignore them.

Visas Visas are required for all except nationals of ECOWAS countries and cost US$60–80. Vaccination certificates are obligatory. Visas are not issued at the border. On arrival you may be asked how long you intend to stay. Whatever you say could be written in your passport and you won't be able to stay for longer, despite what your visa indicates, so always state the duration of your visa.

African embassies

Ⓔ Benin Switchback Lane/80 Volta St, Accra; ☎ 021 77 4860

Ⓔ Burkina Faso 772/3 Farrar St, Asylum Down, Accra; ☎ 021 221988

Ⓔ Guinea 4th Norla St, Labome, Accra; ☎ 021 777921; f 021 760961

Ⓔ Ivory Coast 9 18th Lane, Osu, Accra; ☎ 021 774611/12; f 021 773734

Ⓔ Liberia 10 West Cantonments Rd, Accra; ☎ 021 775641/2; f 021 775987

Ⓔ Mali Bungalow 1, Liberia Rd, West Ridge, Accra; ☎ 021 663276; f 021 666942

Ⓔ Niger E 104/3 Independence Av, Accra; ☎ 021 224962/229011

Ⓔ Nigeria Josef Tito Av, Accra; ☎ 021 776158/9; f 021 774395/7766158/777280

Ⓔ Togo Togo Hse, Cantonments Rd, Accra; ☎ 021 777950/4521

DRIVING AND ROADS Drive on the right. The coastal roads are excellent, but as you move further north they get a little patchy.

Fuel costs Diesel: US$0.85; petrol: US$1.10 per litre.

CLIMATE Hot and dry in the north and humid along the coast. The rains arrive in late April and last intermittently until September.

HIGHLIGHTS The coastline from Accra to Dixcove has former gruesome slave forts along the coast at Elmina and Cape Coast. Inland is the ancient Ashanti capital, Kumasi, known for its massive market and Kente cloth-weaving villages nearby. The Kakum and Mole national parks are worth a visit. The coast has some good beaches – Kokrobite, Busa, Dixcove and Axim – with improving facilities.

WHERE TO STAY

Accra We don't know of any obvious place to camp in central Accra, but you might try the Crystalline Hostel which has rooms around US$15–20, or the Amomomo Beach Garden. Nearby, east of Accra at Coco Beach, is Akwaaba Beach Guesthouse (*www.akwaaba-beach.de*).

Kokrobite is about 25km west of Accra. A very popular place here is Big Milly's Backyard, which charges US$3 for camping. Meals are also available just outside on the beach; you can get a fine toasted egg fry with a taste of the local firewater, *apatechi*. Kokrobite is renowned for the Academy of African Music and Arts (AAMAL) with live music, drumming and dancing every weekend. A new resort has been opened here, rooms US$13.

Anomabu This is 20km east of Cape Coast; camping (US$6 each) is offered at the Anomabu Beach Resort (*www.anomabubeach.com*).

Cape Coast Try the Oasis Guest House, US$8–15 dbl. Also Ko Sa on the beach towards Busua has been suggested.

Elmina The Almond Tree Guest House (*www.almond3.com*) is recommended.

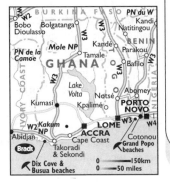

Busua Suggested is Alaska Beach Resort with camping, rooms US$10–15.

Dixcove Options here are Hideout Lodge (*www.hideoutlodge.com*). Camping and bungalows on the beach from US$2–3. Also Green Turtle Lodge (*www.greenturtlelodge.com*); camping from $3; and Safari Beach, all west of Dixcove.

Kumasi The Presbyterian Guesthouse is one place you can camp. Cost is around US$5. It's a beautiful place with huge shady trees, located close to the city centre. Rose's Guest House might be a possible alternative. Kumasi Catering Resthouse has shady grounds but is often full.

North to Burkina There is plenty of savanna forest where you can camp wild.

Bolgatanga The Sand Gardens Hotel is pleasant at US$10 a room.

Mole National Park This is in the northwest of the country. Try the new national parks campsites with prices at US$3 each. The Mole Motel may let you camp at around $3 per person.

OTHER If you own a Land Rover, Accra is the place to get it fixed. Seek advice before diving into the ocean, as Ghana is plagued with dangerous currents. Photographing people is generally not a problem, but always ask beforehand and do not photograph near government institutions. If you're keen to learn the African beat, African Footprint International (*www.africanfootprint.dk*) is a drum and dance workshop located near Cape Coast.

If you need a mechanic in Accra, Roger (Nana) and Godwin (✆ *028 213 803;* e *rogerko2001@yahoo.com*) have been recommended.

FURTHER INFORMATION
Ghana: The Bradt Travel Guide, Philip Briggs
www.ghanaweb.com

GUINEA

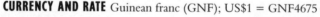

CAPITAL Conakry

LANGUAGE AND TELEPHONE French is the official language. International telephone code +224.

CURRENCY AND RATE Guinean franc (GNF); US$1 = GNF4675

RED TAPE The police in Guinea sometimes host roadblocks at night and hold your papers until you pay a bribe. In other words, don't drive at night. If you do get caught in one of these notorious roadblocks, you shouldn't pay more than US$5 as a bribe. During the day there are very few checks.

Visas Visas are required for all and cost US$130–180. Depending on which country you are in, the Guinean Embassy may ask for a letter of introduction from your own embassy. You will also need a photocopy of the identification pages of your passport. Visas issued in Africa are normally valid for two weeks only, but this depends on where you apply. They are not issued at the border.

Non-African embassies
⊖ France (issues visas for Burkina Faso & Togo), Bd du Commerce, Conakry; ☎ 41 1605

African embassies
⊖ Benin Rue RO 251, Kipe, Conakry; ☎ 29 2688; e cbc-gn@yahoo.fr
⊖ Ghana Corniche Nord, Camayenne, Conakry; ☎ 40 9560
⊖ Guinea Bissau Route de Donka, Conakry; ☎ 42 2136
⊖ Ivory Coast Bd du Commerce, Conakry; ☎ 45 1082

⊖ Mali Pl du Novembre, Coleach Corniche, Conakry; ☎ 46 1418
⊖ Nigeria Av de la Gare, Conakry; ☎ 41 1681/46 1343
⊖ Senegal Corniche Sud, Conakry; ☎ 46 2834/40 9037
⊖ Sierra Leone Carrefour Bellevue, Conakry; ☎ 46 4084

DRIVING AND ROADS Drive on the right. The main road from Conakry to Bamako is generally not too bad but elsewhere the roads are poor and those that are paved are usually pot-holed. The road to to Dalaba and Labé is not too bad. After Labé it is rough into the higher country. In the east roads are exceedingly variable. Guinea does have some fun sections of dirt road for those yearning for the old days in Africa.

Fuel costs Diesel: US$1.00; petrol: US$1.00 per litre.

CLIMATE Guinea has a tropical climate, with a lengthy rainy season between May and October determined by altitude and location.

HIGHLIGHTS Conakry has some pleasant leafy areas and markets. There are beaches on the Iles de Los, Iles de Roume and Iles de Kassa. Most can only be reached by *pirogue* (a small river craft of various sizes). Iles de Los has a mini-resort. You may even get a spontaneous musical performance. Some local outfits teach tourists about the music and you can learn to play the *kora* here. Inland is the Fouta Djalon Plateau with short treks from either Dalaba, a pleasant hill resort, Labé or Pita.

WHERE TO STAY
Conakry For a place with parking, you need to head north of the centre. A good place is the Hotel du Golfe in the Rogbane area and, in the northern area, try Hotel Kaporo. In town is the Hotel Niger, a seedy but cheap place without parking.

Koundara There are two places here where you can park and camp. Hotel Gagan is the quiet one a little further out east and costs US$4. Hotel Niafay is friendly with more space but more noise. Both are reached down a tiny track from the central empty fuel station.

Fouta Djalon Plateau This plateau, with its rolling green hills, cooler climate and excellent hiking, is a must for any visitor to Guinea. Stay with local people in traditional village huts and preferably have a local guide to translate.

Labé Try the wonderful, efficient and friendly Hotel Tata (*www.tatasenegal.com*), with thatched huts in the garden and some parking places. Delightful Madame Raby still runs the place. Rooms cost from US$18 and camping is possible.

Dalaba The Pension Tangama is a relaxing place with parking. Up the hill overlooking the valley is the more upmarket Sib Hotel Fouta with camping in the garden and great panoramic views across the rolling hills.

Mamou Look out for Hotel Baly with a courtyard.

Kindia On the way out of town on the east side, but not signposted unless you are going north, is the Hotel Flamboyant. This is a great retreat with extensive gardens. Camping is allowed, or take a room. The pool has yet to be filled.

Kankan Look for the Hotel Bate (e *hotelbate@yahoo.fr*). The annexe is cheaper (US$24) and the air conditioning works at times. There's good secure parking and the lively markets are not far. It's a quiet retreat and has a bar and restaurant. Beware of hidden one-way streets near the hotel – the police are probably badly paid!

Mali border There is Relais Tata on the Guinean side.

Kissidougou On the road out west towards Faranah is the pleasant Hotel Savannah with parking in a yard opposite, where you can cook and probably camp if you wish. We witnessed Guinea being thrashed by Ivory Coast here after Guinea had beaten Morocco in the 2008 African Cup of Nations. We could have watched Portsmouth v Arsenal in a shed with television and generator 20km out of town in a village.

Macenta Look for Hotel Bamala.

Nzérékoré The cramped but secure Hotel Chez Aida is in a quiet area northwest of the markets, up a little hill.

OTHER Guinea is a great country for outdoor enthusiasts, particularly cyclists and hikers, and is also well known for its music. The Fouta Djalon is the most obvious option; remember to carry adequate water and food with you. The eastern forest area is remote and there are still areas of dense rainforest with narrow muddy roads that are passable in the dry season. There is also the great biking/hiking Pita–Télimélée route, which was part of the Paris–Dakar rally in 1995. Hotels are still excellent value so it's not necessary to rough it all the time.

FURTHER INFORMATION
West Africa, Rough Guides
www.guineenews.org

GUINEA BISSAU

CAPITAL Bissau

LANGUAGE AND TELEPHONE Portuguese is the official language. International telephone code +245.

CURRENCY AND RATE West African franc (CFA); US$1 = CFA415

RED TAPE You may find intermittent roadblocks, but locals, including government personnel, are extremely friendly.

Visas Visas are required for all except nationals of Cape Verde and Nigeria. They cost around US$20–50 and are valid for one month. Visas are not issued at the border.

Non-African Consulate

🇪 **French Consulate** (issues visas for Burkina Faso, Central African Republic, Chad, & Togo) Bairro de Penha, Av de 14 Novembro, Bissau; ☎ 20 1312

African embassies

🇪 **Gambia** Av de 14 Novembro, Bissau; ☎ 25 1099 or 20 3928

🇪 **Guinea** Corner of Rua Osvaldo Veira & Rua 12, Bissau; ☎ 21 2681/20 1231

🇪 **Mauritania** Rua Eduardo Mondlane, Bissau; ☎ 20 3996

🇪 **Nigeria** Av 14 Novembro, no 6, Bissau; ☎ 20 2564

🇪 **Senegal** 43 A Rue Omar Terrijos/Praça dos Heróis Nacionais, Bissau; ☎ 21 2944/21 1561

DRIVING AND ROADS Drive on the right. The roads are generally poor; those that are paved are usually pot-holed.

Fuel costs Diesel: US$1.30 per litre. Petrol: US$1.40.

CLIMATE The hottest months are April to May, with the coolest months from December to January. Rains are from July to September.

HIGHLIGHTS Explore the Portuguese colonial areas of Bissau. In the north are the coastal mangrove swamps around Cacheu, with its tiny ruined fort. More offbeat is a visit by boat to the Bijagos Islands.

WHERE TO STAY

Bissau Finding somewhere to park or camp will be difficult. Try one of the hotels, perhaps the top-end Hotel Bissau or maybe Hotel 24 de Septembro out of town.

Bijagos Archipelago These are a group of islands off Guinea Bissau. Assuming you can find secure parking for the vehicle for a night or two, your best bet is to pack an overnight bag and head over to one of the following two islands, which have some accommodation. Bolama Island is the closer to the mainland, but accommodation is basic. Bubaque Island, at the centre of the archipelago, is one of the easiest to reach. The best part is said to be Praia Bruce beach on the southern end of the island, with some basic places to stay. Ask other travellers about any new developments.

Cacheu Try the Hotel Baluarte if it's reopened, where the rates for camping accommodation will need to be negotiated.

OTHER Guinea Bissau is one of the poorest countries in Africa. If you are invited to stay by a local person, always offer to pay for your accommodation and/or meal.

FURTHER INFORMATION

West Africa, Rough Guides

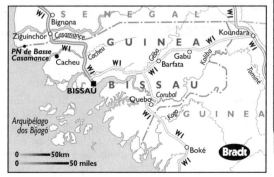

IVORY COAST (CÔTE D'IVOIRE)

☞ **WARNING!** Due to the recent civil unrest in much of the country, we strongly advise against overland travel. Seek sound travel advice if you do intend to visit. The political stalemate makes visiting dangerous. Expect security problems travelling overland for some time to come. Parts of Abidjan are notorious for crime, with rogue elements.

CAPITAL Yamoussoukro is the official capital, though Abidjan remains the commercial and diplomatic centre.

LANGUAGE AND TELEPHONE French is the official language. International telephone code +225.

CURRENCY AND RATE West African franc (CFA); US$1 = CFA415

RED TAPE With a sporadic civil war in the country, you can expect a lot of hassles throughout.

Visas Visas are required for all except nationals of ECOWAS countries and cost US$50–80. Vaccination certificates are obligatory. Visas are not issued at the border. A Visa Touristique Entente covering Benin, Burkina Faso, Ivory Coast, Niger and Togo is theoretically available, but tracking it down via a relevant embassy or consulate is difficult.

Non-African embassy
🅔 **France** (issues visas for Chad) Rue Lecour, Plateau, Abidjan; ☏ 20 20 05 04/20 20 04 04

African embassies
🅔 **Benin** Rue de Jardins, Deux Plateaux, Abidjan; ☏ 22 41 44 13
🅔 **Burkina Faso** I Av Houdaille, Plateau, Abidjan; ☏ 20 21 15 01
🅔 **Ghana** Res le Corniche, Bd Général de Gaulle, Plateau, Abidjan; ☏ 20 33 11 24
🅔 **Guinea** Immeuble Crosson Duplessis, Av Crosson Duplessis, Abidjan; ☏ 20 32 94 94
🅔 **Liberia** 20 Av Delafosse, Plateau, Abidjan; ☏ 20 32 46 36

🅔 **Mali** 46 Bd Lagunaire, Abidjan; ☏ 20 32 31 47; f 20 21 55 14
🅔 **Niger** 23 Bd Angoulvant, Marcory, Abidjan; ☏ 20 26 28 14
🅔 **Nigeria** Bd de la République, Plateau, Abidjan; ☏ 20 21 19 82/ 20 22 26 58
🅔 **Togo** Near Rue du Commerce, Plateaux, Abidjan; ☏ 20 32 09 74

DRIVING AND ROADS Drive on the right. Good surfaced roads on main routes with mainly good dirt roads elsewhere.

Fuel costs Diesel: US$1.30; petrol: US$1.50 per litre.

CLIMATE There are two climatic regions. In the south, the temperature remains at a steady 30°C all year round but rainfall is heavy at times. There are four seasons: a long dry season from December to April; a long rainy season from May to July; a short dry season from August to September; and a short rainy season from October to November. The north has a broader temperature range, with a rainy season from June to October and a dry season from November to May.

HIGHLIGHTS Grand Bassam, with its colonial-era buildings, has a stretch of bustling beachfront cafés and entertainment. Abidjan offers contrasting affluence and poverty. It once had a huge market for secondhand spares, plus great supermarkets with goodies such as imported cheeses – costly but worth the taste sensation. Things are not so rosy today, though.

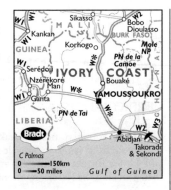

Yamoussoukro is fascinating, full of contrasts, with deserted streets, concrete structures and eight-lane highways lined with thousands of lights ending abruptly in the jungle. The Basilique de Notre Dame de la Paix, which resembles St Peter's in Rome, is the white elephant of Africa, built by President Houphouët-Boigney at a cost of a mere US$300 million. There is nothing else quite like it. Upcountry, Korhogo, the capital of the Senoufo, is famous for its wooden carvings and Korhogo cloth (mud-coloured designs painted on fabric). In December there are several festivals. Try to visit the pottery and blacksmith quarters, with temples for each of the crafts. Also visit Komoé National Park.

WHERE TO STAY

Abidjan Abidjan has six sections – Plateau, Treichville, Marcory, Adjame, Cocody and Deux Plateaux. Camping is not a safe option anywhere near town. Try asking at the Hotel Golf (e *golfhotel@golfhotel-ci.com*), east of the centre along the shores of the Ebrie Lagoon.

There is still a fair selection of hotels, from budget to top of the range, but secure parking is a big problem.

Grand Bassam Grand Bassam is south of Abidjan and frequented mostly by expatriates during the weekend, so visit during the week. Camping is not safe, as crime is rampant, so look around the hotels for a place to park. Try Taverne la Bassamoise or Hotel Boblin la Mar.

Yamoussoukro There is no camping in Yamoussoukro and you will have to ask one of the hotel managers if you can stay in their courtyard. Try the Hotel Sialou-Mo.

Korhogo There is no camping facility in Korhogo, but budget accommodation is available. It's just a matter of finding secure parking for your vehicle.

OTHER A photographic permit is not required. But be very careful until the political problems have calmed down. Bouaké is still probably best avoided, being at the centre of the rebel movement. Camping accommodation may be hard to find.

FURTHER INFORMATION
West Africa, Lonely Planet

CAPITAL Nairobi

LANGUAGE AND TELEPHONE English and Swahili are the official languages. International telephone code +254.

CURRENCY AND RATE Kenyan shilling (KES); US$1 = KES61.20

RED TAPE You may need to take an armed officer, or join the convoy if it's reinstated, from Isiolo to Moyale to get to Ethiopia or vice versa. See pages VIII–IX and 44, for further details. You may need a foreign road permit if you stay more than a week: US$30 for one month and US$100 for three months.

Visas Visas are required by most visitors except nationals of some Commonwealth countries. Passport holders of Australia, New Zealand, Sri Lanka and the UK *do* need visas. Other nationalities should check, as recent changes have been made. Getting a Kenyan visa in advance in Tanzania, Uganda or Ethiopia is simple and hassle-free. Costs vary from US$55–70+. It may still be possible to get visas at the border if coming from Tanzania or Uganda, but check beforehand.

Non-African consulate

E French Consulate (issues visas for most French-speaking African countries) Barclays Plaza, Loita St, Nairobi; ✆ 339978

African embassies

E Democratic Republic of the Congo Electricity Hse, Harambee Av, Nairobi; ✆ 229771

E Djibouti 2nd Floor, Comcraft Hse, Haile Selassie Av, Nairobi; ✆ 339633

E Egypt 24 Othaya Rd, off Gitanga Rd, Kileleshwa, PO Box: 30285, Nairobi; ✆ 3870298/3870278/3870360; f 3870383; e egypt@wananchi.com

E Eritrea 2nd Floor, New Rehema Hse, Westlands, Nairobi; ✆ 443164; f 443165

E Ethiopia State Hse Av, PO Box: 45198, Nairobi; ✆ 273 2050–52; f 273 2054–3; e ethioemb@kenyaweb.com

E Malawi Westlands, off Waiyaki Way, PO Box 30453, Nairobi; ✆ 440569; f 440568

E Mozambique Bruce Hse, 3rd Floor, Standard St, Nairobi; ✆ 221979/214191; mozambique@africaonline.co.ke

E Nigeria PO Box 30516, Nairobi; ✆ 228321/228322

E Rwanda Kilimani, Kahahwe Rd, Nairobi; ✆ 575977; f 575976

E South Africa, 17/18th Floor, Lonrohho Hse, Standard St, Nairobi; ✆ 215616/7 or 282710; f 223687; sahc@africaonline.co.ke

E Sudan Minet-ICDC Building, Mamlaka Rd, Nairobi; ✆ 720854; f 722253

E Tanzania Re-Insurance Plaza, Aga Khan Walk (moving from Continental Hse, Harambee Av), Nairobi; ✆ 331056; f 721874; e tanzania@users.africaonline.co.ke

E Uganda Uganda Hse, Baring Arcade, Kenyatta Av, Nairobi; ✆ 311814; f 311806; e ugahicom@todays.co.ke orugahicom@todaysonline.com; www.ugandahighcommission.co.ke

E Zambia Nyerere Av, Nairobi; ✆ 718494

E Zimbabwe Minet-ICDC Bldg, Mamlaka Rd, Nairobi; ✆ 721049/721071

DRIVING AND ROADS Drive on the left. Many of the roads in Kenya are excellent, but some are deteriorating fast. The roads get worse the further north you go. Around Mount Kenya some sections are quite rough, as is some of the coast road to Mombasa. Watch out for some bad driving locally.

Fuel costs Diesel: US$1.55; petrol: US$1.80 per litre.

CLIMATE Coastal areas are tropical and hot, but tempered by monsoon winds. The wettest months are April, May and November; the hottest are February and March; the coolest are June and July. The lowlands are hot and dry. Much of Kenya, however, stands at over 1,500m (4,500ft) and has a more temperate climate with four seasons. There is a warm and dry season from January to March; a rainy season from March to June; a cool, cloudy and dry season from June to October; and a rainy season from November to December.

HIGHLIGHTS Visit the famous national parks: Masai Mara, Amboseli, Tsavo and Nakuru, to mention but a few. Climb Mount Kenya and visit the different lakes: Naivasha, Bogaria, Baringo and, if safe, Lake Turkana. Along the coast are many good beaches and resorts from Mombasa to Lamu. Also watch out for the various colourful tribes: Samburu, Turkana, Rendille and Masai. Eating in Kenya is a highlight, too. There is great ice cream, a cheese factory in Eldoret and superb bacon and eggs in Nairobi.

WHERE TO STAY

Nairobi Most overlanders end up at either one of these camps. Upper Hill Campsite (✆ *675 0202;* e *upperhill_campsite@yahoo.co.uk; www.upperhillcampsite.com*) (GPS co-ordinates (Universal): S 1° 18.000 E 36° 48.719) is on Menengai Road, just off Hospital Road, which is within walking distance of the city centre; camping costs US$3 and double rooms were US$13. Others stay at Rangi's in Langata, which is a little way out of town; ask around. The bar is reported to be superb. There are plenty of cheap hotels near Tom Mboya Street, but no parking. As for eating, which most overlanders do all day long in Nairobi, the most famous restaurant is Carnivore, specialising in all types of game meat, on Langata Road. For morning coffee, the Thorn Tree Café at the New Stanley has been *the* place forever. Indaba Campsite is another option with a basic restaurant. It's small but has a workshop.

Eldoret There is a good campsite just outside Eldoret called the Naiberi River Campsite, with the most comfortable bar imaginable. Camping costs US$6–7.

Mount Elgon Camping is pleasant at the Delta Crescent Farm, 28km from Kitale near the park entrance. US$3 each.

Turbo On the way to Uganda is the Spring Park Hotel, a nice local camp and hotel, very cheap, safe and clean.

Kericho The main options here are the Kericho Tea Hotel with camping at US$3 each, or try the hotels. All are good value, including Kericho Garden Motel and Kericho Lodge.

Nakuru Look for Kembu Camping, 20km from town going towards Njoro and Molo. Camping US$4. Also here is Acacia Cottages, camping US$3 each. On the lake is Mbweha Camp, again for around US$3 per person.

Lake Naivasha The lake area makes a good break from the chaotic lifestyle in Nairobi. Try Fisherman's Camp, which has huge acacia trees, an incredible amount of birdlife, loads of water activities and a great bar. Camping costs about US$6. Also look for Top Camp, Crayfish Camp, Burch's Marina and Fish Eagle Inn.

Lake Baringo Try Robert's Camp on the lakeside; cost about US$5 each.

Lake Bogoria At the Lake Bogoria Hotel is posh camping at US$8 each.

Mount Kenya For all information on Mount Kenya, go to the Naro Moru River Lodge, which also offers camping at US$5 per person. It is about 1.5km off to the left on the main Nairobi to Nanyuki road. In Naro Moru town there is Mount Kenya Camping and Hostel, Blue Line Hostel and it's also OK to camp at the Mount Kenya Guides' place.

Nanyuki North of Nanyuki is Timau River Lodge, which has cottages and camping; cost US$5 each. Also look for the Nanyuki River Camel Camp.

Lodwar In town is Nawoitorong Guesthouse with cheap camping options. *En route* and north of the Marich Pass is Mtelo View Campsite, a nice retreat.

Maralal On the way to Lake Turkana, Maralal is high up in the hills and above the Lerochi Plateau. It is also famous for its camel derby, which takes place every October. The best place to stay is the Yare Safari Club and Campsite.

Up to Lake Turkana Bush sleeping is the best option, but check the latest security warnings. The road up to Lake Turkana crosses volcanic outcrops, which means there are lots of sharp stones that make it slow going. On Lake Turkana, in Loyangalani, there were a number of campsites: El Molo, Sunset Strip, Gametrackers and the Oasis Lodge.

Moyale You can camp outside the friendly customs office or stay on the Ethiopian side at the Bekele Mola Motel.

Marsabit The national park campsite is very expensive and run-down. The best place in town is the Jey Jey Motel, with cheap clean rooms, and safe parking. Double room US$6–8. It is just off the main road. They do a superb greasy egg and toast breakfast; yes it's sad isn't it, those little pleasures?

Isiolo There is a campsite on the main road about 10km south of town, Rangeland Camping.

Mombasa and the coastline The options are endless, but not in Mombasa town. Most people rave about Tiwi beach, south of Mombasa. Twiga Lodge is an old favourite. The only problem is finding safe parking facilities for your vehicle. There are various beach bungalows offering accommodation; prices range from US$3 to US$25 per person, depending on what you want. Diani beach has camping and a lodge.

Malindi Further north up the coast is Silversands Campsite. Also here is KW's Compound and Malindi Marine Park Campsite. Both from US$2 each.

Lamu As this is an island, vehicles have to be parked at Mokowe – check security here.

National parks Most of Kenya's national parks allow vehicles and have camping facilities. Be aware that the cost of taking a foreign-registered vehicle into most national parks is high. It can cost you over US$100 per day (US$30 per person park fee and US$30–40 per vehicle plus US$10–20 per person camping). Smartcard electronic ticketing is now used – usually on sale at the main gates, but allow time for the process. Another option is to organise a tour of the various national parks in Nairobi. Get some advice from Upper Hill Campsite regarding the best and most economical tours available.

OTHER Nairobi has one of the worst reputations regarding crime and petty theft. Watch your back and find out from the locals which areas are being targeted. Don't walk around at night.

FURTHER INFORMATION
Kenya: The Bradt Travel Guide, Claire Foottit
www.kenyaweb.com
www.kenyalogy.com
www.nairobi.com – news about Kenya
www.kenyalastminute.com

LESOTHO

CAPITAL Maseru

LANGUAGE AND TELEPHONE English and Sotho are the official languages. International telephone code +266.

CURRENCY AND RATE The maloti (LSL) is the local currency, but South African rand are universally accepted. The current rate is US$1 = LSL7.79

RED TAPE None of any significance, except visas. Lesotho is within the South African customs area.

Visas Visas are not required by citizens of the Commonwealth and South Africa. Other visitors should check.

African embassies
❸ South Africa Bank of Lesotho Towers, Kingsway;
📞 2231 5758; e sahcmas@leo.co.ls

DRIVING AND ROADS Drive on the left. Many of the roads in western Lesotho are good and tarred, if a little narrow in places. The roads get worse the further you go from Maseru into the eastern mountain regions. Be warned, crossing the Sani Pass is only possible in summer and could be nerve-racking for some.

Fuel costs Diesel: US$1.20; petrol: US$1.40 per litre.

CLIMATE Lesotho has a varied climate affected by a wide range of altitudes. The dry season is June to August, with a wet season from October to April.

HIGHLIGHTS Lesotho is a mountainous enclave within South Africa. It shares the delights of the Drakensberg range, but is much more isolated. Hiking and horseriding are the main activities. Sani Pass is literally a high point. The culture is very strongly retained.

WHERE TO STAY

Maseru The luxury Hotel Lesotho Sun on the hill above town may allow parking/camping. If not, try Lancer's Inn off Kingsway; they have some rondavels.

Teyateyaneng Try the Pitseng Guesthouse. Camping costs US$9 for car plus two people. Also nearby is Blue Mountain Resort, a more upmarket establishment.

Malealea South of Maseru with hiking options, camping is possible at the Malealea Lodge.

Sani Pass Camping at the Sani Top Chalet complex.

FURTHER INFORMATION

East and Southern Africa: The Backpacker's Manual, Philip Briggs (Bradt Travel Guides)

LIBERIA

☞ *MILD WARNING!* Overland travel to the country is now possible. The main roads between Monrovia, Gbarnga and Ganta are secure at the time of publication. Due to the ongoing rebuilding of the country's infrastructure, it would be wise to check how things are, particularly if and when the UN troops leave.

CAPITAL Monrovia

LANGUAGE AND TELEPHONE English is the official language. International telephone code +231.

CURRENCY AND RATE Liberian dollar (LRD); US$1 = LRD62.50. US dollars are freely interchangeable in shops, hotels, fuel stations, etc.

RED TAPE There are lots of roadblocks where friendly UN troops will smile and wave you on. The local police are also very friendly. Occasionally we had to fill in paperwork or hand over copies of passports, but everything was good natured. There is no longer any need to report to immigration in Monrovia.

Visas Visas are required for all and cost US$70–100. Vaccination certificates are obligatory. Visas are not issued at the border.

African embassies

🄴 **Ghana** 15th St, Sinkor, Monrovia; ☎ 223461 or 06 518 269
🄴 **Guinea** Tubman Bd, Monrovia
🄴 **Ivory Coast** 8th St, Sinkor, Monrovia; ☎ 227436

🄴 **Nigeria** Tubman Bd, Monrovia; ☎ 226550
🄴 **Sierra Leone** 15th St, Sinkor, Monrovia; ☎ 226250/06 515 061

DRIVING AND ROADS The road from Bo Waterside, the border with Sierra Leone, is mostly very good to Monrovia. Heading upcountry, the road is generally in good shape to Gbarnga, but after to Ganta there are some poor sections. There are always isolated pot-holes along the whole stretch, so don't take your eyes off the road ahead. Elsewhere little road construction is being undertaken. Roads are not busy outside of Monrovia, which has jams at rush hour.

Fuel costs Diesel: US$0.95; petrol: US$1.00 per litre (note prices at pumps are quoted in gallons at US$3.55 or US$3.45).

CLIMATE Liberia has a fairly wet climate, with the drier season from November to April.

HIGHLIGHTS Liberia is a revelation. It has most of the last remaining concentration of wet tropical rainforest in west Africa. Monrovia is being slowly reconstructed and the beaches nearby are pleasant – Silver Beach, St Martin's and, yes, 'Thinkers' beach! Firestone rubber plantations (some now up and running) here were the largest in the world before the troubles. The people are some of the friendliest in west Africa.

WHERE TO STAY

Monrovia With an influx of UN, NGO and development people, hotel prices are very high. At present camping is not a feasible option, but parking in the grounds of a benevolent hotel could be the only other choice. We splashed out on an air-conditioned room at My Hotel in the centre mainly because it had a well-guarded parking area and a massive generator. There is nowhere to camp at the popular Mamba Point. A 'cheaper' possibility in central Monrovia is the Metropolis Hotel (rooms around US$50–80 but no parking). African Palace Hotel is around US$80 but no parking. Kamoma Hotel on the main road seven miles east of Monrovia is recommended for cheaper rooms and maybe camping. Even further out is the Red Light area (that's the name, really!) with cheaper local places, but safe parking is an issue.

Bo Waterside There is no town here, just the border village, with no accommodation. We camped at the police station 10–15 minutes east of the border and gave a donation freely so the boys (and girls) could pay for fuel for the generator in order to watch the football.

Robertsport A new eco-resort is under development, so ask locally if it has opened. The road is west of Monrovia and on the south side coming from the Bo Waterside border.

Salala About 110km from Monrovia on the Gbarnga road is the small settlement of Salala. The Oasis Lodge is a secure and friendly place with camping for US$25 in the grounds or a room from US$35.

Totota About 90 miles from Monrovia is the amazing CooCoo Nest at Tubman Farms, which has rooms, a cafe and a deserted zoo. It's now run by a Lebanese man and is a useful halfway-house stop.

En route The Sata Guesthouse is signposted along the road before Gbarnga.

Gbarnga We did not see any suitable place, as it's off the main road, but there should be something if you're stuck, because the town is developing and there are plenty of UN people about.

Ganta The town is more a large village, but along the main road north before the end of it is the Hotel Alvinos on the 'Guinea road' where you need to turn off for Nzérékoré in Guinea.

OTHER Car parts are to be found in the Randall Street area of Monrovia and on the road from Bo Waterside on the way into town. Toyota is well represented here, but there are hundreds of secondhand-parts shops too. In the same area is Prestige Motors, the Land Rover dealer, but they don't hold much stock. The area around the US Embassy in Monrovia is blocked off.

FURTHER INFORMATION
www.liberian-conection.com

LIBYA

Note: Libya has become established as a tourist destination. Apart from idiosyncrasies, it is generally very safe. Driving in the far south, close to the border areas of Algeria, Niger and Chad, may present some security issues.

CAPITAL Tripoli

LANGUAGE AND TELEPHONE Arabic is the official language. International telephone code +218.

CURRENCY AND RATE Libyan dinar (LYD); US$1 = LYD1.188

RED TAPE If all your paperwork is in order, you should not experience any major hassles. Currently tourists in their own vehicles need to travel with a guide or with a guide in his own vehicle. This could change in future, so check before travelling.

Visas Visas are required for all. Nationals of Israel or those with an Israeli stamp in their passport will not be admitted. All visitors also need permission from the Libyan People's Bureau, ie: the embassy, which means that a tourist visa needs to be sponsored by a Libyan tour company. You will also need to have all the details of your passport translated into Arabic. Visas now cost US$190 and are valid for one month. You will be required to register within 48 hours at the first police station you come across in Libya. Regulations change constantly, so check before travel.

African embassies
🅔 **Egypt** Sharia al Fateh, Tripoli; ✆ 21 660 5500
🅔 **Nigeria** P.O. Box 4417, Tripoli; ✆ 21 214 3036
🅔 **Sudan** 68 Mohamed Ali Mosadak St, Tripoli; ✆ 21 477 8052; f 21 477 4781; e sudtripoli@hotmail.com

🅔 **Tunisia** Sharia al Jabah, Bin' Ashur, Tripoli; ✆ 21 333 1051

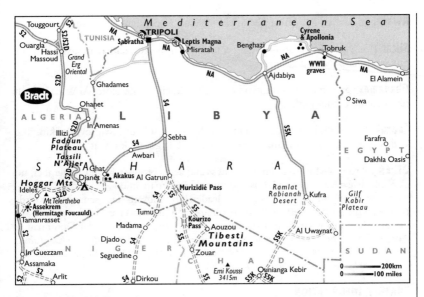

DRIVING AND ROADS Drive on the right. The roads on major routes are good and the rest are desert pistes and tracks. Main roads are quite busy along the northern coast near Tripoli; driving standards are rather erratic, to be kind!

Fuel costs Diesel: US$0.11; petrol: US$0.10 per litre. Libya has the cheapest fuel available in Africa. Sometimes travellers who only top up their tanks are not charged for the fuel.

CLIMATE The best time to visit is during the northern spring and autumn months from October to early March, although you might come across the *ghibli,* which is a hot, dry and sand-laden wind that can raise the temperatures to 40°C or more.

HIGHLIGHTS Tripoli has a fascinating old city medina. The magnificent Roman ruins of Leptis Magna and Sabratha should not be missed, plus the ancient Greek cities of Cyrene and Apollonia. In the west are the old granaries at Nalut and the old mud city of Ghadames. The war graves at Tobruk are sobering. In the Sahara are the 'Dune Lakes' close to Awbari and the Akakus Mountains near Ghat. Visit the prehistoric rock art and see the superb desert scenery, including some rock arches. You can't miss the billboards with the great leader's face adorned with blue sunglasses.

WHERE TO STAY Wild camping is the most pleasant option throughout Libya, and away from settlements this is not a problem. Always carry adequate fuel and water when visiting the Sahara. Even in the larger towns it's best to park up for the day, do what needs to be done, and leave in the early afternoon to find a camping spot. There are hotels in most major cities, but prices are high and you might be charged in foreign currency.

Tripoli Rather difficult and expensive, so stay at Sabratha or camp on the beach at Zuara near the Tunisian border.

Leptis Magna There is a place to camp just outside the entry gate to the ruins. Across the road to the west is a hotel with its name in Arabic. It also allows camping.

Awbari In Awbari the Africa Camp is a pleasant place, right below the dunes.

Siltar It is possible to camp in the grounds with the Roman statues, which your guide will know about.

Ghadames On the road into town before the old city is the Hotel Al Waha, which has a secure compound.

Tobruk There is a hotel with parking on the south side of town, overlooking the wide open area before the main business area. The guides know it.

OTHER Libya is a Muslim country, so dress and act appropriately, and remember, no alcohol whatsoever is allowed. It is also advisable not to mention any personal political views or criticism of the country's leadership. Libyans are sensitive towards photography, so be careful what you photograph and never ever take pictures of women. For an invitation from a Libyan travel agent, contact Abdel Doumnaji at Africa Tours in Sebha (*Omar Al Mokhtar St, PO Box 396, Sebha, Libya;* ➘+ *218 71 637 600;* f *+218 71 631 084/+218 71 625 594;* m *+218 92 513 23 04;* e *africatours.ly@hotmail.com; www.africatours.ly*).

FURTHER INFORMATION
Africa on a Shoestring, Lonely Planet
www.libya.com

MALAWI

CAPITAL Lilongwe

LANGUAGE AND TELEPHONE English and Chichewa are the official languages. International telephone code +265.

CURRENCY AND RATE Malawi kwacha (MWK); US$1 = MWK145

RED TAPE None of any significance. There are occasional roadblocks, which just check vehicle particulars and your travel itinerary.

Visas Visas are not required for most nationalities. A visitor's stamp is issued at the border.

African embassies
ⓔ Mozambique 2nd Floor, Commercial Bank Bldg, City Centre, Lilongwe; ➘ 774 100/784 100; f 771 342
ⓔ South Africa Kangombe Bldg, Lilongwe; ➘ 773 722/783 722
ⓔ Zambia Plot 40/2 Capital Hill, Lilongwe; ➘ 731 911/772 590
ⓔ Zimbabwe 7th Floor, Gemini Hse, Independence Dr, Lilongwe; ➘ 774 997/784 988

DRIVING AND ROADS Drive on the left. Roads throughout Malawi are generally in good condition, but there is surprisingly little traffic, especially in the north of the country.

Fuel costs Diesel: US$1.30; petrol: US$1.60 per litre.

CLIMATE The climate in Malawi is generally very pleasant. The rainy season is from November to March, when it can be quite grey and overcast some days.

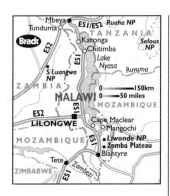

HIGHLIGHTS The main highlight is of course the long lake, with quite a few pleasant beaches, specifically Chitimba, Nkhata Bay, Chintheche, Mangochi and Senga Bay. However, there is a very high risk of contracting bilharzia if you go swimming in its attractive waters. Close to the lake is the Nyika plateau and colonial Livingstonia. Further south are the Zomba Plateau, Liwonde National Park with an array of wildlife, and Mount Mulanje.

WHERE TO STAY

Lilongwe The Mabuya Camp (formerly Kiboko Camp) is a good place to meet other travellers and get a feel for what to see in Malawi, with suggested campsites along the way. The cost is around US$5 each. Other places are Land and Lake Safaris, Annie's Coffee Pot and James' Joint.

Karonga On the beachfront is the large compound, with some shade, of the Mafwa Lakeshore Lodge and Campsite. Camping costs US$5.

Chitimba There are various places: Chitimba Campsite, Mdokera beach and Namiashi Resort, Florence Resthouse with camping, Mayuni Safari Camp, Sangilo Lodge and camp, and Ngara Resort, also with camping.

Nyika Park There is a camping area (US$6 each) near the expensive Chelinda Camp chalet complex.

Livingstonia At the time of our visit, during the rainy season, the road up from Chitimba was unusable. It is apparently better to get there from Rumphi from the south. The Lukwe Permaculture camp, an eco-friendly campsite, is reported to be a good place to stay.

Nkhata Bay Try The Big Blue for camping, also Butterfly Lodge and Njaya Lodge and camp. The Mayoka Village is a picturesque place with pleasant rooms.

Kasungu National Park Stay at Lifupa Lodge with camping for US$5 each.

Nkhotakota In town is Special Pick and Pay Resthouse with camping; south of town are Sani Beach Resort and Nkhotakota Safari Lodge, both with camping. In the nearby wildlife reserve are Bua River Camp and Chipata Camp, and further south is Ngala Beach Lodge.

Chintheche We stayed at Kande beach, which is lively in season. Access is down a very narrow sandy track that floods after rain, so beware. Camping costs US$8 for two. Others with camping include Chintheche Inn, Nkhwazi Lodge, Kaniya Cottage and Flame Tree Lodge, Sambani Lodge and London Lodge. South are two excellent spots at Nkhawazi Lodge and Makuzi beach.

Mzuzu Suggested is Mzoozoozoo, a hostel with camping. In nearby Nyika National Park camping is available at the Chelinda Campsite.

Salima Options here are Steps Campsite and Hippo Hide Resthouse.

Senga Bay Rather hard to find, but just before 'town', is Cool Runnings. It's signposted by a smiley-face logo in places and is a shady, grassy campsite with cottages if you prefer, and lakeside restaurant. There are several other places with camping, so take your pick from Wheelhouse Marina, Carolina Resort, Baobab, Sangalani and Tom's Bar.

Mangochi North of Mangochi are a number of places to stay. They include Nkopola Lodge and Palm Beach Resort.

Cape Maclear There is plenty of accommodation along the beachfront of Cape Maclear. Look for Emanuel's, Fat Monkey, Gaia Lodge or Steven's Place. For a quieter alternative, particularly if you are bringing a vehicle, try the Golden Sands Rest Camp. Camping costs US$4 per person. You should expect to party at Cape Maclear. Bilharzia and malaria are both rampant in this area, so be very, very wary of swimming and cover up fast afterwards!

Blantyre Though sometimes full, Doogle's on Mulomba Place is a great place with a good atmosphere, bar, food and excellent internet service. Camping costs US$4 per person. The area outside is not safe at night, but there's no need to leave the premises. Otherwise try at the Limbe Country Club further out to the east.

Liwonde/Liwonde National Park Near town is Shire Camp. Within the park, the best place to stay is Chinguni Hills Campsite for US$5 each. Otherwise there is the popular Mvu Lodge and Camp which has a restaurant and open-plan bar overlooking the river. Camping will cost US$10 for two and they can also arrange boat rides on the river.

Zomba Plateau The Zomba Plateau is in the highlands and is a little cooler, with great hiking opportunities. You will need to find secure parking if hiking up to the plateau. The Chitinji campsite on the top of the plateau is run by the local community and will cost you next to nothing. Also try the Forest Campsite or Zomba Forest Lodge on the lower slopes, accessed by a dirt road.

Mount Mulanje Camping is about US$5 per person at the Mulanje Golf Club and at the Likhubula Forest Lodge.

OTHER In the past, under the Hastings Banda regime, if you were a man with long hair it was sheared off at the border there and then. Fortunately, since then Malawi has calmed down considerably and is today a relaxed country in which to travel. Do not get caught with the local grass, known as 'Malawi Gold'. The police are clamping down on users and dealers. In some campsites you will find notes on signboards saying 'Hi, I am from England and am currently in jail for carrying drugs. I really just need somebody to talk to.' You have been warned.

And, we repeat, there is a **high risk of bilharzia** in the beautiful blue waters of the lake.

FURTHER INFORMATION
Malawi: The Bradt Travel Guide, Philip Briggs
www.malawi.com

MALI

CAPITAL Bamako

LANGUAGE AND TELEPHONE French is the official language. International telephone code +223.

CURRENCY AND RATE West African franc (CFA); US$1 = CFA415

RED TAPE Tourism has become quite important to the economy in Mali and, as a result, travel is much easier.

Visas Visas are required for all. A one-month visitor's visa can cost US$50–70, depending on where you apply for it. There is no Mali embassy in Britain. Registering with the police does not seem to be necessary any more, but check with other travellers what the current status is. Visas were being issued at the border in 2008, but you'd better check beforehand somewhere in case. Vaccination certificates are obligatory.

African embassies

E Algeria Bamako; ☎ 220 5176

E Burkina Faso Rue 224, off Route de Koulikoro or Route de Guinea, Bamako; ☎ 221 3171; f 221 9266; e ambfaso@datatech.toolnet.org

E Ghana Off Route de Hamdalaye, Bamako; ☎ 229 6083; f 229 6084

E Guinea Immeuble Saibou Maiga, Quartier de Fleuve, Bamako; ☎ 222 2975/8006

E Ivory Coast Lumumba Sq, Bamako; ☎ 221 2289; f 222 1376

E Mauritania Rue 218, off Route de Koulikoro, Bamako; ☎ 221 4815

E Nigeria BP 57, Bamako; ☎ 277 2512

E Niger Was at Av Mamadou Konate, Bamako; ☎ 601 9239

E Senegal 341 Rue 287, north of Route de Koulikoro, Bamako; ☎ 221 8274; f 224 6452

DRIVING AND ROADS Drive on the right. The main road between Bamako and Gao through Mopti is mostly good with a few variable sections. The exciting but very corrugated desert piste from Douentza to Timbuktu will shake your bones to bits! The possibly unsafe northern track to Gao is lonely and very sandy. The roads into Senegal and Mauritania are now finished and sealed. The road south to Kankan in Guinea is almost done.

Fuel costs Diesel: US$1.30; petrol: US$1.40 per litre. Carry extra supplies on desert routes including to Timbuktu (fuel can normally be obtained in Douentza and Timbuktu itself), in case of shortages.

CLIMATE Mali spans the desert and Sahel areas, creating differences across the country. The three main seasons are the rainy season June to September/October; cool dry season October/November to February; hot dry season March to June. The *harmattan*, sand-laden winds, blow from January through March.

HIGHLIGHTS Mali is one of the highlights in west Africa. It has everything that encapsulates Africa: colourful markets and people, deserts, mud architecture, river life and dramatic escarpments. Bamako has great bustling markets. Ségou, Djenné and Mopti have traditional mud-brick architecture and mosques, the one at Djenné particularly spectacular. The Bandiagara Escarpment in the Dogon country is a cultural feast, with some trekking. Gao and Timbuktu, on the edge of the

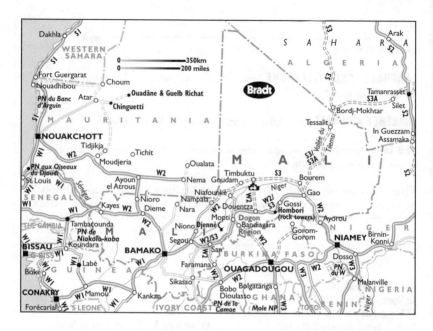

Sahara, are famous for their history. Getting to Timbuktu and, unlike the early explorers, getting back, is still a memorable journey even today.

WHERE TO STAY

Bamako It is possible to camp at the Hotel Djamilla (US$12 for two) south of the river not far from the old bridge (to the south) in their pleasant garden, but it's often noisy with 'car sellers.' Another place is the Hotel Djoliba, where there is space for overland trucks. It's south of the old bridge, on the same side as the Djamilla. Much further out (18km) but very pleasant is the Campement Kangaba (US$14 for two). This is down a dirt track on the north of the Ségou road where the dual carriageway ends, not far before a check-post; it is signposted. It might be too quiet for some, but the French food and bar are good.

Also south of the river on the way to Ségou with a nice shady garden is Hotel Les Colibris: US$45 or more in a bungalow.

Look out also for Joan and André Charette at Le Cactus (bar, restaurant, hotel, camping) (*PO Box 2619, Bamako;* ☎ *(223) 279 0709;* 📱 *(223) 613 6455;* e *acharmaca@ yahoo.com*). They are at GPS N12°32.18 W8°02.76: 12km from the new bridge (on the right bank).

If you're coming from Kankan late in the day and don't want to face the chaos in Bamako, there is a campement in the village of Sibi below some amazingly beautiful rocky outcrops.

Bougouni On the southwest side of town is Hotel Piedmont. Head south along a good tar road from the roundabout with a fuel station; this is out of the town centre on the Bamako road. Rooms and sloping camping space here.

Selingue Look for Hotel Woloni.

Ségou The Hotel l'Auberge, a popular watering hole in Ségou, has parking in its annexe. They also run the Hotel de l'Independence just out of town on the road to

Mopti, which has secure parking, with camping possible (US$12 for two) and rooms from US$25.

Bla A small OK dirt road leads to a campement close to the Bani River.

San Camping is allowed at the Hotel/Campement Teriya for US$6 each. Also before town from Ségou is the new Hotel Santoro, which has a pool and a little space to camp if you don't want a room.

Djenné The only place to stay is Le Campement near the grand mosque (which is a must-see). Your vehicle is safe in the car park and sleeping on the roof costs US$6 per person. Also, you can camp at Chez Baba near the main market, US$6, and on the roof of Hotel Faguibine out of town.

Mopti Other than being an impressive town, Mopti is the gateway to the Dogon country. The old favourite in town, the Campement Hotel du Mopti, is still there, but it's now smack in the middle of a noisy intersection area. It's the only real camping option if you want to be in town, though. There is also the Hotel Ya Pas de Probleme, but the on-street parking is not at all good, so it's best to stay out at Sevaré (see below). Hotel Kanaga is the plush super deluxe spot in town, with parking.

Sevaré Without doubt the best place for overlanders is the friendly Hotel Via Via, with camping in a pleasant courtyard, rooms and a great restaurant. You can just about camp at Mac's Refuge for around US$9 each, but you are not allowed to cook. The included breakfast yoghurt is excellent, though.

Dogon country
Bandiagara Before town is the Auberge Toguna with camping from US$4. Hotel Le Village also has space for camping.

Sangha Campement Hotel Sangha, also known as La Guina, is a relaxing place with a garden. The Gite de la Femme Dogon is another nice spot.

Bankass Look for the Hotel Les Arbres with camping in the garden, as well as the Campement Hogon.

Koro A recent addition here is the base camp set up by Aventure Dogon (e *contact@afrikhorizons.com; www.aventure-dogon.com*). You can also contact Olivier on (French mobile) **m** +33 6 80 02 14 57.

Dogon trekking For your travels in Dogon country, all fees, including accommodation, should be arranged with your guide beforehand. Meals are not included, but costs are minimal at each of the villages you stop in. Accommodation is a mattress on the roof, a wonderful experience as you hear the village sounds, or in village campements (US$3 plus tax US$2). Take some time in choosing your guide and in negotiating the fees. You will initially be hassled, but once a guide has been chosen, the rest should disappear. There is a guides association in Bandiagara for a list of qualified guides but it's hard to find. Guide fees from US$20 plus negotiable daily costs. For porters allow US$6–7 per day.

Douentza Offering fixed nomad tents and camping (US$10), Chez Jerome is the most efficient place at present, with good open-air showers. Across the road, the Auberge Gourma has camping for US$6 per person. Campement Hogon is another possibility. The Hotel Falaise west of town has a great garden and is developing the space in front for campers.

Hombori Look out for the Campement Tondako, with a pleasant compound, thatched huts and a restaurant serving excellent local food (camping US$6 for two). The views are great. Also here are Campement Mangou Bagni and Campement Kaga Tondo/Chez Lelele, who can organise elephant-tracking safaris. Out of town 13km, below the fantastic Hand of Fatima outcrop, is the rustic Campement Manyi.

Gossi Here is the basic Gossi Campement for those hoping to locate the elephants of the Gourma area.

Gao Try Sahara Passion (e *spassion@malinet.ml*). Camping Euro is the latest addition. Camping Bangu, Campement Yarg and Campement Tila Fanso are other alternatives.

Bambara Maounde On the way to Timbuktu, there is a rustic campement here if you need it.

Timbuktu The wonderfully renovated traditional building housing the Auberge Le Caravanserail has a sandy yard for campers for US$12 for two. Suitable for all budgets and with safe vehicle parking, it also has beautiful rooms and a superb restaurant. It's on the corner of rues 164/139, west of the road into town from the Niger ferry, a couple of sandy streets over and about 0.5km south of the post office. If it's full you will probably have to try the Hotel Bouctou for camping and a secure parking area. The hard-to-find Sahara Passion is hiding somewhere in the back streets in the north of town. On the south side of the Niger River, about 35km south in Tiboraghene, is Campement Ténéré, for those stuck here after ferry hours. If you are camping in the bush, be sure to keep some distance from settlements, or the police may disturb you. Other more upmarket hotels in Timbuktu are Hotel La Maison, Hotel Colombe and Hotel du Desert near the Auberge Le Caravanserail.

Niono du Sahel For those coming from or going to Mauritania, this is the first or last chance for a beer. In town is a scruffy car yard on the south side, with even scruffier rooms. There is also a dubious hotel in the main street. Much better, and well away from the centre, 2km west along the dusty sandy little road beside the hotel and across a riverbed, is the Centre de Djamana complex and radio station, transmitting live. Parking is outside in the street, but it seems safe enough. Locals come here to sit on the sand and watch television.

OTHER Mali is a great place for overlanding. Sadly, there have been incursions by armed rebels in northern Mali, particularly in the Adra des Iforhas region around Kidal. Other northern border areas may also be insecure, so find out from other travellers and locals what the latest status is. Bamako is also a very large place these days, with the usual petty crime, vendors, cars, people and animals using every part of the road and pavement. Ideally it's best to walk everywhere rather than drive, but distances are great. Don't expect to escape the interest of tourist guides, touts and onlookers these days. In town you should be fairly safe parking outside the Burkina Faso Embassy north of the new bridge. If you need parts for your Land Rover, Prestige Motors is south of the river; it is partly signposted but you may have to ask the way.

FURTHER INFORMATION
Mali: The Bradt Travel Guide, Ross Velton
www.mali.com is now www.afribone.com

Toguna Adventure in Bamako (contact Karen) (✆ *223 229 5366/69;* m *621 5079;* e *togunaadventure@afribonemali.net; www.geocities.com/toguna_adventure_tours*)

MAURITANIA

CAPITAL Nouakchott

LANGUAGE AND TELEPHONE Arabic is the official language. International telephone code +222.

CURRENCY AND RATE Ouguiya (MRO); US$1 = MRO256.41

RED TAPE You will have to buy insurance at the border, even if you have a valid insurance for west Africa. Customs will charge €10 for 'tax', so have the right notes. Some of the desert settlements impose a 'right of passage tax' on visitors. Alcohol is not permitted except at expensive European restaurants in Nouakchott.

Visas Visas are required for all except Western nationals. On application you may need to show your vaccination certificate and get a letter of introduction from your embassy. Three-month visas cost US$80. Visas were not issued at the border in spring 2008, though reportedly you can now get a three-day transit visa at the border. However, we do not recommend this, as it is a long way back to Rabat or Bamako if the border officials change their policies. There are embassies in Rabat (see under *Morocco*; €20 for a single-entry visa) and in Bamako, where it's currently a same-day service and no air tickets are required anymore.

African embassies

🇪 **Egypt** Rue de l'Ambassade de Sénégal, Nouakchott; ✆ 529 2192
🇪 **Mali** North of Av Palais des Congres, BP 5371 Nouakchott; ✆ 525 2078/525 4078
🇪 **Morocco** Av du Général de Gaulle, Nouakchott; ✆ 525 1411
🇪 **Senegal** Rue de l'Ambassade de Sénégal, Nouakchott; ✆ 525 7290

DRIVING AND ROADS Drive on the right. Roads are generally in good condition on all major routes. Watch out for sand drifts over the roads. Around Atar some tracks are very rocky. The Saharan pistes are very remote between Oualata and Tichit, Chinguetti and Tidjikja, so taking a guide is a good plan. Do not drive alone in these areas.

Fuel costs Diesel: US$1.10; petrol: US$1.30 per litre.

CLIMATE Most of the country has a true desert climate, very dry and extremely hot throughout the year. The far south has occasional rains.

HIGHLIGHTS Most travellers cross through Mauritania from Mali to Morocco or vice versa. However, it is worth visiting the Adrar region around Atar, with its rocky plateaux and the Terjit oasis. The Chinguetti and Ouadâne oases are beautiful and surreal, being partially abandoned. Further south, the old oasis towns of Tidjikja, Rachid and Tichit are remote and see few visitors. Oualata, with its intriguing houses, is another exciting sight near the Mali border, but check the security situation before you go. The Parc National du Banc d'Arguin has spectacular birdlife. The best time to visit the park is during the nesting period from April to July and October to January. The park is quite hard to get to, but information can be obtained from the park's head office in Nouadhibou. You will need to take a guide.

WHERE TO STAY

Nouakchott Convenient and pleasant is La Nouvelle Auberge (US$12 for two) west of the main street near a fuel station and roundabout. Camping is also possible at the Auberge Menata (e *auberge.menata@voila.fr*), which is in a quiet but central street and has parking space. Ask for Olivia. Also popular is the Auberge du

Sahara (*www.auberge-sahara.com*) east of the Stade Olympique on the road north to Nouadhibou. Auberge Awkar is another suitable place on offer nearby. All these places also have rooms.

Nouadhibou Look for Camping Abba, well south past the main area of town. This is one of the best choices here. Prices from US$6 each. For a treat at a colonial-style retreat, why not try Hotel El Jazira?

Gare du Nord At 240km between Nouadhibou and Nouakchott is a fuel station/tyre repair man/restaurant/shop/mosque, with camping permitted. This is the only proper building on this road. There is also Auberge Michelin a hundred miles south of Nouadhibou, just a collection of shacks.

Atar Look out for the Camping Bab Sahara, otherwise try the Toile Maure Campement, 2km or so out of town.

Chinguetti The Auberge la Rose des Sables is a pleasant spot and has been going for years. Newer places are Auberge des Caravanes and Le Maure Bleu (*www.maurebleu.com*).

Terjit Try the Auberge Oasis or Auberge des Caravannes.

Tidjikja Apart from the desert there are two relatively expensive hotels at US$30 or more, including Auberge des Caravanes.

Ayoun el Atrous There are said to be a couple of hotels, but we did not see any sign of them when we drove through. Since people had been kidnapped there within the not-too-distant past, we decided not to hang around and ask. Parking, it seemed, might be a problem.

Kiffa The Hotel El Emel has friendly camping in the pleasant courtyard for 3000MRO. It's just west of town on the road out, set back to the north. Rooms are available as well as meals, if booked earlier, and drinks.

Boutilimit The spacious, pleasant complex with bungalows under thatch on the east side of the main road northwards from the centre is called the Auberge Touristique.

For some of Mauritania, desert sleeping is the only option.

OTHER The new road from Guergarat, the Moroccan border, to Nouakchott is now open. If you take the piste from Nouadhibou to Choum and Atar beside the railway, keep on the south side of the tracks to avoid possible old landmines.

The officials on both sides of the border with Senegal at Rosso and to a degree at Diama are currently extorting high 'taxes' (€40–100 in all).

With the demise of the classic trans-Saharan routes through Algeria, groups were visiting the country in increasing numbers until the cancellation of the Paris–Dakar rally in January 2008. We await the next season to see how it goes.

The clean, Moroccan mechanic-staffed BMW/Land Rover dealer in the southwest quarter of Nouakchott is liable to overcharge. The crumby sandy workshops in the Ksar area are probably just as good if you are desperate. Toyota have a centre near Camping Abba in Nouadhibou.

FURTHER INFORMATION
West Africa, Rough Guides
www.mauritania.com is for sale

MOROCCO

CAPITAL Rabat

LANGUAGE AND TELEPHONE Arabic is the official language. International telephone code +212.

CURRENCY AND RATE Dirham (MAD); US$1 = MAD7.30

RED TAPE Officials were often extremely helpful and kind, but we can't guarantee that they are always like that. When crossing the Sahara it is advisable to have several copies of the *Personal details* document in *Appendix 2*, page 316, plus copies of your passport and driving licence, as these are required at roadblocks in Morocco and Western Sahara. Alternatively, take a copy of your passport photo page, write all the relevant information on it, then make a multitude of copies of this. Be sure to **STOP** at all police road check-posts at the 'Halte Gendamerie' signs, or they may fine you. **Don't move on** until they wave at you to do so.

Visas Most visitors to Morocco do not require visas and can remain in Morocco for 90 days on entry. There are some exceptions to this rule (Israel, South Africa and others), so check before travelling.

African embassies
🅔 **Algeria** 46 Bd Tariq ibn Zayid, Rabat; ☎ 037 76 54 74
🅔 **Ivory Coast** 21 Rue de Tedders, Rabat; ☎ 037 76 31 51; f 037 76 27 92
🅔 **Mali** 58 Cite Olm Ext-Streissi 11, Rabat; ☎ 037 75 91 25

🅔 **Mauritania** 6 Rue Thami Lamdawar, Souissi II Villa, Rabat; ☎ 037 65 66 78; f 037 65 66 80
🅔 **Senegal** 17 Rue Qadi Amadi, Rabat; ☎ 037 75 41 38
🅔 **Tunisia** 6 Av de Fès, Rabat; ☎ 037 73 05 76

DRIVING AND ROADS Drive on the right. Roads are generally in good condition on all major routes, apart from the more remote desert tracks.

Fuel costs Diesel: US$1.15; petrol: US$1.30 per litre. In Tantan and further south the fuel is almost half price.

CLIMATE Morocco has a variety of climates: Mediterranean in the north, Atlantic in the west, continental in the interior and desert in the south. The Atlas Mountains can get very cold for much of the year outside the summer months. Rain is likely sometimes in winter and snow can be heavy in the mountains.

HIGHLIGHTS The Atlas Mountains are famous for their Berber villages and stunning landscape, including the Todra Gorge. Then there are the historical towns of Tangier, Fès, Meknès, Chefchaouen and Marrakech. The famous Djemaa el-Fna, a huge fair in the square of the old city of Marrakech, comes to life in the early afternoon. Between Ouarzazate and Zagora is the road of the kasbahs, with fortified mud citadels. Check out the massive citadel of Ait Benhaddou. The fringes of the Sahara in the south offer good, if limited off-road opportunities. The coastline includes the cities of Casablanca, with some Art Deco buildings, and Rabat, famous for its magnificent architecture and lack of tourists. Essaouira and Taroudannt are two other places of interest.

WHERE TO STAY In Morocco it is sometimes more convenient to stay in towns than on the outskirts, where many campsites have retreated. There are hundreds of pensions available in all major towns; parking is the main snag, though, as there are not so many guarded places. A double will cost around US$20–30. Most serve breakfast. Another speciality of Morocco is the riad, a town house usually located within the old medinas. Rooms are invariably tastefully decorated around quadrangles and the owners are the congenial hosts. Again, parking is the main difficulty with these places, but some are close to secure parking compounds. Campsites are often reasonably convenient, though these days most of them have been invaded and taken over by white campervans escaping the winter cold in Europe.

Tangiers Look for Camping Miramonte in a pleasant green area about 3km west of town. There is a rumour, though, that it may be closed in winter.

Tetouan Head for the coast at Martil, where you will find the pleasant Camping Al Boustane just north along the coast from the centre (US$7 for two).

Chefchaouen Famous for its supply of hashish, this town in the Rif Mountains is a relaxing place. The town has a Hispanic look of whitewashed houses and tiled roofs. The only campsite is Camping Municipal about 3km from the centre: US$10 for two. There are many budget hotels here and most serve delicious green tea.

Ouazzane The Motel Rif Camping is on the east side of the main road near the town, 4km south.

Fès This is the oldest imperial city in Morocco. There are two options regarding camping – Camping Diamant Vert, which is about 8km out on the south side, with a limited bus service into town, and the more expensive, but only 4km out, Camping International.

Meknès Look for Camping Agdal just near the Ville Imperial. It's very convenient, quiet, secure and also full of campervans. Volubilis, the old Roman ruins, are close to Meknès.

Asilah Campervans (and any other riff-raff like Land Rovers!) are allowed to park outside the city walls at a designated spot. A fee of €2 is charged. The two

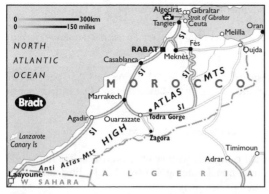

campsites appear to be closed in winter. There are no toilet or washing facilies here, but there is a restaurant nearby.

Rabat The Camping de la Plage at Salé beach is the only camping option in Rabat until it's built over (it's rumoured to be closed very soon). Camping costs US$4 per person. It's across the river from the old medina of Rabat. For a splurge, try the Riad Dar al Batoul (**e** *albatoul@menara.ma; www.riadbatoul.com*).

Casablanca The only camping option was way out of town on the road to El-Jadida. It was called Camping de l'Oasis. Driving around here is a nightmare and most people continue on the motorway to Marrakech.

Atlas Mountains On the way across the mountains is Telouet, just east of Tizi-N-Tichka, where you will find Camping Auberge Tasga. On the southern side is the Dadès Gorge at Boumalne, with the Auberge le Soleil Bleu. There are many nearby Berber villages and a walk here is worthwhile. Along the gorge look for Camping d'Ait Oudina, Camping La Gazelle du Dadès and Camping Berbere de la Montagne. Camping in the gorge can be dangerous after rain and is not secure.

Tinerhir For Todra Gorge there is a good campsite at Tinerhir called Camping Ourti. Also try staying at Hotel Tomboctou (*www.hoteltomboctou.com*).

Marrakech About 10km out of town off the main road to Casablanca is Camping Le Relais de Marrakech. It has clean facilities that work, large nomad tents available, tasty food and a swimming pool. It's off to the west of the main road; take the Safi road then turn off on a small road to the right. Close by, but right on the noisy main road, are Camping Ferdaous and Camping International. There are many riads in the old medina area and other cheaper hotels, but parking your precious vehicle in a car park some distance away will be your main concern.

Essaouira On the south side is Camping Sidi Magdoul (US$5 per car). Further out, look for Camping Le Calm.

Agadir The town's municipal camping site is popular with campervan retirees from Europe. It's OK, if a little crowded.

Ouarzazate On the road to Tinerhir is Campsite Municipal just outside town, east of the big kasbah but within walking distance. Camping costs US$7 per vehicle. There is also a place to camp 14km north of town near the Ait Benhaddou turnoff. Not cheap but with secure parking south of the Oued is the amazing Kasbah Dar Daif (**e** *contact@dardaif.ma; www.dardaif.ma*). They are also very helpful if you need any vehicle repairs.

Ait Benhaddou There are a couple of small sites for campers.

Taroudannt The Riad El Aissi (e *riad_elaissi@yahoo.com; www.riadelaissi.com*) is 3km from town.

Tata Try the municipal campsite in the centre, which is fine for US$6 per car. For a taste of luxury, take a room at the atmospheric Maison d'Hotes Dar Infiane, south of town in a palmerie.

Akka There is a camping place, 4X4 Campers, south of town on the west side.

Zagora It has several designated campsites with shady palm trees. These include Camping Auberge Prends ton Temps, Camping Auberge Les Jardins and several others.

Agdz A superbly atmospheric place, the Kasbah de la Palmeraie offers not only camping in the palmeraie but also rooms in the kasbah. It's north of the main plaza along a rough road.

Erfoud and Merzouga There is camping near the Oued Ziz, on the left before town if you're coming from Errachidia. For a big splurge book into Hotel Kasbah Tizimi (e *katizimi@iam.net.ma; www.kasbahtizimi.com*); good food; double room US$50. In Merzouga there are many places to stay, with a few offering tented places as well as rooms. Try Kasbah Mohayut for normal camping.

Tiznit The town has a camping site on the north side.

Guelmime There is one camping place before town on the right side coming from Agadir. It has a dubious reputation but looks OK.

Fort Bou Jerif (e *contact@boujerif.com* or *pierregerbens2@yahoo.com; www.fortboujerif.com*) Heading south to Laayoune, about 40km west of Guelmime (the last 9km is on a very rough dirt road), is this fabulous place; from US$6 with your own tent. Taste the camel tajine for a real treat!

For places further south, see the *Western Sahara* section, page 305.

OTHER To ease the hassle factor from the hashish touts, it is best to dress conservatively and respect the culture, although you will see tourists running around with next to nothing on. Hashish is illegal and the fines for being caught with it are heavy. Beware of car-based hash sellers who block roads.

FURTHER INFORMATION
Morocco, Barnaby Rogerson (Cadogan)
www.marocnet.com

MOZAMBIQUE

CAPITAL Maputo

LANGUAGE AND TELEPHONE Portuguese is the official language. International telephone code +258.

CURRENCY AND RATE New metacal (MZN); US$1 = MZN24.28. The plural of metacal is metacais.

RED TAPE There are always rumours regarding traffic officials and roadblocks in Mozambique. We had no problems but were frequently asked if we had two warning triangles, which we did. More likely now is that officials at roadblocks want to practise their language skills and have a quick English lesson – 'Hello, how are you? Where are you going?'

Visas Visas are required for all and cost US$80–100 except South Africans. You also have to pay a border tax of US$10. It is better to pay in South African rand if you are coming in that way, as it is cheaper than paying in metacais. Visas may be issued at the border, but don't bank on it.

Non-African embassy
❸ France (visas for French-speaking African countries) Av Julius Nyerere, Maputo; ❧ 21 491774

African embassies
❸ Congo CP 4743 Av Kenneth Kaunda 783, Maputo; ❧ 21 490 142
❸ Malawi 75 Av Kenneth Kaunda, Maputo; ❧ 21 492676
❸ Nigeria 821 Av Kenneth Kaunda, Maputo; ❧ 21 490991
❸ South Africa 745 Av Eduardo Mondlane, Maputo; ❧ 21 491614/490 059

❸ Swaziland 608 Av Kwame Nkrumah, Maputo; ❧ 21 492451
❸ Tanzania Ujamaa Hse, 852 Av Martires de Machava, Maputo; ❧ 21 490110;
e safina@zebra.uem.mz
❸ Zambia 1286 Av Kenneth Kaunda, Maputo; ❧ 21 492452
❸ Zimbabwe 242 R Damiao Gois, Maputo; ❧ 21 490404/490025

DRIVING AND ROADS Drive on the left. The main north–south highway through Malawi, Tete, Beira and Maputo is mostly OK, but some quite long sections are breaking up. The state of roads in the north is not known. There is very little traffic and there are virtually no fuel stations between the main towns. Carry enough fuel and water. (Make sure your vehicle insurance is valid; you will probably have to buy more at the border anyway.)

Fuel costs Diesel: US$1.20; petrol: US$1.30 per litre.

CLIMATE The dry season is from April to September, when it is cool and pleasant. The wet season is from October/November to March, when it is hot and humid. It is generally drier in the north.

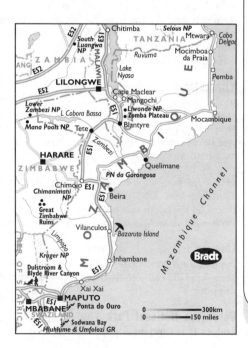

HIGHLIGHTS Hectic Maputo still has some fine colonial buildings and good nightlife. There are some beautiful beaches on the southern coast close to Inhambane at Tofo, plus Vilanculos and the lovely islands of the Bazaruto Archipelago. The northern beaches, Pemba and Ilha do Moçambique, are more remote and less inhabited. In the central bushland is the once popular Parc del Gorongosa.

WHERE TO STAY

Maputo The only place to stay in town in Maputo is at Fatima's Place on 1317 Mao Tse Tung Road. Two vehicles can be parked in the garage and there is a security guard at night. Fatima herself is the owner and full of news about Maputo and surrounding areas. A double chalet costs around US$15. Meals and drinks are available. On the main road north of Maputo (on the west side of the road) is the spacious and relaxing Camping Casa Lila run by an Englishman from Kenya. It has an excellent bar and restaurant. Camping costs US$12 for car plus two people.

Ponta do Ouro to Belene There are a number of proper camping places along the southern coast: Campismo Ninho, Ponta do Ouro Campsite, Ponta Malongane Resort, Jay's Lodge, Complex Turistico Parque Flora and Complexo Palmeiras are some of them.

Xai Xai Camping by the beach is found at the Xai Xai Caravan and Camping Park; US$5 each.

Inhambane It is probably best to camp at the Maxixe Campismo place across the estuary on the main road. It is signposted. Ferries sometimes run infrequently, so check first.

Tofo There are quite a few places here, but access is tricky because of the rather deep soft sand around here. Fatima's Nest, owned by Fatima from Maputo, has a place with camping; cost US$4 each. Further along the beach is the sandy Bamboozi 'Resort' with camping. Cost US$9, car plus two people. Camping is also offered at Turtle Cove in Tofinho.

Vilanculos The Camping Vilanculos is a well-run, grassy, shaded campsite close to the beach. It is popular with South Africans, but has no restaurant. It costs around US$16 for two people in a car. Another place with camping is Baobab Beach Backpackers. Vilanculos is a favourite spot for travellers. Day excursions can be planned to the Bazaruto Archipelago, where the diving is said to be excellent.

Tete The best choice for camping/parking is at the Indian-run Motel Tete. Camping costs US$10 for car plus two people. There are also simple camping places on the north side of the river east of the big bridge. Try A Piscina, Piscina o Paraiso Zambezi Misterioso and also the Jesus e Bom – none of these three is great.

Chimoio It's possible to camp at the windmill-style Hotel Moinho, which is popular for its restaurant and bar. It is out of town on the road to Beira. Camping costs US$10, car plus two people. Also suggested is Pink Papaya, which has camping.

Gorongosa National Park This is beginning to redevelop and Chitengo Safari Lodge offers camping for US$4 per person.

Beira The only place for overland campers is the Biques Campsite, which charges US$4 each.

The north
Chocas One of Charlie and Illya's highlights was an area called Chocas, 21km south of Ilha do Moçambique, towards Mossaril. Previously camping on the beach was the only option, but now Verandas offers cheap camping. Water is available from wells in the village and fish is sold every morning, fresh from the ocean.

Ilha do Moçambique It is possible to drive across to the island, as there is a 3km bridge that joins it to the mainland. There are no camping facilities on the island, so if you intend to stay the night, it is best to ask one of the restaurateurs or hoteliers to let you park in their yard. Camping is possible on the mainland at Camping Casuarinas at a cost of around US$4–5 each with vehicle.

Pemba North of Ilha do Moçambique is Pemba, where you could stay for days. Try the Nacole Jardim, where camping is offered for US$10 each. At Wimbe beach is Russell's Place (e *russelbott@yahoo.com*), run by Margot and Russell. Camping costs US$6 per person. Further up from Pemba the roads become worse and the going is slow, but the whole northern area is wild and untamed.

Pangane A quiet place with camping, Camagamento Pangane is pleasant. Nearby are a number of tranquil islands slowly being developed within the Quiramba National Park. Some islands have luxury resorts, while others offer cheaper places. On Ibo is Casa Janine; rooms cost US$15–20 and camping US$5–6, but be sure to find secure parking on the mainland.

OTHER A bridge between Mwambo (Mozambique) and Mtwara (Tanzania) has reportedly been planned for ages. There does seem to be a ferry at least, which runs at high tide only. Check timings the day before. It is said to cost US$10, but ferries are invariably negotiable upwards. We have no current information though, so before trying to head north into Tanzania, check the status of the border crossing and the river crossing for vehicles.

Do not photograph anything remotely resembling or near to a government institution.

FURTHER INFORMATION
Mozambique: The Bradt Travel Guide, Philip Briggs and Danny Edmunds
www.mozambique.mz

NAMIBIA

CAPITAL Windhoek

LANGUAGE AND TELEPHONE English and Afrikaans are the official languages. International telephone code +264.

CURRENCY AND RATE Namibian dollar (NAD); US$1 = NAD7.87. The Namibian dollar has the same value as the South African rand, which can be used for most transactions in Namibia. It is best to use up Namibian dollars before leaving because the reverse is not true; they cannot be used in South Africa.

RED TAPE Refreshingly little, but avoid the mining area around Lüderitz, as the police who patrol this area can be a bit over-zealous. To visit a mining area, you need a special permit arranged by the mining company in Windhoek, but it could be hard to come by.

Visas No visas are required by nationals of Australia, Canada, Republic of Ireland, New Zealand, South Africa, the UK, the USA, and most other southern African and western European countries.

African embassies

E Angola Angola Hse, 3 Dr Agostinho Neto St, Windhoek; ✆ 227535; f 221498

E Botswana 101 Nelson Mandela Av, Klein, Windhoek; ✆ 221941/2; f 236034

E Congo 9 Corner St, Windhoek; ✆ 226958

E Egypt 10 Berg St, Windhoek; ✆ 221501/2; f 228856

E Ghana 5 Nelson Mandela Av, Windhoek; ✆ 220536/221341; f 221343

E Kenya Kenya Hse, Robert Mugabe Av, Windhoek; ✆ 226836; f 221409

E Malawi 56 Bismarck St, 13254 Windhoek 9000; ✆ 221391/2/3

E Nigeria High Commission, 4 Omuramba Rd, Eros, Windhoek; ✆ 232103/5; f 221639

E South Africa RSA Hse, corner Jan Jonker Strasse & Nelson Mandela Dr, Klein Windhoek, Windhoek; ✆ 250711; f 224140

E Zambia 27 Sam Nujoma Dr, corner of Republic Rd, Windhoek; ✆ 237610; f 228162

E Zimbabwe Corner Independence Av & Grimm St, Windhoek; ✆ 228134; f 226 859

DRIVING AND ROADS Drive on the left. The roads are in excellent condition except for parts of the Namib Desert, Kaokoland and Kuadom Reserve. Most secondary roads are gravel/sand/dirt, but are well maintained and quite fast. Having said that, drive carefully – it would be easy to slide off if going too fast.

Fuel costs Diesel: US$1.45; petrol: US$1.60 per litre.

CLIMATE Overall the country is fairly dry. It gets quite hot in summer (October to April). Any rainfall occurs during the summer months. Winter is cool and the evenings can get quite cold. The coastal region of the Namib Desert is cool, damp and rain-free, with mist for much of the year.

HIGHLIGHTS Namibia has a long list of highlights, including Windhoek. The amazing orange/red dunes of the Namib Desert, seen as well at Sossusvlei, are spectacular. Swakopmund and Lüderitz have relics of the German colonial period. In the north is Kaokoland, with its beautiful scenery and Himba people. Then there are the national parks, including the world-famous Etosha, plus the Waterberg Plateau, the Skeleton Coast, Fish River Canyon, Kalahari Gemsbok and Namib Naukluft, all with varied wildlife.

WHERE TO STAY

Windhoek A popular campsite is at Daan Viljoen Game Park, 18km west of town. You can pre-book at the NWR (Namibia Wildlife Resorts) in Windhoek, which handles all park bookings, or you can just turn up. Camping costs US$20+ per site. Alternatively, Arebbusch Travel Lodge in Olympia, on the road south to Rehoboth, charges US$10 per person to camp. In town are various backpacker places, of which we stayed/camped at the Cardboard Box and the Chameleon. Camping US$12–13 all in; double room US$18 upwards. Another is Backpackers Unite. Out of town to the east is Trans Kalahari Caravan Park and to the northwest is Elisenheim Guest Farm.

Okahandja The Okahandja Lodge offers campers a spot for US$7 each. Nearby at the dam is the Von Bach Campsite, US$16 per site.

Spitzkoppe There is a proper site now with an ablution block. It's possible to camp amongst these amazing boulders and craggy peaks. It is not far north of the main Swakopmund road.

Swakopmund Although not as ethereal a town as Lüderitz, Swakopmund is attractive and interesting. In town try Desert Sky Backpackers, a well-organised place with parking. Just on the southern end of town there is Gulls Cry Camping. Other camping options are all out of town: try Alte Brücke Restcamp and, further south, El Jada Restcamp. Closer to Walvis Bay you can camp at Long Beach Resort; there are several other possibilities along the coast to the north.

Skeleton Coast National Park/Henties Bay Bucks Camping Lodge is a top-end option. There are other sites at Mile 14 and Jakkalsputz Campsite. Heading north, you find Mile 72 Campsite and Mile 108 Campsite. At Torra Bay is Torra Bay Campsite with standard rates around US$8 per site plus US$4 each.

Kaokoland Facilities are developing rapidly in this region, with quite a number of good places. Brandberg, Uis/Ughab, Organ Pipes region, Twyfelfontein, Khorixas and north along C34 all have designated places and more expensive choices. Bush sleeping is, however, still a great option as you head north towards Angola. At Epupa Falls you can sleep under the palm trees, or in the enclosed campsite. Due to the influx of tourists, the Himba's lifestyle has been threatened. Do not give them alcohol, though you will be asked for it continually.

Etosha National Park (*www.nwr.com.na*) The gem of northern Namibia, Etosha offers lodges and camps at Namutoni, Halali and Okaukuejo. The park entry fee is US$6 per person and US$6 per vehicle (entry to most Namibian parks costs around NAD30–40). Camping costs US$30 plus for a maximum of eight people. There are also a lot of options around the park itself to suit all pockets. Booking advised.

Grootfontein Look out for Roy's Camp out of town in a pleasant location. It's along the B8 then the D2885. Camping costs US$5–6 each. Farm walks, fresh meat and food.

Ondangwa Around 10km out of town is the Nakambale Museum and Restcamp, a local project with cultural interest. At Ruacana Falls is the Hippom Pools Campsite.

Rundu Look out for the Sarasunga River Lodge, which offers camping for US$5 per person. Also the N'Kwazi Lodge near Rundu has camping and trips across the river into Angola. Some 35km east is Mbamba Campsite and another 50km east is Shankara Lodge with camping.

Caprivi Strip At Popa Falls there is camping at several places, including Ngepi Camp for US$7 each, Suclabo Lodge, N'Goabaca Community Campsite and Popa Falls Restcamp. The area is developing fast and new places are being built along the strip. In the Kwando River zone are Bun Hill, Nambwa Campsite, Mazambala Island Lodge, Camp Kwando. Further east at Katima are Zambezi River Lodge, Kalizo Lodge and Caprivi River Lodge (Land Rover owners get a discount) but it's not cheap. Finally, at the border is Salambala Community Campsite.

Gobabis The new Goba-Goba Lodge and Rest Camp overlooking the Black Nossob River charges around US$17 for a site for two.

Border with Botswana If you are coming from Ghanzi in Botswana, where there are no camping places, wild or otherwise, due to fencing, a new campsite is open on the Namibian side close to the border. It is called Buitepos Camping/East Gate Rest Camp.

Route C26 Conveniently placed are Weissenfels Guest Farm, where camping is US$13 per person, and Hakos Guest Farm, which is a cheaper option at US$6 each.

Naukluft Mountains About 10km from Bullsport on the D854 is the Naukluft Campsite. Other places are Naukluft View Camping and Hauchabfontein Camping, as well as more expensive rest camp options.

Namib Naukluft Park There are a number (8 or 9) of designated camping areas for those fully independent. Book through Namib Naukluft Campsites (*www.nwr.com.na*).

Solitaire The one-horse/house town of Solitaire has a pleasant campsite and lodge. Their apple strudel is divine and the homemade bread is superb. Camping costs US$14, car plus two people. Not far away, camping is also available at Solitaire Guest Farm.

Sesriem The Sesriem Campsite has some shade. Cost around US$20 for a large pitch. Further out a newer option is the Sossusvlei Campsite and also Footloose Camping. Camping is not permitted at nearby Sossusvlei itself.

Lüderitz Lüderitz is a surreal German colonial relic set on the edge of the Namib Desert. The only place to camp is the windy Shark Island Campground north of town, which costs US$8 per site. Try Lüderitz Backpackers for less windy conditions.

Duwisib Where the castle is and also the Duwisib Campsite; US$8 per site plus US$3 per person.

Helmeringhausen This is another one-horse/hotel town; the hotel is a great place to stop or stay, with more delicious apple strudel.

Betta Coming on the desert road south from Sesriem to Helmeringhausen there are many very expensive farm lodges. For a cheap option try Betta Camp. Betta is a one-house town.

Keetmanshoop The town has the municipal Keetmanshoop Rest Camp, a caravan/camping park.

Grunau Camping at Grunau Motors for US$11 a pitch.

Fish River Canyon National Park The park has a very nice campsite, Hobias Camping, costing US$20 for a site. Further south you can also camp at Ai Ais Hot Springs resort.

Close to the Fish River Canyon Set amongst some ancient boulders and tastefully done is the Canyon (or Cañon) Lodge. This is expensive and sheer luxury. They also run a place north of Hobias on the west side of the road, called Cañon Roadhouse, which has camping. Another place nearby is Koelkrans Campsite.

OTHER Do not photograph anything remotely close to a government institution. Crime is on the increase in larger towns, but campsites have also been targeted; lock your valuables away at night.

FURTHER INFORMATION
Namibia: The Bradt Travel Guide, Chris McIntyre
www.namibiaweb.com
www.nwr.com.na

NIGER

☞ *WARNING!* In 2007 new tensions arose in the Aïr/Agadez region, so check for the latest security information. Currently Niamey and the western areas are safe. East, beyond Birnin-Konni and possibly to Zinder, you will need to check.

CAPITAL Niamey

LANGUAGE AND TELEPHONE French is the official language. International telephone code +227.

CURRENCY AND RATE West African franc (CFA); US$1 = CFA415

RED TAPE One of the friendliest countries we have travelled in, Niger has little red tape. However, the exception is when coming from Algeria. Perhaps understandably, the border officials at Assamaka are prone to need a little something extra to do the paperwork; it is jolly hot work lifting a pen and disturbs the lethargy of the place! The old practice of getting the passport stamped in every town has all but finished, except in Arlit and places like Bilma.

Visas Visas are required for all except nationals of the countries of ECOWAS. One-month visas are issued within 48 hours and cost US$50–60. They are easily obtained from the countries bordering Niger (though not Mali). You'll need one

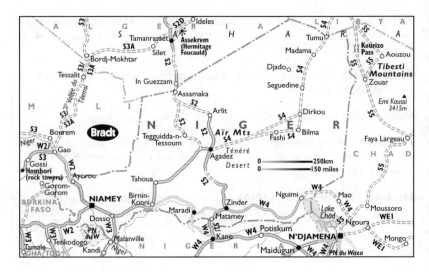

to four photos for each application. Visas can be obtained in Paris for those heading south. Vaccination certificates are obligatory. Visas are not issued at the border.

Non-African embassy
❸ France (issues visas for some French-speaking African countries) Route de Tondibia, Yantala, Niamey; ☏ 72 2722/2431–2; f 72 2518

African embassies
❸ Algeria Bd des Ambassades, north of Rte de Tillabéri, Niamey; ☏ 72 3583
❸ Benin Rue des Dallois; Niamey; ☏ 72 2860/3919
❸ Chad Av du General de Galle, off Route de Tillabéri, Niamey; ☏ 75 3464

❸ Libya BP 683, Niamey; ☏ 72 4019
❸ Mali Koira Kano, west along & beyond Bd de Liberta/l'Indépendance, Niamey; ☏ 75 4290/41; f 73 3346
❸ Nigeria Bd des Ambassades, Niamey; ☏ 73 2410

DRIVING AND ROADS Drive on the right. Roads are generally in good condition, particularly along major routes: Niamey, Maradi to Zinder and via Tahoua to Agadez and Arlit. Agadez to Zinder still has about 150km of piste. Remoter routes are desert pistes and tracks.

Fuel costs Diesel: US$1.30; petrol: US$1.40 per litre.

CLIMATE The climate is hot and dry, except for a brief rainy season in July and August. The coolest months are December to February, when the *harmattan* blows the dust off the desert.

HIGHLIGHTS The Grand Marché in Niamey and market days in Filingué and Zinder are very colourful. Agadez is a fabulous place, with colourful Tuareg markets and traditional mud architecture: the mosque, Sultan's Palace, Hotel de l'Aïr and Vieux Quartier in particular. Taking an expedition into the remote areas of the Aïr Mountains, Crabe d'Arakao, Adrar Chiriet, Temet and/or the Ténéré Desert with Fashi, Bilma and the Djado Plateau, is possible but quite expensive. For safety reasons, it is obligatory to have a guide with vehicle from a local tour operator and a travel permit for the area. Guides are expensive, but you can go in convoy and share the guide. It is worth every penny and is one of the most beautiful areas of Africa. It is also a wonderful introduction to the Tuareg culture. The Tuareg, the blue men of the desert, are a nomadic tribe and famous for their salt caravans to the Bilma oasis. The camel caravans continue to this day; trucks were tried but they kept breaking down, so the old faithful camels are back at work.

WHERE TO STAY

Niamey The one campsite here, Camping Touristique, needed repair and may be getting it soon. It's west along Boulevard des Sy et Mamar. Try asking at the Grand Hotel if you can park/camp; it has lots of space and is a great place for sundowners by the river. Also try Hotel Sahel further up the road. Hotel Maourey is a good place in town, but it has no parking.

Dosso The best and most entertaining place is the Hotel Djerma, with good parking, pool, colourful ladies and lively atmosphere. The steaks are great. Is the pool still empty?

Park du W The park has a number of camping places like Campement Nigercar, Campement de Boumba and Campement de Karey Kopto for US$3–6.

Birni N'Konni Look for Relais Camping Touristique along the main road; US$3.

Zinder There is a campsite called Camping Touristique just north of town – ask locals for details. It is rumoured to double as a brothel, so beware! The Hotel Amadou Kourou Daga, which has an artisan shop and shady space, may allow parking/camping. Close by is the Auberge Mourna if you want a room.

Tahoua Try the Hotel l'Amitié. It seemed to be called La Giraffe as well.

Agadez The Camping L'Escale is a huge campsite 4km northwest of town, with lots of shade and great toilet and shower facilities, costing US$12 for two. It's also possible to park in the grounds of the classic Hotel de l'Aïr, with its rooftop café and view of the mosque. The friendly Hotel Agreboun can squeeze in one car. La Tende allows camping; it's northwest of town.

Aïr Mountains There is now Campement de Timia and Campement de Tasselot around Timia. In the north at Iferouane are Camping Oasis les Arbres and Auberge Tidargo (Chez Sidi) all with camping choices.

Arlit There is now a small campsite in town. But you may prefer to desert-camp north of town; go at least 20km away on the way to Assamaka, where you will find some low scrubby bushes you can just about hide behind (this route is sadly unsafe for the time being though). Midway between Agadez and Arlit (about 130km from Agadez) is an ancient rock art site east of the main road. Bush camping is allowed close by, but it costs CFA500 to enter the site.

OTHER Dress conservatively, as dress is taken very seriously in this Muslim country. Always ask permission before taking photographs and stay clear of all government institutions. You may need to register with the local police in the odd places like Arlit; check if this is still the case. This is referred to as '*vu au passage*'.

FURTHER INFORMATION
Niger: The Bradt Travel Guide, Jolijn Geels
www.expeditionworld.com

9

☞ **WARNING!** There have been intermittent violent clashes between Muslims and Christians. Seek sound travel advice before entering Nigeria. Most of the time things are quiet. Avoid the Niger delta around Port Harcourt while low-key kidnappings of oil workers is ongoing.

CAPITAL Abuja

LANGUAGE AND TELEPHONE English is the official language. Main local languages are Hausa and Yoruba. International telephone code +234.

CURRENCY AND RATE Naira (NGN); US$1 = NGN118.55

RED TAPE Apart from getting the visa in the first place, roadblocks are evident throughout Nigeria, sometimes within 5km (3 miles) of each other. These are police, traffic police, forestry police, fund raisers(!) and military police. We have heard that policemen and many government employees are often not paid for long periods at a time. Some may ask for a *dash*, a little 'gift' for services rendered. It's up to you to decide each case on its merits.

Visas Visas are required for all except nationals of ECOWAS countries. The cost depends on your nationality, but can be from US$100–150 and more for double entry. You will also need two or three photographs and, if you get it in Africa, maybe a letter of introduction from your embassy. Even then you may only get a 48-hour visa to be extended in the country with yet more hassles. Yellow fever vaccination certificates are obligatory. Visas are not issued at the border. Getting one in your own country is strongly advised, but still a far from simple procedure.

Non-African consulate

❸ French Consulate (issues some visas for French-speaking African countries) 1 Oyinkan Abayomi Dr, Ikoyi Island, Lagos; ☎ 269 3427/260 3300

African embassies

❸ Angola 31 Pope John Paul St, Matama Area, Abuja; ☎ 413 41645

❸ Benin 4 Abudu Smith St, Victoria Island, Lagos; ☎ 261 4385. In Abuja; ☎ 523 8424

❸ Burkina Faso 15 Norman Williams St, Ikoyi Island, Lagos; ☎ 268 1001

❸ Cameroon 5 Elsie Fermi Pearse St, Victoria Island, Lagos; ☎ 261 2226/. Currently easier in Calabar near the border.

❸ Chad 10 Mississipi St, Maitama, Abuja; ☎ 413 0751

❸ Gabon 8 Norman Williams St, Ikoyi, Lagos; ☎ 268 4566

❸ Gambia 162 Awolowo Rd, SW Ikoyi, Lagos; ☎ 268 2192

❸ Ghana 21–23 King George V (Island Club) Rd, Lagos Island, Lagos; ☎ 260 0015

❸ Ivory Coast 4 Abudu Smith St, Victoria Island, Lagos; ☎ 261 0936; f 261 3822

❸ Mali Plot 465 Nouakchott St, Abuja; ☎ 523 0494

❸ Niger 15 Adeola Odeku St, Victoria Island, Lagos; ☎ 261 2300. Also in Abuja; ☎ 413 4434 & maybe a consulate in Kano.

❸ Senegal 12–14 Kofo Abayomi Cl, Victoria Island, Lagos; ☎ 261 7449

❸ Togo Plot 976, Oju Olobun Close, Victoria Island, Lagos; ☎ 261 1762

DRIVING AND ROADS Drive on the right. Main roads are generally in good condition, but once on side roads watch out for pot-holes and worse.

Fuel costs Diesel: US$0.50; petrol: US$0.60 per litre.

'At the time of writing there was no fuel available.' That's what Charlie and Illya wrote in the third edition of this guide and it still applies in many parts almost ten years later. Sometimes fuel is found in stations, but often the only fuel available is on the black market at US$0.70 per litre or more. It's totally crazy when you think that oil is Nigeria's major source of income.

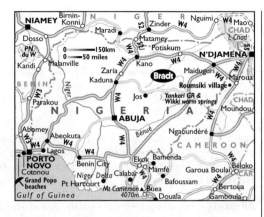

CLIMATE The south is hot and humid, with a long rainy season from March to November. The north has far greater extremes of temperature, as a result of the Saharan influence. It can be blisteringly hot. The rains last from April to September, with a shorter wet season in the far north.

HIGHLIGHTS Most travellers enjoy the north of the country. The crime and heavy concentrations of the population in the south deter many people. Highlights of the north include Kano, Jos and the Yankari Game Reserve. Kano is famed for its old city, Sultan's Palace, mosques, dye pits and the narrow streets lined by the remains of the old city wall. The Jos Plateau is 1,200m (3,600ft) above sea level and has a relatively cool climate all year round. It is green and surrounded by rolling green hills, but check in case there has been any civil unrest recently. Benin City in the south is famed for its bronzes. In the far southeast near Cameroon is Calabar town, where many travellers 'relax' for a while getting their visas, and the cattle ranching area of Obudu.

WHERE TO STAY

Kano The only campsite in Kano, just off Bompai Road, is the Kano State Tourist Camp, which is friendly, secure and helpful. Camping costs US$5 per person. Hussein or Mohammed can fix any problems with vehicle or fuel supplies etc.

Sokoto If you find yourself here, then head to the Sokoto Guest Inn with big chalets in a garden setting.

Jos Jos has no campsite, so you'll have to ask at one of the larger hotels whether it is possible to park there for a night or two. Plateau Hotel has parking and Hill Station Hotel has colonial charm in a leafy area.

Potiskum Try the FNC College. Double room costs from US$10.

Maiduguri There are a few hotels. Try at the Maiduguri International Hotel, which has parking in large gardens but quite expensive rooms.

Bama Try the government resthouse/bungalows out of town towards the border. Rooms must have been wonderful before independence. Double room with bathroom (bath, toilet, bidet but no water) and sitting room cost us US$7 in 2004 but it's sure to have risen by now.

Abuja We stayed at the Hotel Luna about 20km west of town near the main road junction. There is parking and it's friendly. A double room costs US$10 but again will be more now. Some overland trucks have camped at the Sheraton near Wuse market. Also the Lakeview Hotel allows camping with various forms of entertainment.

Lagos If you have to stay in Lagos, it's expensive, even for many of the grimmer places. Michael's Guesthouse claims to have parking, but the rooms are very expensive. It could be easier to stay at Eleko Beach, 60km east of town, where there are said to be beach huts.

Abeokuta If you have come through the Ketou/Meko border from Benin, you will pass this historic Yoruba town. Parking and cheaper rooms are available at the Mokland Inn at 7 Oba Alake Road.

Ibadan Secure parking can be found at the Plaza Park Hotel near the university, just east of Oyo Road. Rooms from US$30.

Oshogbo For a quiet retreat, try the Ambassador Guest House, 6km west of town. It's not cheap, though. A cheaper alternative is the Hotel Heritage International.

Benin City There is parking of a sort at the Central Hotel. Otherwise there is the Edo-Delta Hotel with a church on site. Also mentioned is Hotel Felona, where the bacon and eggs may tempt you.

Calabar Camping at Paradise City Hotel. The nearby sanctuaries for drill monkeys are worth a visit and it should be possible to stay at Rhoko Camp.

Yankari Within the park, roughly 45km from the gate, is Wikki Camp for about US$5 each plus vehicle charge.

Obudu Cattle Ranch and Afi Drill Ranch These are two nice places to camp close to the Cameroon border, but the access roads are steep and difficult in the rain. Obudu is expensive.

Gboko Try Lemba Lodge within a secure compound.

OTHER To avoid any hassles in Nigeria, ensure that all paperwork is in order and be patient. Do not photograph any government institutions. Dress conservatively, particularly in the north where there is more of a Muslim influence.

Room costs have risen significantly, even if standards have not. Be aware that there are frequent and long-lasting power cuts throughout the country. So, although you may have a suite of rooms (for US$15–30 or so) with a luxurious bathroom, you will probably have no water except in a bucket and no air conditioning except the breeze when you head outside to sleep on the roof of your vehicle.

For an excellent mechanic in Abuja, look for Cyprian Ogbodo.

FURTHER INFORMATION
Nigeria: The Bradt Travel Guide, Lizzie Williams
www.motherlandnigeria.com

☞ **WARNING!** Although travel within the country is currently safe, borders with the DRC and Burundi remain sensitive. Access is normally via Uganda and Tanzania. Always heed local advice and don't wander off the beaten track alone in unpopulated areas of the northwest or south. Check the current situation before travelling.

CAPITAL Kigali

LANGUAGE AND TELEPHONE Kinyarwanda, French and English are all official languages; English is less widespread outside Kigali. International telephone code +250.

CURRENCY AND RATE Rwandan franc (RWF); US$1 = RWF553.70.

Banks in Kigali can generally handle travellers' cheques (you'll get a poorer rate for them than for cash) and maybe even some Visa (card) transactions. The official and private forex bureaux only change cash – US dollars or euros are best. Elsewhere in the country, you're best off with cash. Moneychangers operate at border crossings. All main towns have Western Union offices if you need funds sent from home.

RED TAPE Not a great deal. There are occasional police checkpoints, but they don't seem to target overlanders. Your vehicle may be checked for roadworthiness – carry two warning triangles and a fire extinguisher.

Visas At present visas are not required (for stays of under three months) by nationals of the UK, Germany, Sweden, Canada, USA, Hong Kong, Burundi, DRC, Mauritius, South Africa, Tanzania and Uganda, but check in case any unfriendliness develops with these countries. For others they cost around US$50–70 and are currently obtainable at the border. You must buy separate car insurance at the border as you enter.

African embassies

Ⓔ **Burundi** Bd de l'Umuganda, Kigali; ☎ 517 529/587 940/3
Ⓔ **Kenya** Bd de l'Umuganda, Kigali; ☎ 583 332/6

Ⓔ **Tanzania** Av de la Paix, Kigali; ☎ 505 400; f 505 402
Ⓔ **Uganda** Av de la Paix, Kigali; ☎ 572 115/7; f 573 551

DRIVING AND ROADS Drive on the right. Roads linking main cities and border points are generally surfaced and relatively good; some smaller roads are narrow and twisty, and may be muddy (or in some areas impassable) after rain. Ask local advice, particularly in the wet season. If you don't like negotiating steep hairpin bends, stay away.

Fuel costs Diesel: US$1.40; petrol: US$1.60 per litre.

CLIMATE Rwanda is a high, hilly country and not too hot. Rainy seasons are March/May and October/November. The hottest months are August and September.

HIGHLIGHTS There are three national parks: the Volcanoes Park in the northwest (mountain gorillas, golden monkeys, Dian Fossey's grave, crater walks, trekking), Akagera Park in the east (hilly savanna, lakes, hippos, giraffe, elephant, antelope, fish eagles) and Nyungwe Forest in the southwest (chimps, colobus and l'Hoest's monkeys, orchids, birds). The National Museum of Rwanda in Butare is one of east Africa's best, with extensive displays on Rwandan history and culture. Visits to interpretive genocide memorials are possible. The tranquil lakeside towns of Kibuye and Gisenyi offer stunning views of Lake Kivu and boat trips to some islands. Permits to visit the amazing mountain gorillas (US$350) must be bought in advance from the Rwanda Tourist Board in Kigali (*Office Rwandais du Tourisme et des Parcs Nationaux (ORTPN)*, BP 905; ✆ 576514; e *ortpn@rwanda1.com* & *info@rwandatourism.com*; *www.rwandatourism.com*). It's at the junction of Boulevard de la Révolution and Avenue de l'Armée; go there for also maps, guides and other information.

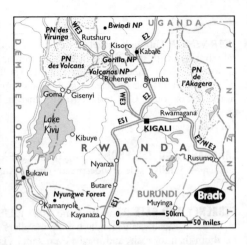

WHERE TO STAY Rwanda is a very densely populated country and secluded spots are hard to find. All three national parks have basic (but not cheap) campsites nearby. In most towns there's a small hotel or guesthouse where you can ask to camp in the grounds.

Kigali The One Love Guesthouse (*Rue de Kinamba;* ✆ *575412*) and maybe the Episcopal Church Guesthouse (*Av Paul VI;* ✆ *573219*) offer secure parking and you may be able to camp (their rooms aren't expensive anyway).

Gisenyi It should be possible to stay at the Hotel Palm Beach on the shore of the lake or in rondavels at the Paradis Malahide in Rubona. Otherwise there is the Methodist Church Centre de'Accueil in a quiet location to the north.

Lake Kivu There was lakeside camping in Kibuye at the Kibuye Guest House. The steep, twisting Gisenyi – Kibuye road is rough going in places, but the views are amazing. In Cyangugu you can stay at the Home St François for a budget option.

Musanze (formerly Ruhengeri) The Hotel Ituze is suitable for those with their own vehicles; rooms from US$10.

Parc National des Volcans Try at the Kinigi Guest House near the park or a campsite near the ORTPN park office. Ask the Rwandan Tourist office (*www.rwandatourism.com*).

Lake Muhazi Beside Lake Muhazi in the east there's camping near Gahini at the Seeds of Peace Centre and Jambo Beach (on the main eastern Kigali–Uganda road); and on the northern shore at some idyllic small bar-restaurants (accessed via the Byumba road).

Kibungo If you are *en route* to Kigali from Tanzania, you might need a place here. Sunset Guesthouse has been suggested.

Nyungwe National Park The park has the Uwinka Reception Centre Campsite and is in a forest setting with trails.

OTHER Be tactful about photos – always ask, always respect the answer, and remember that this is a country still emerging from deep trauma. Supportive tourism is a way to help.

FURTHER INFORMATION
Rwanda: The Bradt Travel Guide, Philip Briggs and Janice Booth
www.rwandatourism.com
www.newtimes.co.rw Rwanda's English-language newspaper

SENEGAL

☞ ***WARNING!*** Periodic disturbances still occur in the Casamance region, so check before travelling there.

CAPITAL Dakar

LANGUAGE AND TELEPHONE French is the official language. International telephone code +221.

CURRENCY AND RATE West African franc (CFA); US$1 = CFA415

RED TAPE Roadblocks are frequent; the police are often over-zealous if you are in a vehicle or on a motorbike. Always adhere to all the rules and try to avoid handing over original documents.

Visas US and EU citizens do not need a visa, nor do citizens of most Commonwealth countries. Australians and New Zealanders are among those who do, however. A visa costs US$20–50, depending on the country of application. Visitor's entry permits are issued at the border. A yellow fever certificate is obligatory.

Non-African embassies
🄴 **French Consulate** (issues visas for most French-speaking African countries) 1 Rue Assane Ndoye, Dakar; ☎ 839 5100

African embassies
🄴 **Burkina Faso** Liberty extension, Dakar; ☎ 823 9290/827 9509
🄴 **Cameroon** 157 Rue Josef Gomis, Dakar; ☎ 823 2195
🄴 **Gambia** 11 Rue de Thiong, Ponty, Dakar; ☎ 821 7230
🄴 **Ghana** Point E, Dakar; ☎ 869 4053
🄴 **Guinea** Rue 7, Point E, Dakar; ☎ 824 8606
🄴 **Guinea Bissau** Rue 6, Point E, Dakar; ☎ 824 5922
🄴 **Ivory Coast** 2 Av Albert Sarraut or Rue 7, Point E, Dakar; ☎ 821 3473/869 0270
🄴 **Mali** Route de la Corniche Ouest, Dakar; ☎ 824 6252/823 4893
🄴 **Mauritania** Rue 37, Kolobane, Dakar; ☎ 822 6238

DRIVING AND ROADS Drive on the right. Roads are generally in good condition, except to Tambacounda.

Fuel costs Diesel: US$1.50; petrol: US$1.70 per litre. Expensive!

9

CLIMATE Dry from December to May; hot, humid and wet from May to June. The dry season is shorter in the south and east.

HIGHLIGHTS Dakar has some beaches not far from town for lazing and good nightlife; be careful late at night. Take a boat trip to the historic former slaving centre, Ile de Gorée. Ferries leave from the wharf area in Dakar every one to two hours. The cost is around US$10 return per person.

Hike in the Casamance region when it's safe and enjoy the beautiful beaches of Cap Skiring. Visit the Siné-Saloum Delta and the Parc National de Niokolo-Koba. Highlights of the north include the old town of St Louis and the magnificent birdlife of the area. Touba is a pilgrimage centre with massive modern mosques. Senegal is also famed for its musicians, such as Youssour N'Dour and Salif Keita.

WHERE TO STAY In the old days there were many tourist campements, but these are slowly evaporating or being upgraded. Finding good budget options is becoming harder.

Dakar The options for budget rooms and maybe camping are all out of town at Yoff along the north coast, close to the beach at Lac Rose. Try at Campement Lac Rose Palal. You could also see if Via Via (e *viavia@sentoo.sn*) is operating. At Malika, about 20km out, there used to be Campement Touristique de Malika Peul.

Siné-Saloum Delta The delta is often overlooked by visitors and is a wild, beautiful area of mangrove swamps, lagoons, forests, dunes and sand islands. In Palmarine is Campement Villeois de Sessene. Near Djiffer, camping accommodation was available at La Pointe du Sangomar, on the western edge of the delta at the tip of a narrow spit of land called Pointe de Sangomar. Rooms here are now reported to cost around US$18. From here you are able to hire pirogues to reach the beautiful islands of Guior and Guissanor.

St Louis The Zebrabar, south of town on a road off to the right ahead and then down various small lanes, is the best place to stay. It's very pleasant, with beautiful natural surroundings, as well as a popular bar and restaurant. Follow the signposts. If you head south for 5km towards the Parc National de la Langue de Barbarie, famed for its birdlife, look for Hotel Dior at the Hydrobase. Finding anywhere to camp in town is not possible, but there are a number of hotels, including the famous Hotel de la Poste (*www.hotel-poste.com*) (US$60 plus).

Touba Try the Campement Touristique le Baol; it's 10km south of town in Mbaka. Watch out for the inquisitive goats here and mosquitoes. Camping US$7. Bungalows are also available, as well as a restaurant.

Koungheul *En route* to Tambacounda, along the nightmarish pot-holed RN1 road, is the French-run hunting retreat of Campement Bambouck, with camping and bungalows. A good spot to break for tea before your nerves are shattered by the awful bone-shaking road.

Tambacounda There are two hotels out of town on the way in from Dakar. Camping may still be tolerated, but neither is cheap. For rooms Relais de Tamba is negotiable around US$35–60 and the Oasis Oriental Club is a bit more.

Casamance The best bet for accommodation is to stay at one of the local campsites called Campements Touristiques (Campement Villageois) where prices are standard at US$6 for a bed. Camping costs would need to be negotiated. At Elinkine and on the Ile de Karabane there are basic campements. Cap Skiring has a couple of better campements.

Oussoye Has a couple of long-standing traditional mud-built and cool village campements.

OTHER The beaches at Cap Skiring are some of the nicest in Africa. This area is worth a week's visit. However, do check the security situation in this area before you visit. Watch out for the police around St Louis, who seem hell-bent on fining foreigners for anything, real or otherwise. The officials at the border with Mauritania are notorious for extra 'taxes'.

FURTHER INFORMATION
West Africa, Rough Guides
www.homeviewsenegal.com
www.earth2000.com

SIERRA LEONE

☞ *WARNING!* With the civil war in Sierra Leone now part of history, it is again feasible to travel overland into the country. Travel in very isolated parts of the border regions of the country areas may still be a bit too adventurous. Seek local advice.

CAPITAL Freetown

LANGUAGE AND TELEPHONE English is the official language. International telephone code +232.

CURRENCY AND RATE Leone (SLL); US$1 = SLL3000

RED TAPE Following the recent civil war, there are still some road checkpoints, but not as many as you might expect.

Visas Visas are required for all, and cost around US$80–100 depending on your nationality. They are not issued at the border.

Non-African embassies
❺ **France** (issues visas for some French-speaking African countries) 13 Lamina Sankoh St, north of Siaka Stevens Rd, Freetown; ☎ 222 477

African embassies
❺ **Gambia** Wilberforce St, Freetown; ☎ 225 191
❺ **Ghana** Warpole St, Freetown; ☎ 223 461
❺ **Guinea** Carlton Carew Rd, Freetown; ☎ 232 496
❺ **Liberia** 2 Spur Rd, Wilberforce, Freetown; ☎ 230 991
❺ **Mali** Wilkinson Rd, Freetown; ☎ 231 781/230 284
❺ **Nigeria** Siaka Stevens St, Freetown; ☎ 224 229
❺ **Senegal** Upper East St, Freetown; ☎ 222 948

DRIVING AND ROADS Drive on the right. The condition of the roads is improving. Sealed roads now head east from Freetown almost all the way to Kenema; there are also a few tarmac sections heading north towards Guinea. Elsewhere the state of disrepair is likely to be bad.

Fuel costs Diesel: US$1.10; petrol: US$1.10 per litre. Sold and priced locally in gallons.

CLIMATE The main rainy season is from June to September, with the rest of the year much drier.

HIGHLIGHTS Sierra Leone once had a thriving beach-holiday tourist industry, which may now be redeveloped. Freetown, although formerly run-down and crowded, is beginning to experience a revival now that the war has finished. Its often unlit, seedy streets have a certain vibrant charm! Close by are a number of good beaches: Lumley, Lakka, River No 2 and Tokey. Banana Island, and Bunce Island with its old fort, may be revived. In the Loma Mountains is Mount Bintumani, the highest point in west Africa at nearly 2,000m, set in a forest reserve. Also, when things improve, there is the Ooutamba Kilimi National Park. For something completely different, visit the central town of Bo, famous as a diamond centre. The road to Liberia is a highlight for those desperate to use their 4x4 capacity.

WHERE TO STAY

Freetown Hotels are expensive here, probably due to too many expats hanging around. Out of town along Lumley Beach and with low-roofed underground parking, try Cockle Bay Guest House from US$35 for a room. You can just get a vehicle into the yard of Franjia Guesthouse (US$40) if pushed, but it's not so friendly. Not far from Franjia is the YSC Complex, where there is internet and a café. It might be possible to camp there, too, as there is a lot of secure space. The once tourist-filled Mama Yoko Hotel is now the UN HQ. Power cuts are frequent in Freetown, so air conditioning and fans are often superfluous. As things settle down, new places should open further down the coast – one day.

Coast There are a few options, but none are very developed and the road is shocking. River No 2 is one of the best places and it's shady. Showers are open air for bathers and it gets deserted after dark. Camping costs US$8; rooms are apparently US$50. Sussex Beach is another possibility, but its access road is an obstacle course. Toyeh Bay is said to have a camping place, but there did not seem to be good parking during our visit. It should improve. At Kent there is parking/camping, but it's all very primitive.

Bo Head east out of town to the relaxing and well-run Countryside Guest House with a pool and restaurant; it's also a good spot to catch up with your laundry and car washing.

Kenema You can try Ruby Motel with parking. Heading south, Joru and Zimmi are just mud-hut villages, so don't expect to find a hotel building anywhere.

Makeni If you want to come here, look out for Buya's Motel.

OTHER There is a great Lebanese supermarket for food stocks/soups etc next to the Malian Consulate on Wilkinson Road, close to Franjia Guesthouse and above

Cockle Bay. For motor parts, try MotorCare in Freetown. When visiting Bo, the former RUF headquarters, exercise a low profile when taking photographs. Of course it's tempting to take pictures of diamond shops, isn't it!

FURTHER INFORMATION
Sierra Leone: The Bradt Travel Guide, Katrina Manson and James Knight
www.sierra-leone.org

SOMALIA

☞ **WARNING!** Sadly things have still not changed in Somalia, although a tentative new government of 'almost' national unity backed by Ethiopian troops is struggling to improve security, despite rebel groups and terrorists. Due to the ongoing civil war in Somalia, overland travel is not possible. Basic information has been included.

CAPITAL Mogadishu

LANGUAGE AND TELEPHONE Somali is the official language. International telephone code +252.

CURRENCY AND RATE Somali shilling (SOS); US$1 = SOS1427

RED TAPE No current information. Who needs red tape with so many guns about?

Visas Visas are required for all, but, with the current state of the country, anyone can probably enter without a visa, though it is not recommended. There are some reports that the breakaway northern Somaliland area around Hargeysa may give visas, but then again it may still not be safe either.

African embassies No African embassies are open or functioning.

DRIVING AND ROADS Drive on the right. If the Michelin map is to be believed, the roads from Mogadishu to Hargeysa were relatively new just before the troubles.

Fuel costs Unknown.

CLIMATE Much of Somalia is hot and dry, but there are intermittent rains in the south from March to September.

HIGHLIGHTS Formerly, parts of the capital, Mogadishu, were quite picturesque, but the city has suffered from the ongoing conflict. In the far north, the mountains between Berbera and

Hargeysa are said to be spectacular, but it is not clear if the area is safe yet. Many years ago, some of the people were noted for their friendly welcome. There must be hundreds of miles of attractive coast, but with little chance of anyone except pirates seeing them for the time being.

WHERE TO STAY

Hargeysa Two hotels are said to be open and used by aid workers: Ambassador Lion and Hotel Maansour.

OTHER The virtually independent region of northern Somalia called Somaliland has been much safer than the south and might be possible to visit with prior checking about the security situation. If you have made it to Djibouti, you may hear more up-to-date news. Daallo Airlines (*www.daallo.com*) fly to Hargeysa.

For Somaliland, check information from the British Embassy (e *britishembassy.addisababa@fco.gov.uk*) and their representation in London (e *slrmission@btinternet.com*).

FURTHER INFORMATION
Africa on a Shoestring, Lonely Planet

SOUTH AFRICA

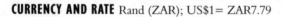

CAPITAL Pretoria (administrative) and Cape Town (legislative)

LANGUAGE AND TELEPHONE English and Afrikaans are the official languages, with another nine local official languages. Those spoken most are Zulu, Xhosa and Sotho. International telephone code +27.

CURRENCY AND RATE Rand (ZAR); US$1= ZAR7.79

RED TAPE If you are intending to sell your vehicle in South Africa, you have to discharge your *carnet* by officially importing the vehicle or bike. To do this, you need a current valuation of your vehicle or bike, based on which you will pay import duty. Passports must be valid for at least six months after your date of departure from South Africa.

Visas Visas are not required for most holiday visitors. You'll be issued with an entry permit on arrival. If you are applying for an extended-stay or work visa, which are issued free, allow a couple of weeks for the process. Visas are not issued at the border. With overland travel you may have to convince the immigration officer that you have sufficient funds for your stay, but crossing borders is usually hassle-free.

African embassies

e **Angola** 153 Oliver St, Brooklyn, Pretoria; ⟍ 012 342 0049

e **Botswana** 24 Amos St, Colbyn, Pretoria; ⟍ 012 430 9640

e **Burundi** 1090 Arcadia St, Hatfield, Pretoria; ⟍ 012 342 4881

e **Congo** 960 Arcadia St, Hatfield, Pretoria; ⟍ 012 342 5508

e **Democratic Republic of the Congo** 960 Arcadia St, Hatfield, Pretoria; ⟍ 012 342 5508

e **Kenya** 302 Brooks St, Menlo Park, Pretoria; ⟍ 012 342 5066/362 2249

e **Lesotho** 1 T Edison St, Pretoria; ⟍ 012 460 7640

e **Malawi** Lynwood, Brooklyn, Pretoria; ⟍ 012 477 827/8/9

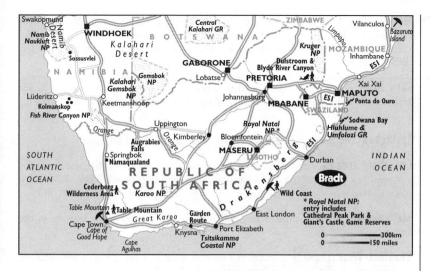

Ⓔ Morocco Pretoria; ✆ 012 343 0230
Ⓔ Mozambique Beckett St/529 Edmond St, Arcadia, Pretoria; ✆ 012 401 0300; f 012 326 6388
Ⓔ Namibia Sunnyside, 702 Church St, Arcadia, Pretoria; ✆ 012 481 9100; f 012 343 7294; e secretary@namibia.org.za
Ⓔ Rwanda 1090 Arcadia St, Hatfield, Pretoria 0083; ✆ 012 342 1740; f 012 342 1743
Ⓔ Sudan 1203 Pretorius St, Hatfield, Pretoria; ✆ 012 342 0599; f 012 342 4539

Ⓔ Swaziland 715 Government Av, Arcadia, Pretoria; ✆ 012 344 1917
Ⓔ Tanzania 822 George Av, Arcadia, Pretoria; ✆ 012 342 4371
Ⓔ Zambia 570 Ziervogel St, Arcadia, Pretoria; ✆ 012 326 1847; f 012 326 2140
Ⓔ Zimbabwe 798 Merton Av, Arcadia, Pretoria; ✆ 012 342 5125; f 012 342 5126

DRIVING AND ROADS Drive on the left. Roads are in excellent condition.

Fuel costs Diesel: US$1.55; petrol: US$1.40 per litre.

CLIMATE The climate is extremely varied and quite localised. The summer (wet season) is from September to April in the north. Winters can be cold, particularly at night. In Cape Town the winter months (May to August) are wet and it can be very windy along the coast. June and July are the best months for game viewing. The Indian Ocean coast is driest from June to September.

HIGHLIGHTS South Africa is such a vast country that months could be spent exploring it. Highlights include the Kruger National Park and surrounding area, as well as Karoo National Park and Augrabies Falls. Of course Cape Town, Table Mountain, Cape of Good Hope and the vineyards in the surrounding area, including Stellenbosch, should be seen. East is the Garden Route along the southern coast, including Knysna, and for all surfers, Jeffreys Bay, which is reputed to have some of the best waves in the world. Oudtshoorn has ostrich farms and the Kango Caves. In the great Karoo are quirky Matjiesfontein with its oddball Lord Milner Hotel and railway station, plus Graff Reinet and the Mountain Zebra National Park. Natal has lush green rolling hills and incredible beaches along its coastline. The Drakensberg Mountains are spectacular, with Giant's Castle, Golden Gate park, etc, as is the Cederberg Wilderness Area. Durban is known for its beaches and cosmopolitan flavour, and nearby is the wilder region of the Transkei.

WHERE TO STAY The options are limitless and the country is well set up for camping. Facilities are excellent. Costs are US$5–10 per person, depending on the site. There are also a lot of backpacker places where parking is not usually too difficult. Here are a few pointers.

Cape Town There is a campsite at Muizenberg, south of town in the eastern beach area, on the way to the Cape. It's called Zandvlei Caravan Park and costs US$9 for a car plus two.

Springbok The Springbok Caravan Park is on the ring road just south of town.

Cederberg area Camp at The Baths. It's off the main road from Citrusdal and has a natural hot pool and tranquil surroundings. Camping costs US$10. A beautiful place to stay.

Stellenbosch Try the Stumble Inn Backpackers. We parked safely outside in the street.

Beaufort West There is a municipal caravan park just on the southern edge of town. Camping for a car plus two people costs US$8.

Gariep Dam Beside the lake is a superb campsite costing US$9 for car plus two people, for a site with private kitchen and bathroom.

Bloemfontein North of the city is the Reyneke Park with camping areas, a peaceful spot. Cost US$12 for two.

Pretoria We stayed at the North South Backpackers in Hatfield, where the vehicle just fitted in through the archway. It's well guarded and costs US$11 to camp/park.

Johannesburg Africa's Zoo Lodge (*233A Jan Smuts Av, Parktown North;* ❯ *011 880 5108; www.zoolodge.co.za*) has been recommended.

Pietermaritzburg The pleasant out-of-town Msundzi Caravan Park has nice camping and is about 5km out on the east side of town.

Top of the Oliviershoek Pass With a wonderful view across the whole range of the Drakensberg Mountains is the relatively inexpensive Windmill Resort. It has rondavel bungalows for a little luxury, and a comfortable bar, too. Across the road, down a steep narrow track, is Amphitheatre Backpackers.

Durban It's best to head for the beaches to the north and south, as Durban is not safe for parking overnight, or even in the daytime in many areas.

OTHER Crime is on the increase in most major towns, so watch your bags and always carry minimal valuables. Most accommodation and camping places in South Africa offer to place all valuables in a safe. It is not advisable for any white person to enter a black township unless with a guide or tour company.

FURTHER INFORMATION
East & Southern Africa: The Backpacker's Manual, Philip Briggs (Bradt Travel Guides)
Johannesburg: The Bradt City Guide, Lizzie Williams
South Africa: The Bradt Budget Guide, Paul Ash
www.southafrica.co.za

SUDAN

☞ **WARNING!** Despite peace agreements, visiting the south remains a risky venture, with landmines being the biggest hazard. The routes across Darfur remain off-limits. Eventually things may improve, but probably not during the lifetime of this guide. Thankfully the routes from Eygpt to Khartoum and south into Ethiopia are safe.

CAPITAL Khartoum

LANGUAGE AND TELEPHONE Arabic is the official language. International telephone code +249.

CURRENCY AND RATE US$1 = SDG2.062 (SDG1 = 100 dinar).

In 2007 Sudan changed its currency again to the Sudanese pound (SDG). The Sudanese dinar is being phased out, but people may refer to the old currency for some time to come.

RED TAPE Sudan is wonderful to travel through, but famous for its bureaucracy. Obtaining the relevant permits is a time-consuming and frustrating task, but you have little choice. Stay within the restrictions of any permits needed, generally all in Arabic, as these may be checked on the road.

The first thing you must obtain is an Alien's Registration Stamp in your passport. This will take time and energy, as you search for the correct office in which to get the correct stamp, and then move on to the next office, and the next... And let's not forget finding the bank, where you must exchange cash in order to pay the US$20 or so for this purpose.

After this, you may need an 'Alien's Movement Permit', which states the towns and the route you intend to take. Any deviation may cause you trouble, so decide on your route before you apply. These documents were formerly required for all travel within Sudan, but we did not need one in 2004 to travel from Khartoum to Gedaref and the Ethiopian border. However, things seem to change constantly, so check at the border and in Khartoum before going too far away.

If you cross one of the land borders, you may have to obtain your permit there; again, check if it is needed. Permits issued at borders were normally only good for travel to Khartoum, where you then needed to obtain another permit for onward travel. These permits should cost about US$20. It is worth photocopying this permit along with your passport to hand out at the police checks. It can save you some time and form-filling. At each town where you stay the night you are supposed to check in with the local police. This can become tedious, especially as the offices are often closed. It is better to camp in the bush, stopping only briefly in the towns for supplies or sightseeing.

You may need to obtain a currency declaration form at the border. We did not in 2004. Also remember you cannot change any travellers' cheques in Sudan, but US dollars cash are no problem.

Visas Visas are required for all and the process can be lengthy in Europe, particularly in London, as your application will first be approved by Khartoum. It could take months. One-month entry visas cost almost US$110. Visas were said to be easy to obtain in Cairo and Addis Ababa. They are not issued at the border.

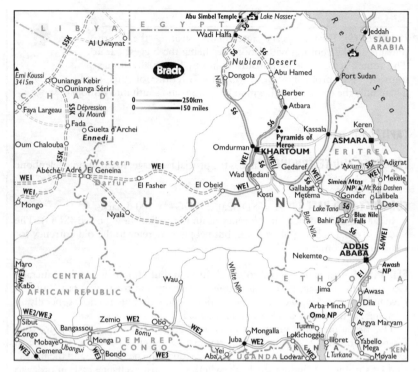

Non-African consulate

ℰ French Consulate (issues visas for most French-speaking African countries) Sharia 13, New Extension, Khartoum; ✆ 471082

African embassies

ℰ Chad Sharia 17, New Extension, Khartoum; ✆ 471084

ℰ Egypt Sharia al-Gamhuriyya, Khartoum; ✆ 772190

ℰ Eritrea Khartoum 2, Street 39, Khartoum; ✆ 483834; f 483835

ℰ Ethiopia Sharia Al Qasr, New Extension, Khartoum 2, northwest of the cemetery, Khartoum; ✆ 471156/11 or 451156; f 471141

ℰ Kenya Sharia 3, New Extension, Khartoum 2; ✆ 483834/940386

ℰ Libya Block 18 Riyadh, Khartoum; ✆ 222547

ℰ Niger Sharia 1, New Extension, Khartoum

ℰ Saudi Arabia Sharia 29, New Extension, Khartoum; ✆ 472583

ℰ Uganda Sharia Abu Qarga, Khartoum; ✆ 797867

DRIVING AND ROADS Drive on the right. The major tarred roads leading from Khartoum to El Obeid, Gedaref, Port Sudan and Atbara are in good condition. The road from Omdurman to Dongola is now sealed and being extended. All other roads into the hinterland are desert pistes and tracks.

Fuel costs Diesel: US$0.60; petrol: US$0.70 per litre. The further north or west you go, the more expensive fuel becomes.

CLIMATE The summer months in Sudan are extremely hot and dry, reaching 45°C+. The best time to visit is during the winter months from December to mid March, when temperatures still reach 40°C but evenings are cool and pleasant.

Should the south open up, don't go during the wet season, April to September, as roads become grim.

HIGHLIGHTS The main highlight of Sudan is its amazingly welcoming and diverse people: Arab, Nubian, Dinka, Shilluk, Nuer, etc. Khartoum, the confluence of the Blue and the White Niles, has Kitchener's old steamboat, teashops, an impressive central mosque, and the Mahdi's Tomb in Omdurman. It offers fine dining at one of the restaurants along the waterfront. Further north is the Nubian Desert and the ancient pyramids of Meroe, reputed to be the oldest in the world.

Along the Red Sea, near Port Sudan and Suakin, are some reportedly excellent diving areas, with fishing excursions possible. On the way to Port Sudan is the town of Kassala, located in some spectacular rocky countryside. It could be visited on the way to Eritrea if things improve in the region. Other places that may eventually become safe are further south: the Dinder National Park and the Nile route to Juba, through the swamps of the Sudd, a naturalist's haven. In the deepest darkest southwest is Wau, an isolated, end-of-the-world settlement close to the Central African Republic. To the west, but sadly off-limits due to the Darfur problems, are the volcanic mountains of Jebel Marra near El Fasher.

WHERE TO STAY Throughout Sudan bush sleeping is the best option, but keep a good distance from settlements.

Khartoum There are two places that offer camping. The best and most convenient is the Blue Nile Sailing Club, on the southern bank of the Blue Nile near the church. It costs about US$11 for a vehicle and two people. An added bonus is the imposing presence of Kitchener's steamboat, marooned here since 1898. The other place, which we did not use, is on the road south to Wad Medani, some 10km out. It's not easy to find and has limited shade. Hotels in town to consider are the Hotel Falcon (US$40) and the Akropole, which is very expensive (US$90–150) but worth a visit. It's been run by George the Greek since time began.

Wadi Halfa You might get invited to stay with the customs man, Kamal Hassan Osman, a well-known local character who has a spacious but simple house. Otherwise there is the grotty Hotel Nile or, much better, stay in the desert, which is not always so easy, with so much paperwork to sort out here. See box on *Wadi Halfa* on page 194, *Chapter 8*.

Atbara The Nile Hotel has been recommended; there's little else.

Meroe Wild camping is permitted in the area. There is also a tastefully designed, Italian-run luxury tented camp and restaurant complex. It is not cheap.

Dongola The best place is Olla Hotel. Others are the Haifa Hotel and the Lord Hotel, but the desert might be preferable.

Gedaref The only decent spot is the Hotel El Motwakil, which claims to have guarded parking; it's US$28 a double. You can bush camp south of town on the grassy plains, but be careful of bush fires, which are common in the dry season.

Kassala The best hotel is the Hipton, with good views of town and the impressive granite Taka Mountain domes. Rooms are from US$27.

Port Sudan You may be able to park/camp in the grounds of the Baasher Palace Hotel.

El Obeid Parking is possible at the El Madina Hotel.

Juba The town has only expensive accommodation options. Campers were previously requested to bed down at the police station.

OTHER Photography is a sensitive issue and photographic permits are sometimes needed for both a camera and a video camera. Don't take photos of anything with even the slightest military connection, including airports, government buildings, post offices, bridges, policemen and even fuel stations.

Ferries run from Port Sudan to Jeddah in Saudi Arabia. Those coming south through the Middle East may need to get a visa in Jordan at the Sudan Embassy (*Area No 13135, El Malfuf Easterm, Oman Mountain St, Maviada, Amman;* ✆ *6 644 251/2;* f *6 664 187*).

FURTHER INFORMATION
Sudan: The Bradt Travel Guide, Paul Clammer

SWAZILAND

CAPITAL Mbabane

LANGUAGE AND TELEPHONE English and Swati are the official languages. International telephone code +268.

CURRENCY AND RATE Lilangeni (SZL) (plural emalangeni), but South African rand are universally accepted. US$1 = SZL7.79.

RED TAPE None of any significance. Swaziland is within the South African customs zone.

Visas Most nationalities do not need a visa. Others should check to see if they are available at the border.

African embassies
❸ **Mozambique** Mountain Inn Rd, Mbabane; ✆ 404   ❸ **South Africa** The Mall, Mbabane; ✆ 404 4651
3700

DRIVING AND ROADS Drive on the left. The main roads are good and secondary roads are mostly fine.

Fuel costs Diesel: US$1.50; petrol: US$1.65 per litre.

CLIMATE Swaziland has a climate generally moderated by altitude. The drier but cool season is from May to August. The main rains are from November to April.

HIGHLIGHTS On the way from Mozambique are the well-manicured sugar plantations and the Hlane Royal Park. A roadsign reads 'Motorists, beware of elephants. Cyclists and pedestrians, beware of lions!' Not far from Mbabane is the beautiful green Ezulwini valley, ancestral home of the royal family. The Mlilwane

Wildlife Sanctuary near Lobamba is a delightful stop. Do go for morning or afternoon tea at Reilly's Rock and enjoy the sumptuous colonial house, slumping in the supersoft armchairs while the overnight guests are out. Other reserves or parks include Malolotja Nature Reserve and Mkhaya Game Reserve for black rhinos.

WHERE TO STAY The country is small, so almost any central location will give access to most places of interest.

Mbabane The Cathmar cottages are north of town near Pine Valley.

Manzini Try Swaziland Backpackers, or Myxo's Place, which offers village visits.

Mlilwane Wildlife Sanctuary There is a lovely campsite in the park with well-kept gardens, bar, restaurant and inquisitive warthogs. Reilly's old house in the park is a superb colonial relic, moderately expensive but good for morning biscuits and tea. Entry costs US$4 each, and camping costs US$12, car plus two people.

OTHER With increasing crime in neighbouring South Africa, it's refreshing to visit Swaziland for its peace and tranquillity (except perhaps Mbabane and Manzini at night). Some game parks can only be paid for in rand or local currency, not other cash, even dollars.

FURTHER INFORMATION
Southern Africa, Lonely Planet

TANZANIA

CAPITAL Dodoma

LANGUAGE AND TELEPHONE English and Swahili are the official languages. International telephone code +255.

CURRENCY AND RATE Tanzanian shilling (TZS); US$1 = TZS1190

RED TAPE Watch out for radar and hefty speeding fines. Yes, even in Africa, but no cameras as yet!

Visas Visas are required for all except nationals of some Commonwealth countries, Scandinavia and the Republic of Ireland: US$80. Things change though, so check. A visitor's pass for up to three months maybe issued at the border, costing US$50, depending on nationality. A transit visa for US$40 may be available.

Non-African consulate
❸ French Consulate (issues visas for most French-speaking African countries) Ali Hassan Mwinyi Rd, Dar es Salaam; ✆ 266 6021

9

African embassies

🄴 **Algeria** 34 Ali Hassan Mwinyi Rd, Dar es Salaam; ☏ 211 7619; f 211 7620

🄴 **Angola** 78 Lugalo Rd, Upanga, Dar es Salaam; ☏ 211 7674

🄴 **Burundi** Plot 1007, Lugalo Rd, Dar es Salaam; ☏ 213 8608; f 212 1499

🄴 **Democratic Republic of the Congo** 438 Malik Rd, Dar es Salaam; ☏ 266 6010

🄴 **Kenya** Old Bagamoyo Rd, Dar es Salaam; ☏ 270 1747; f 270 1747

🄴 **Malawi** Zambia Hse, Sokoine Dr/Ohio St, Dar es Salaam; ☏ 213 6954/7260–1

🄴 **Mozambique** 25 Garden Av, Dar es Salaam; ☏ 211 6502/251. Consulate in Zanzibar.

🄴 **Rwanda** 32 Ali Hassan Mwinyi Rd, Dar es Salaam; ☏ 211 5889; f 211 5888; e ambadsm@minaffet.gov.rw

🄴 **South Africa** Mwaya Rd, Msasani, Dar Es Salaam; ☏ 260 1800/0484

🄴 **Sudan** 64 Ali Mwinyi Rd, Dar es Salaam; ☏ 211 7641; f 211 5811

🄴 **Uganda** 25 Msasani Rd, Dar es Salaam; ☏ 266 7391; f 266 7224; e ugadar@intafrica.com

🄴 **Zambia** 5–9 Sokoine Dr/Ohio St, Dar es Salaam; ☏ 211 8481; f 211 2977

🄴 **Zimbabwe** NIC Hse, Sokoine Dr or New Life Hse, Ohio St, Dar es Salaam; ☏ 211 6789

DRIVING AND ROADS Drive on the left. The main roads are mostly in good condition. Arusha to Dar es Salaam and on to Mbeya is fine. The road from Arusha to Ngorongoro is being tarred and should soon be completed as far as Karatu. The road south from Arusha to Dodoma was said to be atrocious.

Fuel costs Diesel: US$1.55; petrol: US$1.75 per litre.

CLIMATE It's hot and humid along the coast (particularly December to March). The rains are from March/April to May and in November. Inland the rains are January to April. On the central plateau it is warm and drier. The highlands are a little cooler, even cold at times.

HIGHLIGHTS In the north, Arusha is the gateway to the fabulous Serengeti National Park and Ngorongoro Crater. Climbing Mount Kilimanjaro, Africa's highest mountain, is good for those with the inclination and fitness. Bagamoyo, north of Dar es Salaam, is a historic sight with nice beaches close by. Zanzibar has Stone Town with its beautiful winding roads and stunning beaches. In the south are the Ruaha National Park and Selous Game Reserve. Much of the central highland area is very green after the rains and quite wild. South of Dar es Salaam, along a poor remote road, is the former Arab/Omani trading port of Kilwa Kiswani.

WHERE TO STAY

Dar es Salaam Accommodation options are limited and the best bet is to go 20km (12 miles) north along the Bagamoyo road to Kanduchi beach, where there is the Silversands Hotel and Campsite. South of town is Kipepeo Camping and Kim Beach Campsite where costs are US$3 each. In Dar you could try the Safari Inn but parking will be a problem in the city. Bahari Lodge and Campsite is running down, but the setting gorgeous. Power cuts are common in Dar.

Bagamoyo The Travellers' Lodge is one suitable place and another is Badeco Beach Hotel, which has camping.

Zanzibar Various ferries and local pirogues leave daily and hourly from the main wharf in Dar es Salaam. Yellow fever vaccination certificates are obligatory before a ticket is issued. Make sure you find a safe place to park your vehicle before you head over to the island. It's worth the effort, as Zanzibar is really beautiful. There is plenty of accommodation, ranging from hotels to pensions. Budget, but not shoestring, are the following: Hotel Kiponda, Flamingo Guesthouse, Victoria House and St Monica Hostel.

Arusha Stay at the Masai Camp (2.5km outside on the old Moshi road). The cost is US$4–5 each. If it's full of overland trucks, don't expect a quiet night in the bush. The Meserani Snake Park has camping west of town (US$4 each) with workshop and bar, and another place is Arusha Vision Camping.

Mombo Tembo Lodge and Campsite is the place to stay here. US$4 each, with hiking nearby.

Lake Manyara There are a number of camping options here outside the park around the village of Mto Wa Mbu. Look for Panorama Campsite, Twiga Camp and Lodge, National Park Bandas Campsite, Migunga Campsite, Kiboko Bush Camp, Jambo Campsite, Wild Fig Camp and, a cheaper place, Camp Vision Lodge.

Karatu Further along from Lake Manyara is the small town of Karatu. The Safari Inn camping has a nice open garden and good facilities including restaurant/bar. Cost is US$9 for two. Kudu Campsite is another choice.

The Serengeti and Ngorongoro Crater As in Kenya, taking your own vehicle into the national parks is quite expensive. Of course, you do retain the freedom to vary your plans with your own transport. In some circumstances, though, it might be easier to organise something with a tour company from Karatu or Arusha. Taking a tour might cost in the order of US$85–140 per person per day, depending on the number of people. It should include all park fees, accommodation and meals.

Ngorongoro Crater Ngorongoro is a magical place in fine weather. The Simba Camp has been used for some years. Facilities are basic and costs high at US$20 per person, but the views are great. Park entry is US$50 per person per 24 hours, plus a vehicle fee of US$200 (4x4).

Serengeti Covering 15,000 square miles, the Serengeti is a vast park. From Ngorongoro Crater the track passes Olduvai Gorge, famous for its early human remains, and heads to Seronera, the central area with most accommodation. Entry is US$50 for 24 hours plus a vehicle charge of US$40; trucks US$100. The lodges are very expensive but camping in designated areas is possible for US$20 per person per day. Further north is Lobo, with camping. The wildebeest migrations are amazing in this northern zone. Across the border in Kenya is the Masai Mara. West from Seronera is a track to Mwanza and Lake Victoria. It used to get horribly sticky and muddy in the rainy season. If you make it this way, look for the Serengeti Stop Over, a new place with camping near Lake Victoria;

cost US$5 each. It's not unusual to see game around this place, without any entry fees for that night.

Lake Natron There are a couple of camping areas. Riverside Campsite and Waterfall Campsite both charge US$10 per person.

Moshi The Honey Badger Camp for US$5+ is a nice place. Also here is Golden Shower Restaurant and Key Hotel for camping.

Kilimanjaro A good base for climbing Kilimanjaro is the well-known Marangu Hotel in Moshi. It is 10km south of the main gate to the national park and near the start of the most popular route up the mountain. The safe and attractive campsite, with hot showers and pool, costs US$3–4 per person per night. Climbs can be organised here. A more expensive option is Coffee Tree Camping, which also organises climbs. Other choices are Gilman's Camping Site and Amin's Cottages.

A five-day trek will probably cost well over US$500 and up to US$800 per person all in. Beware of the altitude and do not climb higher if you are suffering from prolonged headaches, nausea and loss of appetite – the effects of pulmonary and cerebral oedema can be fatal.

Tanga If you are coming from or going to Mombasa you could pass through Tanga. Look for the Kiboko Guesthouse and Campsite or the Inn by the Sea Hotel on the Ras Kozone Peninsula.

Pangani South of Tanga, look for the Argovia Tented Camp and Campsite with a great location. Another option is the Ushongo Beach Resort.

Same The Elephant Motel south of town allows camping in its large grounds, and has showers. Camping costs US$6 for a car plus two people.

Morogoro Try the New Acropole Hotel for camping out in the yard, or take a room. The bar is lively at night, with lots of expatriates. It is Canadian-run and very friendly.

Selous Game Reserve Overlanders can rest up at the Ndovu Campsite, a new set-up. Two other rather rustic places with few facilities are Lake Tagalala and Beho Beho Camp.

Mikumi National Park Try Malela Nzuri Campsite just off the main road on the east side of the park. Three other national park campsites are found here near the main gate, but at US$20 per person they are expensive for the limited facilities they offer.

Kisolanza Farm/Iringa (e *kisolanza@cats-net.com*) This is a wonderful stop 40km south of Iringa. The farmhouse has been restored and has a spacious campsite under the trees. If you want more luxury for a change, stay in one of the beautiful new bungalows. Local farm produce and delicious steak can be bought, to cook yourself. There is a cosy bar, but no restaurant. Camping costs US$6 for car plus two people. Closer to Iringa is the Riverside Camp, appropriately beside a river.

Mbeya Staying at the Karibuni Centre out of town is a possibility.

Matema Beach You can stay on the Lake Nyasa shores here at the Matema Lutheran Conference Centre and Retreat, where camping is US$3 plus.

Kilwa Masoko If you have come from Mozambique, you could end up here. The budget option is the New Mjaka Guesthouse. The Omani ruins of Kilwa Kisiwani are some of the best in east Africa.

Mtwara South along the coast is this small town, where Beach Villas are at the beautiful Shangani beach.

OTHER Formerly, UK citizens could not get entry permits at the border, but this seems to be a quirk of the past. We still advise prior checking, though. Most nationalities do need visas, but the majority can be obtained on arrival at the border. The fees vary a lot, from US$10 to US$50 for an entry permit/visa.

FURTHER INFORMATION
Tanzania: The Bradt Travel Guide, Philip Briggs
Zanzibar: The Bradt Travel Guide, Chris and Susie McIntyre
www.tanzania-web.com

TOGO

CAPITAL Lomé

LANGUAGE AND TELEPHONE French is the official language. International telephone code +228.

CURRENCY AND RATE West African franc (CFA); US$1 = CFA415

RED TAPE At the southern border of Togo, officials may try to charge you for having your *carnet* stamped and the bureaucracy is very time-consuming. Touts here are awful too and you may not be left alone. Just ignore them. Crossing the Burkina border in the north in either direction is easy, with no obstructive officials. The military can be officious at times.

Visas Visas are required for all except nationals of ECOWAS countries. They are available at Togo embassies or at French consulates where Togo has no other representation. The main borders issue a seven-day pass, cost US$20. A yellow fever certificate is required.

Non-African consulate
🇪 **French Consulate** (issues visas for most French-speaking African countries) Rue de la Marina, Av de Gaulle, Lomé; ✎ 221 2576

African embassies
🇪 **Ghana** Route de Kpalimé, Lomé; ✎ 221 3194
🇪 **Mali** Try at Quartier Ablogame, Rue de la Paix, Lomé; ✎ 213 458

🇪 **Nigeria** 311 Bd du 13 Janvier (Bd Greulaire), Lomé; ✎ 221 3455
🇪 **Niger** Consulate only; ✎ 221 6373/6313

DRIVING AND ROADS Drive on the right. The main roads are in generally good condition. Traffic in Lomé is horrendous, with very few signposts.

Fuel costs Diesel: US$1.10; petrol: US$1.10 per litre.

CLIMATE The rainy season is April to July, with shorter rains in October and November. The temperature is generally pleasant in the dry season, but still hotter inland.

HIGHLIGHTS Lomé has a fetish market. Along the coast from Lomé is Lake Togo, with watersports, and Togoville with voodoo culture. For hiking there are the beautiful hills of Kpalimé. Visit the fortified, tiered, conical compounds (tata houses) of the Tamberma people and the hilly scenery of the Kandé area. From Kandé it's about 16km to Nadoba, the main village. Niamtougou, which has a good market, is another base for visiting these unusual constructions.

WHERE TO STAY

Lomé Near Robinson Plage there was camping at Le Ramatou. About 12km east of Lomé town camping and rooms can be found at Chez Alice on the beachfront. Camping costs US$5 per person.

Lake Togo This shallow lake, 30km (18 miles) east of Lomé, is popular for watersports. On the lake's northern shore lies Togoville, the centre of Togo's voodoo culture. There is rumoured to be a new campsite in the immediate vicinity.

Kpalimé Chez Fanny, 2km from town, might allow 'vehicle camping'. Kpalimé is a great base for hiking enthusiasts.

Sokode The Campement Tchaoudjo has rooms from around US$8.

Kandé is the main town for visiting the amazing Tamberma tata houses. There is the basic but friendly Auberge Oxygène, which has a large bar with cold drinks. Rooms are cheap (US$12) and there is space to camp, too. It is possible to 'sleep' on the floor of one of the Tamberma houses if you're 'young at heart'.

Dapaong There are two branches of the Hotel Tolérance here; each has good parking and nice rooms (US$15) if you want one. Amazingly there is one on either side of town, on the main road, which is very long.

Atakpamé The best hotel in Togo, perhaps, is the Hotel Sahelian. If you're heading south, it's on the left side of the road just before town. Everything works and it has secure parking/camping. Rooms with air conditioning from US$25.

OTHER After the troubles of 2005, things are much better now. However, visitors should still keep a close eye on developments, avoid crowds and keep a low profile if the situation deteriorates.

FURTHER INFORMATION
West Africa, Rough Guides and Lonely Planet

TUNISIA

CAPITAL Tunis

LANGUAGE AND TELEPHONE Arabic is the official language. International telephone code +216.

CURRENCY AND RATE Tunisian dinar (TND); US$1 = TND1.17

RED TAPE None of any significance. Visitors with vehicles will have the fact stamped into their passports.

Visas Nationals of most western European countries can stay in Tunisia for up to three months without a visa. Citizens of the USA, Canada, Germany and Japan can stay up to four months. Nationals of Australia, New Zealand and South Africa may need a visa. Visas are not issued at the border and should be applied for at any Tunisian embassy or consulate beforehand. Costs from US$5–15. Israeli nationals are not allowed into the country. Visitor's entry permits are issued at the border.

Non-African consulate

ⓔ French Consulate (issues visas for most French-speaking African countries) Pl de l'Indépendance, Tunis; ☏ 24 5700

African embassies

ⓔ Algeria 18 Rue de Niger 100 2, Tunis
ⓔ Egypt Av Mohammed V, Tunis; ☏ 79 1181
ⓔ Ivory Coast Rue Fatima El Fehria, Mutuelle-Ville, Tunis; ☏ 79 6601; f 79 8852
ⓔ Libya 35 Rue Alexander Dumas, Tunis; f ☏ 04 23332

ⓔ Mali 117 Av Jurgurtha, Mutuelle-Ville, Tunis; ☏ 79 2589
ⓔ Morocco 39 Rue du 1er Juin, Mutuelle-Ville, Tunis; ☏ 78 7103
ⓔ Sudan 30 Av de l'Afrique, Tunis; ☏ 23 8544; f 75 0884

DRIVING AND ROADS Drive on the right. The roads are generally in good condition. There are a limited number of tracks and pistes in the south near the borders of Algeria and Libya; some are restricted. Watch your speed if a minor road joins the major road you're on; the area around the junction may have a lower speed limit and sometimes there are police checks.

Fuel costs Diesel: US$0.70; petrol: US$0.90 per litre.

CLIMATE Tunisia has a Mediterranean climate in the north with cool, sometimes rainy, winters. In the south it is hotter, with a dry desert climate inland.

HIGHLIGHTS Tunisia has a number of ancient Roman sites, including that of Carthage (near Tunis), Dougga and Bulla Regia. El Djem has a gem of a Roman amphitheatre. Beaches are found south of Hammamet and on the island of Djerba. In the south are the oasis towns of Douz, where you will find organised camel trips to 'nomadic' camps, plus Tozeur and Nefta with

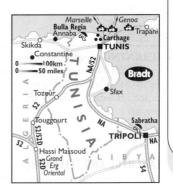

9

picturesque palmeries. The vast Chott el Jerid is a shimmering salt lake. In contrast, the lunar landscape of Matmata near Gabès conceals a once-busy community living underground, in caves chiselled out of the rock – you can visit their dwellings.

WHERE TO STAY There are a few campsites throughout Tunisia.

Tunis The Hotel Amilcar, north of town and close to Sidi Bou Said, is on the beach with fine views. It has safe parking and camping might be allowed. It is also possible, and currently safe, to sleep in your car at the ferry port in La Goulette.

Nabeul It is possible to camp at the Hotel Les Jardins close to the beach.

Hammamet There is a nice camping place with olive trees and a small hotel; take the southern motorway exit to Hammamet, and it's at the first crossroads next to a fuel station.

Gabès The slightly run-down youth hostel has camping in its large grounds. It's hard to find, though. When driving north to south, turn left off the main road at a roundabout with fuel station (near the new bypass ring road), then fork left almost immediately down a narrow road through a dry riverbed on the northwest of town, passing some markets. Turn left at the end and it's on your left.

Tozeur There is a shady pleasant camping place south of town in the palmerie: Camping Beau Rivages.

Nefta Try the Hotel Marhaba, which allows camping in the grounds.

Degache There is a pleasant campsite in the palmeries.

OTHER Tunisia is easy-going by Muslim standards, particularly in areas frequented by tourists, but outside these areas life is still conservative and revolves around the mosque, *hammam* (local baths) and cafés. Act and dress appropriately.

FURTHER INFORMATION
Tunisia, Barnaby Rogerson (Cadogan)
www.tunisiaonline.com

UGANDA

WARNING! Uganda is generally a safe destination, but with one exception. Northeast Uganda was dominated by the LRA (Lord's Resistance Army) and some areas may still be unsafe despite a new peace agreement. Always check the latest conditions before heading to this area.

CAPITAL Kampala

LANGUAGE AND TELEPHONE
English is the official language. International telephone code +256.

CURRENCY AND RATE Ugandan shilling (UGX); US$1 = UGX1515

Money can be changed in Kampala. There are some ATMs, but they only accept Visa credit cards. Cash dollars (US) and cash advances can be obtained at the banks.

RED TAPE The border process is normally efficient and quick. There could be some roadblocks close to the Democratic Republic of the Congo border and in the north with remnant elements of the LRA rebellion.

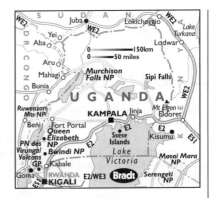

Visas Visas are not required for nationals of Denmark, Finland, France, Germany, Israel, Japan, Sweden and most Commonwealth countries – India, New Zealand and Nigeria are exceptions. Visas cost US$50. They can be obtained at the border and are valid for 30 days. Students/ISS cardholders can get a discount.

Non-African consulate

❸ French Consulate (issues visas for most French-speaking African countries) 19 Lumumba Av, Kampala; ☎ 342 120

African embassies

❸ Burundi Anington Rd, Kampala; ☎ 235 850
❸ Democratic Republic of the the Congo 20 Phillip Rd, Kololo, Kampala; ☎ 230 610
❸ Ethiopia Kira Rd, near National Museum, Kampala; ☎ 348 340; f 341 885
❸ Kenya 41 Nakasero Rd, Kampala; ☎ 258 235–9; f 258 239; e kenhicom@africaonline.co.ug

❸ Rwanda 2 Nakayima Rd, Kampala; ☎ 344 045; f 258 854; e ambakampala@minaffet.gov.rw
❸ South Africa 2b Nakasero Rd, Kampala; ☎ 343 543
❸ Sudan 21 Nakasero Rd, Kampala; ☎ 243 518
❸ Tanzania 4/6 Kagera Rd, Kampala; ☎ 256 272; e tzrep@imul.com

DRIVING AND ROADS Drive on the left. The main roads are in generally good condition. Upcountry the condition of some dirt roads can be badly affected by wet weather.

Fuel costs Diesel: US$1.95; petrol: US$1.65 per litre.

CLIMATE Uganda's position on the Equator is tempered by its high altitude, giving it a very pleasant climate. The rainy seasons are March to June and October to December.

HIGHLIGHTS An undoubted highlight of Uganda is tracking gorillas in the rainforests, but it's not a cheap activity. See Murchison and Sipi falls, Queen Elizabeth National Park, go trekking in the Ruwenzori Mountains and relax for a few days on Ssese Island. There is also white-water rafting on the Nile, while staying in Jinja. Lake Bunyoni (near Kabale) is a very tranquil and relaxing place to spend a couple of days.

WHERE TO STAY

Kampala The Kampala Backpackers Hostel and Campsite (*www.backpackers.co.ug*), Kalema Road in Lungujja, just off Naktete Road and west of town, has a relaxed atmosphere. Camping costs US$3–4 per person. Also look for Red Chilli Hideaway and Camping (*www.redchillihideaway.com*). About 4km east of town is the new campsite Andrew's Farm.

Entebbe There are two places here, Bussi Island on the lakeshore for US$3–4 each and Kisubi Beach Resort for US$2 per person.

Jinja Apart from Speke (after he left Burton), most people stop over in Jinja for the white-water rafting. In or close to town you can stay at either Explorers Backpackers or the Timton Hotel for camping. Not far out (9km) is Bujagali Falls. Here you can stay at Explorers' Campsite or Speke Camp. Also good is Nile High, US$5 for camping. Three companies were offering rafting: Adrift, Equator Rafting and Nile River Explorers. There is also a campsite at Mabira Forest.

Mount Elgon/Sipi Falls To get to Sipi Falls you'll need to climb a steep and treacherous road up into the mountains, but it's worth the effort. Sipi Falls and the surrounding area are beautiful, with green, hilly outcrops and villages dotted around the countryside. You can stay at the Crow's Nest Campsite, which is eco-friendly and has a superb view of Sipi Falls. Camping costs US$3 per person. Nearby are Moses' Campsite and Lacama Lodge.

Masaka Look for Masaka Backpackers with camping for US$3 per person.

Ssese Islands You'll have to leave your vehicle behind, but camping on Buggala Island is available. There is a 50-minute ferry from Kabassese. A new ferry operates from the Nakiwogo port near Entebbe. Campers can stay at Hornbill Campsite, and there are various choices if you want a room.

Lake Mburo National Park It has variously priced tented camps and basic camping.

Mbarara The Agip Motel has a grassy site and secure area for camping.

Kisoro The Rugigana Campsite is popular with overland trucks.

Lake Bunyoni Bunyoni Overland Camp has excellent camping spots right on the lakeside. The camp is well maintained, with a pleasant bar and hot showers. It is becoming a popular overlanders' spot, so it can be a bit crowded and noisy at times. Developments here have ensured a wide choice from luxury to basic. Try one of the following: Bushara Island Camp, Nature's Prime Island, Kalebas Campsite, Crater Bay Cottage and Byoona Amagara Island Retreat. None will break the budget.

Fort Portal This is the base for exploring the Ruwenzori peaks. In town the Ruwenzori Travellers' Inn is highly recommended. Otherwise it is best to head towards the Kibale Forest National Park, south of Fort Portal, and look out for the Safari Hotel, on your right at Nkingo village. Camping costs US$2. For the Ruwenzori National Park, stay in Kasese or at Ruboni Campsite, a community-run place, for US$3 per person. Kibale Forest National Park has Chimp Valley Resort and Safari Hotel as cheaper places.

Bwindi The campsites are near the Buhoma Gate of the national park. The Buhoma Community Rest Camp costs US$3 and the Bwindi Gorilla's Nest Rest

Camp is US$6. Also just outside the park is the Lake Kitandara Bwindi Camp, another cheap choice.

Mgahinga There is a community campsite just near the national park entrance gate with a spectacular setting. Check out the other option, Mount Mgahinga Rest Camp nearby – it's only US$180 per person for a double room. For Nkuringo stay at the Nkuringo Campsite for US$5 per tent.

Murchison Falls National Park Red Chilli has a place with camping (US$6); others are Rabonga Camp, Top of Murchison Falls, Sambiya Lodge and Nile Safari Camp. The falls are particularly spectacular.

Queen Elizabeth National Park There is abundant wildlife here. You will need to be self-sufficient and carry all your supplies with you. During the rainy season the roads in either park can be treacherous. Camping with basic facilities costs US$6 per person. There is also self-catering, where facilities include a basic hut and a staffed kitchen. A number of private campsites have opened across the area: Kookabura, Mweya, Channel 1&2. The entry charge is US$20 per person and US$20 per vehicle.

OTHER

For gorilla trekking The three options are Bwindi National Park, Mgahinga National Park and now Nkuringo, part of Bwindi. Most opt for Bwindi, as they have three groups of gorillas that have been habituated, while Mgahinga has only one. It can get cold up in the mountains, so come prepared. Entry fees are from US$30 per night. Gorilla-tracking permits are now US$500. Contact the UWA (Uganda Wildlife Association) office (*Kiira Rd, Kampala;* \ *0414 355000; www.safari-uganda.com/uganda/bwindi*) for up-to-date prices and entry fees.

FURTHER INFORMATION

Uganda: The Bradt Travel Guide, Philip Briggs
www.myuganda.co.ug
www.visituganda.com
www.ugandatourism.org/lodges.php

WESTERN SAHARA

CAPITAL Laayoune

LANGUAGE AND TELEPHONE Arabic is the official language. International telephone code +212.

CURRENCY AND RATE Dirham (MAD); US$1 = MAD7.30

RED TAPE Officials are often extremely helpful. When crossing the Sahara it is advisable to have many copies of the *Personal details* document in *Appendix 2*, page 316, plus copies of your passport and driving licence, as these are required at roadblocks in Western Sahara and in Morocco.

Visas Most visitors to Western Sahara/Morocco do not require visas and can remain in Morocco for 90 days on entry. Some nationalities do need visas, so it's still best to check.

African embassies Currently the same as those listed for *Morocco*, page 265.

DRIVING AND ROADS Drive on the right. Roads are generally in good condition on all major routes, apart from more remote desert tracks. Some areas are off-limits to foreigners.

Fuel costs Diesel: US$0.60; petrol: US$0.70 per litre.

CLIMATE Western Sahara has a continental climate, with extremes in the interior and desert in the south. The south is generally hotter and inland nights can be cold in winter. Mist often hangs around along the coast, where cold currents hit hot shores.

HIGHLIGHTS The nominal capital, Laayoune, has some older mosques and buildings, but is fundamentally a fairly modern town. The beach is not far away at Laayoune Plage. The Atlantic coast is a bleak and often windswept region, but has a stark beauty of its own. Dakhla is the main point of interest in the south. Visiting Smara is now possible and some have taken the desert piste to/from Assa, east of Tan Tan. If it ever opens up, the desert inland could be a wild region to explore.

 WHERE TO STAY There are now several recognised campsites. Desert camping is also an option, but don't end up stopping by accident in any military zone that is not clearly defined.

Tan Tan Along the coast there are a couple of small, narrow but spectacular inlets where parking is allowed. Cost is US$1.50.

El Ouata/Tan Tan Plage At the road junction is a restaurant/fuel station, Les Deux Chameaux. Rooms are available and there is camping in the yard behind.

Sidi Afkhenir There is camping within the courtyard at Le Courbine d'Argent. Twenty-two kilometres south of the town on the north side of the road is the amazing blue lagoon, La Lagune de Nella, where camping is allowed for a small fee.

Laayoune There's nothing suitable here, although camping cars can park near the airport.

Dawra North of Laayoune is Camping le Bedouin (e *le_roi_bedouin@hotmail.com* or *leroibedouin@altern.org; www.geocities.com/leroibedouin*). A beautiful site on the edge of a salt lake amidst wild scrubby dunes.

Boujdour Camping down by the beach at Camping Sahara Line, Plage de Boujdour is excellent, with good hot showers and laundry facilities. A high wall shelters the site from the pervasive wind. Also, 20km south of town is a police check-post and tarmac road down to an isolated beach. Camping is allowed here on the beach.

Dakhla Dakhla is set at the end of an amazingly beautiful sandy peninsula. A few kilometres from the turn-off is a place to camp on the south side – look for all the white campervans! There is also a walled campsite Camping Moussafir about 6km before the centre of town. In the town itself is the sumptuous hotel, Sahara Regency (e *sahararegency@yahoo.fr; www.sahararegency.com*).

Motel Barbas This small, friendly settlement offers travellers shelter 80km from the border. Rooms, restaurant and free parking are found here. Rooms from MAD100–150.

OTHER Western Sahara was previously known as Spanish Sahara. In 1975 the Spanish colonists left. Morocco and Mauritania then raised claims to the territory, because of phosphates in the area. The native Saharawi people have been in conflict since that time through their Polisario movement.

Morocco virtually annexed the northern two-thirds of Western Sahara in 1976, and the rest of the territory in 1979, following Mauritania's withdrawal. A guerrilla war, with the Polisario Front contesting Rabat's sovereignty, ended in a 1991 ceasefire; a referendum on final status has been repeatedly postponed. In May 2003 the area was granted limited autonomy under Moroccan sovereignty. Over the next few years, some democratic reforms and institutions should be established, followed by a referendum of the Saharawi peoples. The problem is defining who is eligible to vote, and this is the daunting task that the UN has so far been unable to complete.

No permanent solution has been found as yet.

FURTHER INFORMATION
Morocco, Barnaby Rogerson (Cadogan)
www.marocnet.com

ZAMBIA

CAPITAL Lusaka

LANGUAGE AND TELEPHONE English is the official language. International telephone code +260.

CURRENCY AND RATE Zambian kwacha (ZMK); US$1 = ZMK3528.
Most tourist places and hostels quote their rates in US dollars and can be paid in cash US dollars. Money can be changed in Lusaka at one of the many exchange bureaux. In other parts of the country it is far more difficult, so stock up on your kwachas in Lusaka.

RED TAPE Not too much, but there is a 'carbon tax' for vehicles: an average 4x4 costs US$45 (depending on weight).

Visas All visitors except citizens of some Commonwealth countries need a visa. British and Republic of Ireland citizens do need visas and may need to get them in advance. A single-entry visa costs, depending on nationality, US$50 (EU) – US$100 (USA & Canada) – US$150 (UK).

African embassies
e **Angola** 6660 Mumana Rd, Lusaka; ✆ 290346; f 292592

e **Botswana** Pandit Nehru Rd, Lusaka; ✆ 252058/250019; f 253895

ⓔ Democratic Republic of the Congo 1124 Parirenyetwa Rd, Lusaka; ☎ 235679/229044
ⓔ Malawi 31 Bishops Rd, Kabulonga, Lusaka; ☎ 265764/437573; f 260225
ⓔ Mozambique Kacha Rd, Lusaka; ☎ 239135/220333; f 220345
ⓔ Namibia 30B Mutende Rd, Woodlands, Lusaka; ☎ 260407/8; f 263858; e namibia@coppernet.zm

ⓔ South Africa 26 Cheetah Rd, Kabulonga, Lusaka; ☎ 260999/260349
ⓔ Tanzania Ujaama Hse, 5200 United National Av, Lusaka; ☎ 227698/253223; e tzreplsk@zamnet.zm
ⓔ Zimbabwe 4th Floor, Ulendo Hse, Cairo Rd, Lusaka; ☎ 229382; f 227474

DRIVING AND ROADS Drive on the left. Many roads are being rebuilt, but there are speed traps and cops everywhere (fine for overtaking on a white line US$80 – a legitimate fine!).

Fuel costs Diesel: US$2.20; petrol: US$2.20 per litre. Very expensive!

CLIMATE It is sunny but cool from May to September and hot from October to November. The rains are from November to April (most parks and other resorts shut down during this time, as the majority of roads are impassable).

HIGHLIGHTS Victoria Falls is the most imposing sight. You can try white-water rafting and bungee jumping if you need more adrenalin highs than you get from just driving on Zambian roads. Try taking an easy canoe ride down the Zambezi if you actually want to enjoy the surroundings. A trip to the South Luangwa National Park, which has a varied array of wildlife, is highly recommended, and in the north are the Kalambo Falls.

WHERE TO STAY

Lusaka Lusaka has now grown beyond recognition; there are several large shopping centres and ATMs throughout the city. Supermarkets and restaurants abound. There are two camping options a little out of town. Eureka Camping Park is 10km south of the city on Katue Road. Camping costs US$6–7 each. It has a bar and restaurant as well as a large grassy camping area with lots of shelters for cooking. Chalets are also available. Pioneer Campsite is signposted 5km south of the Great East Road, 18km east of the city centre, 3km east of the airport turn-off. Both have nearby transport into Lusaka. Camping is also possible at the Chachacha Guesthouse (*www.chachasafaris.com*).

Livingstone/Victoria Falls
(Zambia side) Entrance to the falls is US$10 per person. There are plenty of backpacker places in Livingstone that also offer camping. Their names are liable to change periodically, even if the premises don't. Jolly Boys is now located behind the museum in town. It's clean and has a great atmosphere, but is often packed. There is a tiny camping area but it's OK for independent campers; dorms and rooms are also available. Camping costs US$5, dorms

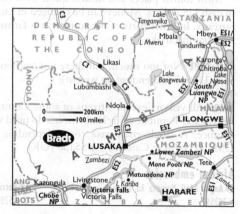

from US$8, rooms from US$28. The Grotto (e *grotto@zamnet.zm*) is still a favourite campsite, with a large grassy area, pool, bar, hot showers with plenty of water and power. Camping costs US$5. Another possibility is The Waterfront. The camping area here could do with more maintenance, but the bar/restaurant/chalets are very nice, though rather expensive. Camping here costs US$8 per person; rooms from US$28–50 per person.

Upstream from Victoria Falls is Bovu Island. It is popular, so it may be worth checking beforehand (↘ 323 708; e *jungle@zamnet.zm*). Camping costs US$4 per person.

Kazungula/Shesheke At Shesheke is Brenda's Best Baobab, which comes highly recommended, with prices from US$6.

Lake Kariba Look out for Eagle's Rest, but beware of crocodiles!

Kafue National Park Not all that cheap, but providing camping are Kainugu Campsite and Puku Pans Campsite. Cheaper are the designated 'self-service' camp spots run by the national park, called Mupasha and Amanzimtoti.

Chipata There is Chachacha Backpackers with camping here. Other places *en route* to South Luangwa are Bridge Camp and at Petauke is Zulu Kraal Campsite. The Mama Rulla is probably still the best campsite in Chipata, with a small bar, large camping area and lots of showers (hot if you ask for the fire to be lit). Camping costs US$7; rooms from US$35. Internet here costs US$1.50 per 15 minutes. (There is now a Barclays bank in town too, with an ATM that actually worked.)

South and North Luangwa National Park Park entry is US$25 per person, with a foreign registered vehicle costing an extra US$30. In general the wildlife is prolific, but the season may dictate the actual abundance of animals you find. There are also reasonable camping opportunities just outside the park; facilities are good at each of the camps. Camping costs US$5 per person. Choices abound, but most are expensive, so check out Wildlife Camp. Flatdogs is set to go upmarket. In the North Park is Natangwe Community Campsite.

Croc Valley It was a part of the old croc farm. Off the main road about 2km from South Luangwa Park entrance on the right, it is a very friendly campsite. A new bar and restaurant with pool and hot showers are being built. There is a large grassy area to camp on and another camping area for overland trucks is in the process of being built. With a fantastic setting right on the river's edge, you have chances to see elephants, hippos, zebra, etc wandering through the campsite. Camping US$5 per person.

Lower Zambezi National Park There is a community campsite near Chongwe.

Mpika The DDSP Compound has been suggested. No other details are available.

Kasanka National Park Area Two places exist that are cheap: Pontoon Campsite and Fibre Campsite. At Lake Waka Waka is a tranquil place to bush camp.

OTHER Zambia is developing very fast, but unfortunately crime is now on the increase, particularly in Lusaka. Do not walk anywhere at night; take a taxi. Be careful around Victoria Falls after dark and watch out for petty theft. The country is getting very expensive, but most things do now work.

The following list concerning Livingstone activities on the Zambian side of the falls has been sent to us by Deborah Thiele (*www.AfricaExpeditionSupport.com*): full-day rafting – US$140, jet boat – 30 minutes US$90, gorge swing – US$115 full day, bungee jump – US$90 per jump, tandem bungee jump – US$130, canoe Upper Zambezi – half day US$95/full day US$105, walk with lions – 45 minutes US$120, sunset/booze cruise – US$40 (including drinks and barbecue dinner).

FURTHER INFORMATION
Zambia: The Bradt Travel Guide, Chris McIntyre
www.zambia.co.zm

ZIMBABWE

☞ **WARNING!** At the time of writing, after the farcical elections of 2008, there are still sporadic violent disputes in Zimbabwe. Check locally if possible before contemplating a trip to the country. Most travellers who have visited have stated that tensions are running high. There is no fuel in most of Zimbabwe.

CAPITAL Harare

LANGUAGE AND TELEPHONE English, Shona and Sindebele are the official languages. International telephone code +263.

CURRENCY AND RATE Zimbabwe dollar (ZWD). Rampant inflation is now the norm, so rates will fluctuate dramatically.

RED TAPE With the current problems in Zimbabwe, there are now major roadblocks and frequent police checks.

Visas Visas are required for most nationalities. They vary in cost; some are free, others are US$40–50. Yellow fever vaccination certificates are obligatory. A visitor's entry pass may be issued at the border.

African embassies

❺ **Angola** Doncaster Hse, 26 Speke Av, Harare; ☏ 479 0070/5

❺ **Botswana** 22 Phillips Av, Belgravia, Harare; ☏ 472 9551/479645; f 470 8459

❺ **Kenya** 95 Park Lane, Harare; ☏ 479 2901

❺ **Malawi** Malawi Hse, 11 Duthie Rd, Alexandra Pk, Harare; ☏ 479 8584/470 5611

❺ **Mozambique** 152 Herbert Chitepo Av, Harare; ☏ 425 3871; f 425 3875

❺ **Namibia** 31A Lincoln Av, Avondale or Borrowdake Rd, Harare; ☏ 488 5800; e namhighcom@primenet.co.zw

❺ **South Africa** Temple Bar Hse, 7 Elcombe Av/2nd St, Belgravia, Harare; ☏ 475 3147

❺ **Tanzania** Ujamaa Hse, 23 Baines Av, Harare; ☏ 472 1870; e tanrep@icon.co.zw

❺ **Zambia** 6th Floor, Zambia Hse, 48 Union Av, Harare; ☏ 477 3777; f 479 0856

DRIVING AND ROADS Drive on the left. Roads were in relatively good condition.

Fuel costs Diesel: US$1.50; petrol: US$1.70 per litre. These are old figures and, due to severe shortages, could change drastically.

CLIMATE Because of its generally higher altitude the country has a temperate climate. The rainy season is December to March and cool season May to September.

HIGHLIGHTS In the east are the highlands and Chimanimani National Park. Perhaps the best-known site is the Great Zimbabwe ruin near Masivingo. In the northwest is the Lake Kariba district, with its lake of dead trees. Victoria Falls offers a variety of activities, from white-water rafting to helicopter rides over the falls. Other national parks are Hwange, Mana Pools, Matobo and Matusadona.

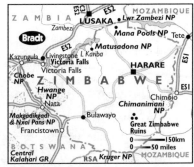

WHERE TO STAY

Harare Most overlanders used to head for Backpackers and Overland Lodge on Twentydales Road. Camping cost US$3. You might also try the Hillside Lodge or York Lodge in Newlands. Don't walk around at night.

Bulawayo The municipal caravan park and camp site and Packers Rest were said to be good for camping. Don't walk around at night.

Mutare Look for the municipal caravan and camping park on Harare Road. Don't walk around at night.

Chimanimani National Park Mutekeswane Base Camp is the place to stay. Formerly, Heaven Mountain Lodge was a great place to stay before trekking up the mountain. You can leave your vehicle at the park entrance and take all necessary goods with you while trekking the area for a few days. You'll need to be self-sufficient; camping is possible in the various caves and lodges dotted around the area. Park entry fees were US$5 per day.

Victoria Falls Many travellers went to the Victoria Falls Restcamp and Lodges or Victoria Falls Backpackers. Other places were Club Shoestring and Tokkie Lodge. Facilities are reasonable and all are within walking distance of the action; be careful after dark though. Camping cost US$4–5 per person. There was an entrance charge of US$20 to visit the Victoria Falls Park, but it is likely to have increased.

Great Zimbabwe National Park Park entry fees were US$5 and the campsite in the actual ruins was shady and comfortable, with excellent facilities. Camping used to cost US$5–6 for a site. Watch out for the vervet monkeys; they'll steal anything.

OTHER The economic situation in the country is very bad, so expect shortages of fuel and supplies. So far tourists have not been affected directly, but seek the latest advice. Zimbabwe has a significant tsetse-fly problem, particularly along Lake Kariba. You will see blue-and-silver screens dotted along the side of roads, which attract the flies. Tsetse flies can give a very vicious bite, so beware. You may also come across tsetse-fly control stations, where two people with a butterfly net in either hand search every part of your vehicle for the elusive fly. This is a genuine search; you are very unlikely to be asked for any 'donation', but the experience may keep you amused for days. And don't wear blue; it's the flies' favourite colour.

FURTHER INFORMATION
East and Southern Africa: The Backpacker's Manual, Philip Briggs (Bradt Travel Guides)
www.zimbabwe.net

A hazy sunshine greeted us as we parked by the seaside. A couple of tour buses pulled up for the view. At this point we were more troubled by our lack of communication with the shipping agents. The internet had crashed at the café. How and when were we going to get the Land Rover home? It's a pity that we took in the significance of the view from the car park too hurriedly. It should have been a moment to savour.

Table Mountain was clearly in the picture: the symbolic end of our trip, which had taken us from the Sudan Embassy in London to Cape Town.

Well, we had made it, but nobody else knew that. American tourists poured from the coach; if it was Wednesday, it must be Cape Town.

Appendix I

FRENCH AND ARABIC TRANSLATION LIST You may well speak normal conversational French, but possibly the technical terms for vehicle parts will not spring easily to mind. We have listed (in alphabetical order) all relevant vehicle parts in French. As for Arabic, it's probably safe to assume you know nothing, as we did! *Salaam Aleikum* with a smile can get you a long way, but you can still find yourself stuck in smaller towns, sometimes even in major cities, if you do not know the translation of a specific vehicle part, spare or tool. The Arabic translation is phonetic, ie: the way one would say it rather than spell it. We have used more of a general dictionary, including some vehicle parts, spares and tools.

French

accelerator jet	*gicleur de pompe*	cotter pins	*bagues d'appui*
alternator	*alternateur*	crankshaft	*vilebrequin*
anti-roll bar	*barre de stabilisateur*	crescent spanner	*clé plate*
armature	*induit de démarreur*	crown wheel and	*couple conique*
axle casing	*corps de pont*	pinion	
ball bearings	*roulement à billes*	CV joint	*joint homocinétique*
ball joint	*rotule*	cylinder block	*bloc-cylindres*
battery	*batterie*	cylinder head	*culasse*
bearing	*coussinet*	diesel	*gazole*
body	*carrosserie*	differential	*différentiel*
bolt	*boulon*	dipstick	*jauge d'huile*
brake hose	*flexible de frein*	disc brakes	*freins à disque*
brake lining	*garniture de frein*	distance recorder	*compteur kilométrique*
brake master	*maître-cylindre*	distributor	*allumeur*
cylinder		engine mounting	*tampon*
brake shoe	*mâchoires de frein*	exhaust valve	*soupape d'échappement*
brush	*balai*	fan	*ventilateur*
bumper	*pare chocs*	fan belt	*corroie de ventilateur*
camshaft	*arbre à cames*	float	*flotteur*
carburettor	*carburateur*	float chamber	*cuve à niveau constant*
chassis	*chassis*	flywheel	*volant*
clutch	*embrayage*	fracture in tyre	*déchirure*
clutch master	*pompe d'embrayage*	fuel gauge	*indicateur de niveau,*
cylinder			*jauge*
clutch plate	*disque d'embrayage*	fuel line	*canalisation*
clutch slave cylinder	*recepteur d'embrayage*	fuel pump	*pompe à essence (gazole)*
coil	*bobine d'allumage*	fuel tank	*réservoir*
condenser	*condensateur*	fuse	*fusible*
conrod	*bielle*	gasket	*joint*
contact points	*jeu de contacts, rupteur*	gearbox	*boîte de vitesses*

313

generator	dynamo	ring spanner	clé à oeillet
gudgeon pin	axe de piston	rocker	culbuteur
hammer	marteau	rockershaft	axe de culbuteur
handbrake cable	cable de frein à main	rotor arm	rotor de distributeur
handbrake lever	levier de frein à main	rubber bush	coussinet en caoutchouc
heater plug	bougie de préchauffage	screwdriver	tournevis
hose	durite	set of pads	jeu de mâchoires
ignition switch	contacteur d'allumage	shock absorber	amortisseur
inlet valve	soupape d'admission	slow idle jet	gicleur de ralenti
jack	cric	socket	douille
leaf spring	lame de ressort	socket spanner	clé à tube
leakage	fuite	solenoid	solenoid, bendix
limited slip	différentiel autobloquant	spanner	clé
differentials		spare wheel	roue de secours
lock nut	contre écrou	spark plug	bougie
locking washer	arrêtoir	speedo cable	flexible de tachymètre
main jet	gicleur d'alimentation	speedometer	compteur, tachymètre
manifold	collecteur	spring	ressort de suspension
needle valve	pointeau	starter motor	démarreur
nut	écrou	steering column	colonne de direction
oil cooler	radiateur d'huile	steering wheel	volant de direction
oil filter	filtre à huile	thermostat	thermostat
oil seal	bague d'étanchéité	third gear	pignon de la troisième
patch	rustine		vitesse
petrol	essence		(1st première,
petrol cap	bouchon de réservoir		2nd deuxième,
piston	piston		4th quatrième)
piston ring	segment	throttle valve	papillon
pitman arm	levier de direction	tie road	barre de connexion
pliers	pince	torque spanner	clé dynamométrique
pressure plates	plateau de pression	tube	chambre à air
prop shaft	arbre de transmission	tyre	pneu
pulley	poulie	tyre lever	démonte pneu
puncture	crevaison	universal joint	cardan de roue
push rod	tige de culbuteur	valve cover	couvercle de culasse
(motor/engine)		valve guide	guide de soupape
push rod	tige de poussoir	valve spring	ressort de soupape
(transmission)		water pump	pompe à eau
push rod tube	couvercle de tige	wheel	roue
radiator	radiateur	wheel hub	moyeu de roue
rear axle	pont arrière	wheel rim	jante
regulator	régulateur	windscreen	pare-brise
release bearing	butée d'embrayage		

Arabic When reading the imitated pronunciation, stress the part of the word that is underlined. Pronounce each word as if it were an English word and you should be understood sufficiently well.

General

accident	haad_e_thah	camel	j_a_mal
accommodation	m_a_skan	campsite	moA_skar
border	hod_ood_	coffee	q_a_hwah
bread	khobz	doctor	tab_ee_bh

314

drinking water	maa' lesh-shorb	reply to greeting	al laikoum salaam
east	sharq	riverbed	oued
encampment made up of tents	douar	road	shaarea
		road or piste	tric
exchange rate	seAr at-taHweel	sick	mareed
flat stony plain	hammada	Sir	Sidi (only used for a person of higher standing than oneself)
Go away!	Emshee!		
greeting	Salaam al Laikoum		
How long will it take?	Qad aysh waqt tastaghreq be-taakhoz?	small shops	souks
How much?	Kem?	small rock standing in the plain	gara
journey	rehlah		
map	khareetah	south	janoob
married	motazawaj	Stop!	Geff!
morning	sabaah	tea	atai
mountain	jebel	thank you	shokrahn
night	layl	tip	baqsheesh
no (response)	laa	valley between dunes	gassi
north	shemaal		
office	maktab	water	mey
passport	jawaaz safar	west	gharb
policeman	shortee	Where can I park?	Wayn awqef as-sayaarah?
police station	noqtat ash- shortah		
post office	maktab bareed	yes	noam

Vehicle

accelerator	dawaasat al-banzeen	inner tube	anboob daakhelee
anti-freeze	modaad let-tajmeed	long (as in How long?)	taweel
battery	bataareeyah		
brake	faraamel	mechanic	meekaaneekee
breakdown	Ta Atal	motorbike	daraajah bokhaareeyah
camshaft	amood al-kaamah	oil	zayt
car	sayaarah	park (as in park the vehicle)	hadeeqah
carburettor	karboraateere		
clutch	debreiyaaj	piston	makbas
diesel	deezel	puncture	thaqb
distributor	destrebyooter	radiator	raadiyateer
drive	yasooq	screwdriver	mafakk
to drive	yasooq	seatbelt	hezaam al-maqad
engine	moHarrek	spanner	meftaah sawaameel
exhaust	shakmaan	spares	qetaa ghiyaar
fan belt	sayr al-marwahah	spark plug	belajaat
funnel	qomA	speedometer	adaad as-sorah
garage (for fuel)	mahattat banzeen	spring	soostah
garage (for repairs)	garaaj meekaaneekee	steering wheel	ajalat al-qiyaadah
gears	geer	to tow	yashab
handbrake	faraamel	transmission	naql al-harakah
ignition	jehaaz al-eshAal	tyre	'etaar or taayer
indicator	mo'asher	wheel	ajalah

Appendix 2

PERSONAL DETAILS

Wherever you plan to go in Africa, it's worthwhile having some copies of the following information sheet in order to speed up some of the bureaucracy. Use A4 paper, then use this and copies of your passport and driving licence for presentation as required. Of course, the information can be written out at each police post, but the officials don't mind the copied material, so why waste time? Alternatively, make a photocopy of your passport photo page and copy the relevant information below on to the same page before photocopying it again many times.

Surname ....

Name ....

Date of birth ....

Place of birth ....

Nationality ....

Passport number ....

Date of issue ....

Date of expiry ....

Place of issue ....

Profession ....

Permanent address ....

Father's name ....

Mother's name ....

Purpose of visit ....

Vehicle make and plate numbers ....

Driving licence number ....

Appendix 3

Below is an example of a useful checklist so that you can see at a glance whether you have everything you will need.

Item	Have or not	Details	Cost
FINANCES			
Travellers' cheques			
US dollars			
British pounds			
Euros			
Other denominations			
Credit cards			
ROUTE PLANNING			
Where, ie: planned route			
For how long			
Suggested itinerary			
Guidebooks and maps			
Africa guidebooks			
North Africa			
West Africa			
Central Africa			
East Africa			
South Africa			
Africa maps			
Bartholomew (Continental Travel Map) Africa			
Michelin 741 – North and West			
Michelin 745 – North East			
Michelin 746 – Central and South Africa			
Michelin 743 – Algeria & Tunisia			
Michelin 742 – Morocco			
Michelin 747 – Ivory Coast			
BUREAUCRACY			
Visas			
For which countries			
Cost estimate			
Can get beforehand			
Other			

Item	Have or not	Details	Cost
Paperwork			
Passport			
Validity			
Number of unused pages			
Vaccination certificates			
Cholera			
Diphtheria			
Hepatitis A and B			
Meningitis			
Polio			
Rabies (optional)			
Tetanus			
Tuberculosis			
Typhoid			
Yellow fever			
NB: Certificate signed by GP/clinic			
Other			
Bond or insurance			
Carnet de passage (carnet) organised for every country mentioned that you will visit			
International certificate for motor vehicles, ie: *carte grise* (grey card)			
Insurance			
Medical insurance			
Vehicle insurance (optional)			
International driving licence			
References			
in English			
in French			
Passport photos			
VEHICLE SELECTION			
4x4/2WD			
Type			
Registration number			
Chassis number			
Engine number			
Other			
Motorbike			
Type			
Registration number			
Chassis number			
Engine number			
Other			
Bicycle			
Type			
Other			

Item	Have or not	Details	Cost
4X4/2WD			
Preparation			
Sleeping requirements			
Tent			
Rooftop tent			
Inside the vehicle			
Mattresses			
Pillows			
Sleeping bags			
Covers for pillows, etc			
Roof rack			
Security			
Padlocks and hasps			
Windows			
Curtains			
Safety box			
Alarm system (optional)			
Bull bar			
Baffle/bash plate			
Suspension			
Heavy-duty suspension fitted			
Spare battery and split charge system			
Oil cooler			
Raised air intake			
Tyres			
Spare tyres			
Inner tubes			
Valves			
Foot or electrical tyre pump			
Tyre repair kit			
Pressure gauge			
Fuel and water tanks			
Capacity			
Fuel			
Water			
Storage boxes			
Seat covers			
Steering-wheel cover			
Stereo			
Type and make			
Serial number			
Canopy			
EQUIPMENT			
Recovery gear			
Electronic or manual winches			
Type and make			
Guarantees			
High-lift jack			
Hydraulic jack			

Item	Have or not	Details	Cost
Blocks of wood to jack on			
Sand ladders			
Towing points			
Towing straps			
Shackles			
Compass and/or Global Positioning System (GPS)			
Type and make			
Mounting and storage system			
Serial number			
Guarantee			
Shovel or sand spades			
Axe or machete			
Warning triangles (2)			
Jerrycans			
Carrying capacity for:			
Fuel			
Water			
Oil			
Fire extinguisher			
Water			
Water purification (eg: Chloromyn T, Puritabs)			
Water filter			
Type			
Capacity of filter before replacement			
Guarantee			
Table and chairs			
Mosquito net/s			
Refrigerator			
Type and make			
Runs on 12V DC or 240V AC or gas or all three			
Serial number			
Guarantee			
Lighting			
Car lights			
Fluorescent strip light			
Map light			
Torch and batteries			
Cooking equipment			
Petrol stoves			
Kerosene stoves			
Container for kerosene			
Meths burners			
Container for methylated spirits			
Gas stoves			
Gas bottle fitted			
Cooking utensils			

ITEM	HAVE OR NOT	DETAILS	COST
Saucepan			
Deep straight-edged frying pan			
Cooking pot or cast-iron pot			
Kettle			
Pressure cooker or wok (optional)			
Decent sharp knife			
Wooden spoon			
Strainer (optional)			
Tin-opener			
Bottle-opener			
Chopping board			
Plates and bowls (plastic or enamel)			
Mugs (plastic)			
Assortment of cutlery			
Matches and/or firelighters			
Fire grill (optional)			
Cleaning up			
Plastic bowl			
Washing-up liquid			
Washing-up cloth			
Scourer (optional)			
Drying-up cloth			
Spares and tools			
Workshop manual			
3 x oil filters			
4 x fuel filters			
2–3 x air filters			
Engine oil (enough for two changes)			
5 litres of gearbox and differential oil			
Grease			
1–2 litres brake and clutch fluid oil			
1–2 litres coolant (you can use water)			
Heater plugs/spark plugs			
One spare diesel injector			
Set of engine gaskets			
Set of all oil seals			
Set of wheel bearings			
Set of engine mounts			
Set of radiator hoses			
Accelerator cable			
2 x fanbelts			
Set of brake pads			
Brake master cylinder rubbers			
Clutch master and slave cylinder rubbers (as above)			
Wheel cylinder kit – rubbers (or kit for disc brakes)			
Water pump			

Item	Have or Not	Details	Cost
Lift pump			
Suspension rubbers and bushes			
Condenser			
Distributor cap			
Contact breaker points			
Spare fuel cap			
Spare radiator cap			
U-bolts centre bolts for leaf springs			
Main leaf springs (coil springs rarely break with careful driving)			
Track rod ends			
Clutch plate			
Wheel nuts			
Water temperature sensor unit			
Sump/gearbox drain plugs			
Propshaft UJ			
Brake hose			
Alternator (complete or at least the brushes)			
Fuses			
Light bulbs			
Other optional parts			
Starter (for remoter areas)			
Fan (for remote areas)			
Injector pipes			
Injector pump (for remote areas)			
Injector pump solenoid if applicable			
Useful items			
Funnel (make sure it fits the filler of your fuel tank)			
Jubilee clips			
Cable ties			
Electrical tapes			
Electrical wires			
Masking tape/duct tape			
Assortment of wire			
Assortment of nuts, bolts and washers			
Plastic fuel line and connectors			
Contact adhesive			
Prately putty/flexible 'bathroom' sealant			
2m fuel hoses (long enough to be used as a siphon)			
Rapid araldite/plastic metal glue			
Plastic padding/instant fibreglass			
Instant gasket paste			
Exhaust repair putty			
Gasket paper			
Can of WD40 or Q20			
Radiator sealant			

Item	Have or not	Details	Cost
Towing eye/cable			
Assorted small sheet metal, short drain piping, square tubing etc			
Assorted bits of rubber, inner tube, old stockings			
Old rags – lots and lots			
Tools			
Good set of spanners (imperial or metric as required)			
Good set of sockets with power bar and ratchet			
Extra large sockets (check sizes needed)			
Assortment of screwdrivers			
Adjustable spanner			
Mole wrench (large and small)			
Pipe wrench			
Grease gun			
Metal and rubber hammers			
Torque wrench			
Pliers (various)			
Circclip removers			
Multi-size puller			
Jump leads			
Set of feeler gauges			
Hacksaw and spare blades			
Multi-meter electrical tester			
Flat metal file			
Small round file			
Coarse flat file			
Hand drill and kit (9V cordless drills can be connected directly to your battery)			
Tyre levers			
Tyre valve tool			
Set of Allen keys			
Centre punch/assorted punches and metal drifts			
Wet and dry sandpaper			
Length of pipe (to extend your power bar for those stubborn nuts)			
Arc welding rods – a few			
G clamp/small vice to attach to bumper			
Magnetic retrieving tool			

MOTORBIKE

Spares and tools			
Repair manual			
1 x spare rear tyre			
1 x front and rear heavy duty inner tubes			

Item	Have or not	Details	Cost
1 x good-quality puncture repair kit with lots of patches			
1 x small mountain bike pump			
A few spare spokes			
Connecting links for chain			
1 x clutch lever			
1 x brake lever			
1 x clutch cable			
1 x throttle cable(s)			
1 x air filter			
3 x oil filters			
1 x fuel filter			
2 x spark plugs			
Fuel hose and jubilee clips			
Bulbs and fuses			
Electrical wire and connectors			
Assorted nuts, bolts and washers			
Main gaskets			
Duct tape			
Assorted cable ties (lots)			
Spare bungee rope/straps			
Instant gasket			
Silicon sealant			
Epoxy glue			
Liquid steel			
Loctite (for nut threads)			
Small tub of grease			
About 1 litre engine oil (for top-up and oiling air filter)			
Standard small toolkit (combination spanners, $^3/_8$" drive ratchet + relevant sockets, screwdrivers)			
Leatherman's or Swiss Army knife			
Feeler gauges			
File			
Spark plug spanner			
Tyre levers			
Personal equipment			
Jacket with built-in shoulder and elbow pads			
Spine protector with a waist band			
Full-length motorcross-style boots (optional)			
Helmet and goggles			
Gloves			

BICYCLE

Spares and tools

Item	Have or not	Details	Cost
Panniers – Overlander by Carradice			
2 x spare tyres			
10 x inner tubes			

ITEM	HAVE OR NOT	DETAILS	COST
Puncture repair kit			
Cables			
Brakepads			
Grease and oil			
Bearings			
Wires and straps			
Pliers			
Set of Allen keys			
Cable cutter			
Spoke tensioner			
Set of spanners			
Screwdriver			
Bottom bracket tensioner			
Front bearing spanner			
Spokes			
Box of nuts and bolts, etc			
Chain link extractor			
Toothbrush			
Personal equipment			
Helmet			
Gloves			
Sunglasses			
2 x whistles (as a warning and signal)			
Compass			

CAMPING: MOTORBIKE/BICYCLE

Tent			
Sleeping mat			
Sleeping bag			
Nylon string			
Towel			
Torch			
Thermarest mattress			
Cooking			
Stove, eg: MSR high-quality petrol stove or Coleman's multi-fuel cooker			
2 x spoons			
2 x plastic bowls			
2 x plastic cups			
Saucepan			
Penknife			
Water			
2 x Travelwell military water purifiers			
2 x 10-litre water bags			
Water bottle			
Filter			
Food			
Salt and pepper			
Herbs and spices			

ITEM	HAVE OR NOT	DETAILS	COST
Tea and coffee			
Sugar			
Powdered milk			
Muesli/cereals/oats			
Jam/marmalade			
Rice and pasta			
Tubes of tomato puree			
Stock cubes			
Marmite/Vegemite			
Tinned meat			
Tinned vegetables and fruit			
Packets of instant foods, ie: ready-made pasta, etc			
Oil			
Vinegar			
Flour or cornflour			
Dried beans			
Mustard			
Kendal Mint Cake			
Dried mushrooms or other			
Dried fruit and nuts			
Biscuits and crackers			
Boiled sweets			
Packets of dried food (specific for cyclists and bikers)			
Instant mashed potato			
Small packets Parmesan cheese			

MEDICAL KIT

Seek medical advice before use of any medicaments and read the instructions.

Analgesics (painkillers)

Aspirin for sore throat and mild pain			
Paracetamol for mild pain and temperature			
Ibuprofen for joint inflammation and pain			
Paracetamol/codeine for moderate pain			

General

Stemetil for severe nausea, vomiting and vertigo			
Loperamide for acute diarrhoea			
Oral-rehydration sachets for dehydration			
Senokot tabs for constipation			
Lozenges for sore throats			
Indigestion tabs for excessive acid and indigestion			
Antihistamines for allergies			

Item	Have or Not	Details	Cost
Pseudoephedrine (Sudafed) for nasal and sinus congestion			
Clove oil for toothache			
Antibiotics			
Amoxycillin for chest, ear, cellulitis and urinary tract infection (general antibiotic)			
Ciprofloxacin for gut and urinary tract infections			
Tinidazole for amoebic dysentery and giardia			
Flucloxacillin for skin infections			
Erythromycin for skin and chest infections (if allergic to penicillin)			
Mebendazole for thread-, round- and hookworm infections			
Malaria (prevention and treatment)			
Anti-malarial tablets			
Treatment for malaria			
Bilharzia			
Biltracide			
Eye, ear and nose			
Chloramphenicol for eye infections			
Normal saline sachets for eye wash			
Eye bath as an eye-wash unit			
Ear drops			
Nose drops			
Powder and creams for the skin			
Hydrocortisone for skin allergies and insect bites			
Lactocalamine for sunburn, itching and rashes			
Daktarin cream for fungal infections			
Cicatrin powder for wound infections (antibiotic)			
Magnesium sulphate for treatment of boils			
Comprehensive first-aid kit			
Granuflex dressing for tropical ulcers			
Gauze swabs for cleaning wounds			
Melolin of varying sizes for non-sticky wound dressing			
Micropore or zinc-oxide tape used as surgical tape			
Assortment of plasters			
Crêpe bandage for muscular injuries			
Steristrips for wound closures			

Item	Have or not	Details	Cost
Wound dressing for heavily bleeding wounds			
Triangular bandage for securing broken limbs			
Safety pins			
Steripods (disposable antiseptic sachets)			
Water gel or Jelonet dressing for burns			
Scissors			
Tweezers			
Disposable gloves			
Lancets (sterile needles which can be used for popping blisters)			
Betadine as antiseptic solution			
Sterile surgical equipment (optional)			
Sterile surgical gloves			
Scalpel (disposable)			
Mersilk suture of varying sizes			
Suturing forceps			
Stitch cutter			
Dental needles			
Syringes of varying sizes			
Variety of needles			
Pink and green Venflon for intravenous administration			
Sterile gauze to cleanse area of sterilisation			
Medical set for intravenous administration			
Other items for the medical kit			
Thermometer			
Permethrin mosi-net treatment			
Repellent coils to burn at night			
Insect repellent			
Anti-itch cream			
Flu medication			
Medication for personal ailments			
Condoms, pill or other			
Tampons			

PERSONAL KIT

Clothes

Jeans			
T-shirts			
Light cotton trousers			
Skirt			
Tunic dress			
Smarter trousers			
Long-sleeved shirts			
Short-sleeved shirts			
Swimming costumes			

ITEM	HAVE OR NOT	DETAILS	COST
Wraparound skirts (also used as towels)			
Light scarf or shawl			
Sweatshirts			
Thick jerseys			
Woolly hats			
Hiking boots			
Sandals			
Raincoats			
Socks and underwear			
Toiletries			
Soap			
Shampoo			
Flannel			
Toothbrush & toothpaste			
Towels (or sarongs)			
Portable washing machine			
Bucket with lid			
Washing liquid/powder			
Nylon or other string			
Clothes pegs			
Miscellaneous			
Pens and pencils			
Writing paper			
Diary or other writing material			
Address book			
Games/playing cards			
Books and magazines			
Music on either tapes or CD			
Short-wave radio			
Pocket calculator			
Swiss Army knife or Leatherman's			
Hammock			
Binoculars and various books on fauna, flora and wildlife			
Driver's logbook			
Gifts			
Photographic equipment			
Dust-proof storage system			
Camera			
Polaroid camera			
Lens/es			
Cleaning gear			
Film			
Other			
Serial number(s)			

Appendix 4

VISA REQUIREMENTS AT A GLANCE

For details see country entries. Prices quoted by UK embassies.

COUNTRY	VISA REQUIREMENTS	APPROX COST
Algeria	Required for all except nationals of other Arabic countries; if you have a stamp from Israel, South Africa, Malawi or Taiwan in your passport the visa application will be rejected; 30-day tourist visas are available	US$55 single
Angola	Required for all; visa applications are referred to Direçao de Emigraçao e Fronteiras (DEFA) in Luanda. Very problematic to obtain, whether in London or Africa.	US$80 single, US$155 double
Benin	Required for all except nationals of the Economic Community of West African States (ECOWAS); 48-hour entry visas are available and can be extended in Cotonou	US$85 15 days single
Botswana	Not required for nationals of USA, UK, Germany, Netherlands and most Commonwealth countries	n/a
Burkina Faso	Required for all except for nationals of ECOWAS	US$50 single
Burundi	Required for all nationals	US$60 single
Cameroon	Required for all	US$115 single
Central African Republic (CAR)	Required for all; nationals of France, Australia, New Zealand and the Republic of Ireland need to get permission from Bangui before entry	US$70–100
Chad	Required for all except French and German citizens. Valid up to three months.	US$50–100
Congo (People's Republic)	Required for all except nationals of France	US$140
Democratic Republic of Congo (DRC)	Required for all	US$85
Djibouti	Required for all	US$75
Egypt	Required for all except nationals of Arab countries and Malta	US$30–40 single
Equatorial Guinea	Required for all	US$65–80
Eritrea	Required for all	US$50
Ethiopia	Required for all except Kenyan nationals	US$50–65 multiple entry 3 months
Gabon	Required for all; all applications need to be referred to Libreville and can take up to a week to issue	US$100 single
Gambia	Required for all except for nationals of Commonwealth countries.	n/a

Ghana	Required for all except nationals of ECOWAS	US$60–80 single 3 months
Guinea	Required for all	US$130–180 (multiple)
Guinea Bissau	Required for all except nationals of Cape Verde	US$20–50
Ivory Coast (Côte d'Ivoire)	Required for all except nationals of ECOWAS; US passport holders don't need visas for stays up to 90 days	US$50–80
Kenya	Required for all except nationals of most Commonwealth countries (nationals of Australia, New Zealand and UK do need visas)	US$55 single
Lesotho	Required for all except nationals of Commonwealth countries and South Africa	n/a
Liberia	Required for all	US$70–100 single
Libya	Required for all; independent tourist visas not issued to nationals of Australia, New Zealand, Great Britain, USA or Canada without approval of Libyan People's Bureau; all details of your passport must be translated into Arabic; nationals of Israel are not permitted entry; an Israeli stamp in your passport will deny you entry.	US$190 single
Malawi	Not required for most nationals	n/a
Mali	Required for all except nationals of France	US$50–70 single
Mauritania	Required for all except nationals of France and Italy and Arab League countries	US$30–80 multiple entry
Morocco	Not required for most nationals except Israel and South Africa	n/a
Mozambique	Required for all	US$80–100
Namibia	Not required for most nationals	n/a
Niger	Required for all except nationals of ECOWAS	US$50–60 single
Nigeria	Required for all except nationals of ECOWAS	US$140
Rwanda	Not required for nationals of several countries	n/a
Senegal	Not required for nationals of the EU, Commonwealth countries and USA	n/a
Sierra Leone	Required for all	US$80–100 single
Somalia	Required for all	n/a
South Africa	Not required for most nationals	n/a
Sudan	Required for all	US$110 single
Swaziland	Not required except for nationals of Germany and France	n/a
Tanzania	Required for all except nationals of some Commonwealth countries, Scandinavia and Iceland	US$80 single
Togo	Required for all except for nationals of ECOWAS 7-day transit visas available at the border	US$70 single US$20
Tunisia	Not required for most nationals	n/a
Uganda	Required for all except nationals of Denmark, Finland, France, Germany, Israel, Japan, Sweden and most Commonwealth countries (nationals of New Zealand, Nigeria and India require visas)	US$50 single
Zambia	Required for all except nationals of Commonwealth countries (British and Irish nationals require visas)	US$150 single
Zimbabwe	Now required for most nationals	n/a

Appendix 5

FURTHER INFORMATION
BOOKS
History and politics

Butcher, Tim *Blood River* Vintage, 2008. A new travelogue by the *Daily Telegraph* correspondent, following the Congo River in the footsteps of the early reporter for the same newspaper, Henry Morton Stanley.

Goldsworthy, David *Tom Mboya: The Man Kenya Wanted To Forget* Heinemann, 1982. Fascinating book on the former Kenyan trade union leader and politician who was murdered in 1969. Provides an insight to Kenya's history in the 1950s and 1960s.

Mandela, Nelson *A Long Walk to Freedom* Little, Brown, 1995. The autobiography of Nelson Mandela and the ANC. Great insight into the apartheid era of southern Africa.

Marable, Manning *African and Caribbean Politics* Verso, 1987. A good overview to African history and politics, with particular reference to Ghana.

Matar, N I *Islam for Beginners* Writers and Readers, 1992. A brief introduction to the basic precepts of Islam.

Moorehead, Alan *The Blue Nile* Hamish Hamilton, 1972. The story of the exploration and history of the Blue Nile River.

Moorehead, Alan *The White Nile* Penguin, 1972. The story of the exploration and history of the White Nile River.

Odinga, Oginga *Not Yet Uhuru* Heinemann, 1967. Autobiography of the man who went from being Kenya's vice-president under Jomo Kenyatta to a leading opposition force in exile.

Panaf Books *Kwame Nkrumah*. An introduction to the man who led Ghana to freedom in 1956 and also led the Pan-African liberation movement.

Panaf Books *Sékou Touré*. The story of Guinea's unique road to independence and of its charismatic first leader.

Pakenham, Thomas *The Scramble for Africa* Abacus, 1992. A briskly readable and well-indexed account of Africa's development – and its colourful cast of characters – from 1876 to 1912.

Sankara, Thomas *Thomas Sankara Speaks* Pathfinder, 1988. Key speeches by the inspiring and popular former president of Burkina Faso.

Reader, John *Africa: A Biography of the Continent* Penguin, 1998. The complete reference book: Africa from its origins until the end of the 20th century, presented vividly and accessibly.

Travel guides
Bradt guides (www.bradtguides.com)

Algeria Jonathan Oakes
Angola Mike Stead and Sean Rorison
Benin Stuart Butler
Botswana: Okavango, Chobe, Northern Kalahari Chris McIntyre
Burkina Faso Katrina Manson and James Knight
Cameroon Ben West

Congo and Democratic Republic of Congo Sean Rorison
East African Wildlife Philip Briggs
East & Southern Africa: The Backpacker's Manual Philip Briggs
Eritrea Edward Denison
Ethiopia Philip Briggs
Gabon, São Tomé & Príncipe Sophie Warne
Gambia, The Craig Emms/Linda Barnett
Ghana Philip Briggs
Johannesburg Lizzie Williams
Kenya Claire Foottit
Malawi Philip Briggs and Mary-Anne Bartlett
Mali Ross Velton
Mozambique Philip Briggs and Danny Edmunds
Namibia Chris McIntyre
Niger Jolijn Geels
Nigeria Lizzie Williams
North Africa: The Roman Coast Ethel Davies
Northern Tanzania Philip Briggs
Rwanda Janice Booth/Philip Briggs
São Tomé & Príncipe Kathleen Becker
Sierra Leone Katrina Manson and James Knight
South Africa: Budget Travel Guide Paul Ash
Southern African Wildlife Mike Unwin
Sudan Paul Clammer
Tanzania Philip Briggs
Uganda Philip Briggs
Zambia Chris McIntyre
Zanzibar Chris and Susie McIntyre

Others

Africa on a Shoestring Lonely Planet, 2004. The classic budget travellers' guide to Africa. A mine of information, although you do have to remember that, with a vast number of contributors, its accuracy does vary considerably. Not very helpful on places to stay if you have your own vehicle to worry about.

de Villiers, Marq and Hirtle, Sheila *Into Africa* Weidenfeld & Nicolson in Great Britain, Jonathan Ball Publishers in South Africa, 1997

Oliver, Roland *The African Experience*, Pimlico, 1991

Philips *Essential World Atlas,* in association with the Royal Geographical Society and the Institute of British Geographers, 1998

Running Press *The Quotable Traveler*, 1994

Scott, Chris *Desert Biking: A Guide to Independent Motorcycling in the Sahara* The Travellers' Bookshop 1995. A mine of information for those planning a trip by motorbike – although specifically covering the requirements of desert biking rather than for a comprehensive African trip. Lots of advice on bikes and equipment, as well as details of a number of north African routes.

Scott, Chris *Adventure Motorcycling Handbook* Trailblazer 2005

Scott, Chris *Sahara Overland* Trailblazer, 2004

St Pierre White, Andrew *The Complete Guide to a Four Wheel Drive in Southern Africa* National Book Printers, 1998/1999

Werner, David et al *Where There Is No Doctor: Village Health Care Handbook for Africa* Macmillan Education 1994

The Rough Guide to West Africa Rough Guide, 2008. A substantial and excellent country-by-country guide to this extraordinary region.

Language
Berlitz *Arabic for Travellers*
Berlitz *Swahili Phrase Book and Dictionary*
Eyewitness Travel Guides *Arabic Phrasebook*
Lonely Planet *Swahili Phrasebook*

Wildlife Enthusiasts may need information tailored to a specific country or area; in this case see recommendations in the appropriate travel guides.

Briggs, Philip *East African Wildlife* Bradt
Kingdon, Jonathan *The Kingdon Field Guide to African Mammals* Academic Press, 1997. Recommended by Philip Briggs, author of many Bradt Africa guides, as 'the most detailed, thorough and up-to-date of several field guides covering the mammals of the region'.
Perlo, Bervan *Illustrated Checklist to the Birds of Eastern Africa* (Collins, 1995) and *Illustrated Checklist to the Birds of Southern Africa* (Collins, 1999) between them cover bird species recorded in countries including Eritrea, Ethiopia, Kenya, Uganda, Rwanda, Tanzania, Zambia, Malawi and South Africa.
Unwin, Mike *Southern African Wildlife* Bradt

Other useful reading
Barker, Hazel *Senile Safari: A Journey from Durban to Alexandria*. A retired couple's drive through Africa. Available from the author (*18 Louisa Rd, Birchgrove, Sydney, Australia;* ℳ *+61 2 810 5040*).
Davies, Miranda and Longrigg, Laura (eds) *Half the Earth: Women's Experience of Travel Worldwide* Thorsons 1986. Excellent collection of guidance and personal encounters by women travellers, based on their experiences around the world.
Hibbert, Christopher *Africa Explored* Penguin, 1982
Melville, K E M *Stay Alive in the Desert* Roger Lascelles, 1984. All you need to know about desert survival, but in far more detail than most travellers will ever need.
Pryce, Lois *Red Tape & White Knuckles* Century, 2008. The story of Lois Pryce's solo motorbike trip from London to Cape Town.
Simon, Ted *Jupiter's Travels* Penguin, 1980. The classic story of a round-the-world journey by motorbike, including the trip from Tunis to Cape Town. As this was undertaken in 1974 to 1978, hard information is rather out of date, but the spirit of the book makes it unmissable.

Easy reads
Blixen, Karen *Out of Africa* Putnam & Co Ltd, 1937 (1st edition)
Foden, Giles *The Last King of Scotland* Faber & Faber, 1999 and *Ladysmith* Faber & Faber, 2000. *The Last King of Scotland* revolves around Idi Amin through the eyes of his personal physician, and has been made into a film. *Ladysmith* is about the British occupation of this small town in southern Africa. Both are superb reads.
Galman, Kuki *I Dreamed of Africa* Penguin, 2007. This author has written several novels regarding her time with her family in Kenya.
Godwin, Peter *Mukiwa* Picador, 2007. Rhodesia 1964 as seen through a young boy's eyes and his steady growth to the freedom of Rhodesia, now known as Zimbabwe.
Mail and Guardian Bedside Book, 1999. A selection of superb journalism from Africa's best.

SOURCING AFRICAN LITERATURE AND MAPS All of the above-mentioned books can be ordered through Amazon on www.amazon.co.uk or www.amazon.com. All Bradt guides are available via www.bradtguides.com. Old, out-of-print books (in bookshops worldwide) can sometimes be tracked down via www.usedbooksearch.co.uk.

UK

Africa Book Centre Ltd 38 King St, London WC2E 8JT; ℄ 020 7240 6649/0845 458 1581; f 020 7836 1975; www.africabookcentre.com

Blackwells 100 Charing Cross Rd, London WC2H 0JG; ℄ 020 7292 5100; f 020 7240 9665; e london@blackwell.co.uk; www.blackwells.co.uk. For all literature & maps. Many shops countrywide.

Stanfords 12–14 Long Acre, London WC2E 9LP; ℄ 020 7836 1321; f 020 7632 8928; www.stanfords.co.uk

Map World Direct Ltd 25 Saltersford Lane, Alton, Staffs ST10 4AU; ℄ 01538 703842; e service@map-guides.com; www.map-guides.com

USA

Book Passage 15 Tamal Vista Bd, Court Madera, CA 94925 ℄ 415 927 0960; f 415 924 3838; e messages@bookpassage.com; www.bookpassage.com. Also in San Francisco: 1 Ferry Bldg #42, San Francisco, CA 94111; ℄ 415 835 1020

The Savvy Traveller 310 South Michigan Av, Chicago, IL 60604; ℄ 888 666 6200 (toll free); f 312 913 9866; e mailbox@thesavvytraveller.com; www.thesavvytraveller.com

Wide World Books and Maps 4411A Wallingford Av North, Seattle, WA 98103; ℄ 888 534 3453 (toll free) or 206 634 3453; f 206 634 0558; e travel@speakeasy.net; www.wildworldtravels.com

South Africa

Exclusive Books Shop U30, Hyde Park Corner, Jan Smuts Av, Craighall, Johannesburg/Gauteng; ℄ 011 325 4298; f 011 325 5001; e hydepark@exclusivebooks.co.za; www.exclusivebooks.co.za. Has 29 other stores, too.

Facts & Fiction Shop 346–350, Rosebank Mall, Bath Av, Rosebank, Johannesburg/Gauteng; ℄ 011 447 3039/3028; f 011 447 3062; e rosebankmall@exclusivebooks.co.za; www.exclusivebooks.co.za. There is also a branch in Gaborone, Botswana (e nikid@exclusivebooks.co.za).

MAPS See page 6.

MAGAZINES

Trailbike and Enduro Magazine (TBM). A UK-based monthly publication with up-to-date information on the latest trailbikes. For information and subscriptions, ℄/f 080 8840 4760 or 5066.

WEBSITES
Expedition planning

www.expeditionworld.com Some photos taken by the authors on their Africa trips
www.africanet.com Africanet (general information on Africa including history and politics)
www.bradtguides.com Bradt Travel Guides
www.wtgonline.com Columbus World Travel Guide
www.africa-overland.net, **www.overlandclub.com** Independent Africa Overland Club (a general overview on travelling overland in Africa)
www.sites.netscape.net/kingmill/africa Kingsmill (a personal journey into Africa, including crossing Sudan)
www.klaus.daerr.de/sahara Klaus Daerr Expedition (in German only but excellent information on the Sahara)
www.sahara-overland.com Sahara Travel Information (specific to Saharan countries, with travellers' tales and much more)
www.geocities.com/MotorCity/1197/driving.html Tips for driving in Africa

Off-road

www.4x4mag.co.uk Internet magazine – particularly good classified section on used vehicles
www.4x4offroad.co.uk Of general interest regarding off-road issues
www.4xforum.co.za Offering information on all aspects of four-wheel driving in Africa
www.muddymotor.com For some fun before leaving, perhaps

Biking

www.adventure-motorcycling.com
www.berndtesch.de
www.horizonsunlimited.com

For luggage and accessories

www.davidlambeth.co.uk
www.adventure-spec.com
www.acerbis.com
www.touratech.de
www.wunderlich.de
www.xr-only.com
www.kriega.com
www.metalmule.com
www.coreuk.co.uk
www.longroad.co.uk

Other

www.africa.com
www.africaguide.com An excellent source of general information on individual African countries
www.africanconnections.com
www.africanet.com
www.africaonline.com
www.allafrica.com News from all over the continent
www.ananzi.co.za
www.arab.net
www.ase.net A useful source of information on accommodation
www.autotrader.co.za
www.backpackafrica.com
www.escapeartist.com
www.finance.yahoo.com/currency
www.freightquote.com
www.geography.about.com
www.horizonsunlimited.com Good for all overlanders, whether in 4x4s or on motorbikes or bicycles.
www.i-cias.com
www.infoplease.com
www.interknowledge.com
www.loisontheloose.com
www.odci.gov CIA website including details of every African country
www.places.co.za For countries in southern Africa and, strangely, the Maldives
www.safarinow.com
www.sas.upenn.edu/African_Studies An excellent site from the University of Pennsylvania
www.travelinafrica.co.za Includes visa information in some detail
www.travel.state.gov/travel
www.wncountries.com World news for every country
www.worldtravelguide.net
www.yellowpages.co.za

WIN £100 CASH!
READER QUESTIONNAIRE

**Send in your completed questionnaire for the chance to win
£100 cash in our regular draw**

All respondents may order a Bradt guide at half the UK retail price – please
complete the order form overleaf.
(Entries may be posted or faxed to us, or scanned and emailed.)

We are interested in getting feedback from our readers to help us plan future Bradt
guides. Please answer ALL the questions below and return the form to us in order
to qualify for an entry in our regular draw.

Have you used any other Bradt guides? If so, which titles? . . . .
. . . .

What other publishers' travel guides do you use regularly? . . . .
. . . .

Where did you buy this guidebook? . . . .

What was the main purpose of your trip to Africa (or for what other reason did you
read our guide)? eg: holiday/business/charity etc. . . . .
. . . .

What other destinations would you like to see covered by a Bradt guide?
. . . .

Would you like to receive our catalogue/newsletters?

YES / NO (If yes, please complete details on reverse)

If yes – by post or email? . . . .

Age (circle relevant category) 16–25   26–45   46–60   60+

Male/Female (delete as appropriate)

Home country . . . .

Please send us any comments about our *Africa Overland* guide or other Bradt Travel
Guides. . . . .
. . . .
. . . .
. . . .

Bradt Travel Guides
23 High Street, Chalfont St Peter, Bucks SL9 9QE, UK
✆ +44 (0)1753 893444 f +44 (0)1753 892333
e info@bradtguides.com
www.bradtguides.com

CLAIM YOUR HALF-PRICE BRADT GUIDE!

Order Form

To order your half-price copy of a Bradt guide, and to enter our prize draw to win £100 (see overleaf), please fill in the order form below, complete the questionnaire overleaf, and send it to Bradt Travel Guides by post, fax or email.

Please send me one copy of the following guide at half the UK retail price

Title	Retail price	Half price
... .	....	....

Please send the following additional guides at full UK retail price

No	Title	Retail price	Total
...	....	....	....
...	....	....	....
...	....	....	....

Sub total ....
Post & packing ....
(£2 per book UK; £4 per book Europe; £6 per book rest of world)
Total ....

Name . . . .

Address. . . . .

Tel . . . .   Email . . . .

☐ I enclose a cheque for £ . . . . made payable to Bradt Travel Guides Ltd

☐ I would like to pay by credit card. Number: . . . .

Expiry date: . . . / . . .   3-digit security code (on reverse of card) . . . . .

Issue no (debit cards only) . . . . .

☐ Please add my name to your catalogue mailing list.

☐ I would be happy for you to use my name and comments in Bradt marketing material.

Send your order on this form, with the completed questionnaire, to:

Bradt Travel Guides AO5
23 High Street, Chalfont St Peter, Bucks SL9 9QE
✆ +44 (0)1753 893444   f +44 (0)1753 892333
e info@bradtguides.com   www.bradtguides.com

Index

Page numbers in **bold** indicate major entries; those in *italic* indicate maps.